MATHEMATICS
MADE   SIMPLE

MATHEMATICS
MADE SIMPLE ®

NEW, REVISED EDITION

BY

ABRAHAM SPERLING, Ph.D.

Assistant Professor, the College of the City of New York

AND

MONROE STUART

MADE SIMPLE BOOKS
®
DOUBLEDAY & COMPANY, INC.
GARDEN CITY, NEW YORK

Library of Congress Cataloging in Publication Data

Sperling, Abraham Paul, 1912-
Mathematics made simple.

(Made simple books)
Includes index.
1. Mathematics—1961-   . I. Stuart, Monroe.
II. Title. III. Series.
QA39.2.S684   1981   510
AACR2
ISBN: 0-385-17481-0
Library of Congress Catalog Card Number 80-2627

ABOUT THIS BOOK

Mathematics made simple was first published in the 1940s. It was designed especially for students in high school and college or for those who aspired to better jobs or to improve professional skills or to advance in the Armed Forces. This book serves as a review of arithmetic and an introduction to algebra, geometry, and trigonometry. The exercises and answers in this book provide readers with opportunities to test their mastery of each step in the four common branches of mathematics.

Examples were given with purposely small numbers so that the reader could concentrate on the principle involved instead of being distracted by needlessly long calculations.

Special other features that make this survey of mathematics especially useful should be noted. In the section that gives answers to the exercises, the examples given as problems are explained step by step so the reader can see exactly how the answers were arrived at, a feature making this book ideal for home study without the help of an instructor.

The chapter on denominate numbers (weights, measures, etc.) was designed to make it as useful as possible for the practical application for those who make cost estimates in businesses, construction work, or other jobs.

Among the tables in this book are the following: Decimal Equivalents of Sixty-fourths; Weights, Measures, Money; Equivalents of U. S. Standard and Metric Values; Simple and Compound Interest; Squares and Square Roots, Cubes and Cube Roots, Common Logarithms, and Four-place Values of Natural Trigonometric Functions (by intervals of 10′).

A final feature that adds interest consists in the two tests with which the book starts and ends. Test No. 1 is typical of the qualifying and classification tests given by governmental, industrial and commercial organizations. Check up your knowledge with Test No. 1 before you begin (consider 70 percent the passing mark) and then note with pride and satisfaction how greatly that knowledge has increased when you apply it to the final test!

In 1962 this book was revised with chapters added on "Combinations and Permutations" and "The Theory of Probability."

For this new edition some essential updating has been done. Cities that are now a part of our fifty states are no longer identified as "foreign." Foreign currency has changed in form (no more shillings and sixpence in England). But in areas with constant changes—money, taxation, interest rates—many of the examples remain the same. The purpose of this handy volume is to teach principles. For daily, weekly, or annual variations in values and rates, it is appropriate to consult the financial section of the newspaper.

Today many jobs require and many schools and colleges permit the use of pocket calculators. Some general directions have been added to this edition to make sure that the use of the calculator does not reduce mastery of the basic principles or understanding of the mathematical processes.

A NOTE ON THE USE OF CALCULATORS

The availability and relatively low cost of small hand-held calculators has replaced the laborious pencil-and-paper process of computation. Today, arithmetical and algebraic calculations in most offices and work places and in many classrooms are done with the aid of a calculator. In most cases it has replaced the use of the sliderule, for the calculator has all of its capabilities and applies logarithmic principles to members of many digits or those requiring many decimal places.

There are many models and types of calculators. Each has a distinctive design according to its manufacturer, even calculators that are relatively simple and offer few special features. It is worthwhile to become familiar with location of the keys so that calculations can be made quickly and correctly. The different arrangements from one model to another can lead to serious errors. Practice makes perfect, so one must practice because a calculator provides correct answers only when used as directed in the manual provided by the manufacturer. The right keys must be pressed in the proper order. Most models display an error symbol (E) and stop further calculations, as in cases when a number is divided by zero, or when the integer portion of the quotient in percentage calculation is 17 digits, and in other instances. A calculator's algebraic entry system allows a problem to be entered in the same order as it is written as in the four fundamental arithmetical calculations which follow:

Addition

$123 + 456 = 579$

Subtraction

$789 - 456 = 333$

Multiplication

$12.3 \times 4.5 = 55.35$

Division

$12.3 \div 4.5 = 2.7333333$

Besides the basic arithmetical processes, a calculator provides discounts, square roots, reciprocals, chain, and mixed calculations, all generally arrived at by touching the right key or keys. A mixed calculation example follows:

$12 + (34 \times 56) - 789 = 1127$

A student should remember that his or her aim is to understand and master the principles of the problem. The calculator is a helpful tool, not a crutch.

Although often appealing when seen in a store, a calculator that displays the time, the date, rings alarm bells, or other features is not essential to the understanding of decimals, fractions, powers, and roots.

6

TABLE OF CONTENTS

CHAPTER TWELVE

CHAPTER THIRTEEN

CHAPTER FOURTEEN

CHAPTER FIFTEEN

10 *Contents*

MATHEMATICS
MADE   SIMPLE

TEST NO. 1

1 The rudder of an airplane broke off. The part that broke off represented $\frac{2}{5}$ of the length. A piece 6 feet long was left intact. What was the length of the part that broke off?

(A) 2 ft. _____   (c) 6 ft. _____
(B) 4 ft. _____   (d) 8 ft. _____

2 The crew of a boat was increased by $\frac{2}{7}$ of its original number. They then had 117 men. How many men did they have originally?

(A) 84 _____   (c) 91 _____
(B) 77 _____   (d) 105 _____

3 In order to reach a building 99 ft. tall, a fireman's ladder had to be increased by 32% of its length. How long was it?

(A) 67 ft. _____   (c) 70 ft. _____
(B) 67.32 ft. _____   (d) 75 ft. _____

4 Train travel is $2\frac{1}{2}$ times as fast as boat travel. How long would it take to go 600 miles by boat if it takes a train 10 hrs.?

(A) $10\frac{1}{3}$ hrs. _____   (c) $14\frac{1}{2}$ hrs. _____
(B) 25 hrs. _____   (d) 15 hrs. _____

5 A factory has enough oil to last 20 days if 2 drums are used daily. How many drums less must be used daily to make the oil last 30 days?

(A) $\frac{1}{3}$ _____   (c) $\frac{2}{3}$ _____
(B) $\frac{1}{2}$ _____   (d) 1 _____

6 A man took a loan for 1 year and 4 months at 6% interest. At the end of that time he paid $432, which included the loan plus the interest. How much did he originally borrow?

(A) $397.60 _____   (c) $400.00 _____
(B) $398.00 _____   (d) $406.08 _____

7 The formula $C = \frac{5}{9}(F - 32)$ gives Centigrade temperature in terms of Fahrenheit. What is the Centigrade equivalent for a temperature of 113° on the Fahrenheit scale?

(A) 144° _____   (c) 81° _____
(B) 96° _____   (d) 45° _____

8 The value of 36 coins, dimes and quarters only, is $6.60. Find the number of quarters.

(A) 16 _____   (c) 24 _____
(B) 20 _____   (d) 26 _____

9 If it takes 9 men 15 days to complete a construction job, how long would it take if 5 men worked on the job?

(A) 27 days _____   (c) 21 days _____
(B) $8\frac{1}{3}$ days _____   (d) 29 days _____

10 An airplane is to be built with a cowling 6 feet in length, a tail as long as the cowling plus $\frac{1}{4}$ the length of the body, and a body as long as the cowling and tail together. What will be the overall length of the airplane?

(A) 16 ft. _____   (c) 48 ft. _____
(B) 32 ft. _____   (d) 60 ft. _____

CHAPTER ONE

WHOLE NUMBERS

Arithmetic is the science of numbers.

A **whole number** is a digit from 0 to 9, or a combination of digits, such as 17, 428, 1, 521. Thus it is distinguished from a division or part of a whole number, such as a fraction like $\frac{5}{7}$ or $\frac{10}{9}$.

ADDITION OF WHOLE NUMBERS

You should be able to add whole numbers rapidly. In order to do this you must add mentally. Here are sample tests used for classification purposes. Speed and accuracy count.

You should get a score of 22 out of 25 correct, and should not take longer than two and one-half minutes. If you are not up to this level, use the exercise on the following page for practice.

TEST NO. 2

MENTAL ADDITION

A

1 $12 + 3 =$	6 $36 + 6 =$	11 $53 + 13 =$	16 $139 + 46 =$	21 $495 + 179 =$
2 $16 + 4 =$	7 $74 + 9 =$	12 $64 + 28 =$	17 $178 + 57 =$	22 $697 + 267 =$
3 $11 + 7 =$	8 $21 + 18 =$	13 $59 + 17 =$	18 $274 + 89 =$	23 $673 + 568 =$
4 $24 + 5 =$	9 $14 + 15 =$	14 $65 + 38 =$	19 $457 + 76 =$	24 $878 + 595 =$
5 $25 + 7 =$	10 $32 + 19 =$	15 $118 + 48 =$	20 $326 + 134 =$	25 $1,578 + 673 =$

B

26 $11 + 4 =$	31 $35 + 6 =$	36 $63 + 16 =$	41 $149 + 36 =$	46 $479 + 195 =$
27 $15 + 3 =$	32 $64 + 9 =$	37 $54 + 38 =$	42 $178 + 67 =$	47 $687 + 257 =$
28 $13 + 6 =$	33 $19 + 18 =$	38 $69 + 27 =$	43 $264 + 79 =$	48 $693 + 578 =$
29 $23 + 5 =$	34 $13 + 19 =$	39 $75 + 38 =$	44 $467 + 66 =$	49 $888 + 585 =$
30 $25 + 8 =$	35 $32 + 29 =$	40 $118 + 58 =$	45 $336 + 144 =$	50 $1,468 + 724 =$

C

51 $13 + 5 =$	56 $47 + 7 =$	61 $63 + 18 =$	66 $139 + 46 =$	71 $579 + 115 =$
52 $35 + 3 =$	57 $74 + 9 =$	62 $64 + 38 =$	67 $168 + 47 =$	72 $677 + 237 =$
53 $43 + 4 =$	58 $21 + 28 =$	63 $79 + 27 =$	68 $254 + 89 =$	73 $683 + 568 =$
54 $52 + 6 =$	59 $15 + 17 =$	64 $85 + 48 =$	69 $346 + 74 =$	74 $878 + 595 =$
55 $35 + 7 =$	60 $42 + 39 =$	65 $116 + 38 =$	70 $457 + 134 =$	75 $1,558 + 723 =$

Speed Test

PRACTICE IN SIGHT ADDITION

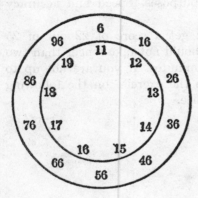

1   Add 1 to each figure in the outer circle; add 2 to each figure; add 3 to each figure; add 4, 5, 6, 7, 8, 9. Thus mentally you will say 1 + 5 = 6, 1 + 15 = 16, 1 + 25 = 26, and so on going around the entire circle. Then add 2 + 5, 2 + 15, 2 + 25, 2 + 35, etc. Continue this until you have added every number from 1 to 9 to every number in the outer circle.

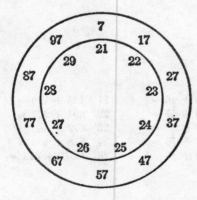

2   Add 11 to each figure in the outer circle. Thus mentally you will say 11 + 6 = 17, 11 + 16 = 27, 11 + 26 = 37, 11 + 36 = 47, and so on around the entire outer circle. Repeat this process for numbers from 12 through 19.

3   Follow same procedure as above using numbers from 21 through 29 as shown in the inner circle.

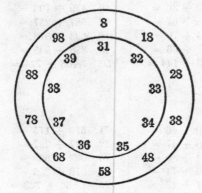

4   Follow same procedure as above using numbers from 31 through 39 as shown in the inner circle.

COLUMN ADDITION
Practice Exercise No. 1

This exercise is designed to present forty graded examples in column addition. Add Column I from *A* to *B*, then from *B* to *C*, then from *C* to *D*, then from *D* to *E*. Repeat for Columns II, III and IV. Next add Column I from *A* to *C*, from *B* to *D*, from *C* to *E*. Repeat for the other columns. Add Column I from *A* to *D*, then from *B* to *E*. Repeat process. Finally add each column from *A* to *E*. The complete answers will be found on page 175.

	I	II	III	IV
A	6,737	8,956	6,276	1,712
	7,726 ⎫10	7,735 ⎫9	2,985 ⎫10	1,814
	2,884 ⎭	6,544 ⎭	4,355 ⎭	2,523
	8,825	5,459	5,734	4,411
	2,201 ⎫10	4,893 ⎫9	3,756 ⎫9	4,515
	4,669 ⎭	6,876 ⎭	7,843 ⎭	5,115
	1,608	8,574	2,263 ⎫8	1,220
B	2,599	8,328	8,545 ⎭	1,418
	5,511	1,681	9,477	1,541
	5,522	6,418	1,668	1,825
	8,113	4,527	6,322	4,236
	2,037	2,772	9,755	1,547
	8,474	7,858	4,281	2,625
	7,745	6,785	5,727	1,608
	3,355	5,274	2,466	4,838
C	4,505	4,654	8,515	1,638
	5,754	5,737	3,594	1,518
	2,256	4,862	5,676	2,417
	4,445	6,143	1,229	3,514
	6,652	3,688	8,163	4,656
	1,868	6,471	2,223	2,181
	6,244	2,423	7,662	3,435
	5,471	1,584	6,141	1,615
D	4,649	7,845	8,759	2,344
	6,456	2,417	3,443	4,011
	5,554	7,989	5,682	9,122
	3,566	8,016	1,317	3,517
	4,273	5,703	8,831	1,833
	8,622	4,298	4,247	2,328
	2,488	1,683	4,042	4,244
	4,229	5,316	1,761	1,613
E	3,698	6,235	9,278	8,999

ACQUIRING SPEED

One way to acquire speed in column addition is to learn to group successive numbers at sight in such a way as to form larger numbers. Learn first to recognize successive numbers that make 10. In Column I of the preceding exercise are many combinations of two numbers adding up to 10. Practice again on this column, picking out these combinations as you go along.

Similarly in Column II you will find many combinations making 9, while in Column III you will recognize groups adding to 10, 9 and 8. Practice such grouping with these columns also.

If your work calls for any considerable amount of column addition, learn to group numbers that add to other sums—11, 12, 13, 14, 15, etc., as well as any total at all that is less than 10. You need not limit yourself to groups of only two numbers. Learn to combine three or even more numbers at sight.

Persons who are exceptionally rapid at addition, add two columns at a time (some do even three). Adding two columns at once is not as difficult as it may seem. Column IV of the preceding exercise has been specially designed as fairly easy practice in two-column addition. Try it! If you find that this method is not beyond your abilities, practice using it as occasions arise.

PARTIAL TOTALS

In actual work when you have long columns to add, write down your entire sum for each column separately instead of merely putting down a single digit and carrying the others. For instance, partial totals for Column I of the exercise would be set down thus:

$$\begin{array}{r} 166 \\ 137 \\ 152 \\ \underline{142} \\ 158736 \end{array}$$

By this procedure you treat each column as an individual sum and to that extent simplify the work of checking.

HORIZONTAL ADDITION

The method of partial totals is especially useful where the figures to be added are not arranged in column form—especially when they are on separate pieces of paper, such as invoices, ledger pages, etc.

In such a case you first go through the papers adding up only the figures in the units column; then you go through them again for the tens, for the hundreds, etc., setting down each successive partial total one place to the left. This procedure is usually very much quicker than the alternative one of listing the figures to be added.

Practice Exercise No. 2

Add the following, using the method of partial totals.

1   67 + 28 + 24 + 12 + 55 + 82 + 87 + 34 =

2   524 + 616 + 546 + 534 + 824 + 377 + 882 + 665 =

3   551 + 473 + 572 + 468 + 246 + 455 + 264 + 455 =

4   2,642 + 6,328 + 2,060 + 9,121 + 3,745 + 5,545 + 6,474 + 5,567 =

5   2,829 + 7,645 + 1,989 + 1,237 + 4,555 + 4,652 + 8,419 + 6,463 =

6   28,988 + 76,546 + 88,164 + 27,654 + 54,636 + 21,727 + 85,415 + 69,754 =

SUBTRACTION OF WHOLE NUMBERS

Subtraction is the process of finding the difference between two numbers. This is the same as finding out how much must be added to one number, called the **subtrahend,** to equal another, called the **minuend.**

For instance, subtracting 12 from 37 leaves a difference of 25 because we must add 25 to the subtrahend 12 to get the minuend 37. This may be written: 37 − 12 = 25; or:

$$
\begin{array}{rl}
37 & \text{(minuend)} \\
-12 & \text{(subtrahend)} \\
\hline
25 & \text{(difference)}
\end{array}
$$

The **minus sign** (−) indicates subtraction.

Here are several ways in which subtraction is indicated in verbal problems. They all mean the same as *subtract 4 from 16.*

a. How much must be added to 4 to give 16? Ans. 12
b. How much more than 4 is 16?   Ans. 12
c. How much less than 16 is 4?   Ans. 12
d. What is the difference between 4 and 16? Ans. 12

The circle arrangement on page 16 may be used for practice in subtraction. In each case subtract the smaller number from the larger.

DIFFERENT METHODS OF SUBTRACTION

There are two different routines for subtraction in accepted use—the *borrow* method and the *carry* method.

Use whichever method you were taught at school, since that is the one which will come most easily to you. To understand the difference between the two methods consider their application to the example: from 9624 subtract 5846.

The **borrow method** proceeds thus:

$$
\begin{array}{r}
851 \\
9\llap{/}624 \\
5846 \\
\hline
3778
\end{array}
$$

This may be read: subtracting 6 from 14 leaves 8, 4 from 11 leaves 7, 8 from 15 leaves 7, 5 from 8 leaves 3.

The **carry method** goes like this:

$$
\begin{array}{r}
9624 \\
5846 \\
695 \\
\hline
3778
\end{array}
$$

This may be read: subtracting 6 from 14 leaves 8, 5 from 12 leaves 7, 9 from 16 leaves 7, 6 from 9 leaves 3.

The *borrow method* is used by the vast majority of people in this country today, although the *carry method* was widely taught in our schools at one time.

MULTIPLICATION OF WHOLE NUMBERS

Multiplication is a short method of adding a number to itself a given number of times.

The given number is called the **multiplicand.** The number of times it is to be added is called the **multiplier.** The result is called the **product.**

For instance, 4 times 15 means 15 + 15 + 15 + 15, or 60. This may be written: 4 × 15 = 60; or:

$$
\begin{array}{rl}
15 & \text{(multiplicand)} \\
\times\,4 & \text{(multiplier)} \\
\hline
60 & \text{(product)}
\end{array}
$$

The **sign of multiplication** is ×; it is read *times.*

To multiply well and to use this ability in

Table I

MULTIPLICATION TABLE FROM TWO TO TWELVE

No.	×2	×3	×4	×5	×6	×7	×8	×9	×10	×11	×12
1	2	3	4	5	6	7	8	9	10	11	12
2	4	6	8	10	12	14	16	18	20	22	24
3	6	9	12	15	18	21	24	27	30	33	36
4	8	12	16	20	24	28	32	36	40	44	48
5	10	15	20	25	30	35	40	45	50	55	60
6	12	18	24	30	36	42	48	54	60	66	72
7	14	21	28	35	42	49	56	63	70	77	84
8	16	24	32	40	48	56	64	72	80	88	96
9	18	27	36	45	54	63	72	81	90	99	108
10	20	30	40	50	60	70	80	90	100	110	120
11	22	33	44	55	66	77	88	99	110	121	132
12	24	36	48	60	72	84	96	108	120	132	144

solving problems you must know by heart the product of any two numbers from 1 to 12. Above are tables of multiplication from 2 to 12; if you don't know all of them, memorize them now.

SHORT CUTS

There are so many short cuts in multiplication that they are an interesting study in themselves and throw a great deal of light on the general subject of the properties of numbers. It is beyond the plan of this book to treat this subject in detail, but the interested student may profitably experiment for himself with the devices presented on this page. More are considered in the chapters dealing with decimals and algebra.

Expanded multiplication table. Acquire a more extensive knowledge of the multiplication table. Aim to master it to 25 × 25. It is easy to learn 13 ×, 15 ×, 20 × and 25 × 25. Gradually include other numbers, as in Table 1A.

Small multipliers of two places. Multiply 326 by 127:

$$
\begin{array}{r}
326 \\
127 \\
\hline
2282 \\
3912 \\
\hline
41402 \\
\end{array}
\quad \text{instead of} \quad
\begin{array}{r}
2282 \\
652 \\
326 \\
\hline
41402 \\
\end{array}
$$

That is, multiply at once by 12, instead of multiplying first by 2 and then by 1.

Multipliers involving multiples of each other. Multiply 456 by 279.

$$
\begin{array}{r}
456 \\
279 \\
\hline
4104 \\
12312 \\
\hline
127224 \\
\end{array}
\quad \text{instead of} \quad
\begin{array}{r}
4104 \\
3192 \\
912 \\
\hline
127224 \\
\end{array}
$$

Recognizing that 27 in the multiplier is 3 × 9, you here multiply the 4104 by 3 instead of doing two separate calculations of 7 × and 2 ×.

Multiplying by 11. Multiply 24 by 11. 2 + 4

Mathematics Made Simple

Table IA

OTHER MULTIPLICATION TABLES

No.	×13	×14	×15	×16	×19	×21	×24	×25
1	13	14	15	16	19	21	24	25
2	26	28	30	32	38	42	48	50
3	39	42	45	48	57	63	72	75
4	52	56	60	64	76	84	96	100
5	65	70	75	80	95	105	120	125
6	78	84	90	96	114	126	144	150
7	91	98	105	112	133	147	168	175
8	104	112	120	128	152	168	192	200
9	117	126	135	144	171	189	216	225
10	130	140	150	160	190	210	240	250
11	143	154	165	176	209	231	264	275
12	156	168	180	192	228	252	288	300
13	169	182	195	208	247	273	312	325
14	182	196	210	224	266	294	336	350
15	195	210	225	240	285	315	360	375
16	208	224	240	256	304	336	384	400
17	221	238	255	272	323	357	408	425
18	234	252	270	288	342	378	432	450
19	247	266	285	304	361	399	456	475
20	260	280	300	320	380	420	480	500
21	273	294	315	336	399	441	504	525
22	286	308	330	352	418	462	528	550
23	299	322	345	368	437	483	552	575
24	312	336	360	384	456	504	576	600
25	325	350	375	400	475	525	600	625

= 6. Place a 6 between the 2 and the 4 and write the answer, 264. If the two numbers of the multiplicand add up to more than 10, add 1 to the hundreds figure in the answer. Multiply 48 × 11. 4 + 8 = 12. Make the first figure of the answer 5 and place the 2 of the 12 between 5 and 8 instead of between 4 and 8. Answer, 528.

Multiplying by "near" figures. To multiply 36 × 49, recognize that 49 is *near* 50. Then, since 50 × 36 = 1800 mentally, 49 × 36 must be only 36 less, or 1800 − 36 = 1764. Similarly, to multiply 3746 × 9988, recognize that 9988 is only 12 less than 10,000. Therefore, write down 37,460,000 and subtract 44,952 which is 12 × 3746, to get 37,415,048, the quick answer.

Practice Exercise No. 3

Use short-cut methods where applicable.

1	32 × 47 =	6	1112 × 893	11	4562 × 1211
2	123 × 43 =	7	1457 × 369	12	3765 × 648
3	182 × 52 =	8	48 × 48	13	87 × 87
4	217 × 21 =	9	83 × 53	14	96 × 46
5	136 × 24 =	10	115 × 115	15	997 × 327

DIVISION OF WHOLE NUMBERS

Division is the process of finding how many times one number, called the **divisor**, goes into another number, called the **dividend.** Hence, division is "multiplication in reverse," but its answer is called the **quotient.**

For instance, since 15 × 4 = 60, the dividend 60 divided by the divisor 4 produces the quotient 15. This may be written: 60 ÷ 4 = 15, or:

$$\text{(divisor) } 4\overline{)60} \quad \begin{array}{l}15 \text{ (quotient)}\\ \text{(dividend)}\end{array}$$

The sign of division is ÷, and is read *divided by*.

If the answer in the above case were not at once obvious, it could be obtained as follows: 6 ÷ 4 = 1 with 2 left over; write 1 above 6 and carry over the 2 to make the next partial dividend 20; then 20 ÷ 4 = 5, so write 5 over the 0 obtaining the exact quotient 15.

When a divisor does not thus go into a dividend an exact number of times, the last number left over is called the **remainder.** For instance, 63 ÷ 4 = 15 with the *remainder* 3.

The method of the above examples is called **short division** because the intermediate steps can be carried out mentally. The method

called **long division** is exactly the same, but its intermediate steps are written out as follows:

```
                    279   (quotient)
(divisor)  456)127229    (dividend)
           912
           ───
           3602
           3192
           ────
            4109
            4104
            ────
               5  (remainder)
```

The last digits, 2 and 9, of the dividend in such an example are said to be "brought down" in the intermediate steps.

COMPUTING AVERAGES

To find the average of several quantities, *divide their sum by the number of quantities.*

EXAMPLE: What was the average attendance at a church if the daily attendance from Monday through Friday was as follows: 462, 548, 675, 319, 521?

SOLUTION:

```
 462
 548
 675
 319
 521
────
2525
```

EXPLANATION: Add the quantities and divide the sum of 2525 by the number of days, 5. The average attendance is the quotient 505.

2525 ÷ 5 = 505. ANS.

Practice Exercise No. 4

1	7,258 ÷ 19 =	6	45,522 ÷ 54 =
2	13,440 ÷ 35 =	7	42,201 ÷ 46 =
3	21,492 ÷ 53 =	8	66,822 ÷ 74 =
4	19,758 ÷ 37 =	9	53,963 ÷ 91 =
5	47,085 ÷ 73 =		

CHECKING ANSWERS

Additions are checked by adding in the opposite direction.

Subtraction is checked by adding the subtrahend to the remainder. The sum should equal the minuend. In other words, in a completed subtraction example, the sum of the middle and bottom figures should equal the top figure.

Simple multiplication may be quickly checked by reversing multiplicand and multiplier.

Prove	36	by	57
	57		36
	252		342
	180		171
	2052		2052

Simple division may be checked by multiplying divisor by quotient and adding the remainder, if any.

For long examples in multiplication, however, a good method of checking is that which is known as *casting out nines*. The same method is also applicable in principle to addition and subtraction, but nothing would be gained by using it for the latter, while for the former it would be cumbersome.

CASTING OUT NINES

This method of checking does not present an absolute proof of correctness but only a presumable one. It can fail, however, only if the solution of an example contains two errors that exactly offset one another. Since the chance of this happening is negligible, the method may be considered almost completely reliable.

The method of casting out nines is based on a peculiar property of the number 9. This is that—

The sum of the digits of a number (or the sum of these digits minus any multiple of 9) is equal to the remainder that is left after dividing the original number by nine.

No.	Sum of digits	Remainder after ÷ 9
21	3	3
32	5	5
62	8	8

		Sum of digits minus multiple of 9	
27	9	0	0
54	9	0	0
72	9	0	0
156	12	3	3
8765	26	8	8

In the cases of 27, 54 and 72, note that *when the nines have been cast out of the multiple of 9 the remainder is 0.*

In the case of 156 and 8765, note that you need only add the digits in the figure representing the sum of the original digits to arrive at the desired remainder.

In applying the method of casting out nines we are concerned only with the *remainders*. By the principles explained above check the remainders here given:

	Remainder		Remainder
24	6	1466	8
36	0	16975	1
58	4	206534	2
138	3	7898875	7
257	5	56879876	2

The application of the method to multiplication and division is very simple and rapid, but before proceeding to explain this it will be well to do the following exercise.

Practice Exercise No. 5

What are the remainders after nines have been cast out of the following?

1	35	6	3,465	11	365,727
2	87	7	5,624	12	584,977
3	126	8	8,750	13	862,425
4	284	9	46,824	14	7,629,866
5	982	10	65,448	15	8,943,753

To check multiplication, *multiply the remainders representing the original numbers, cast nines out of this product and compare the remainder with the remainder representing the answer.*

EXAMPLES:

						Remainders
(1)	35	—	8			
	× 24	—	× 6			
	140		48	—	3	
	70					
	840	—			3	✓
(2)	54	—	0			
	× 38	—	× 2			
	432		0	—	0	
	162					
	2052	—			0	✓
(3)	97653	—	3			
	84296	—	× 2			
	585918		6	—	6	
	878877					
	195306					
	390612					
	781224					
	8231757288	—			6	✓

Note from the second of these examples that if *either* of the original numbers has a remainder of 0, the answer will have a remainder of 0.

The third example illustrates how easily the method may be applied to the most difficult multiplications.

If an answer is wrong, the method will also help you to find out quickly *where* the mistake has been made, since the casting out of nines can be applied to every step of the procedure. This is illustrated by the following example which has been purposely made incorrect.

Remainders should equal

358		7
246		3
2148	6 × 7 or	6
wrong 1442	4 × 7 or	1
716	2 × 7 or	5
wrong 88168	3 × 7 or	3

To check division, *subtract from the dividend any regular fractional remainder, then check the multiplication of quotient by divisor.*

EXAMPLE: Is $705,776 \div 728 = 969\frac{344}{728}$ correct?

Remainders after casting out 9's

705776		
− 344		
705432	—	3
969	—	6
× 728	× 8	
48	— 3	✓

The 3s check, therefore the answer may be considered correct.

Practice Exercise No. 6

Check by casting out nines whether each of the following is right or wrong.

1 $92 \times 61 = 5,612$
2 $88 \times 72 = 6,336$
3 $72 \times 37 = 2,665$
4 $35 \times 99 = 3,465$
5 $6,284 \times 192 = 1,236,528$
6 $1,938 \times 421 = 815,898$
7 $664 \times 301 = 199,864$
8 $736 \times 428 = 315,008$
9 $893 \times 564 = 502,652$
10 $1,084 \times 839 = 892,706$
11 $985 \times 916 = 902,260$
12 $3,241 \times 326 = 956,566$
13 $47,974 \div 83 = 578$
14 $21,954 \div 67 = 327\frac{45}{67}$
15 $88,445 \div 95 = 931$
16 $90,159 \div 123 = 732\frac{64}{123}$
17 $229,554 \div 234 = 981$
18 $307,395 \div 345 = 890$
19 $59,448 \div 96 = 619\frac{1}{4}$
20 $66,822 \div 86 = 779$
21 $47,320 \div 52 = 910$
22 $45,414 \div 62 = 732\frac{30}{62}$
23 $78,027 \div 93 = 839$
24 $31,806 \div 38 = 839$

Practice Exercise No. 7

ADDITION, SUBTRACTION, MULTIPLICATION, AND DIVISION

Note: For each problem multiple answers are given, of which only one is correct. After you solve the problem check the answer that agrees with your solution.

1 A dealer bought 3 loads of coal weighing 6,242 lbs., 28,394 lbs. and 143,686 lbs. How much did he buy in all?

(A) 76,324 ____
(B) 178,322 ____
(C) 268,422 ____
(D) 165,432 ____

2 If your Army pay is $152 a month, how much will you earn in a year?

(A) $1,800 ____
(B) $1,884 ____
(C) $1,824 ____
(D) $1,956 ____

3 A company marched 48 miles in 5 days. The first day they marched 12 miles, the second day 9 miles, the third day 7 miles, the fourth day 9 miles. How many miles did they march the last day?

(A) 11 ____
(B) 8 ____
(C) 16 ____
(D) 20 ____

4 How many packs of cigarettes can you buy for $3.00 at the rate of 2 for 60 cents?

(A) 5 ____
(B) 10 ____
(C) 15 ____
(D) 20 ____

5 If an automobile travels 450 yards in 15 seconds, how many feet does it go in $\frac{1}{3}$ of a second?

(A) 30 ____
(B) 90 ____
(C) 60 ____
(D) 10 ____

6 Your grades on 5 tests were 80%, 90%, 70%, 60% and 50%. What is the average of your 5 grades?

(A) 80 ____
(B) 70 ____
(C) 75 ____
(D) 85 ____

7 A barracks is 100 feet long, 50 feet wide and 10 feet high. Estimate the cost of heating it at the rate of $25.00 per 1,000 cubic feet per season.

(A) $125 ____
(B) $250 ____
(C) $1,250 ____
(D) $2,250 ____

8 It takes 5 lbs. of cement to cover 10 sq. ft. How many lbs. of cement will be needed to cover a rectangular area 25 ft. by 10 ft.?

(A) 25 ____
(B) 150 ____
(C) 200 ____
(D) 125 ____

Note: In solving problems such as No. 8 always *determine first what one unit will do.* In this case:

If 5 lbs. cover 10 square feet, then 1 lb. covers 2 square feet.

9   Before leaving his 142-acre estate, Mr. Curran sold 22 acres to Mr. Brown, 30 acres to Mr. Jones, 14 acres to Mr. Smith and 16 acres to Mr. Ives. How many acres did he have left?

  (A) 30 ____   (c) 50 ____
  (B) 40 ____   (D) 60 ____

10   Two machinists operating the same lathe work 10 hrs. each on a day- and on a night-shift respectively. One man turns out 400 pieces an hour, the other 600 pieces per hour. What will be the difference in their output at the end of 30 days?

  (A) 10,000 ____   (c) 60,000 ____
  (B) 6,000 ____   (D) 40,000 ____

11   You are given 12 days to drive to a destination 2,400 miles away. For the first 6 days you do 200 miles a day. Due to an accident you can't drive for 2 days. What is the average number of miles per day that you have to drive to reach your destination on time?

  (A) 100 ____   (c) 300 ____
  (B) 200 ____   (D) 400 ____

12   If, out of your annual pay of $4,800, you pay $20 weekly on your car, send home $10.00 weekly, and pay a monthly insurance of $20.00, how much will that leave you to spend on a monthly basis?

  (A) $200 ____   (c) $250 ____
  (B) $400 ____   (D) $150 ____

CHAPTER TWO

COMMON FRACTIONS

Although the product of any two whole numbers (Chapter One) is always another whole number, the quotient of two whole numbers may, or may not, be a whole number. For instance, $2 \times 3 = 6$, and $6 \div 3 = 2$; but $2 \div 3$ and $3 \div 2$ do not come out as whole numbers. In these latter cases, therefore, we call the quotients **fractional numbers,** or, for short, **fractions.**

LANGUAGE OF FRACTIONS

More particularly, a **common fraction** is one in which the dividend, called the fraction's **numerator,** is written over the divisor, called the fraction's **denominator,** with a slanting or horizontal line between them to indicate the intended division. Thus, in common fraction form:

$$2 \div 3 = 2/3 \quad \text{or}$$

with 2 as the numerator over 3 as the denominator.

From this example we see that $\frac{2}{3}$ by definition means $2 \div 3$, or "2 divided by 3." Likewise, $\frac{3}{2}$ by definition means $3 \div 2$, or "3 divided by 2." However, we shall soon see that, arithmetically:

$$\frac{2}{3} = 2 \times \frac{1}{3}, \quad \text{and} \quad \frac{3}{2} = 3 \times \frac{1}{2}.$$

For this reason we commonly read the symbol "$\frac{2}{3}$" as "*two thirds*," and the symbol "$\frac{3}{2}$" as "*three halves*," etc.

A **proper fraction** has a value less than 1 (one) because, by definition, it has a numerator smaller than its denominator. Examples: $\frac{2}{3}, \frac{1}{4}, \frac{3}{5}$.

A so-called **improper fraction** has a value greater than 1 because, by definition, it has a numerator larger than its denominator. Examples: $\frac{3}{2}, \frac{7}{4}, \frac{31}{9}$. But it is quite "proper" arithmetically to treat these fractions just like others.

A **mixed number** consists of a whole number and a fraction written together with the understanding that they are to be added to each other. Examples: $1\frac{3}{4}$ which means $1 + \frac{3}{4}$, and $2\frac{5}{7}$ which means $2 + \frac{5}{7}$.

A **simple fraction** is one in which both numerator and denominator are whole numbers, as in all the above examples of fractions.

A **complex fraction** is one in which either the

numerator or the denominator is a fraction or a mixed number, or in which both the numerator and the denominator are fractions or mixed numbers. Examples are:

$$\frac{1}{4} \, , \quad \frac{2}{\frac{2}{4}} \, , \quad \frac{\frac{1}{4}}{3} \, , \quad \frac{1\frac{1}{2}}{2} \, , \quad \frac{2}{3\frac{1}{4}} \, , \quad \frac{1\frac{1}{2}}{2\frac{3}{4}} \, .$$

A FUNDAMENTAL RULE OF FRACTIONS

In much of our work with fractions we need to apply the **fundamental rule** that: *When the numerator and denominator of a fraction are both multiplied or divided by the same number, the value of the fraction remains unchanged.* Examples are:

$$\frac{1}{2} = \frac{1 \times (2)}{2 \times (2)} = \frac{2}{4} = \frac{2 \times (25)}{4 \times (25)} = \frac{50}{100} \, , \text{ etc.;}$$

or

$$\frac{50}{100} = \frac{50 \div (10)}{100 \div (10)} = \frac{5}{10} = \frac{5 \div (5)}{10 \div (5)} = \frac{1}{2} \, , \text{ etc.}$$

From these examples we see that any common fraction can be written in as many different forms as we wish, provided always that the numerator, divided by the denominator, yields the same quotient. That particular form of a fraction which has the smallest possible whole numbers for its numerator and denominator is called **the fraction in its lowest terms.** Thus the above fraction $\frac{50}{100}$, or $\frac{5}{10}$, or $\frac{2}{4}$, is $\frac{1}{2}$ in its lowest terms.

REDUCTION OF FRACTIONS

To change a fraction to its lowest terms, divide its numerator and its denominator by the largest whole number which will divide both exactly.

EXAMPLE: Reduce $\frac{12}{30}$ to its lowest terms.

SOLUTION: $\frac{12}{30} = \frac{12 \div 6}{30 \div 6} = \frac{2}{5}$, ANS.

When you do not at once see the largest number which can be divided exactly into a large numerator and denominator, reduce the fraction by repeated steps, as follows:

EXAMPLE: Reduce 128/288 to lowest terms.

SOLUTION: $\frac{128}{288} = \frac{128 \div 4}{288 \div 4} = \frac{32}{72} = \frac{32 \div 8}{72 \div 8}$

$$= \frac{4}{9} \, , \text{ ANS.}$$

This is equivalent to:

$$\frac{128}{288} = \frac{128 \div 32}{288 \div 32} = \frac{4}{9} \, , \text{ ANS. (the same)}$$

When a fraction has been reduced to its lowest terms, the numerator and the denominator of the fraction are said to be *prime to each other*.

Numbers are **prime to each other** when there is no other whole number that is contained exactly in both of them. Thus 8 and 15 are *prime to each other* because there is no number that will divide both of them without a remainder.

A number that cannot be divided by any other number at all except 1, is called a **prime number.** Thus 1, 2, 3, 5, 7, 11, 13, 17 and 19 are prime numbers. But 4, 6, 8, 9, 10, 12, 14, 15, 16, 18 and 20 are not prime numbers because each of these can be divided by one or more smaller numbers.

A number that is contained exactly in two or more other numbers is called a *common divisor* of these numbers.

GREATEST COMMON DIVISOR

The largest number that is contained exactly in two or more other numbers is called the **greatest common divisor (GCD)** of these numbers.

A knowledge of how to find the greatest common divisor of two or more numbers is necessary in order to perform various operations with fractions.

There are two methods of doing so—the **factoring method** and the **direct division** method. The *factoring method* is the handier where the numbers involved are small, and it has the added advantage that it can be applied at a single operation to more than two numbers.

To find the greatest common divisor by factoring, *arrange the numbers in a line and divide them by any prime number that is exactly* *contained in all of them; divide the quotients in the same way; continue thus to divide the quotients until a quotient is obtained which contains no common divisor; multiply the divisors that have been used to arrive at the desired greatest common divisor.*

EXAMPLE: Find the greatest common divisor of 42, 60 and 84.

SOLUTION:

$$\begin{array}{r} 2)\overline{42,\ 60,\ 84} \\ 3)\overline{21,\ 30,\ 42} \\ \overline{7,\ 10,\ 14} \\ 2 \times 3 = \text{GCD} \end{array}$$

EXPLANATION: The greatest common divisor of two or more numbers is equal to the product of all the *prime* factors (divisors) that are common to *all* of them. 7 and 14 are divisible by 7, and 10 and 14 by 2; but no number will divide all three of these quotients. Hence the only prime factors are 2 and 3.

The foregoing method is not readily applicable when the numbers are large and thus not subject to easy analysis. In such cases the following method is employed.

To find the greatest common divisor by direct division, *divide the larger number by the smaller, then divide the remainder into the smaller, and continue to divide remainders into previous divisors until no remainder is left; the last divisor used is the desired greatest common divisor.*

EXAMPLE: What is the greatest common divisor of 323 and 391?

SOLUTION:

$$\begin{array}{r} 323)391(1 \\ 323 \\ \hline 68)323(4 \\ 272 \\ \hline 51)68(1 \\ 51 \\ \hline 17)51(3 \\ 51 \qquad 17 = \text{GCD} \end{array}$$

EXPLANATION: Since the greatest common divisor is contained in both 391 and 323 it must be contained in the difference between these numbers or 68; it must also be contained in any multiple (product) of 68 as well as in the difference between such a multiple and 323. Hence it must be contained in 51. Hence it must be contained

in 68, 51 and in the difference between them or 17. Since no smaller number is contained in 17, this must be the required greatest common divisor.

If the successive divisions continue until a remainder of 1 is obtained, this means that the original numbers have no common divisor.

If more than two numbers are originally given, *find the greatest common divisor of any two of them, then find the greatest common divisor of this result and another of the original numbers, continuing in this way until all the original numbers have been used. The last divisor is the required greatest common divisor.*

Practice Exercise No. 8

Find the GCD of the following:

1	12, 16, 28	6	48, 60	11	24, 32, 104
2	12, 72, 96	7	63, 99	12	36, 90, 153
3	14, 21, 35	8	54, 234	13	48, 120, 168
4	15, 45, 81	9	33, 165	14	64, 256, 400
5	32, 48, 80	10	256, 608	15	81, 117, 120

Practice Exercise No. 9

Reduce the following fractions to lowest terms.

1	$\frac{8}{12} =$	6	$\frac{16}{44} =$	11	$\frac{20}{36} =$
2	$\frac{8}{20} =$	7	$\frac{10}{12} =$	12	$\frac{42}{126} =$
3	$\frac{6}{15} =$	8	$\frac{13}{52} =$	13	$\frac{15}{18} =$
4	$\frac{9}{15} =$	9	$\frac{10}{16} =$	14	$\frac{144}{244} =$
5	$\frac{12}{32} =$	10	$\frac{18}{56} =$	15	$\frac{8}{56} =$

To raise the denominator of a given fraction to a required denominator, *divide the denominator of the given fraction into the required denominator, then multiply both terms of the given fraction by the quotient.*

EXAMPLE: Change $\frac{1}{4}$ to sixty-fourths.

$$64 \div 4 = 16$$

$$\frac{1}{4} = \frac{1 \times 16}{4 \times 16} = \frac{16}{64}$$

EXPLANATION: 64 is the required denominator; 4 is the given denominator; 1 and 4 must each be multiplied by the quotient 16 to give the stepped-up fraction.

Practice Exercise No. 10

Change the following fractions to equivalent fractions having the indicated denominator.

1   $\frac{1}{4}$ to 8ths =   9 $\frac{3}{8}$ to 24ths =
2   $\frac{1}{3}$ to 12ths =   10 $\frac{2}{5}$ to 45ths =
3   $\frac{2}{5}$ to 20ths =   11 $\frac{2}{9}$ to 36ths =
4   $\frac{4}{5}$ to 81sts =   12 $\frac{11}{12}$ to 60ths =
5   $\frac{3}{8}$ to 48ths =   13 $\frac{14}{25}$ to 75ths =
6   $\frac{2}{7}$ to 49ths =   14 $\frac{9}{11}$ to 88ths =
7   $\frac{4}{32}$ to 64ths =   15 $\frac{5}{12}$ to 96ths =
8   $\frac{5}{13}$ to 78ths =   16 $\frac{7}{17}$ to 68ths =

To change an improper fraction to a whole or mixed number, *divide the numerator by the denominator and place the remainder over the denominator.*

EXAMPLE: Change $\frac{19}{5}$ to a mixed number.

$$\frac{19}{5} \text{ means } 19 \div 5 \qquad 5)\overline{19} \atop 3\frac{4}{5} \qquad \frac{19}{5} = 3\frac{4}{5}$$

Practice Exercise No. 11

Change to whole or mixed numbers:

1   $\frac{12}{5}$ =   4 $\frac{43}{5}$ =   7 $\frac{32}{14}$ =   10 $\frac{21}{7}$ =
2   $\frac{14}{7}$ =   5 $\frac{52}{8}$ =   8 $\frac{28}{6}$ =   11 $\frac{82}{41}$ =
3   $\frac{19}{12}$ =   6 $\frac{114}{76}$ =   9 $\frac{19}{4}$ =   12 $\frac{96}{6}$ =

To change a mixed number to an improper fraction, *multiply the whole number by the denominator of the fraction, add the numerator to this product and place the sum over the denominator.*

EXAMPLE 1: $2\frac{7}{8} = \frac{8 \times 2 + 7}{8} = \frac{23}{8}$,   Ans.

EXAMPLE 2: $4\frac{3}{5} = \frac{5 \times 4 + 3}{5} = \frac{20 + 3}{5}$

$$= \frac{23}{5}, \text{ Ans.}$$

Practice Exercise No. 12

Change to improper fractions:

1   $2\frac{3}{4}$ =   4 $5\frac{3}{5}$ =   7 $19\frac{8}{7}$ =   10 $13\frac{3}{7}$ =
2   $3\frac{1}{4}$ =   5 $12\frac{2}{3}$ =   8 $16\frac{1}{6}$ =   11 $14\frac{1}{5}$ =
3   $4\frac{4}{5}$ =   6 $18\frac{3}{4}$ =   9 $12\frac{2}{7}$ =   12 $22\frac{2}{5}$ =

ADDITION AND SUBTRACTION OF FRACTIONS

Just as you cannot add or subtract numbers of feet and numbers of yards until you have first reduced both to a common unit such as feet, yards, or inches, you cannot add or subtract unlike fractions until you have first reduced them to a common denominator.

To add unlike fractions, *first change them to equivalent fractions with the same denominator. Then add the numerators and put the sum over the common denominator.*

EXAMPLE 1: Find $\frac{1}{2}$ plus $\frac{3}{4}$.

SOLUTION:

$$\frac{1}{2} + \frac{3}{4} = \frac{2}{4} + \frac{3}{4} = \frac{2+3}{4} = \frac{5}{4}, \text{ or } 1\frac{1}{4}, \text{ Ans.}$$

EXAMPLE 2: Find $\frac{1}{3}$ plus $\frac{3}{4}$.

SOLUTION:

$$\frac{1}{3} + \frac{3}{4} = \frac{4}{12} + \frac{9}{12} = \frac{4+9}{12} = \frac{13}{12}, \text{ or } 1\frac{1}{12}, \text{ Ans.}$$

EXPLANATION: The smallest number that contains both 3 and 4 is 12. We find that number by thinking of multiples of 4, the higher of the two denominators, as 4, 8, 12, 16. We stop as soon as we come to the first number that also contains 3. Then we work as follows:

For $\frac{1}{3}$: $12 \div 3 = 4$; so $\frac{1}{3} = \frac{4 \times 1}{4 \times 3} = \frac{4}{12}$.

For $\frac{3}{4}$: $12 \div 4 = 3$; so $\frac{3}{4} = \frac{3 \times 3}{3 \times 4} = \frac{9}{12}$, etc.

LOWEST COMMON DENOMINATORS

The 12 in the foregoing calculation is called the **lowest common denominator** of the fractions and is abbreviated **LCD**.

The term *lowest common denominator* is limited to use in connection with fractions. Numerically it is identical with the **least common multiple (LCM)** of the given denominators. The latter term has a more general use in mathematics. The *least common multiple* of two or more numbers is the smallest number that can be exactly divided by all the given numbers. Thus 12 is the least common multiple of 3 and 4; 45 is the least common multiple of 9 and 15. When applied to fractions, 12 is the least common *denominator* of $\frac{1}{3}$ and $\frac{1}{4}$; 45 is the least common denominator of $\frac{1}{9}$ and $\frac{1}{15}$.

To find the least common multiple of two numbers, *first determine their greatest common divisor; divide the numbers by this, and multiply together the resulting quotients and the greatest common divisor.*

EXAMPLE 1: What is the least common multiple of 12 and 16?

$$2\overline{)12,\ 16}$$
$$2\overline{)\ 6,\ \ 8}$$
$$3,\ \ 4$$

GCD = 2 × 2 = 4.

LCM = 4 × 3 × 4 = 48.

EXAMPLE 2: What is the least common multiple of 54 and 81?

$$54\overline{)81(1}$$
$$\underline{54}$$
$$27\overline{)54(2}$$
$$\underline{54}$$

GCD = 27.

$$27\overline{)54,\ 81}$$
$$2,\ \ 3$$

LCM = 27 × 2 × 3 = 162.

The least common multiple of more than two numbers can be found by factoring, but in this case we must be careful not only to use the divisors that are contained in all the given numbers but also any divisors that may be contained in two or more of them.

EXAMPLE 3: What is the least common multiple of 6, 8, and 12?

$$2\overline{)6,\ 8,\ 12}$$
$$2\overline{)3,\ 4,\ \ 6}$$
$$3\overline{)3,\ 2,\ \ 3}$$
$$1,\ 2,\ \ 1$$

LCM = 2 × 2 × 3 × 2 = 24.

EXPLANATION: In the examples given above which dealt with only two numbers, we multiplied the greatest common divisor by the quotients obtained by dividing the original numbers. To do so in this example would be wrong. The greatest common divisor of all the numbers is 2, but the quotients 3, 4 and 6 contain other common divisors that must be considered. 3 and 6 contain 3; 4 and 6 contain 2. We therefore continue the division, simply bringing down such numbers as cannot be divided by any given divisor, until no groups with a common divisor remain in the quotient.

This method may be stated as follows:

To find the least common multiple of more than two numbers by factoring, *divide all the numbers or any groups of two or more of them by such prime common divisors as may be contained in them and multiply together these divisors and the final quotients.*

To find the least common multiple of more than two numbers which cannot be readily factored, *find the least common multiple of two of them, then the least common multiple of this result and another of the given numbers; continue in this way until all the original numbers have been used.*

To subtract unlike fractions, *first change them to equivalent fractions with their LCD. Then find the difference of the new numerators.*

EXAMPLE: Find $\frac{3}{5} - \frac{1}{3}$.

SOLUTION: LCD is 15. $\therefore \dfrac{3}{5} = \dfrac{9}{15}; \dfrac{1}{3} = \dfrac{5}{15}.$

Hence:

$$\frac{3}{5} - \frac{1}{3} = \frac{9}{15} - \frac{5}{15} = \frac{9-5}{15} = \frac{4}{15}, \quad \text{Ans.}$$

To find the LCD when no two of the given denominators can be divided by the same number, *multiply the denominators by each other; the result is the LCD.*

EXAMPLE: Find $\frac{1}{2} + \frac{1}{3} + \frac{1}{5} + \frac{1}{7}$.

SOLUTION: 2 × 3 × 5 × 7 = 210 LCD.

$$\frac{1}{2} = \frac{105}{210}; \frac{1}{3} = \frac{70}{210}; \frac{1}{5} = \frac{42}{210}; \frac{1}{7} = \frac{30}{210};$$

$$\frac{105 + 70 + 42 + 30}{210} = \frac{247}{210} = 1\frac{37}{210}, \quad \text{Ans.}$$

To add and subtract mixed numbers, *treat the fractions separately; then add or subtract the results to or from the whole numbers.*

EXAMPLE: From $8\frac{1}{3}$ subtract $6\frac{3}{4}$.

SOLUTION: LCD of $\frac{1}{3}$ and $\frac{3}{4}$ = 12.

$$\tfrac{1}{3} = \tfrac{4}{12}; \tfrac{3}{4} = \tfrac{9}{12};$$

$$8\tfrac{4}{12} = 7 + \tfrac{12}{12} + \tfrac{4}{12} = 7\tfrac{16}{12};$$

$$\begin{array}{r} 7\frac{16}{12} \\ -6\frac{9}{12} \\ \hline 1\frac{7}{12} \ \text{Ans.} \end{array}$$

EXPLANATION: Since $\frac{9}{12}$ is greater than $\frac{4}{12}$, it is necessary to borrow 1 from the 8, which becomes 7; then $7 + \frac{12}{12} + \frac{4}{12} = 7\frac{16}{12}$; subtracting $6\frac{9}{12}$ we get $1\frac{7}{12}$. Ans.

Practice Exercise No. 13

Do the following examples:

1. $\frac{7}{8} + \frac{3}{4}$
2. $\frac{8}{9} - \frac{2}{3}$
3. $\frac{7}{8} - \frac{3}{5}$
4. $\frac{5}{6} + \frac{8}{9}$
5. $\frac{3}{4} + \frac{5}{12} - \frac{2}{3}$
6. $\frac{7}{8} - \frac{1}{2} - \frac{1}{4}$
7. $5\frac{1}{2} + 3\frac{3}{4}$
8. $3\frac{2}{3} + 1\frac{5}{6} + 2\frac{1}{4}$
9. $15\frac{1}{9} + 8\frac{5}{6}$
10. $12\frac{7}{8} - 6\frac{1}{3}$
11. $9\frac{1}{3} - 7\frac{3}{4}$
12. $16\frac{3}{8} - 9\frac{5}{6}$

MULTIPLICATION AND DIVISION OF FRACTIONS

To multiply a fraction by a whole number, *multiply the* NUMERATOR *by the whole number. The product will be the new numerator over the old denominator.*

Thus, $\quad 6 \times \frac{2}{3} = \frac{6 \times 2}{3} = \frac{12}{3} = 4$, ANS.

To divide a fraction by a whole number, *multiply the* DENOMINATOR *of the fraction by the whole number. The quotient will be the old numerator over the new denominator.*

Thus: $\quad \frac{2}{3} \div 5 = \frac{2}{3 \times 5} = \frac{2}{15}$, ANS.

$$\frac{1}{5} \div 2 = \frac{1}{5 \times 2} = \frac{1}{10}, \quad \text{ANS.}$$

To multiply one fraction by other fractions, *place the product of the numerators over the product of the denominators; then reduce.*

$$\frac{2}{3} \times \frac{1}{5} \times \frac{3}{6} = \frac{2 \times 1 \times 3}{3 \times 5 \times 6} = \frac{6}{90} = \frac{1}{15}.$$

To multiply mixed numbers, *change the mixed numbers to improper fractions.*

Thus: $\quad 1\frac{3}{4} \times 2\frac{2}{3} \times 1\frac{1}{2} = \frac{7}{4} \times \frac{8}{3} \times \frac{3}{2}$

$$= \frac{7 \times 8 \times 3}{4 \times 3 \times 2} = \frac{168}{24} = 7, \quad \text{ANS.}$$

To divide a whole number or a fraction by a fraction, *invert the* DIVISOR *and* MULTIPLY.

Inverting a fraction means turning it upside down. Thus, $\frac{2}{3}$ inverted is $\frac{3}{2}$; $\frac{2}{5}$ inverted becomes $\frac{5}{2}$.

Inverting a whole number means putting a 1 above it. Thus, 2 becomes $\frac{1}{2}$; 16 becomes $\frac{1}{16}$.

EXAMPLE 1: $\quad \frac{1}{2} \div \frac{2}{3} = \frac{1}{2} \times \frac{3}{2} = \frac{3}{4}$, ANS.

EXAMPLE 2: $\quad \frac{4}{7} \div \frac{2}{5} = \frac{4}{7} \times \frac{5}{2} = \frac{20}{14} = 1\frac{6}{14}$
$$= 1\frac{3}{7}, \quad \text{ANS.}$$

CANCELLATION

Cancellation is a short cut in the process of multiplication of fractions. It consists of taking out common factors in the numerator and denominator before dividing out.

Thus in the calculation
$$\overset{1}{\cancel{2}} \quad \overset{1}{\cancel{3}} \quad \overset{1}{\cancel{4}}$$
$$\frac{\cancel{2}}{\cancel{4}} \times \frac{\cancel{3}}{\cancel{6}} \times \frac{\cancel{4}}{\cancel{3}} = \frac{1}{3},$$
$$\underset{1}{} \quad \underset{3}{} \quad \underset{1}{}$$

the 4's cancel each other, the 3's cancel each other, and the 2 in the numerator is contained 3 times in the 6 in the denominator, leaving 3.

Cancellation can be applied only to multiplication and division of fractions; *never to addition and subtraction of fractions.*

Compare: $\quad \frac{10}{25} \times \frac{4}{3} \times \frac{12}{8} =$

Long method: $\dfrac{10 \times 4 \times 12}{25 \times 3 \times 8} = \dfrac{480}{600} = \dfrac{48}{60} = \dfrac{4}{5}.$

Cancellation: $\dfrac{\overset{2}{\cancel{10}}}{\underset{5}{\cancel{25}}} \times \dfrac{4}{3} \times \dfrac{\overset{1}{\cancel{12}}}{\underset{2}{\cancel{8}}} = \dfrac{4}{5}.$

Practice Exercise No. 14

Do the following examples:

1. $\frac{3}{7} \times \frac{3}{5} =$
2. $\frac{3}{8} \times \frac{2}{3} =$
3. $\frac{2}{15} \times \frac{4}{21} \times \frac{7}{8} \times 5 =$
4. $\frac{14}{15} \times \frac{9}{28} =$
5. $\frac{3}{16} \times 12 =$
6. $\frac{15}{16} \times \frac{7}{90} =$
7. $\frac{5}{6} \times \frac{5}{9} =$
8. $\frac{7}{27} \times \frac{9}{14} =$
9. $18 \div \frac{1}{2} =$
10. $\frac{3}{5} \div \frac{1}{15} =$
11. $\frac{2}{3} \div \frac{1}{2} =$
12. $\frac{4}{5} \div \frac{1}{8} =$
13. $1\frac{2}{3} \times \frac{3}{4} =$
14. $2\frac{1}{2} \times 1\frac{3}{4} =$
15. $3\frac{1}{2} \div \frac{1}{4} =$
16. $1\frac{1}{8} \div \frac{3}{16} =$
17. $\dfrac{\frac{2}{3} + \frac{1}{4} + \frac{1}{2}}{\frac{5}{8} - \frac{1}{6} - \frac{1}{4}} =$
18. $\dfrac{\frac{2}{3} \div \frac{1}{5}}{\frac{1}{4} \times \frac{1}{3}} =$
19. $\dfrac{2\frac{1}{2} + 3\frac{1}{3}}{4 + \frac{2}{3}} =$
20. $\dfrac{\frac{1}{4} \text{ of } 8}{1\frac{1}{2} \text{ of } 3} =$
21. $\dfrac{\frac{1}{5} + \frac{8}{14} + \frac{3}{7}}{\frac{3}{7} \div 10} =$
22. $\dfrac{\frac{1}{6} + \frac{2}{5} + \frac{3}{4} + \frac{1}{3}}{\frac{7}{12} - \frac{1}{6} + \frac{1}{3}} =$

To simplify complex fractions, *convert the numerators and denominators to simple frac-*

tions, then follow the rules for adding, subtracting, multiplying or dividing simple fractions.

Thus:

$$\frac{\frac{1}{2}+\frac{3}{4}}{2+\frac{1}{2}}=\frac{\frac{5}{4}}{\frac{5}{2}}=\frac{\overset{1}{\cancel{5}}}{\cancel{4}_{2}}\times\frac{\overset{1}{\cancel{2}}}{\cancel{5}_{1}}=\frac{1}{2},\text{ Ans.}$$

$$\frac{1\frac{2}{3}\times 2\frac{1}{4}}{\frac{1}{2}\div\frac{2}{3}}=\frac{\frac{5}{3}\times\frac{9}{4}}{\frac{1}{2}\times\frac{3}{2}}=\frac{\frac{45}{12}}{\frac{3}{4}}=\frac{\cancel{45}}{\cancel{12}}\times\frac{\cancel{4}}{\cancel{3}}=5,\text{ Ans.}$$

In performing cancellation, when the quotient of any division is 1, this figure may be written down as in the preceding examples; but this is not strictly necessary.

LARGER NUMBERS INVOLVING FRACTIONS

To multiply a whole number and a mixed number together, *perform separate multiplications and add the results.*

EXAMPLE 1: Multiply 17 by $6\frac{3}{4}$.

$$\begin{array}{r}17\\6\frac{3}{4}\\\hline 102\\12\frac{3}{4}\\\hline 114\frac{3}{4},\text{ Ans.}\end{array}$$

EXPLANATION: We multiply 17 first by 6, the whole-number part of the multiplier, and then by the fractional part, $\frac{3}{4}$; this is simply taking $\frac{3}{4}$ of it. Finally we add the results.

EXAMPLE 2: Multiply $17\frac{3}{5}$ by 4.

$$\begin{array}{r}17\frac{3}{5}\\4\\\hline 2\frac{2}{5}\\68\\\hline 70\frac{2}{5},\text{ Ans.}\end{array}$$

EXPLANATION: We first multiply $\frac{3}{5}$ in the multiplicand by 4, the multiplier; thus, 4 times $\frac{3}{5}$ is $\frac{12}{5}$, equal to $2\frac{2}{5}$, which is in effect taking $\frac{3}{5}$ of the multiplier 4. We then multiply the whole number part, 17, by 4. Finally we add the two products.

To divide a mixed number by a whole number, *divide the whole-number part of the*

dividend, reduce any remainder to a single fraction and divide this by the divisor.

EXAMPLE: Divide $17\frac{3}{8}$ by 6.

6)$17\frac{3}{8}$
2 with $5\frac{3}{8}=\frac{43}{8}$, remainder.
Next: $\frac{43}{8}\times\frac{1}{6}=\frac{43}{48}$.
Then: $2+\frac{43}{48}=2\frac{43}{48}$, Ans.

EXPLANATION: Having divided the whole number as in simple division, we have a remainder of $5\frac{3}{8}$, which we reduce to an improper fraction and divide by the divisor. Annexing this result to the quotient 2, we obtain $2\frac{43}{48}$ for the answer.

To divide a whole number by a mixed number, *reduce the divisor and dividend to equivalent fractions having the same denominator; then divide the numerator of the dividend by the numerator of the divisor.*

EXAMPLE: Divide 25 by $4\frac{3}{5}$.

$$\begin{array}{c|c}4\frac{3}{5} & 25\\5 & 5\\\hline 23)125(5\frac{10}{23}\\115\\\hline 10\end{array}$$

EXPLANATION: We first reduce the divisor and dividend to fifths, and then divide as in whole numbers. By multiplying divisor and dividend by the same number, 5, their relation to each other is the same as before, and the quotient is not changed. The answer here is $\frac{125}{23}=5$ and $\frac{10}{23}$.

Practice Exercise No. 15

1	$9\frac{3}{8}\times 5=$	11	$17\frac{3}{5}\div 7=$
2	$12\frac{2}{5}\times 7=$	12	$18\frac{3}{7}\div 8=$
3	$9\times 8\frac{11}{12}=$	13	$27\frac{11}{12}\div 9=$
4	$10\times 7\frac{1}{8}=$	14	$31\frac{1}{10}\div 11=$
5	$11\frac{9}{7}\times 8=$	15	$78\frac{4}{5}\div 12=$
6	$7\frac{6}{11}\times 5=$	16	$36\div 9\frac{3}{8}=$
7	$23\frac{7}{12}\times 6=$	17	$97\div 13\frac{11}{12}=$
8	$8\frac{3}{5}\times 5=$	18	$342\div 14\frac{47}{131}=$
9	$9\times 6\frac{3}{8}=$	19	$113\div 21\frac{1}{7}=$
10	$12\times 637\frac{1}{2}=$	20	$19\div 2\frac{3}{7}=$

To find what part one number is of another, *make the first number the numerator and the second the denominator of a fraction; reduce to lower terms if possible.*

Thus, 5 is $\frac{5}{8}$ of 8, because 1 is $\frac{1}{8}$ of 8, and 5 is 5 times 1.

Again, 2 is $\frac{4}{7}$ of $3\frac{1}{2}$, because if we write the relation as a complex fraction we get $\dfrac{2}{3\frac{1}{2}}$, and multiplying both numerator and denominator by 2 gives us $\frac{4}{7}$.

Similarly, to find what part $3\frac{1}{2}$ is of $5\frac{1}{6}$, we reduce both to twelfths. $3\frac{1}{2} = \frac{42}{12}$; $5\frac{1}{6} = \frac{62}{12}$; $\frac{42}{12} = \frac{21}{31}$.

To find a number when a specified fractional part is given, *divide the given number by the specified fraction.*

EXAMPLE: 360 is $\frac{5}{6}$ of what number?

SOLUTION: $360 \times \frac{6}{5} = 432$, Ans.

EXPLANATION: Since 360 is $\frac{5}{6}$ of the number, $\frac{1}{6}$ will be determined by dividing 360 by 5, and the whole number will be found by multiplying this sixth part by 6. The necessary calculations are performed at once by simply inverting the specified fraction and then multiplying.

Practice Exercise No. 15a

1 What part of 11 is 8?
2 What part of 16 is $\frac{3}{5}$?
3 What part of $5\frac{1}{4}$ is 4?
4 What part of $3\frac{1}{2}$ is $2\frac{1}{4}$?
5 160 is $\frac{4}{5}$ of?
6 144 is $\frac{9}{10}$ of?
7 143 is $1\frac{3}{4}$ of?
8 $1\frac{5}{16}$ is $\frac{5}{7}$ of?

Practice Exercise No. 16

PROBLEMS

1 How many sheets of metal $\frac{1}{32}$ inches thick are there in a pile $25\frac{1}{2}$ inches high?

(A) 550 ____   (c) 408 ____
(B) 105 ____   (D) 816 ____

2 If a man can do a piece of work in 16 days how much of it can he do in $\frac{1}{2}$ day?

(A) $\frac{1}{2}$ ____   (c) $\frac{1}{8}$ ____
(B) $\frac{1}{32}$ ____   (D) $\frac{1}{16}$ ____

3 Find the area in square inches of the figure represented by the diagram below.

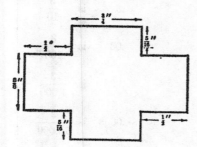

(A) $1\frac{1}{2}$ ____   (c) $1\frac{9}{16}$ ____
(B) $2\frac{1}{32}$ ____   (D) $6\frac{2}{3}$ ____

4 If $\frac{1}{3}$ the length of a beam is 10 feet, how long is the entire beam?

(A) 3 ____   (c) $3\frac{1}{3}$ ____
(B) 30 ____   (D) 9 ____

Note: To find the value of the whole when the fractional part is given, *invert the fraction and multiply it by the given part.*

5 If $\frac{1}{3}$ of a machine's daily output is equal to $\frac{1}{2}$ of another machine's daily output, and if the total day's output is 600 parts, how many parts were produced by the more efficient machine?

(A) 300 ____   (c) 200 ____
(B) 360 ____   (D) 440 ____

6 If it takes 5 hours to do $\frac{2}{3}$ of a job, how long will it take to complete the job?

(A) $7\frac{1}{2}$ ____   (c) 7 ____
(B) $3\frac{1}{2}$ ____   (D) 10 ____

7 Two machines turn out an equal amount of parts daily. One day they both break down; the second to break down turns out $\frac{5}{6}$ of its usual amount while the first turns out $\frac{1}{2}$ of what the second does. What fraction of their usual combined total is lost because of the breakdown?

(A) $\frac{1}{2}$ ____   (c) $\frac{3}{4}$ ____
(B) $\frac{3}{8}$ ____   (D) $\frac{1}{6}$ ____

8 An aviator made 3 flights. The first was 432 miles, the second was only $\frac{1}{2}$ that distance and the third $\frac{1}{3}$ of the original distance. How far would he have to go on a fourth flight to equal $\frac{1}{2}$ the distance covered by the second and third trips?

(A) 180 ____   (c) 360 ____
(B) 450 ____   (D) 275 ____

9 It takes 24 days to complete the first $\frac{1}{4}$ of a ship; 31 days to complete the next $\frac{3}{8}$ of it. If the average rate of speed for this much of the job were maintained, how long would it take to build the entire ship?

(A) 96 ____   (c) 33 ____
(B) 80 ____   (D) 88 ____

10 The distance between New York and California is 3,000 miles. Two trains leave the two cities at the same time. One train travels at the rate of $62\frac{3}{8}$ miles an hour, the other at $69\frac{4}{5}$ miles per hour. How far apart will the two trains be at the end of 5 hours?

(A) 662 ____   (c) 2,220 ____
(B) 2,338 ____   (D) 1,842 ____

CHAPTER THREE

DECIMAL FRACTIONS

Decimal fractions are a special way of writing proper fractions that have denominators beginning with 1 and ending with one or more zeros. *Thus,* when written as decimal fractions,

$$\frac{1}{10}, \quad \frac{2}{100}, \quad \frac{3}{1,000}, \quad \frac{4}{10,000}, \quad \frac{5}{100,000}, \text{ etc.}$$

become

.1,   .02,   .003,   .0004,   .00005, etc.

The period before the digits is the **decimal point;** the digits following it are said *to stand in certain decimal places.*

The word *decimal* means *relating to the number ten,* and to calculate fractions by decimals is simply to extend into the field of fractions the same method of counting that we employ when dealing with whole numbers.

READING DECIMAL FRACTIONS

Read the number after the decimal point as a whole number and give it the name of its last decimal place.

Thus,

.135 is read as *one hundred thirty-five thousandths.*

4.18 is read as *four and eighteen hundredths.*

Another way to read
.135 is *point, one-three-five.*
4.18 may be read *four, point, one-eight.*

Practice Exercise No. 17

Read each number aloud and write it as a common fraction or as a mixed number.

1	.01 =	6	.0008 =
2	.5 =	7	.0608 =
3	.625 =	8	.2341 =
4	2.10 =	9	.04329 =
5	23.450 =	10	18.0200 =

In examples 11 to 20 write the numbers as decimals.

11	$\frac{3}{10}$ =	16	$18\frac{7}{10}$ =
12	$\frac{5}{100}$ =	17	$\frac{300}{1000}$ =
13	$\frac{321}{1000}$ =	18	$\frac{145}{100}$ =
14	$12\frac{1}{100}$ =	19	$\frac{223}{10}$ =
15	$124\frac{3}{10000}$ =	20	$\frac{4330}{1000}$ =

Place of digit	How to read it	Example		
First decimal place	Tenths	.3	is	$\frac{3}{10}$
Second decimal place	Hundredths	.03	is	$\frac{3}{100}$
Third decimal place	Thousandths	.003	is	$\frac{3}{1,000}$
Fourth decimal place	Ten thousandths	.0003	is	$\frac{3}{10,000}$
Fifth decimal place	Hundred thousandths	.00003	is	$\frac{3}{100,000}$

Table II
DECIMAL EQUIVALENTS OF SIXTY-FOURTHS

Fraction	Decimal	Fraction	Decimal
$\frac{1}{64}$	0.015625	$\frac{33}{64}$	0.515625
$\frac{1}{32}$	.03125	$\frac{17}{32}$	.53125
$\frac{3}{64}$	.046875	$\frac{35}{64}$	.546875
$\frac{1}{16}$	.0625	$\frac{9}{16}$	.5625
$\frac{5}{64}$	.078125	$\frac{37}{64}$	.578125
$\frac{3}{32}$	.09375	$\frac{19}{32}$	.59375
$\frac{7}{64}$	.109375	$\frac{39}{64}$	.609375
$\frac{1}{8}$	.125	$\frac{5}{8}$	.625
$\frac{9}{64}$	.140625	$\frac{41}{64}$	.640625
$\frac{5}{32}$	.15625	$\frac{21}{32}$	.65625
$\frac{11}{64}$	.171875	$\frac{43}{64}$	.671875
$\frac{3}{16}$	.1875	$\frac{11}{16}$	.6875
$\frac{13}{64}$	.203125	$\frac{45}{64}$	.703125
$\frac{7}{32}$	.21875	$\frac{23}{32}$	.71875
$\frac{15}{64}$	.234375	$\frac{47}{64}$	.734375
$\frac{1}{4}$	.25	$\frac{3}{4}$	.75
$\frac{17}{64}$	.265625	$\frac{49}{64}$	.765625
$\frac{9}{32}$	.28125	$\frac{25}{32}$	.78125
$\frac{19}{64}$	.296875	$\frac{51}{64}$	.796875
$\frac{5}{16}$	.3125	$\frac{13}{16}$	.8125
$\frac{21}{64}$	.328125	$\frac{53}{64}$	.828125
$\frac{11}{32}$	.34375	$\frac{27}{32}$	.84375
$\frac{23}{64}$	.359375	$\frac{55}{64}$	.859375
$\frac{3}{8}$	.375	$\frac{7}{8}$	.875
$\frac{25}{64}$	.390625	$\frac{57}{64}$	.890625
$\frac{13}{32}$	.40625	$\frac{29}{32}$	.90625
$\frac{27}{64}$	.421875	$\frac{59}{64}$	.921875
$\frac{7}{16}$	.4375	$\frac{15}{16}$	.9375
$\frac{29}{64}$	.453125	$\frac{61}{64}$	.953125
$\frac{15}{32}$	.46875	$\frac{31}{32}$	.96875
$\frac{31}{64}$	.484375	$\frac{63}{64}$	.984375
$\frac{1}{2}$	.5	1	1.

In the last part of Exercise No. 17 you converted fractions to decimals by placing the decimal point and the correct number of ciphers (0's) before the numerator and eliminating the denominator. You could do this because all the denominators were 10s or some multiple of ten such as 100, 1,000, 10,000, etc. It is not possible, however, to do this in all cases. Hence—

To change any common fraction into decimals, *divide the numerator by the denominator and write the quotient in decimal form.*

EXAMPLE 1: Change $\frac{3}{5}$ to a decimal.

SOLUTION: 5)3.0
.6 ANS.

EXAMPLE 2: Change $\frac{3}{8}$ to a decimal.

SOLUTION: 8)3.000
.375 ANS.

Above you will find a table in which the decimal equivalents are worked out for fractions up to 64ths. All of these are frequently used in various types of technical work. Similarly, conversions of decimals to common fractions are often necessary in shop practice.

Practice Exercise No. 18

Using the foregoing table, find the decimal equivalents to the nearest thousandths of the following fractions:

1 $\frac{1}{2}$ =   6 $\frac{17}{32}$ =   10 $8.04 - 7.96 =$

2 $\frac{3}{4}$ =   7 $\frac{28}{32}$ =   11 $72.306 + 18.45 - 27.202 =$

3 $\frac{3}{8}$ =   8 $\frac{14}{16}$ =   12 $14 - 6.3 + 2.739 =$

4 $\frac{5}{16}$ =   9 $\frac{22}{32}$ =   13 $27.65 + 18.402 - 2.39 + 7.63 =$

5 $\frac{9}{16}$ =   10 $\frac{56}{64}$ =   14 $18.0006 + 14.005 + 12.34 =$

15 $93.8 - 16.4327 - 20.009 =$

16 $14.29 - 6.305 - 3.47265 =$

ADDITION AND SUBTRACTION OF DECIMALS

To add or subtract decimals, *place the numbers in a column with the decimal points in a column. Add or subtract as for whole numbers, placing the decimal point in the result in the column of decimal points.*

EXAMPLE 1: Find the sum of 2.43, 1.485, .3, 12.02 and .074.

SOLUTION:

```
  2.43   or    2.430
  1.485        1.485
   .3           .300
 12.02        12.020
   .074         .074
 ------       -------
 16.309       16.309
```

EXPLANATION: Since 1.485 and .074 are three-place numbers, we write zeros after 2.43, .3 and 12.02. This does not change the value but helps to avoid errors.

EXAMPLE 2: Find the difference of 17.29 and 6.147.

SOLUTION:

```
 17.29   or   17.290
 -6.147       -6.147
 ------       ------
 11.143       11.143
```

EXPLANATION: As above, we add a zero to 17.29 to make it a three-place number. This does not change the value, and is not strictly necessary but helps to avoid errors.

Note : *The value of a decimal fraction is not changed if zeros are written at the right end of it.*

Practice Exercise No. 19

Do the following examples:

1 $.2 + .07 + .5 =$

2 $2.6 + 22.4 + .03 =$

3 $22.8 + 5.099 + 613.2 =$

4 $.005 + 5 + 16.2 + .96 =$

5 $15.4 + 22 + .01 + 1.48 =$

6 $28.74 - 16.32 =$

7 $.005 - .0005 =$

8 $1.431 - .562 =$

9 $1.0020 - .2 =$

MULTIPLICATION OF DECIMALS

To multiply decimals, *proceed as in multiplication of whole numbers. But in the product, beginning at the right, point off as many decimal places as there are in the multiplier and in the multiplicand combined.*

EXAMPLE 1: Multiply 3.12 by .42.

SOLUTION:

```
 3.12   (Multiplicand—has two decimal places.)
  .42   (Multiplier—has two decimal places.)
 ----
 624
1248
------
1.3104  Ans. (Product has two plus two, or four
              decimal places.)
```

EXPLANATION: Since there is a total of four decimal places when we add together those in the multiplier and in the multiplicand, we start at the right and count four places; hence we put the decimal point off to the left of the 3, which marks the fourth place counted off.

EXAMPLE 2: Multiply .214 by .303

SOLUTION:

```
  .214
  .303
 -----
  642
6420
-------
.?64842 = .064842,  Ans.
```

EXPLANATION: There are a total of six places in the multiplier and in the multiplicand, but there are only five numbers in the product; therefore we prefix a zero at the left end, and place our decimal point before it to give the required six decimal places. If we needed eight places and the answer came out to five places, we would prefix three zeros and place the decimal point to the left of them.

To multiply a decimal by any multiple of ten, *move the decimal point as many places to the right as there are zeros in the multiplier.*

Thus, $.31 \times 100 = 31$; $.021 \times 100 = 02.1 = 2.1$ (here we drop the zero since before a whole number it is meaningless), .31 × 1,000 = 310 (we add a cipher to make the third place).

Reciprocally: **to divide a decimal or a whole number by 10 or by a multiple of 10,** *we move the decimal point as many places to the* LEFT *as there are zeros in the divisor.*

Thus, 42 ÷ 10 = 4.2; 15.6 ÷ 100 = .156; 61 ÷ 1,000 = .061 (prefixing zero to give the required number of decimal places).

Practice Exercise No. 20

Do the following examples:

1	18.5 × 4 =	16	8.7 × 10 =
2	3.9 × 2.4 =	17	.0069 × 10 =
3	45 × .72 =	18	95.6 × 100 =
4	143 × .214 =	19	.0453 × 100 =
5	.56 × .74 =	20	4.069 × 1,000 =
6	.224 × .302 =	21	.000094 × 10,000 =
7	7.43 × .132 =	22	9.2 × 10 =
8	.021 × .204 =	23	7.49 × 100 =
9	.601 × .003 =	24	534.79 ÷ 100 =
10	.014 × .0064 =	25	492.568 ÷ 1,000 =
11	13.2 × 2.475 =	26	24.9653 ÷ 1,000 =
12	.132 × 2.475 =	27	5.908 ÷ 100 =
13	.236 × 12.13 =	28	.07156 ÷ 1,000 =
14	9.06 × .045 =	29	4956.74 ÷ 10,000 =
15	.008 × 751.1 =	30	.038649 ÷ 100,000 =

DIVISION OF DECIMALS

Law of division: *A quotient is not changed when the dividend and divisor are both multiplied by the same number.*

EXAMPLE 1: 7.2 ÷ .9

7.2 × 10 = 72   Thus, multiplying dividend and
.9 × 10 = 9   divisor by ten gives 72 ÷ 9 = 8.
72 ÷ 9 = 8, ANS.

To check: 8 × 9 = 72, and 8 × .9 = 7.2.

To divide a decimal by a whole number, *proceed as with whole numbers, but place the decimal point in the quotient directly above the decimal point in the dividend.*

EXAMPLE 2: 20.46 ÷ 66.

SOLUTION:

```
        .31  ANS.
  66)20.46
     198
     ───
      66
      66
      ──
       0
```

EXPLANATION: Dividing as with whole numbers, simply place the decimal point in the quotient directly above the decimal point in the dividend. Check the answer by multiplying the quotient by the divisor.

EXAMPLE 3: How many yards in 165.6 inches?

SOLUTION:

```
         4.6  ANS.
  36)165.6
     144
     ───
     216
     216
     ───
       0
```

EXPLANATION: Since there are 36 inches in one yard, we divide the number of inches by 36, pointing off the quotient decimally as in the previous example.

To divide a decimal by a decimal, *move the decimal point of the divisor to the right until it becomes a whole number (i.e. multiply it by ten or a multiple of ten). Next move the decimal point of the dividend the same number of places to the right, adding zeros if necessary.* (Multiplying divisor and dividend by the same number does not change the quotient.) *Then proceed to divide as in Example 2, above.*

EXAMPLE 4: 131.88 ÷ 4.2

SOLUTION:

```
          31.4  ANS.
  4.2)131.8.8
      126
      ───
       58
       42
       ──
      168
      168
      ───
        0
```

EXPLANATION: Division of a decimal by a decimal is simplified if the divisor is made a whole number. In this case the divisor 4.2 was made a whole number by moving the decimal point one place; therefore we also moved the decimal point one place in the dividend. Then placing the decimal point in the quotient directly above the decimal point in the dividend, we proceed as for division of whole numbers.

Check the answer by multiplying the quotient by the divisor or by casting out nines.

It is a corollary of the foregoing that when we are working with two numbers which contain the same number of decimal places, the decimal points may be disregarded and the two numbers treated like whole numbers. This is often useful to remember when working against time.

To carry out a decimal quotient to a given number of places, *add zeros to the right of the dividend until the dividend contains the required number of places.*

EXAMPLE 5: Find .3 ÷ .7 to the nearest thousandth.

SOLUTION:

$$7\overline{)3.0000}$$

   .4285, Ans.—But change to .429 as the answer requested.

EXPLANATION: In examples 1, 2, and 3 the quotients had no remainder. Often division problems do not come out evenly, as in Example 5. We then add zeros to the right of the dividend in order to carry out the division to the number of decimal places required by the work.

As a general rule carry out the division to one more decimal place than is needed. If the last figure is five or more drop it and add one to the figure in the preceding place. (This was done in Example 5, above.) If the last figure is less than five, just drop it entirely.

AVERAGES

In finding averages of several quantities you should round off the result to the smallest part stated in the problem. Thus, if a problem is stated in decimal thousandths, the result should be given in thousandths.

Rule: To find the average of several decimal quantities, *divide their sum by the number of quantities.*

EXAMPLE: Find the average of the following dimensions: 1.734, 1.748, 1.64, and 1.802

SOLUTION:

  1.734 $4\overline{)6.924}$
  1.748   1.731 = 1.73, Ans.
  1.640
  1.802
  6.924

EXPLANATION: Add the quantities and divide the sum, 6.924, by the number of quantities, 4. Carry the answer only to hundredths, since that is the smallest dimension included in the problem.

Practice Exercise No. 21

Carry out answers only as far as three places.

1	.34 ÷ 2	6	1.11 ÷ .3
2	.35 ÷ 7	7	.987 ÷ 21
3	5.4 ÷ 9	8	.2546 ÷ .38
4	47.3 ÷ 10	9	2.83 ÷ .007
5	4.2 ÷ .01	10	.081 ÷ .0022

ALIQUOT PARTS

An **aliquot part** of a number is a part that exactly divides the number. The term is used especially of the decimal values in cents that are exact fractional divisions of one dollar. Everybody should be familiar with the following values.

ALIQUOT PARTS OF ONE DOLLAR

$\frac{1}{8}$	$= 12\frac{1}{2}¢$	$\frac{1}{6}$	$= 16\frac{2}{3}¢$
$\frac{2}{8}$ or $\frac{1}{4}$	$= 25$	$\frac{2}{6}$ or $\frac{1}{3}$	$= 33\frac{1}{3}$
$\frac{3}{8}$	$= 37\frac{1}{2}$	$\frac{4}{6}$ or $\frac{2}{3}$	$= 66\frac{2}{3}$
$\frac{4}{8}$ or $\frac{1}{2}$	$= 50$	$\frac{5}{6}$	$= 83\frac{1}{3}$
$\frac{5}{8}$	$= 62\frac{1}{2}$		
$\frac{6}{8}$ or $\frac{3}{4}$	$= 75$	$\frac{1}{16}$	$= 6\frac{1}{4}$
$\frac{7}{8}$	$= 87\frac{1}{2}$	$\frac{1}{12}$	$= 8\frac{1}{3}$

Problems involving any of these values will usually be simplified if they are worked with common fractions instead of decimals.

To find the cost when the price involves an aliquot part of one dollar, *multiply the cost by the price expressed as a common fraction.*

EXAMPLE 1: What will 1,751 castings cost at $33\frac{1}{3}¢$ each?

SOLUTION: $1{,}751 \times \frac{1}{3} = 583\frac{2}{3} = \$583.67$, Ans.

EXAMPLE 2: What would 15,500 bushels of grain cost at $2.75 per bushel?

SOLUTION: $15{,}500 \times \frac{11}{4} = \frac{170{,}500}{4}$

$$= \$42{,}625, \text{ Ans.}$$

To find the quantity when the total cost is given and the price is an aliquot part of one dollar, *divide the cost by the price expressed as a common fraction.*

EXAMPLE: How many yards of cloth at $83\frac{1}{3}¢$ per yard can be bought for $1,000?

SOLUTION: $1000 \div \frac{5}{6} = 1000 \times \frac{6}{5} = \frac{6000}{5}$

$$= 1{,}200 \text{ yards, } \text{Ans.}$$

Practice Exercise No. 22

1 276 yards @ $16\frac{2}{3}$¢ =
2 344 bushels @ $62\frac{1}{2}$¢ =
3 267 pounds @ $83\frac{1}{3}$¢ =
4 1,908 gallons @ $1.25 =
5 2,514 barrels @ $5.83\frac{1}{3}$ =
6 $6,200 buys how many tons @ $7.75?
7 $1,000 buys how many bushels @ 1.33\frac{1}{3}$?
8 $500 buys how many yards @ $37\frac{1}{2}$¢?
9 $10 buys how many quarts @ $8\frac{1}{3}$¢?
10 $1 buys how many pounds @ $62\frac{1}{2}$¢?

Practice Exercise No. 23

PROBLEMS INVOLVING DECIMALS

1 A laborer mixed 250 lbs. of mortar. .84 of it was sand. How many pounds of sand were used?

(A) 166 ____   (c) 210 ____
(B) 14 ____   (d) 50 ____

2 A square metal box has a perimeter of 8.32″ (inches). If the sides are .04″ thick, what is the perimeter of the inside?

Note: Perimeter is equal to the total distance around an object.

(A) 8.16″ ____   (c) 8.24″ ____
(B) 8.48″ ____   (d) 8″ ____

3 A link pin is supposed to have a diameter of .675″, but one of these was made .0007″ too large. What was its diameter?

(A) .6743 ____   (c) .7675 ____
(B) .6757 ____   (d) .4725 ____

4 Mr. Brown received $44.20 for his eggs. How many dozen did he sell if the price he received was 52 cents a dozen?

Note: 52 cents is equivalent to .52.

(A) 90 ____   (c) 95 ____
(B) 100 ____   (d) 85 ____

5 A 16-story building is 158.72 feet high. How high is it up to and including the 6th story?

(A) 9.92 ____   (c) 66 ____
(B) 26.45 ____   (d) 59.52 ____

6 What would you consider the probable diameter of a lock nut if you measured it four times and obtained the following readings: .641″, .647″, .642″, .646″?

(A) .643″ ____   (c) .645″ ____
(B) .644″ ____   (d) .646″ ____

7 A certain automobile cylinder is $3\frac{3}{8}$″ in diameter. The piston which is to fit into it must have .0045″ clearance. What should the diameter of the piston be?

Note: Use table of fractional equivalents.

(A) $3\frac{7}{8}$″ ____   (c) 3.366″ ____
(B) 3.3695″ ____ (d) 3.420″ ____

PERCENTAGE

(*Discount, Interest, Commission, Profit, and Loss*)

Percentage is a term used in arithmetic to denote that a whole quantity divided into 100 equal parts is taken as the standard of measure. Percentage is indicated by the **percent sign** (%).

Thus *percent*, or %, means a number of parts of one hundred (100). For example, 4% may be written as $\frac{4}{100}$ or .04. Notice that $\frac{4}{100}$ reduces to $\frac{1}{25}$.

Percents may be added, subtracted, multiplied, or divided, just as other specific denominations are treated.

$$Thus: \quad 6\% + 8\% = 14\%$$
$$18\% - 12\% = 6\%$$
$$18\% \div 9\% = 2$$
$$7\% \times 5 = 35\%$$

In the actual working of a problem, when the % sign is not used the percentages must be changed to a common fraction or a decimal.

To change a percent to a fraction, *divide the percent quantity by 100 and reduce to lowest terms.*

$$Thus: \quad 8\% = \frac{8}{100} = \frac{2}{25}$$
$$75\% = \frac{75}{100} = \frac{3}{4}$$
$$80\% = ?$$

Table III

FRACTIONAL EQUIVALENTS OF PERCENTS

$10\% = \frac{1}{10}$	$12\frac{1}{2}\% = \frac{1}{8}$	$8\frac{1}{3}\% = \frac{1}{12}$
$20\% = \frac{1}{5}$	$25\% = \frac{1}{4}$	$16\frac{2}{3}\% = \frac{1}{6}$
$40\% = \frac{2}{5}$	$37\frac{1}{2}\% = \frac{3}{8}$	$33\frac{1}{3}\% = \frac{1}{3}$
$50\% = \frac{1}{2}$	$62\frac{1}{2}\% = \frac{5}{8}$	$66\frac{2}{3}\% = \frac{2}{3}$
$60\% = \frac{3}{5}$	$87\frac{1}{2}\% = \frac{7}{8}$	$83\frac{1}{3}\% = \frac{5}{6}$

Practice Exercise No. 24

Change to fractions.

1 1% =   7 $6\frac{2}{3}$% =
2 2% =   8 $7\frac{1}{2}$% =
3 4% =   9 $\frac{1}{3}$% =
4 7% =   10 $\frac{3}{4}$% =
5 $\frac{1}{2}$% =   11 $1\frac{1}{2}$% =
6 $6\frac{1}{4}$% =   12 $3\frac{1}{2}$% =

To change a percent to a decimal, *remove the percent sign and move the decimal point two places to the left.*

EXAMPLE 1: Change 25% to a decimal.

25% = .25   Moving decimal point two places to the left.

EXAMPLE 2: Change 1.5% to a decimal.

1.5% = .015   To move the decimal point two places to the left, one zero had to be prefixed.

To change a decimal to a percent, *move the decimal point two places to the right and add a percent sign.*

EXAMPLE 1: Change .24 to a percent.

.24 = 24%   Moving the decimal point two places to the right and adding the % sign.

EXAMPLE 2: Change .0043 to a percent.

.0043 = .43%   Note that this is less than 1%.

EXAMPLE 3: Change 2.45 to a percent.

2.45 = 245%   Note that any whole number greater than 1 which designates a percent is more than 100%.

The **terms** commonly used in percentage are **rate** (R), **base** (B), **percentage** (P), **amount** (A), and **difference** (D).

Rate (R) or **rate percent** is the fractional part in hundredths that is to be found.

For example, in 4% of 50 = 2,

$$4\%, \tfrac{1}{25} \text{ or } .04 \text{ is the } rate.$$

The **base** (B) is the whole quantity of which some percent is to be found.

In 4% of 50 = 2, 50 is the *base* or whole quantity.

The **percentage** (P) is the result obtained by taking a given hundredth part of the base.

In 4% of 50 = 2, 2 is the *percentage* or the part taken.

The **amount** (A) is the sum of the base and the percentage.

In 4% of 50 = 2, the *amount* is 50 + 2, or 52.

The **difference** (D) is the remainder of the base left when the percentage is subtracted.

In 4% of 50 = 2, 50 − 2 or 48 is the *difference.*

THE THREE TYPES OF PERCENTAGE PROBLEMS

A. **Finding a percent of a number:** given the base and the rate, to find the percentage.

EXAMPLE 1: Find 14% of $300.

$$
\begin{array}{r}
300 \text{ base} \\
\times\,.14 \text{ rate} \\
\hline
1200 \\
300 \\
\hline
\$42.00 \text{ percentage, \ Ans.}
\end{array}
$$

EXPLANATION: 14% is equal to .14. Multiplying 300 by .14, the product is $42 or 14% of $300.

Percentage = Base × Rate; or $P = B \times R$.

B. **Finding what percent one number is of another:** given the base and the percentage to find the rate.

EXAMPLE 2: 120 is what percent of 240?

$\frac{120}{240} = \frac{1}{2} = 50\%$, Ans.

120 = the percentage.

240 = the base.

50% = the rate.

Rate = Percentage ÷ Base; or $R = \dfrac{P}{B}$.

EXPLANATION: This is another way of saying what fractional part of 240 is 120. Change the answer to percent.

C. **Finding a number when a percent of that number is known:** given the rate and the percentage, to find the base.

EXAMPLE 3: 225 is 25% of what amount?

$25\% = \frac{1}{4}$, $225 \div \frac{1}{4} = 225 \times \frac{4}{1} = 900$, Ans.

225 = the percentage.

25% = the rate.

900 = the base.

Base = Percentage ÷ Rate; or $B = \dfrac{P}{R}$.

EXPLANATION: This is another way of saying $\frac{1}{4}$ of a number equals 225, and asking what does the whole number equal.

The formulas given above make the solution of percentage problems easy if you learn to identify the base, the rate, and the percentage.

Practice Exercise No. 25

1 Find 30% of 620 gallons.

2 Find $12\frac{1}{2}$% of 96 men.

3 What is 4% of 250 lb.?

4 How much is $62\frac{1}{2}$% of $80.00?

5 Find $\frac{1}{2}$ of 1% of 190 tons.

6 8¢ is what percent of 32¢?

7 $7\frac{1}{2}$ inches is what percent of 15 inches?

8 $14 is what percent of $200?

9 $\frac{1}{3}$ is what percent of $\frac{2}{3}$?

10 $\frac{1}{2}$ is what percent of $\frac{2}{3}$?

11 12 = 25% of what number?

12 10 is 20% of what number?

13 8 is $2\frac{1}{2}$% of what number?

14 16% of a sum = 128. What is the sum?

15 What number increased by 25% of itself equals 120?

16 A loaded truck weighs 20,000 lbs. If 80% of this represents the load, how much does the truck weigh?

(A) 2,000 ____   (c) 4,000 ____

(B) 8,000 ____   (D) 16,000 ____

17 A bin weighs 8% as much as its contents. If the contents weigh 275 lbs., what is the weight of the bin?

(A) 22 ____   (c) $22\frac{11}{12}$ ____

(B) $34\frac{3}{8}$ ____   (D) 207 ____

18 A brass bar weighing 75 lbs. is made of 45% zinc and the balance of copper. How many lbs. of copper does it contain?

(A) 55 ____   (c) $33\frac{3}{4}$ ____

(B) $41\frac{1}{4}$ ____   (D) $\frac{3}{5}$ ____

19 What number increased by 75% of itself = 140?

(A) 105 ____   (c) $46\frac{2}{3}$ ____

(B) 215 ____   (D) 80 ____

20 One man in a crew receives a bonus of $5.25, which is 17.5% of the total bonus allowed for the job. What is the total bonus in dollars and cents?

(A) $93.65 ____   (c) $30.00 ____

(B) $433.12 ____   (D) $31.50 ____

21 A truck carrying 6,750 lbs. of coal weighed 9,000 lbs. What percent of the total weight was due to the weight of the truck?

(A) 15% ____   (c) 25% ____

(B) 20% ____   (D) 30% ____

22 A bronze statue with a wooden base weighed 28 lbs. The base weighed $3\frac{1}{2}$ lbs. What percent of the total weight was bronze?

(A) $87\frac{1}{2}$% ____   (c) 9.8% ____

(B) $12\frac{1}{2}$% ____   (D) $83\frac{1}{3}$% ____

23 In a factory 8% of the machines broke down. They were replaced by new ones. How many machines are there in the shop if 144 machines were replaced?

(A) 1,728 ____   (c) 1,440 ____

(B) 1,800 ____   (D) 360 ____

24 If the voltage loss of an electrical transmitting line is 5%, what will be the voltage at the end of the line if the generator voltage is 140?

(A) 147 ____   (c) 28 ____

(B) 7 ____   (D) 133 ____

25 $33\frac{1}{3}$% of a machinist's daily output is equal to 50% of another man's output. The slower man turns out 1,500 machine screws daily. What is the faster man's output?

(A) 500 ____   (c) 2,000 ____

(B) 1,000 ____   (D) 2,250 ____

CHAPTER FOUR

DISCOUNT, COMMISSION, INTEREST, PROFIT, AND LOSS

The arithmetical principles learned in studying the topic of percentage can be applied directly in solving problems in Discount, Commission, Interest, and Profit and Loss. In order to understand problems in those fields it is first necessary to become familiar with the meanings of the terms used in each branch. Here is a table of terms used in connection with these topics, matched according to their equivalence to each other and to those used in dealing with the general subject of percentage.

Table IV

Percentage	Commission	Discount	Interest	Profit and Loss
Base (*B*)	Cost or Selling price	List price	Principal	Cost
Rate percent (*R*)	Rate of commission	Rate	Rate	Percent gain or loss
Percentage (*P*)	Commission	Discount	Interest	Gain or loss in money
Amount	Total cost			
or	or	Net price	Amount	Selling price
Difference (*D*)	Net proceeds			

You will notice that the same basic relationship that holds true for percentage ($P = B \times R$), holds true for all the others.

DISCOUNT

A **discount** is a reduction in the selling price of an article or in the amount of a bill. Discounts are expressed as rates or percents.

The **list price** of an article is the original price.

The **net price** is the list price minus the discount.

To find the amount of a discount, *multiply the list price, or base, by the rate of discount.*

Formula: $P = B \times R$, indicating the first type of percentage problem.

EXAMPLE 1: A used car listed at $925.00 was sold at a discount of 10%. Find the discount.

$B = \$925, R = 10\%$ $P = ?$
$P = B \times R; P = \$925 \times .10 = \$92.50$

To find the net price, *subtract the amount of the discount from the original or list price.*

Formula:

Difference = Base − Percentage.
$$D = B - P.$$

EXAMPLE 2: A file cabinet was listed at $62.50. Find the net price if the discount was 12%.

SOLUTION: $D = ?$ $P = ?$ $R = 12\%$. $B = \$62.50$.

$P = B \times R = \$62.50 \times .12 = \$7.50$.
$D = B - P = \$62.50 - \$7.50$
$\qquad = \$55.00$ net,   ANS.

ALTERNATE SOLUTION: Instead of multiplying the list price by the percent discount and deducting the result, a short method is to deduct the percent discount from 100% and multiply the remainder by the list price to get the net price directly. Thus in the same example we have:

$100\% - 12\% = 88\%$;
$62.50 \times .88 = \$55.00$,   ANS.

Chain discounts is the term used when more than one discount is given. Thus, when two or more discounts are given, the second discount is taken off what remains after the amount of the first discount has been deducted from the list price. The same process is continued in cases where three or more discounts are allowed.

EXAMPLE 3: An oil stove is listed at $400 with discounts of 20%, 10% and 5%. What is the net price?

SOLUTION:

$\$400 \times \frac{1}{5} = \$80$
$\underline{-80}$
$\$320 \times \frac{1}{10} = \$32$
$\underline{-32}$
$\$288 \times \frac{1}{20} = \$14.40$
$\underline{-14.40}$
$\$273.60$ net price,   ANS.

A SHORTER WAY to do this example: Discounts of 20%, 10% and 5% mean selling at 80%, 90% and 95% of the list price; expressed decimally they are .8, .9, and .95. Multiply these in succession. $.8 \times .9 \times .95 = .684$

List price $\qquad$ $400
Net price per dollar $\underline{\quad .684}$ multiplying $.684 \times 400$
$\qquad\qquad$ $273.60 net selling price,   ANS.

The method here shown is generally used in business. In offices where a great many calculations of this kind have to be made, however, matters are expedited by the use of tables which show the net decimal equivalents of chain discounts.

Practice Exercise No. 26

1 What is the selling price of a $129 chair if it is sold at a discount of 25%?

(A) $32.25 _____   (c) $96.75 _____
(B) $85.00 _____   (D) $45 _____

2   How much can be saved by buying at a discount of $66\frac{2}{3}\%$ a table marked $58.50?

(A) $39.00 ____   (c) $48.00 ____
(B) $19.50 ____   (d) $27.00 ____

3   A painter buys 60 rolls of wall paper. The list price is $3.50 a roll. He gets a discount of 8% and an additional 2% for cash. How much did he pay for the wall paper?

(A) $371.00 ____   (c) $210.66 ____
(B) $21.00 ____   (d) $189.34 ____

4   A dealer buys equipment for a baseball catcher. It has a list price of $40. He receives discounts of 40%, 10% and 5%. How much does he have to pay?

(A) $22.00 ____   (c) $20.52 ____
(B) $18.00 ____   (d) $21.60 ____

5   What do discounts of 25%, 8% and 5% amount to on a bill of $300?

(A) $115.45 ____   (c) $120.65 ____
(B) $103.35 ____   (d) $118.25 ____

COMMISSION OR BROKERAGE

Commission or brokerage is the amount of money paid to an agent for buying or selling goods. When the commission is some percent of the value of the services performed, that rate percent is called the rate of commission.

Gross proceeds or **selling price** is the money received by the agent for his employer. In commission or brokerage calculations this is called the **base**.

Net proceeds is the gross proceeds minus the commission.

To find the commission, *multiply the principal amount, or the base, by the rate of commission.*

The **formula** is:

Commission (P) = Base $(B) \times$ Rate (R),

or $\qquad P = B \times R.$

EXAMPLE 1: A real estate salesman sold a lot for $5,000. His commission is $2\frac{1}{2}\%$. How much does he receive?

SOLUTION: $P = B \times R.$
$\qquad B = \$5,000, R = 2\frac{1}{2}\%, P = ?$
$\qquad \$5,000 \times .025 = \$125$ commission, ANS.

EXAMPLE 2: A broker received $200 for selling a piece of property. His rate of commission was 5%. What was the selling price?

SOLUTION: $\dfrac{P}{R} = B.$

$\qquad P = \$200, R = 5\%, B = ?$

$\qquad \dfrac{\$200}{.05} = \$4,000$ selling price, ANS.

Or: $\$200 \div \frac{1}{20} = \$200 \times \frac{20}{1} = \$4,000$, ANS.

Practice Exercise No. 27

1   An agent sells $25,000 worth of property at $1\frac{1}{2}\%$ commission. How much does he receive?

(A) $3,500 ____   (c) $166 ____
(B) $375 ____   (d) $750 ____

2   A salesman sells 100 sets of silverware at $165 per set. At 16% what would his commission be?

(A) $26.40 ____   (c) $2,640 ____
(B) $2,700 ____   (d) $2,000 ____

3   An agent earned $400 commission at a rate of 5% for selling a farm. What was the selling price of the farm?

(A) $8,000 ____   (c) $2,000 ____
(B) $3,800 ____   (d) $6,000 ____

4   For a very difficult sale a commission agent received $37\frac{1}{2}\%$ on a sale. His fee was $600. What was the amount of the sale?

(A) $4,800 ____   (c) $1,200 ____
(B) $1,600 ____   (d) $2,000 ____

INTEREST

Interest problems employ the rules of percentage problems but include the additional factor of *time*.

The **interest** (I) is the amount of money paid for the use of money.

The **principal** (P) is the *base* or the money for the use of which interest is paid.

The **rate** (R) is the percent charged on the basis of one year's use of the money.

The **time** (T) is the number of years, months and days over which the money is used. Note especially that 30 days are considered a month and 360 days are considered a year.

The **amount** (A) is the sum of the principal and the interest.

To find the interest for any given period of time, *multiply the principal by the rate by the time.*

Formula: $I = P \times R \times T.$

EXAMPLE 1: Find the simple interest on $900 for 2 yrs. at 6%.

SOLUTION:

$I = ?, \quad P = \$900, \quad R = 6\%, \quad T = 2.$
$\$900 \times .06 = \$54, \$54 \times 2 = \$108$ interest.

To find the amount, *add the interest (I) to the principal (P).*

Formula: $A = P + I.$

EXAMPLE 2: Find the interest and amount of $400 for 3 years, 3 months and 10 days at 6%.

SOLUTION:

$I = P \times R \times T$ and $A = P + I.$

$$\$400 \times .06 \times 3 = \quad \$72.00$$
$$\$400 \times .06 \times \tfrac{1}{4} = \quad 6.00$$
$$\$400 \times .06 \times \tfrac{10}{360} = \quad \underline{.66\tfrac{2}{3}}$$
$$\$78.67 \text{ interest,}$$

$A = P + I$
$= \$400 + \$78.67 = \$478.67$ amount,   ANS.

INDIRECT CASES OF INTEREST

To find the rate when the principal, interest and time are given, *divide the total interest by the time to get the amount of the interest for one year; then divide this quotient by the principal.*

EXAMPLE 3: What must be the rate of interest on $400 to produce $25 in 6 months?

SOLUTION:

$\$25 \div \tfrac{1}{2} = \$25 \times \tfrac{2}{1} = \$50$ interest for 1 yr.
$\$50 \div 400 = \tfrac{1}{8}$ or $12\tfrac{1}{2}\%$ rate of interest,   ANS.

To find the time when the principal, interest and rate percent are given, *multiply the principal by the rate to obtain the amount of interest for one year; then divide the total interest by the interest for one year.*

EXAMPLE 4: How long will it take for $600 to yield $40 in interest at a rate of 4%?

SOLUTION: $\$600 \times .04 = \$24.00$ interest for 1 yr.
$\$\tfrac{40}{24} = 1\tfrac{16}{24} = 1\tfrac{2}{3}$ years,   ANS.

To find the principal when the interest, the rate percent and the time are given, *divide the interest by the time to get the interest for one year, then divide this by the rate.*

EXAMPLE 5: How much money will you have to lend to get $24 interest at 6%, if you lend it for 6 months?

SOLUTION:

$\$24 \div \tfrac{1}{2} = 24 \times \tfrac{2}{1} = \$48$ interest for 1 yr.

$\dfrac{\$48}{.06} = \$800$ or $\dfrac{\$48}{\tfrac{6}{100}} = \$48 \times \dfrac{100}{6} = \$800,$ ANS.

Note: There are alternate methods for solving interest problems of the above type. See if you can figure them out.

To find the principal when the amount, rate percent and time are given, *divide the given amount by the amount of $1 for the given time at the given rate.*

EXAMPLE: How much would you have to deposit at 4% in order to withdraw $819 at the end of 1 year and 3 months?

SOLUTION:

$1 at 4% for 1 yr. will amount to $1.04
$1 at 4% for $1\tfrac{1}{4}$ yrs. will amount to $1.05
∴ The number of dollars that will amount to $819 is $819 ÷ $1.05 or $780,   ANS.

Note that when dates are given for an interest-bearing period, the time from a given date in one month to the same date in any other month is figured as even months of thirty days each. Thus, from February 5 to March 4 would normally be reckoned as 27 days, but extending the time to the next day, March 5, makes it 30 days or one month.

THE 6% METHOD

When the rate of interest is 6%, use is often made of what is known as the **6%** or **60-day method.** By this method the time is reduced to multiples or fractions of 60 days or of 6 days.

Rule: 1. To find interest for 60 days by the 6% method *move the decimal point in the principal two places to the left.*

2. To find interest for 6 days *move the decimal point in the principal three places to the left.*

3. To find interest for other intervals of time *multiply or divide, as may be necessary, the amounts which are thus found.*

EXAMPLE: What is the interest on $500 for 5 months and 8 days at 6%?

SOLUTION:

5 mo. = 60 da. + 60 da. + 30 da.
8 da. = 6 da. + 2 da.

$ 5.00 int. for 60 da.
  5.00 int. for 60 da.
  2.50 int. for 30 da.
   .50 int. for 6 da.
   .17 int. for 2 da.
$13.17 total int., ANS.

EXPLANATION: Since the interest for 1 year is 6%, the interest for 2 months or 60 days is 1%, and the interest for 6 days is $\frac{1}{10}$ of that for 60 days, or .1%. Taking the given example, the time is divided as shown. Each 60-day period earns 1% or $5.00 of interest. The 30-day period earns $\frac{1}{2}$ of $5.00 or $2.50. For 6 days the interest is $\frac{1}{10}$ of 1% or $.50, and for 2 days it is $\frac{1}{3}$ of $\frac{1}{10}$ of 1% or $.16$\frac{2}{3}$, which is changed to $.17. Adding these figures gives the total interest for the whole period.

ACCURATE INTEREST

The rule of the 30-day month and the 360-day year is most commonly used in business, but the United States Government and the Federal Reserve Bank, as well as certain commercial banks under certain conditions, pay interest on the basis of a 365-day year. Interest on this basis is known as **accurate interest** or **exact interest.**

In figuring this kind of interest the exact number of days in the period is computed. (*For the method of calculating this see page* 56.) Each day is figured as $\frac{1}{365}$ of a year. The total amount of interest paid is naturally somewhat smaller than it would be on the basis of a 360-day year.

EXAMPLE: What is the accurate interest of $292 from January 14 to February 11 at 5%?

SOLUTION:

Jan. 17 da.
Feb. 11 da.
   28

$$292 \times \frac{5}{100} \times \frac{28}{365} = \frac{$112}{100}$$
$$= $1.12 \text{ int., ANS.}$$

EXPLANATION: As interest starts on the 14th day of January, there are 17 interest-bearing days left in that month. These added to 11 days in February make a total of 28 days. Multiplying the principal by the rate by $\frac{28}{365}$ produces the interest.

BANK DISCOUNT

When a bank lends money against a promissory note it collects the interest charges in advance by deducting them from the full value or *face* of the note. This is called **discounting** the note. The amount thus deducted is called the **discount.** The remainder left when the *discount* has been deducted from the *face* of the note is called the **net proceeds** and is what the borrower receives. When the note falls due at **maturity,** the borrower pays back to the bank its full face value.

EXAMPLE 1: A 90-day note for $400 at 6% is discounted when made. Find the discount and the net proceeds.

SOLUTION:

Interest for 60 days = $4.00.
Interest for 90 days = $6.00 discount,
$400 − $6 = $394 net proceeds, } ANS.

EXAMPLE 2: A 90-day note for $400 at 6%, dated April 15, is discounted May 15. Find the net proceeds.

SOLUTION:

Term of discount = 90 da. − 30 da. = 60 da.
Interest for 60 da. = $4.00 discount.
$400 − $4 = $396 net proceeds, ANS.

COMPOUND INTEREST

Compound interest is interest which for each successive interest period is figured on a base that represents the original principal plus all the interest that has accrued in previous interest periods.

To compute compound interest, *add the interest for each period to the principal before figuring the interest for the next period.*

EXAMPLE: What is the compound interest on $5000 for 4 years at 6% compounded annually?

SOLUTION:

 $5000 original principal
    .06 rate
  300.00 interest for 1st yr.
 5000.00
 5300.00 new principal, 2nd yr.
    .06
  318.00 interest for 2nd yr.
 5300.00
 5618.00 new principal, 3rd yr.
    .06
  337.08 interest for 3rd yr.
 5618.00
 5955.08 new principal, 4th yr.
    .06
  357.30 interest for 4th yr.
 5955.08
 6312.38 amt. at end of 4th yr.
 5000.00 original principal
$1312.38 comp. int. for 4 yrs., ANS.

INTEREST TABLES

Simple Interest

Showing the interest on $1,000 at various rates; based on a 30-day month and a 360-day year.

Time	2½%	3%	3½%	4%	4½%	5%	5½%	6%
1 day	0.069	0.083	0.097	0.111	0.125	0.139	0.153	0.167
2 days	0.139	0.167	0.194	0.222	0.250	0.278	0.306	0.333
3 days	0.208	0.250	0.292	0.333	0.375	0.417	0.458	0.500
4 days	0.278	0.333	0.389	0.444	0.500	0.556	0.611	0.667
5 days	0.347	0.417	0.486	0.556	0.625	0.694	0.764	0.833
6 days	0.417	0.500	0.583	0.667	0.750	0.833	0.917	1.000
1 month	2.083	2.500	2.917	3.333	3.750	4.167	4.583	5.000
2 months	4.167	5.000	5.833	6.667	7.500	8.333	9.167	10.000
3 months	6.250	7.500	8.750	10.000	11.250	12.500	13.750	15.000
6 months	12.500	15.000	17.500	20.000	22.500	25.000	27.500	30.000
1 year	25.000	30.000	35.000	40.000	45.000	50.000	55.000	60.000

Compound Interest

Showing the amount of $ at various rates.

Yr.	2%	2½%	3%	3½%	4%	4½%	5%	5½%	6%	7%
1	1.02000	1.02500	1.03000	1.03500	1.04000	1.04500	1.05000	1.05500	1.06000	1.07000
2	1.04040	1.05063	1.06090	1.07123	1.08160	1.09203	1.10250	1.11303	1.12360	1.14490
3	1.06121	1.07689	1.09273	1.10872	1.12486	1.14117	1.15763	1.17424	1.19102	1.22504
4	1.08243	1.10381	1.12551	1.14752	1.16986	1.19252	1.21551	1.23882	1.26248	1.31080
5	1.10408	1.13141	1.15927	1.18769	1.21665	1.24618	1.27628	1.30696	1.33823	1.40255
6	1.12616	1.15969	1.19405	1.22926	1.26532	1.30226	1.34010	1.37884	1.41852	1.50073
7	1.14869	1.18869	1.22987	1.27228	1.31593	1.36086	1.40710	1.45468	1.50363	1.60578
8	1.17166	1.21840	1.26677	1.31681	1.36857	1.42210	1.47746	1.53469	1.59385	1.71819
9	1.19509	1.24886	1.30477	1.36290	1.42331	1.48610	1.55133	1.61909	1.68948	1.83846
10	1.21899	1.28009	1.34392	1.41060	1.48024	1.55297	1.62889	1.70814	1.79085	1.96715
11	1.24337	1.31209	1.38423	1.45997	1.53945	1.62285	1.71034	1.80209	1.89830	2.10485
12	1.26824	1.34489	1.42576	1.51107	1.60103	1.69588	1.79586	1.90121	2.01220	2.25219
13	1.29361	1.37851	1.46853	1.56396	1.66507	1.77220	1.88565	2.00577	2.13293	2.40985
14	1.31948	1.41297	1.51259	1.61870	1.73168	1.85194	1.97993	2.11609	2.26090	2.57853
15	1.34587	1.44830	1.55797	1.67535	1.80094	1.93528	2.07893	2.23248	2.39656	2.75903
16	1.37279	1.48451	1.60471	1.73399	1.87298	2.02237	2.18287	2.35526	2.54035	2.95216
17	1.40024	1.52162	1.65285	1.79468	1.94790	2.11338	2.29202	2.48480	2.69277	3.15882
18	1.42825	1.55966	1.70243	1.85749	2.02582	2.20848	2.40662	2.62147	2.85434	3.37993
19	1.45681	1.59865	1.75351	1.92250	2.10685	2.30786	2.52695	2.76565	3.02560	3.61653
20	1.48595	1.63862	1.80611	1.98979	2.19112	2.41171	2.65330	2.91776	3.20714	3.86968

Money will double itself at *compound interest* in 35.003 years at 2%, in 23.450 years at 3%, in 17.675 years at 4%, in 14.207 years at 5%, in 11.896 years at 6%, in 10.245 years at 7%. These figures are based on annual compounding of interest. If interest is compounded semi-annually or quarterly the periods will be only very slightly shorter. At *simple interest* money doubles itself in 25.000 years at 4%, in 20 years at 5%, in 16.667 years at 6%, in 14.286 years at 7%.

EXPLANATION: We first find the interest on the original principal ($5,000) for one year. This amounts to $300. We add this to $5,000, making the new principal at the start of the second year $5,300. One year's interest on $5,300 comes to $318, which we add to $5,300 to arrive at $5,618 as the new principal at the start of the third year. We continue in this way until we reach the end of the fourth year when we find that principal and interest together amount to $6,312.38. From this we subtract the original principal of $5,000 leaving $1,312.38 as the compound interest for the entire period of 4 years.

To avoid awkward four-place decimals in figuring compound interest multiply the cents in the principal separately (you will usually be able to do it mentally) and if the result comes to more than one cent, add this to the first figure you write down.

TRUE DISCOUNT

True discount (not to be confused with *bank* discount) is the deduction made from the face value of an obligation payable at some future date in order to determine what this obligation is worth at the present time. **Present worth** is the sum of money which, if invested at the same rate as that which applies to the given obligation, will equal the face value of the debt when it becomes due.

Rule: 1. To find present worth *divide the face value of the indebtedness by the amount of $1 for the given time at the given rate.*

2. To find true discount *subtract present worth from face value.*

True discount may apply to obligations bearing either simple or compound interest.

EXAMPLE: What is the present worth of an obligation for $500 payable 2 years and 6 months from now and bearing interest at 6% not compounded. Also, what is the true discount?

SOLUTION:

.06 $\times$ 2$\frac{1}{2}$ = .15 interest rate for 2$\frac{1}{2}$ years.
$1.00 $\times$ .15 = $.15 interest on $1 for 2$\frac{1}{2}$ years.
$1.00 + $.15 = $1.15 amount of $1 for 2$\frac{1}{2}$ years.
$500 $\div$ $1.15 = $434.78 present worth, ⎫
$500 − $434.78 = $65.22 true discount, ⎬ ANS.

EXPLANATION: Since $1 would grow to $1.15 in 2 years and 6 months at 6% simple interest, to find out how many dollars would grow to $500 we divide $500 by $1.15 and get $434.78 as the required amount. The difference between this and $500 is the true discount. This example may

be checked by multiplying $434.78 by .15 to arrive at $65.22 interest at 6% for 2$\frac{1}{2}$ years, corresponding with the same amount calculated as true discount.

Since a sound bond on the day when it matures is worth neither more nor less than its face value, it follows that as such a bond approaches maturity its value on the stock market tends more to coincide with *present worth* as determined by the principles of true discount.

TAXES

MUNICIPAL TAXES

Most of the tax money raised by city, town and village governments is obtained through taxes on *real estate* or *personal property*.

The value of real estate holdings is appraised by tax officers called **assessors**, and the value thus set on any property is called its **assessed valuation**. The local government establishes a **tax rate** (usually once a year), and the taxpayer pays taxes at this rate according to the *assessed valuation* of the property that he owns.

The *tax rate* is determined by taking the estimated expenses of the municipal government for the ensuing year and dividing this by the total of assessed valuations on all property in the municipality. Thus if a town needed $300,000 to operate its various governmental departments as well as to contribute its share to county and state taxes, etc., and if the total of assessed valuations were $10,000,000, it would fix a tax rate of $300,000 $\div$ $10,000,000 or 3%.

It should be noted, however, that municipalities differ with regard to the way in which the tax rate is expressed. A tax rate of 3% might be expressed as 30 mills on $1, or $3.00 on $100, or $30 on $1,000.

A real estate tax rate means little unless account is taken of the relation which the assessed valuation bears to the current market value of the property. A lower tax rate may actually produce higher revenues if assessed valuations are raised accordingly. Thus, if a plot is actually salable at $5,000, tax payments on an assessed valuation of $4,800 at **$3.00 per $100** would be higher than those paid at a rate of $3.25 per $100 on an assessed valuation of $4,200.

FEDERAL TAXES

The United States Government obtains most of its revenue by three forms of taxation. These are:

    1. **Import duties** or **customs**—taxes on goods brought into this country from foreign lands.

    2. **Internal revenue taxes**—taxes on tobacco, alcoholic beverages, gasoline, luxuries, etc.

    3. **Income taxes**—taxes on the earnings of individuals and business concerns.

Import duties are of two kinds: an **ad valorem** duty is one that represents a certain percent of the value of the goods imported; a **specific** duty is one that calls for payment of a certain amount per pound, ton, gallon or other quantity of the goods.

Internal revenue taxes are paid to the government by the manufacturer or the distributor of the taxed commodity. Taxes of this kind are often called **indirect taxes** because the consumer, who ultimately bears the expense, pays them *indirectly* through the merchant from whom he buys the goods.

Income-tax computation has been greatly simplified by the federal government and by many state governments, which provide "short forms" with appended tables for taxpayers who have no unusual deductions to claim and gross incomes, derived wholly from wages, less than a certain specified amount—$5,000 for the federal government, and $10,000 for New York State, in 1960. A taxpayer eligible to use such a form has only to find his gross income in a left-hand column of the table and to trace this line to the right to a column headed by the number of his claimed dependency exemptions. The figure thus found gives his tax obligation, automatically making deductions for his dependents and crediting him with an approximate allowance of 10% for his other possible deductions.

For taxpayers using "long forms," the tax tables in the instruction booklet provided take into consideration the dependency exemptions, but you itemize all other deductions. The difficulty lies not in the arithmetic, but in deciding how and where to use it. Today, in households with two working adults, there are choices between filing joint or separate returns, and the difference in the final amounts can be significant. These decisions are a complete subject in themselves, but the final arithmetic computations usually involve only a few additions and subtractions:

EXAMPLE 1: One year Mr. A had gross earnings from wages of $28,000, his itemized federal deductions were $4,000, and he had four dependents, including himself. What was his federal income tax that year, using the table on page 190?

SOLUTION:

$28,000 gross income from wages
−4,000 itemized deductions
$24,000 net taxable balance
3,219 total tax (from table), ANS.

EXAMPLE 2: Ms. B had the same income as Mr. A plus $900 in medical expenses that year. Compute her deduction for medical expenses, if these were allowed, only in excess of 3% of her gross income. Round off to the nearest dollar if necessary.

SOLUTION:

$28,000 gross income
× .03 = 3%, percentage not deductible
$ 840 amount not deductible

$ 900 actual medical expenses
−840 amount not deductible
$60 deductible medical expenses, ANS.

Long-term capital gains are profits realized from the sale of capital assets held for more than 6 months. Expenses incurred in connection with such sales are fully deductible. Only 50% of the gains are taxed, but the resulting tax advantage of investors over wage earners is even greater percentage-wise because of the graduations in our income-tax structure.

EXAMPLE 3: Mr. C had the same itemized deductions, etc., as Mr. A (Example 1), but his gross income, in the same amount, derived from the sale of capital assets held for more than a year. What was his federal income tax if he incurred $800 expenses in connection with the sale of these assets? Use the same table.

SOLUTION:

$28,000 gross long-term capital gains
− 800 expenses, deductible in full

$27,200 net long-term capital gains
× .60 permitted 60% adjustment factor

$16,320 adjusted gross income
−4,000 itemized deductions

$12,320 net taxable income
−2,400 = $600 × 4 dependency credits

$ 2,110 net taxable income
× .20 = 20% rate on amt. less than $4,000

$ 761 total tax (from table), ANS.

EXAMPLE 4: What percentage of Mr. B's income tax on capital gains (Example 3) was Mr. A's income tax on the same amount of wages?

SOLUTION: 3,219/761 = 4.23 = 423% to the nearest 1%, ANS.

Practice Exercise No. 28

Note: Unless otherwise stated interest is to be considered as simple interest rather than compounded.

1 What is the interest on $188.60 for one year at $4\frac{1}{2}\%$?
- (A) $9.43____
- (B) $18.11____
- (C) $8.49____
- (D) $9.43____

2 Find the interest on $1,850 for 2 years and 6 months at 4% a year.
- (A) $74.00____
- (B) $185.00____
- (C) $111.00____
- (D) $277.50____

3 How much interest will be charged for a loan of $275 for 3 months if the rate is $4\frac{1}{2}\%$ a year?
- (A) $3.09____
- (B) 12.37\frac{1}{2}$____
- (C) $4.12____
- (D) $3.45____

4 I lend $60,000 for 2 years. On $\frac{2}{3}$ of it I receive 4% interest, on the balance I receive 5% interest. What is the total amount of interest money I receive?
- (A) $2,600____
- (B) $5,200____
- (C) $520____
- (D) $5,600____

5 At what rate will $300 yield $67.50 interest in 4 years and 6 months?
- (A) 2%____
- (B) 3%____
- (C) 4%____
- (D) 5%____

6 At what rate will $150 double inself in 14 years?
- (A) $6\frac{1}{3}$____
- (B) $7\frac{1}{7}$____
- (C) $4\frac{1}{9}$____
- (D) $8\frac{1}{4}$____

7 How long will it take $480 to earn $56 interest at 5%?
- (A) $2\frac{1}{3}$ yrs.____
- (B) $3\frac{1}{2}$ yrs.____
- (C) $1\frac{2}{3}$ yrs.____
- (D) 2 yrs.____

8 What principal will yield $36 in 3 months at 3% interest?
- (A) $300____
- (B) $4,800____
- (C) $2,400____
- (D) $1,200____

9 How long will it take to earn $80.00 interest with a deposit of $800 at 6%?
- (A) $1\frac{1}{2}$ yrs.____
- (B) $1\frac{1}{3}$ yrs.____
- (C) $1\frac{3}{4}$ yrs.____
- (D) 2 yrs.____

PROFIT AND LOSS

To find profit or gain, *subtract the cost from the selling price.*

EXAMPLE 1: A man bought a motor for $600 and sold it for $800. How much profit did he make?

SOLUTION: Selling price − cost = profit.
$800 − $600 = $200, ANS.

To find the loss, *subtract the selling price from the cost.*

EXAMPLE 2: A dealer paid $800 for a machine and sold it the following year for $200. How much did he lose?

SOLUTION: Cost − selling price = loss.
$800 − $200 = $600, ANS.

Note: In all profit and loss problems the words *gain* and *profit* have the same meaning and are used interchangeably.

When a percent of profit or loss is given, it is understood, unless stated to the contrary, that this percent is based on the *cost*. *Thus,* if a man states simply that he sold something at a profit of 10%, he is understood to mean that it was sold for an amount equal to its cost plus 10% of its cost. In modern business, however, it is quite customary to figure profit and loss as a percent of *selling price*. This is because commissions, discounts, certain taxes and other items of expense are commonly based on selling price, and in a complicated business it makes for simplicity in accounting to base profit and loss also on selling price.

There are, accordingly, two distinct kinds of profit and loss problems—those in which profit or loss is based on cost, and those in which profit or loss is based on selling price. Before such a problem can be solved it must be known in which of these classes it belongs. Bear in mind, though, that profit or loss is always to be considered as based on cost unless it is stated or otherwise known that it is based on selling price.

PROFIT AND LOSS BASED ON COST

To find the percent gain or loss, *divide the amount gained or lost by the cost.*

EXAMPLE 3: A wrench that cost 80 cents is sold at a profit of 20 cents. Find the percent or rate of profit.

SOLUTION: Gain ÷ cost = % profit.
$\frac{20}{80} = \frac{1}{4}$ or 25%, ANS.

EXAMPLE 4: A book that cost $1.00 is sold for 80 cents. Find the percent loss.

SOLUTION:
Cost − selling price = loss.
$1.00 − $.80 = $.20 loss.
loss ÷ cost = % loss.
$\frac{$.20}{$1.00} = \frac{1}{5}$ or 20%, ANS.

To find the gain and the selling price when the cost and the percent gain are given, *multiply the cost by the percent gain and add the result to the cost.*

EXAMPLE 5: Find the gain if the selling price of a desk that cost $48 represents a profit of $16\frac{2}{3}$%.

SOLUTION: Cost × percent gain = gain.
$48 × $\frac{1}{6}$ = $8, ANS.

To find the loss and the selling price when the cost and the percent loss are given, *multiply the cost by the percent loss and subtract the product from the cost.*

EXAMPLE 6: A damaged chair that cost $110 was sold at a loss of 10%. Find the loss and the selling price.

SOLUTION:
Cost × percent loss = loss:
$110 × $\frac{1}{10}$ = $11, loss, ANS.

Cost − loss = selling price.
$110 − $11 = $99, selling price, ANS.

To find the cost when the profit and the

percent profit are given or to find the cost when the loss and the percent loss are given, *divide the profit or loss by the percent profit or loss.*

EXAMPLE 7: A house was sold at a profit of $9,000. The rate of profit was $37\frac{1}{2}$%. What was the cost of the house?

SOLUTION:
$37\frac{1}{2}$% or $\frac{3}{8}$ of the cost = $9,000.
Cost = $9,000 ÷ $\frac{3}{8}$ = $\cancel{$9,000}^{$3,000} × \frac{8}{3}$
= $24,000, ANS.

ALTERNATE SOLUTION:
$37\frac{1}{2}$% = $\frac{3}{8}$.
If $\frac{3}{8}$ of the cost = $9,000, $\frac{1}{8}$ of the cost = $3,000, and $\frac{8}{8}$ = 8 × $3,000 = $24,000, cost, ANS.

When the rate is reducible to a decimal fraction, *use decimal multiplication or division.*

EXAMPLE 8: A boat was sold at a loss of $120, representing a loss of 6%. What was the cost of the boat?

SOLUTION:
6% of the cost = $120
100% or total cost = $120 ÷ .06
= $2,000, cost, ANS.

To find the cost when the selling price and the percent profit are given, *divide the selling price by 1 plus the percent profit.*

EXAMPLE 9: A table was sold for $80. This figure included a profit of 25%. Find the cost.

SOLUTION:
Profit = 25% or $\frac{1}{4}$ of cost.
Total cost = $\frac{4}{4}$.
∴ Selling price = 1 + $\frac{1}{4}$ = $\frac{5}{4}$ of cost.
$\frac{5}{4}$ of cost = $80.
∴ $80 ÷ $\frac{5}{4}$ = $64, cost, ANS.

To find the cost when the selling price and the percent loss are given, *divide the selling price by 1 minus the percent loss.*

EXAMPLE 10: A silver set was sold for $168; the loss was 4%. How much did the silver set cost?

SOLUTION:
Loss = 4% of cost. Total cost = 100%.
Selling price = 100% − 4% = 96%.

96% of cost = $168.
Cost = $168 ÷ .96 = $175, Ans.

PROFIT AND LOSS BASED ON SELLING PRICE

Modern accounting practice favors the basing of profit and loss on selling price rather than on cost. This is because commissions and other selling expenses are figured as percentages of selling price, and it simplifies accounting to base profit and loss on selling price also.

To find the percent profit or loss, *divide the amount gained or lost by the selling price.*

EXAMPLE 1: A box of candy sells for $1.50 at a profit of 50¢. What percent of profit on selling price does this represent?

SOLUTION: Gain ÷ selling price = % profit.
$.50 ÷ $1.50 = .33⅓ or 33⅓% profit, Ans.

EXAMPLE 2: On every radio selling for $40 a merchant lost $8. What was his rate of loss on selling price?

SOLUTION: Loss ÷ selling price = % loss.
$8 ÷ $40 = .20, or 20% loss, Ans.

To find the profit and the cost when the selling price and the percent profit are given, *multiply the selling price by the percent profit and subtract the result from the selling price.*

EXAMPLE 3: Eggs selling for 60¢ a dozen carry a profit of 15% of selling price. Separate this selling price into cost and profit.

SOLUTION:
Selling price × % profit = profit.
Selling price − profit = cost.
$.60 × .15 = $.09, profit, ⎫
$.60 − $.09 = $.51, cost, ⎬ Ans.

To find the loss and the cost when the selling price and the percent loss are given, *multiply the selling price by the percent loss and add the result to the selling price.*

EXAMPLE 4: At a clearance sale shoes selling at $6.00 are sold at a loss of 25% of selling price. What is the loss and the original cost?

SOLUTION: Selling price × % loss = loss.
Selling price + loss = cost.
$6.00 × .25 = $1.50, loss, ⎫
$6.00 + $1.50 = $7.50, cost, ⎬ Ans.

To find the selling price when the profit and the percent profit are given, or to find the selling price when the loss and the percent loss are given, *divide the profit or loss by the percent profit or loss.*

Note: This rule should be compared with the one under *Profit and Loss Based on Cost.* The two rules are exactly similar except that in one case 100% represents cost while in the other case 100% represents selling price.

EXAMPLE 5: A kind of tape is selling at a profit of 12% of selling price, equal to 18¢ per yard. What is the tape selling at?

SOLUTION: Profit ÷ % profit = selling price.
$.18 ÷ .12 = $1.50, selling price, Ans.

EXAMPLE 6: A loss of $13.50 on a floor-waxing machine represents 15% loss on the selling price. What is the selling price?

SOLUTION: Loss ÷ % loss = selling price.
$13.50 ÷ .15 = $90.00, selling price, Ans.

To find the selling price when the cost and the percent profit are given, *subtract the percent profit from 100% and divide the cost by the remainder.*

EXAMPLE 7: A machine costing $90 to produce is sold at a profit of 40% of selling price. What is the selling price?

SOLUTION:
Cost ÷ (100% − % profit) = selling price.
$90 ÷ .60 = $150, selling price, Ans.

To find the selling price when the cost and the percent loss are given, *add the percent loss to 100% and divide the cost by this sum.*

EXAMPLE 8: Socks that cost 80¢ per pair were sold at a loss of 25% of selling price. What did they sell for?

SOLUTION:
Cost ÷ (100% + % loss) = selling price.
$.80 ÷ 1.25 = $.64, selling price, Ans.

When profits are based on cost, profit is commonly referred to as **mark-up** over selling price, and the percent profit on cost is called **percent mark-up** to distinguish it from *percent profit* (*i.e.*, on selling price).

To reduce percent profit on selling price to percent mark-up (percent profit on cost), *divide profit on selling price by 100% minus percent profit on selling price.*

EXAMPLE 9: 40% profit on selling price is what percent mark-up (percent profit on cost)?

SOLUTION:

% profit on SP ÷ (100% − % profit on SP)
= % profit on cost.
.40 ÷ .60 = .66⅔% or 66⅔% profit on cost, ANS.

To reduce percent mark-up (percent profit on cost) to percent profit on selling price, *divide percent mark-up by 100% plus percent mark-up.*

EXAMPLE 10: A baseball bat marked up 25% carries what percent of profit on selling price?

SOLUTION:

% profit on cost ÷ (100% + % profit on cost)
= % profit on SP.
.25 ÷ 1.25 = .20 or 20% profit on SP, ANS.

To reduce percent loss on selling price to percent loss on cost, *divide percent loss on selling price by 100% plus percent loss on selling price.*

EXAMPLE 11: 20% loss on selling price is what percent loss on cost?

SOLUTION:

% loss on SP ÷ (100% + % loss on SP)
= % loss on cost.
.20 ÷ 1.20 = .16⅔ or 16⅔% loss on cost, ANS.

To reduce percent loss on cost to percent loss on selling price, *divide percent loss on cost by 100% minus percent loss on cost.*

EXAMPLE 12: 33⅓% loss on cost is what percent loss on selling price?

SOLUTION:

% loss on cost ÷ (100% − % loss on cost)
= % loss on SP.
.33⅓ ÷ 66⅔ = ½
= .50 = 50% loss on SP, ANS.

The four foregoing rules may appear confusingly difficult to distinguish, but they will be easily remembered if the student will ask himself whether the percent required in the answer is to be larger or smaller than the one that is given. Where profits are concerned, the percent of selling price is smaller than the percent of cost. Where losses are concerned, the percent of selling price is larger than the percent of cost. If a smaller percent is required in the answer, the given percent is divided by 100% (or 1) plus the given percent. If a larger percent is required in the answer the given percent is divided by 100% minus the given percent. It should also be noted in these examples that when the given percent is added to 100% the sum represents a cost or a selling price corresponding exactly with the *kind* of percent wanted in the answer.

Practice Exercise No. 29

1 Apples cost 5¢ each. They are sold at a 20% profit. Find the selling price of one dozen apples.
  (A) 12¢ ____ (c) 72¢ ____
  (B) $1.00 ____ (D) 60¢ ____

2 The Army bought 10,000 pairs of gloves. They cost $2.50 a pair to manufacture and were sold to the Army at a 6% profit. What was the total selling price?
  (A) $26,500 ____ (c) $1,500 ____
  (B) $25,000 ____ (D) $40,000 ____

3 A dealer paid $200 for 10 books. He sold ⅖ of them at $30 apiece and the remainder at $25 apiece. What was his percent profit?
  (A) 70% ____ (c) 35% ____
  (B) 40% ____ (D) 80% ____

4 A dealer made a profit of 25% in selling a boat for $500. How much did the boat cost him?
  (A) $300 ____ (c) $620 ____
  (B) $380 ____ (D) $400 ____

5 A man having to get rid of his car in a hurry sold it at a 15% loss, which meant that he lost $75. How much did the car cost him originally?
  (A) $575 ____ (c) $500 ____
  (B) $425 ____ (D) $600 ____

6 A department store sold a damaged bedroom set at a 37½% loss. The amount they lost was $90. What was the selling price of the bedroom set?
  (A) $240 ____ (c) $90 ____
  (B) $150 ____ (D) $330 ____

7 A farmer had to sell an inferior crop at a loss of 12½%. He sold it for $259. What did the crop cost him to produce?
  (A) $296 ____ (c) $295 ____
  (B) $281.38 ____ (D) $291.38 ____

8 A furniture dealer sold a piano for $806 at a 24% mark-up. How much did it cost him?
  (A) $871 ____ (c) $612.56 ____
  (B) $650 ____ (D) $604.33 ____

9 If you bought two farms for $10,000 each, and sold one of them at a gain of 18%, and the other at a loss of 18%, how much did you make?
  (A) $1,800 ____ (c) $3,600 ____
  (B) $00 ____ (D) $900 ____

10   You sold two building lots at $3,600 each. On one your rate of profit was 20%, on the other your rate of loss was 20%. How much did you lose on the total transaction?

(A) $00 _____   (c) $300 _____

(B) $900 _____   (D) $600 _____

11   The $4 which a dealer receives for a fountain pen includes 37½% profit. What did it cost him? (*This style of wording indicates that profit is based on selling price.*)

(A) $3.00 _____   (c) $3.37½ _____

(B) $2.00 _____   (D) $2.50 _____

12   A grocer sells $1,000 worth of tea at a profit of 12½% on the selling price. What did it cost him?

(A) $900 _____   (c) $1,125 _____

(B) $875 _____   (D) $800 _____

13   A hardware merchant sells nails at a mark-up of 15%. What percent of the selling price is profit?

(A) 13.04% _____   (c) 30% _____

(B) 17.64% _____   (D) 20% _____

14   15% loss on selling price is what percent loss on cost?

(A) 13.04% _____   (c) 15% _____

(B) 17.65% _____   (D) 85% _____

15   A and B, in neighboring towns, each owns a house that could be readily sold for $11,000. A's house is assessed at $\frac{5}{6}$ of its market value, while B's is assessed at 80% of market value. A pays taxes at the rate of $28 on $1,000; B pays a rate of $28.50. Who pays the more taxes, A or B, and how much more does he pay?

(A) B, $36.67 more _____   (c) A, $5.87 more _____

(B) A, $66.67 more _____   (D) B, $55 more _____

CHAPTER FIVE

DENOMINATE NUMBERS

A **denominate number** is one that refers to a unit of measurement which has been established by law or by general usage. Examples are: 1 *inch*, 8 *pounds*, 3 *seconds*.

A **compound denominate number** is one that consists of two or more units of the same kind. Examples are: 1 *foot* 3 *inches*, 2 *hours* 15 *minutes*, 1 *pound* 14 *ounces*.

Denominate numbers are used to express measurements of many kinds, such as:

a. Linear (length)   d. Weight (pounds)
b. Square (area)   e. Time (seconds)
c. Cubic (volume)   f. Angular (degrees)

This classification is by no means complete. Systems of currency (dollars and cents, pounds sterling and pence, etc.) would, for instance, be considered denominate numbers, and the various foreign systems of weights and measures would of course come under the same head, though they are beyond the scope of this book.

To gain facility in working out arithmetic problems involving denominate numbers it is necessary to know the most common tables of measures, such as are given here for reference. Note the abbreviations used, since these are in accordance with the manner in which the values are usually written.

TABLES OF MEASUREMENTS

1. LENGTH OR LINEAR MEASURE

Linear units are used to measure distances along straight lines.

U. S. OR ENGLISH SYSTEM

12 inches (in. or ″)	= 1 foot (ft. or ′)	320 rods or 8 furlongs	= 1 mile (mi.)
3 feet or 36 inches	= 1 yard (yd.)	1760 yards	= 1 mile
5½ yards or 16½ feet	= 1 rod (rd.)	5280 feet	= 1 mile
220 yards or ⅛ mile	= 1 furlong (fur.)		

NAUTICAL MEASURE

6080.26 feet	= 1 nautical mile or knot	360 degrees = circumference of earth at equator
1.15 land miles	= 1 nautical mile	
3 nautical miles	= 1 league	1 fathom = 6 feet (of depth)
60 nautical miles	= 1 degree (at the equator)	1 hand = 4 inches

METRIC SYSTEM

Unit		Meters		U. S. Value
	1 millimeter (mm.) =	.001	=	.03937 in.
10 millimeters =	1 centimeter (cm.) =	.01	=	.3937 in.
10 centimeters =	1 decimeter (dm.) =	.1	=	3.937 in.
10 decimeters =	1 METER (M.) =	1.	=	39.3707 in.
10 meters =	1 dekameter (Dm.) =	10.	=	32.809 ft.
10 dekameters =	1 hectometer (Hm.) =	100.	=	328.09 ft.
10 hectometers =	1 kilometer (Km.) =	1000.	=	.62137 mi.
10 kilometers =	1 myriameter (Mm.) =	10000.	=	6.2137 mi.

2. SQUARE MEASURE

This is used to measure the area of a surface; it involves two dimensions, length and width.

SQUARE OR AREA MEASURE

144 square inches	= 1 square foot (sq. ft.)
9 square feet	= 1 square yard (sq. yd.)
$30\frac{1}{4}$ square yards	= 1 square rod (sq. rd.)
160 square rods	= 1 acre (A.)
640 acres	= 1 square mile or 1 section (sec.)

SURVEYORS' SQUARE MEASURE

625 square links (sq. l.)	= 1 square rod (sq. r.)
(1 linear link = 7.92″)	
16 square rods	= 1 square chain (sq. ch.)
10 square chains	= 1 acre (A.)
640 acres	= 1 square mile
36 square miles	= 1 township (Tp.)

METRIC SQUARE MEASURE

100 square millimeters (sq. mm.)	= square centimeter (sq. cm.)
100 square centimeters	= 1 square decimeter (sq. dm.)
100 square decimeters	= 1 square meter (sq. m.)
100 square meters	= 1 square dekameter (sq. Dm.) or are (A)
100 square ares	= 1 square hectometer (sq. Hm.) or hectare (H)
100 square hectares	= 1 square kilometer (sq. Km.)

3. CUBIC MEASURE

This is used to find the volume or amount of space within the boundaries of three-dimensional figures. It is sometimes referred to as *capacity*.

CUBIC OR VOLUME MEASURE

1728 cubic inches (cu. in.)	= 1 cubic foot (cu. ft.)
27 cubic feet	= 1 cubic yard (cu. yd.)
1 cubic yard	= 1 load of sand or dirt
128 cubic feet	= 1 cord of wood (cd.)
$24\frac{3}{4}$ cubic feet	= 1 perch of stone (pch.)

LIQUID MEASURE OF CAPACITY

4 gills (gi.)	= 1 pint (pt.)
2 pints	= 1 quart (qt.)
4 quarts	= 1 gallon (gal.)
$31\frac{1}{2}$ gallons	= 1 barrel (bbl.)
2 barrels	= 1 hogshead (hhd.)

APOTHECARIES' LIQUID MEASURE

60 drops or minims (m)	= 1 fluid drachm (f₃)
8 fluid drachms	= 1 fluid ounce (f℥)
16 fluid ounces	= 1 pint (O.)
8 pints	= 1 gallon (cong.)

DRY MEASURE OF CAPACITY

2 pints (pt.)	= 1 quart (qt.)
8 quarts	= 1 peck (pk.)
4 pecks	= 1 bushel (bu.)

METRIC MEASURE OF CAPACITY

1000 cubic millimeters (c.mm.)	= 1 cubic centimeter (c.c.)
1000 cubic centimeters	= 1 cubic decimeter (c. dm.)
1000 cubic decimeters	= 1 cubic meter (c.m.)
10 centiliters (cl.)	= 1 deciliter (dl.)
10 deciliters	= 1 liter (l.) = 1 cubic meter
10 cubic liters	= 1 dekaliter (Dl.)
10 dekaliters	= 1 hectoliter (Hl.)

4. MEASURES OF WEIGHT

These are used to determine the quantity

of matter a body contains. Four scales of weight are used in the U. S.

a. Troy—for weighing gold, silver and other precious metals.

b. Apothecaries'—used by druggists for weighing chemicals.

c. Avoirdupois—used for all general purposes.

d. Metric—used in scientific work.

AVOIRDUPOIS WEIGHT

16 drachms (dr.)	=	1 ounce (oz.)
16 ounces	=	1 pound (lb.)
7000 grains (gr.)	=	1 pound
100 lbs.	=	1 hundredweight (cwt.)
2000 lbs.	=	1 ton or short ton
112 lbs.	=	1 cwt. old measure
2240 lbs.	=	1 long ton

TROY WEIGHT

24 grains (gr.)	=	1 pennyweight (pwt.)
20 pennyweights	=	1 ounce (oz.)
12 ounces	=	1 pound (lb.)
5760 grains	=	1 pound
3.2 grains	=	1 carat (kt.)

The carat, as defined in the table, is used to weigh diamonds. The same term is used to indicate the purity of gold. In this case, a carat means a twenty-fourth part. Thus, 14 Kt. gold means that 14 parts ($\frac{14}{24}$) are pure gold and that 10 parts ($\frac{10}{24}$) are of other metals.

APOTHECARIES' WEIGHT

20 grains (gr.)	=	1 scruple (sc. or ℈)
3 scruples	=	1 dram (dr. or ℨ)
8 drams	=	1 ounce (oz. or ℥)
12 ounces	=	1 pound (lb.)
5760 grains	=	1 pound

METRIC WEIGHT

10 milligrams (mg.)	=	1 centigram (cg.)
10 centigrams	=	1 decigram (dg.)
10 decigrams	=	1 gram (g.)
10 grams	=	1 dekagram (Dg.)
10 dekagrams	=	1 hectogram (Hg.)
10 hectograms	=	1 kilogram (Kg.)
10 kilograms	=	1 myriagram (Mg.)
10 myriagrams	=	1 quintal (Q.)
10 quintals	=	1 tonneau (T.)

5 MEASURES OF TIME

60 seconds (sec. or ″)	=	1 minute (min. or ′)
60 minutes	=	1 hour (hr.)
24 hours	=	1 day (da.)
7 days	=	1 week (wk.)
2 weeks	=	1 fortnight
365 days	=	1 common year
366 days	=	1 leap year
12 calendar months	=	1 year
10 years	=	1 decade
100 years	=	1 century (C.)

6. ANGULAR OR CIRCULAR MEASURE

ANGULAR (∠) OR CIRCULAR (○) MEASURE

60 seconds (″)	=	1 minute (′)
60 minutes	=	1 degree (°)
90 degrees	=	1 right angle (∟) or 1 quadrant
360 angle degrees	=	4 right angles
360 arc degrees	=	1 circumference (○)

7. MONEY

UNITED STATES MONEY

10 mills (m.)	=	1 cent (ct. or ¢)
10 cents	=	1 dime (d.)
10 dimes	=	1 dollar ($)
10 dollars	=	1 eagle (E.)

ENGLISH MONEY

12 pence	=	1 shilling (s.)
20 shillings	=	1 pound or 1 sovereign } (£)
21 shillings	=	1 guinea

Shillings and pence are commonly written simply as numbers with an oblique line between: 5 shillings 6 pence would thus be written 5/6. The guinea is no longer a coin but professional men continue to charge fees in guineas.

REDUCTIONS INVOLVING COMPOUND UNITS

REDUCTION DESCENDING

EXAMPLE: Reduce $5\frac{1}{4}$ bbl. to units of lower denomination.

SOLUTION:

$$5\frac{1}{4} \text{ bbl.} = 165\frac{3}{8} \text{ gal.}$$
$$\frac{3}{8} \text{ gal.} = 1\frac{1}{2} \text{ qt.}$$
$$\frac{1}{2} \text{ qt.} = 1 \text{ pt.}$$
$$5\frac{1}{4} \text{ bbl.} = 165 \text{ gal. } 1 \text{ qt. } 1 \text{ pt.}$$

EXPLANATION: 1 bbl. = $31\frac{1}{2}$ gal. $5\frac{1}{4}$ bbl. = $5\frac{1}{4}$ × $31\frac{1}{2}$ = $165\frac{3}{8}$ gal. 1 gal. = 4 qt. $\frac{3}{8}$ gal. = $\frac{3}{8}$ × 4 = $1\frac{1}{2}$ qt. 1 qt. = 2 pt. $\frac{1}{2}$ qt. = $\frac{1}{2}$ × 2 = 1 pt. Bringing together the whole numbers, we arrive at the answer.

REDUCTION ASCENDING

EXAMPLE: How many yards in 107 ft. 3 in.?

SOLUTION:

$$\frac{107}{3} = 35 \text{ yd.} + 2 \text{ ft.}$$

2 ft. $= \frac{2}{3}$ yd.; 3 in. $= \frac{1}{12}$ yd.

$\frac{2}{3} + \frac{1}{12} = \frac{3}{4}$

107 ft. 3 in. $= 35\frac{3}{4}$ yd.

EXPLANATION: Take out of the given compound units the large number of whole units that are wanted in the answer, and use fractions only to reduce the remainder. The alternative of this method would be to reduce the whole to inches and then divide by 36.

Practice Exercise No. 30

1 How many feet in 24 rd. 7 yd. 1 ft.?
2 How many yards in 10 mi. 36 rd. 8 yd.?
3 How many inches in 14 rd. 11 ft.?
4 How many inches in 10 miles?
5 How many feet in 10 mi. 4 fur. 8 yd.?
6 How many inches in $6\frac{1}{2}$ yd.?
7 How many rods in 6 mi.?
8 How many square inches in 20 sq. yd. 8 sq. ft. 30 sq. in.?
9 How many acres in 960 sq. rd.?
10 How many square feet in 1,728 sq. in.?
11 How many acres in 35 sq. mi.?
12 How many square yards in 543 sq. ft.?
13 How many square yards in 1 sq. mi.?
14 How many acres in 1,742,400 sq. ft.?
15 How many quarts in 1 bbl.?
16 How many quarts in 56 bu.?
17 How many pennyweight in 6 oz. troy?
18 How many ℔ in 1 lb.?

THE FOUR FUNDAMENTAL OPERATIONS APPLIED TO DENOMINATE NUMBERS

ADDITION

EXAMPLE: Add 3 yd. 2 ft. 8 in., 4 yd. 2 ft. 6 in., 3 yd. 2 ft. 4 in.

SOLUTION:

yd.	ft.	in.
3	2	8
4	2	6
3	2	4
12	1	6	ANS.

EXPLANATION: List like units under one another. Add the inches, take out the number of feet contained in them (1) and put down the remainder. Carry 1 to the ft. column and proceed as before.

SUBTRACTION

EXAMPLE: From 6 gal. 2 qt. take 2 gal. 3 qt. 1 pt.

SOLUTION:

gal.	qt.	pt.
6	2	0
2	3	1
3	2	1	ANS.

EXPLANATION: To make the subtraction of pints possible we borrow one unit from the qt. column and subtract 1 from 2. A similar operation is performed with the quarts.

MULTIPLICATION

EXAMPLE: Multiply 6 bu. 3 pk. 6 qt. by 5.

SOLUTION:

bu.	pk.	qt.
6	3	6
		5
34	2	6	ANS.

EXPLANATION: $5 \times 6 = 30$ qt. $= 3$ pk. 6 qt. Carry 3 pk. $15 + 3 = 18$ pk. $= 4$ bu. 2 pk. Carry 4 bu. $30 + 4 = 34$ bu.

DIVISION

EXAMPLE: Divide 17 gal. 3 qt. 1 pt. 1 gi. by 3.

SOLUTION:

	gal.	qt.	pt.	gi.
3)	17	3	1	1
	5	3	1	3	ANS.

EXPLANATION: $17 \div 3 = 5$ with 2 gal. remainder. 2 gal. $= 8$ qt. $8 + 3 \div 3 = 3$ with 2 qt. remainder. Continue this process to the end.

Practice Exercise No. 30a

1 Reduce 27 rd. to units of lower denomination.
2 What fraction of an hour is 22' 30"?
3 Add the following in pounds troy: 2 lb. 8 oz. 12 pwt., 3 lb. 6 oz. and 9 pwt., 4 lb. 5 oz. 6 pwt.
4 Add the following: 50° 37' 23", 40° 28' 42", 18° 17' 53".
5 From 17 bbl. 14 gal. take 6 bbl. 20 gal.
6 From 6 bu. 2 pk. 5 qt. take 2 bu. 3 pk. 7 qt.
7 Multiply 3 tons 750 lb. by 6.
8 Multiply 5 gal. 3 qt. 1 pt. by 7.
9 Divide 6 mi. 6 fur. 12 rd. by 4.
10 Divide 8 bbl. 18 gal. 3 qt. by 3.

LATITUDE, LONGITUDE AND TIME

The **latitude** of a place is its distance north or south of the equator, calculated in degrees, minutes and seconds. (*See table of Angular or Circular Measure above.*) Distance north of the equator is called **north latitude,** and distance south of the equator, **south latitude.**

The **longitude** of a place is its distance east or west of a given **prime meridian**, calculated in degrees, minutes and seconds. Distance east of the prime meridian is called **east longitude**, and distance west of the prime meridian is called **west longitude**.

By international agreement the English-speaking countries and a number of others consider the prime meridian (or the meridian of 0° longitude) to be that which passes through Greenwich, a suburb of London, England.

The 180th meridian of longitude is designated as neither East nor West since the same line on the earth's surface is both 180° east and 180° west of Greenwich.

The latitude and longitude of a place are arrived at by determining its position with relation to the sun and the time of day. Observation of the sun is performed with an optical instrument called, according to its type, a *sextant* or an *octant*. The procedures incident to calculating position from such observations constitute the science of **navigation**.

Differences of latitude or longitude between two places are calculated by the following rules.

1. *If the latitudes of the two given places are both north or both south, subtract the lesser latitude from the greater; but if one is north and the other south, add the two latitudes.*

2. *If the longitudes of the two given places are both east or both west, subtract the lesser longitude from the greater; but if one is east and the other west, add the two longitudes.*

3. *If the sum of two longitudes exceeds 180°, this sum is subtracted from 360° to obtain the correct difference in longitude.*

EXAMPLE 1: The longitude of New York is 74° 0′ 3″ West; of Philadelphia 75° 10′ West. What is their difference in longitude?

SOLUTION:

$$75° \quad 10′ \quad 0″$$
$$74 \quad 0 \quad 3$$
$$\overline{1° \quad 9′ \quad 57″}, \text{ Ans.}$$

EXPLANATION: Since New York and Philadelphia are both west of the prime meridian of Greenwich, their difference in longitude must be the distance by which Philadelphia is farther west than New York. This distance is found by subtracting the lesser longitude of New York from the greater longitude of Philadelphia.

EXAMPLE 2: What is the difference in longitude between New York and Paris? The longitude of the former city is 74° 0′ 3″ West; that of the latter city is 2° 20′ 22″ East.

SOLUTION:

$$74° \quad 0′ \quad 3″$$
$$2 \quad 20 \quad 22$$
$$\overline{76° \quad 20′ \quad 25″}, \text{ Ans.}$$

EXPLANATION: Since the distance from Paris to the prime meridian is 2° 20′ 22″, and from the prime meridian to New York is 74° 0′ 3″ farther on in the same direction, the total distance or difference in longitude between these two places must be the sum of these two distances.

The relation of time to longitude is described in the following.

The daily revolution of the earth on its axis causes the sun to appear to pass from east to west over the 360° of the earth's longitude in 24 hours. Hence in 1 hour, the sun appears to pass over $\frac{1}{24}$ of 360°, or 15° of longitude; in 1 minute of time, $\frac{1}{60}$ of 15°, or 15′ of longitude; and in 1 second of time, $\frac{1}{60}$ of 15′, or 15″ of longitude. Hence 15° longitude corresponds to 1 hour of solar time; 15′ of longitude corresponds to 1 minute of solar time; and 15″ of longitude corresponds to 1 second of solar time.

The solar time (sun time) of any place depends upon the sun's relative position. It is 12 o'clock M, or noon, at a place when the sun crosses its meridian. Hence, if it is noon at our meridian, it is afternoon (P.M. or *post meridian*) at all places east of us, and forenoon (A.M. or *ante meridian*) at all places west of us.

The United States uses what is known as **Standard Time**. The country is divided into four time zones, each approximately 15° of longitude in width. Every place in each of these zones uses the same *standard time* instead of its own local sun time.

The four time zones are designated as Eastern, Central, Mountain and Pacific and use the solar time, respectively, of the 75th, 90th, 105th and 120th meridians of West Longitude.

Foreign standard time. When it is 12 o'clock noon Eastern Standard Time, the standard time in various cities is as follows:

Berlin	6.00 P.M.	Moscow	8.00 P.M.
Calcutta	10.53 P.M.	Paris	5.00 P.M.
Honolulu	6.30 A.M.	Rome	6.00 P.M.
Istanbul	7.00 P.M.	Shanghai	1.00 A.M. next day
Leningrad	8.00 P.M.	Sydney	3.00 A.M. next day
London	5.00 P.M.	Tokyo	2.00 A.M. next day

Daylight saving time originated in England during the First World War. By setting the clock an hour ahead during late spring, summer and early autumn, an hour of daylight is taken off the beginning of the clock-day and added to the evening. Daylight saving time has been a matter of local option in this country except during the Second World War, when the Federal Government established it for the whole year and for the period of the duration under the name of **Standard War Time.**

Argentina, the Bahamas, Bermuda, Canada, and Chile are among the Western Hemisphere countries that use advanced time during at least part of the year.

To find the difference in solar time between two places, *divide the difference in longitude in degrees, minutes and seconds by 15, and the quotient will be the difference in solar time expressed respectively in hours, minutes and seconds.*

EXAMPLE: What is the difference in solar time between New York and Greenwich? The longitude of New York is 74° 0′ 3″ West.

SOLUTION: 15)74° 0′   3″
              4 hr. 56 min. 0 sec.,   ANS.

EXPLANATION: Division is performed in the regular manner used with denominate numbers. The final remainder, $\frac{3}{15}$ or $\frac{1}{5}$ second is discarded.

To find the difference in longitude between two places when their difference in solar time is known, *multiply the difference in solar time in hours, minutes and seconds by 15, and the product will be the difference in longitude expressed respectively in degrees, minutes and seconds.*

EXAMPLE: The difference in solar time between Berlin and Paris is 44 min. $13\frac{3}{5}$ sec. If the longitude of Berlin is 13° 23′ 45″ East, and if Paris is west of Berlin, what is the longitude of Paris?

SOLUTION:

	44 min.	$13\frac{3}{5}$ sec.	
		15	
11°	3′	24″	
13	23	45	East
2°	20′	21″	East, ANS.

EXPLANATION: Multiply the difference in time by 15 to find the difference in longitude, amounting to 11° 3′ 24″. Since Paris is west of Berlin, the longitude of Paris must be 11° 3′ 24″ nearer to the prime meridian, which is also west of Berlin. Hence, the difference in longitude is subtracted from the longitude of Berlin to find the longitude of Paris.

Since time is reckoned both east and west of Greenwich it follows that time on the 180th meridian might be considered either 12 hours earlier or 12 hours later than that of Greenwich. Instead of taking the 180th meridian as the strict dividing line between eastern time and western time, agreement among the nations has established the International Date Line which follows a somewhat zigzag course in the neighborhood of the 180th meridian. This has been done so that Pacific islands in the same group may use the same time. When it is noon at Greenwich it is shortly after midnight on the morning of the same day at places slightly east of the International Date Line, and shortly before midnight on the night of the same day at places slightly west. When it is 1 P.M. at Greenwich it is about 1 A.M. of the same day at the former places and 1 A.M. of the *following day* at the latter places.

ARMED FORCES TIME

In all branches of the Armed Forces, time is reckoned by the 24-hour clock. Starting at midnight, or 0000, the hours are indicated by hundreds. 8 A.M. is 0800; 12 M. is 1200; 1 P.M. is 1300; 11 P.M. is 2300. Minutes are indicated by units—preceded by a 0 if less than 10, since there must always be four digits. 8.10 A.M. is 0810; 12.05 P.M. is 1205; 11.59 P.M. is 2359; 12.01 A.M. is 0001.

TIME BETWEEN DATES

To compute **ordinary interest time between dates in different years,** *consider all months to have* 30 *days and proceed as for subtraction of denominate numbers.*

EXAMPLE 1: What is the ordinary interest time between October 15, 1937 and March 11, 1945?

SOLUTION:

```
       yr.   mo.  da.
      1945    3    11
      1937   10    15
       7      4    26,  ANS.
```

EXPLANATION: The years are considered as quantities of time. 30 days are borrowed from 3 months to make possible the subtraction of 15 days, and 12 months are borrowed from 1945 years to make possible the subtraction of 10 months.

To compute **exact interest time between rates in different years:**

1. *Determine the number of days remaining in the earlier of the given years after the given date, and to this add the number of days in the later of the given years up to the later date.*

2. *Find the number of full years remaining in the interval and add to these the number of days previously determined.*

EXAMPLE 2: For purposes of exact interest, what is the time between October 15, 1937 and March 11, 1945?

SOLUTION:

```
      1937 Oct.  16 da.
           Nov.  30  "
           Dec.  31  "
      1945 Jan.  31  "
           Feb.  28  "
           Mar.  11  "
                 147  "
```

1938 to 1944 inclusive = 7 years
7 yr. 147 da., ANS.

EXPLANATION: Starting with October, 1937, there are 16 days left in October, 30 days in November and 31 in December. Then from the beginning of 1945 there are 31 days in January, 28 in February and 11 in March up to the 11th day of March.

All these days come to a total of 147, and these are added to the 7 full years occurring in the given interval.

A **leap year** of 366 days occurs every four years, with February containing 29 days. Every year evenly divisible by 4 is a *leap year*, except that every year evenly divisible by 100 is *not* a leap year, except that every year evenly divisible by 400 *is* a leap year.

To find the exact number of days between dates in different years:

1. *Find the number of years and days by the method used to determine time for exact interest.*

2. *Multiply the number of years by 365 and add to this the separate number of days as previously found.*

3. *Add one day for every leap year occurring in the full years included in the interval*.

EXAMPLE 3: What is the exact number of days between October 15, 1937 and March 11, 1945?

SOLUTION: By Example 2 we found that this interval contained 7 years and 147 days. Multiplying 365 by 7 and adding 147 we get 2702 days. But 2 leap years occurred among the full years (1940 and 1944). Hence we add two days to make a total of 2704 days.

Practice Exercise No. 30b

1 The latitude of Washington is 38°53′39″ North and that of Montreal is 45° 35′ North. What is their difference in latitude?

2 The longitude of Calcutta is 88° 19′ 2″ East and that of San Francisco 122° 26′ 45″ West. What is their difference in longitude? (Hint—subtract from 360°.)

3 The longitude of New Orleans is 90° 2′ 23″; that of San Francisco is given in Question 2. What is their difference in solar time?

4 When it is 11.48 A.M. solar time in Washington it is 12.15 P.M. solar time in Portland. If the longitude of Washington is 77° 15″ West, what is that of Portland? Which Portland is meant—Maine or Oregon?

5 How many days are there between August 13, 1943 and March 12, 1944?

ENGLISH MONEY

When dealing with English money by itself, calculations are made as with any other kind of denominate numbers. Of special interest and importance, however, is the reduction of English money to equivalent values in United States money.

The **exchange rate** on money expresses the value of the money of one country in terms of the money of another. Thus if the **exchange rate** on English money is $2.00, it means that one pound is considered to be worth $2.00 of our money. Exchange rates vary according to the conditions under which money is wanted and also fluctuate with general conditions in the money market. Current exchange rates are quoted daily in the newspapers.

Note: It should be observed that when an individual buys foreign money on a small scale, he does not secure the full advantage of the exchange rate, since the bank or money broker charges a small commission on the transaction. In the following examples and exercises such commissions are disregarded.

To find the value of English money in United States money *multiply by the current exchange rate.*

EXAMPLE: If the rate of exchange for the pound is $2.00, how much is 15£ 3d. worth in United States money?

$2.00 × 15.3 = $30.60,   ANS.

To find the value of United States money in English money *divide the United States money by the exchange rate in dollars.*

EXAMPLE: With exchange at $2.00, what is $26.25 worth in English money?

$26.25 ÷ $2.00
= £13.13
13£ and 13d.,   ANS.

Practice Exercise No. 30c

1   When the exchange rate is $2.00 what is the value in United States money of 5£ 6d.?

2   At the same rate, what is 10£ worth in American money?

3   At $4.03 to the pound, what was the value in dollars at 3£ 4d.?

SURFACE MEASUREMENTS

The *area* of a rectangular surface is the number of square units which it contains. (*See also page* 119.)

In finding an *area* the unit of measure is a square each side of which is a unit of the same denomination as the given dimensions. Hence to find the area of a rectangular surface 8 feet long and 5 feet wide, the measuring unit will be 1 square foot, since the denomination of the length and width is feet.

To find the area of a rectangular surface *multiply the two dimensions.*

EXAMPLE: How many square yards are in a sidewalk 48 feet long and 11 feet 4 inches wide?

SOLUTION:

11 ft. 4 in. = $11\frac{1}{3}$ ft.
48 sq. ft. × $11\frac{1}{3}$ = 544 sq. ft.
544 ÷ 9 = $60\frac{4}{9}$ sq. yd.,   ANS.

EXPLANATION: Taking 1 square foot as the unit, a sidewalk 48 feet long and 1 foot wide would contain 48 square feet. Hence a sidewalk of equal length and $11\frac{1}{3}$ feet wide must contain $11\frac{1}{3}$ times 48 square feet or 544 square feet. This reduces to $60\frac{4}{9}$ square yards.

To find either dimension of a rectangular surface when the other dimension and the area are given, *divide the area by the given dimension.*

EXAMPLE: If a rectangular field containing 30 acres is 40 rods wide, what is its length?

SOLUTION:

30 acres = 4800 sq. rd.
4800 ÷ 40 = 120 rd.,   ANS.

EXPLANATION: A field 40 rods long and 1 rod wide would contain 40 square rods. Therefore to contain 30 acres or 4800 square rods, a field 40 rods wide would have to be as many rods long as 40 square rods are contained in 4800 square rods.

In estimating the cost of pav.ng, painting, plastering, roofing, etc., the basic procedure is to multiply the area of the surface to be covered by the unit cost per square yard or per square foot. There are a number of special considerations, however, and in any case the cost of such work is likely to be governed by local trade customs and the practices of individual contractors.

In the case of *painting* and *plastering*, **allowances** must be made for openings. That is to say, the area of doors and windows must be deducted from the area represented by the overall dimensions of the walls. Similarly, deductions may have to be made for baseboards, wainscotings and the spaces concealed by tubs, ranges and the like.

In estimating the **quantity of paint** necessary to cover a surface, the area of the surface is divided by the covering capacity of the paint as stated on the can or in the literature of the manufacturer. *Thus,* if a gallon of paint is rated to cover 400 square feet with two coats, a surface of 1,000 square feet would require $2\frac{1}{2}$ gallons for two coats or $1\frac{1}{4}$ gallons for one coat.

In the case of *roofing* the usual unit on which cost is based is the **square.** This measures 10 feet on each side and contains 100 square feet. Roofing materials are usually packaged in bundles, each of which will cover 1 such square.

To find the number of pieces of material necessary to cover a given surface, *divide one of the dimensions of the surface by one of the dimensions of the piece, and the other dimension of the surface by the other dimension of the piece, and multiply these two quotients.*

EXAMPLE: How many tiles 9 inches square will be necessary to floor a room measuring 35 feet by 20 feet?

SOLUTION:

35 ft. = 420 in.   420 in. ÷ 9 in. = $46\frac{2}{3}$
                                   = 47 tiles.

20 ft. = 240 in.   240 in. ÷ 9 in. = $26\frac{2}{3}$
                                   = 27 tiles.

$47 \times 27 = 1,269$ tiles,   ANS.

EXPLANATION: Along the 30-foot side the exact measurement equals $46\frac{2}{3}$ tiles, but it will be necessary to take this as 47 tiles. Similarly a width of 27 tiles must be taken. 27 rows of 47 tiles each come to a total of 1,269 tiles.

Note on **tiling, etc.:** If this example had figured out to $46\frac{1}{3}$ (instead of $46\frac{2}{3}$) in one direction, 27 rows of 46 tiles would give enough left-over thirds of tiles to

make up another 27 rows of thirds. The answer then would have been 46×27 or 1,242 tiles.

An extra-wide mortar joint may make a reduction in the number of rows. In some cases, like shingling, only the *exposed* surface is calculated.

When the material is longer in one direction than the other, it may be necessary to determine which dimension of the material divides the more economically into which dimension of the surface.

To find how many yards of material are needed to cover a given surface, *determine how many strips will be necessary and the length of each strip. The total area of all strips in square yards will be the required yardage.*

EXAMPLE: If 2 inches are to be allowed for turning under on all sides of the room, how many yards of carpet $\frac{3}{4}$ of a yard wide will be required for a room measuring 16 by 19 feet?

SOLUTION:

4 in. = $\frac{1}{9}$ yd.

$\frac{19}{3} \times \frac{4}{3} = \frac{76}{9} = 8\frac{4}{9}$ $\frac{16}{3} \times \frac{4}{3} = \frac{64}{9} = 7\frac{1}{9}$

$6\frac{1}{3} + \frac{1}{9} = 6\frac{4}{9}$ yd. $5\frac{1}{3} + \frac{1}{9} = 5\frac{4}{9}$ yd.

$6\frac{4}{9} \times 8 = 52$ yd. $5\frac{4}{9} \times 9 = 49$ yd.,   ANS.

EXPLANATION: In examples of this kind it is often necessary and always safest to determine in which direction the carpet may be laid more economically. If we divide 16 feet or $\frac{16}{3}$ yards by $\frac{3}{4}$, we get $7\frac{1}{9}$, which means 8 strips. If we divide $\frac{19}{3}$ yards we get $8\frac{4}{9}$ or 9 strips. Allowing 2 inches for turning under on both ends of each strip, we find that in one case the strip would have to be $5\frac{4}{9}$ yards long, while in the other case they would be $6\frac{4}{9}$ yards long. 9 strips of $5\frac{4}{9}$ yards give a smaller total yardage than 8 strips of $6\frac{4}{9}$ yards. Hence we select 49 yards as the correct answer.

Note on **carpet, linoleum, wall paper, etc.:** In laying or applying materials of this kind a certain allowance may have to be made for matching patterns. The matching of pattern, moreover, may work out more economically in one direction than in the other.

Carpet is usually 1 yard or $\frac{3}{4}$ yard wide, and is most commonly sewn together by the dealer making the sale. Linoleum comes in various widths.

Wall paper is calculated on the basis of the *single* roll, which is 8 yards long and 18 inches wide excluding lap. It is actually sold, however, in *double* rolls of 16-yard length. The longer roll minimizes waste in cutting, etc. The quantity of wall paper required for a room can be approximately determined as follows. Measure the distance around the room in yards, and multiply this figure by two to arrive at the number of strips. Determine how long the full strips will be and how many such strips can be cut from a double roll. This number divided into the total number of strips will give the number of double rolls required. For the average room, it is safest to make no allowances for openings as such allowances will be offset by the waste in cutting and matching.

Practice Exercise No. 31

1 What is the difference between 8 square feet and 8 ft. square?

(A) 16 ft. _____   (C) 56 sq. ft. _____
(B) 16 sq. ft. _____   (D) 64 sq. ft. _____

2 A fence surrounding a half-mile race-track is 8 feet high. How many square yards does it contain?

(A) 5,180 _____   (C) 2,346$\frac{2}{3}$ _____
(B) 586$\frac{2}{3}$ _____   (D) 685$\frac{2}{3}$ _____

3 What is the cost of flooring a room 25 feet wide and 33$\frac{1}{2}$ feet long with yard-wide carpet at $9.50 a yard? Make no allowance for turning under or matching pattern.

(A) $171.65 _____   (C) $572.20 _____
(B) $950.00 _____   (D) $1,500.00 _____

4 A farm 360 rods long by 189 rods wide was bought for $36 an acre. How much did this farm cost?

(A) $7,654.50 _____   (C) $15,309 _____
(B) $12,937 _____   (D) $18,627 _____

5 A walk 50 feet long and 5 feet wide is paved with bricks measuring 8 by 4 inches. How many bricks are in it?

(A) 2,250 _____   (C) 3,357 _____
(B) 1,125 _____   (D) 4,500 _____

6 A roof is resurfaced at a cost of $45 per square (100 sq. ft.). If the roof measures 65 × 35 feet, what is the cost of the job?

(A) $102.38 _____   (C) $2,500.00 _____
(B) $2,046.50 _____   (D) $1,023.75 _____

CUBIC MEASUREMENT

The **cubical contents** or the **volume** of a rectangular solid is the number of cubic units which it contains. Another synonymous term is **capacity**. (*See also page 123.*)

The unit of *cubical measure* is a cube each edge of which is a unit of the same denomination as the three given dimensions. Hence to find the cubical contents of a rectangular solid which is 6 feet long, 4 feet wide and 3 feet deep, the measuring unit will be 1 cubic foot, since the denomination of the length, width and depth is feet.

To find the cubical contents of a rectangular solid, *multiply together the three dimensions.*

EXAMPLE: What are the cubical contents of a box 3 feet 8 inches long, 3 feet 6 inches wide and 2 feet 3 inches in length?

SOLUTION:

$3\frac{2}{3}$ ft. × $3\frac{1}{2}$ ft. × $2\frac{1}{4}$ ft. = $28\frac{7}{8}$ cu. ft., ANS.

EXPLANATION: Imagining cubes measuring one foot each way, we find that a row of $3\frac{2}{3}$ such cubes could be laid along the longest dimension of the box. The $3\frac{1}{2}$ feet of width would accommodate $3\frac{1}{2}$ rows of $3\frac{2}{3}$ cubic feet each, and the depth of the box would have room for $2\frac{1}{4}$ layers of $3\frac{2}{3} \times 3\frac{1}{2}$ cubes. Hence the total comes to $3\frac{2}{3} \times 3\frac{1}{2} \times 2\frac{1}{4}$ or $28\frac{7}{8}$ cubic feet.

To find a third dimension of a rectangular solid when the other two dimensions and the cubical contents are given, *divide the cubical contents by the product of the two given dimensions.*

EXAMPLE: A block of stone 7 feet long and 5 feet wide contains 140 cubic feet. What is its height?

SOLUTION:

$140 \div (7 \times 5) = 4$ ft.

EXPLANATION: A block 7 feet long, 5 feet wide and 1 foot high would contain 35 cubic feet. Hence to contain 140 cubic feet, a block of this length and width would have to be as many times 1 foot high as 35 is contained in 140.

Board measure is used in measuring boards, planks and other sawed lumber.

A **board foot** represents one square foot of surface of a board 1 inch or less in thickness; that is, it is considered to be a board 1 foot long, 1 foot wide and 1 inch thick. *Thus*, a board 8 feet long, 2 feet wide and 1 inch (or less) thick would contain 16 *board feet.*

If the board is more than 1 inch thick multiply length by width by thickness. Thickness is measured only by quarter-inches. Lumber of small dimensions is commonly sold by the running foot, big timbers and logs by the cubic foot.

Board measure has no connection with cord measure, which is used for fireplace wood, or sometimes for stone or other bulk material. A *cord* represents the volume of two cubes each measuring 4 feet on an edge.

Practice Exercise No. 32

1 How many cubic inches in 13 cu. ft.?
2 How many cubic inches in 11 cu. yd.?
3 How many cubic inches in 5 cu. yd. 6 cu. ft.?

4 How many cubic feet in 135 cu. yd.?
5 How many cubic feet in 15,552 cu. in.?
6 How many cubic yards in 466,560 cu. in.?
7 How many cubic yards in 11,106 cu. ft.?
8 How many cubic inches in 1 cu. yd.?
9 How many cubic inches in a block 1 ft. × 2 ft. × 3 ft.?
10 How many cubic yards in this block?

COMPARISON OF STANDARD WEIGHTS AND MEASURES

LIQUID MEASURE

1 U.S. gallon	= 231 cubic inches
1 British (imperial) gallon	= 277.27 cubic inches
$7\frac{1}{2}$ gallons	= 1 cubic foot
1 gallon water	= $8\frac{1}{3}$ pounds
1 cubic foot of water	= $62\frac{1}{2}$ pounds

DRY MEASURE

1 bushel (struck)	= 2150.42 cubic inches
1 bushel (heaped)	= 2747.715 cubic inches

The struck bushel (known as the Winchester bushel) is the measure for grains and small fruits. The heaped bushel is the measure for large fruits.

For practical purposes, contents in cubic feet may be multiplied by .8 to give struck bushels or by .63 to arrive at heaped bushels. Dividing struck bushels by .8 or heaped bushels by .63 gives a quotient in cubic feet.

BUSHEL WEIGHTS

The following weights per bushel are those which are commonly accepted. In individual cases values varying slightly from these may be established by state law.

Apples	48 lb.	Corn (on cob)	70 lb.
Barley	48 lb.	Oats	32 lb.
Beans	60 lb.	Peas	60 lb.
Buckwheat	48 lb.	Potatoes	60 lb.
Clover seed	60 lb.	Rye	56 lb.
Corn (shelled)	56 lb.	Wheat	60 lb.

WOOD MEASURE

16 cubic feet	= 1 cord foot
8 cord feet (128 cu. ft.)	= 1 cord

Cord measure is used in measuring wood for fuel.

WEIGHTS

1 oz. avoirdupois =	.9115 oz. troy *or* apothecaries'
1 lb. avoirdupois =	1.2153 lb. troy *or* apothecaries'
1 oz. troy *or* apothecaries' =	1.0971 oz. avoirdupois
1 lb. troy *or* apothecaries' =	.8229 lb. avoirdupois

It should be noted that the basic unit which is the same in all three systems of weight is the grain—supposedly a grain of wheat "from the middle of the ear." The apothecaries' pound and the troy pound are the same since they contain the same number of grains, namely 5,760. The avoirdupois pound is heavier since it contains 7,000 grains. The ounce is also equal in the apothecaries' and troy systems (480 gr.) but the avoirdupois ounce is lighter (437.5 gr.).

WEIGHT OF MATERIALS

The weight of a given volume of a substance can be determined if its **specific gravity** is known. Specific gravity is the relation of its weight to that of water. The following table shows the specific gravities of a number of materials. Weight in pounds avoirdupois per cubic foot may be found by multiplying the values here given by 62.4.

Alcohol	.79	Lead	11.01
Aluminum	2.67	Mercury	13.6
Asphaltum	1.06	Nickel	8.8
Beeswax	.96	Nitric acid	1.32
Benzene	.83	Platinum	21.37
Brass	8.1	Rubber	.93
Carbon, diamond	3.52	Silver	10.42
Carbon, graphite	2.25	Sulphur	2.0
Copper	8.89	Sulphuric acid	1.84
Gold	19.3	Tin	7.18
Hydrochloric acid	1.20	Turpentine	.87
Iron	7.86	Zinc	4.32

Practice Exercise No. 32a

1 How many imperial gallons are there in a United States barrel? Carry to two decimal places.
2 If a tank measuring 10 feet by 6 feet by $4\frac{1}{2}$ feet is filled to running over, what is the weight of water it contains?
3 How many bushels of wheat would be contained in this same space?
4 What would be the weight of this wheat?
5 How many pounds troy would this weight be equivalent to?
6 How many pounds would a bar of lead one inch square and one foot long weigh? Carry to two decimal places.

THE METRIC SYSTEM

Since the metric system is based on decimal values, exactly like United States money, all ordinary arithmetical operations may be performed by simply moving the decimal point.

Consider the quantity of 4.567 meters. It is made up of the following units:

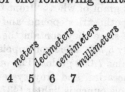

meters	decimeters	centimeters	millimeters
4	5	6	7

We may read this quantity as 4.567 meters, or as 45.67 decimeters, or as 456.7 centimeters or as 4,567 millimeters.

When it comes to dealing with square and cubic measures we must simply bear in mind that instead of moving the decimal point one place for each successive change in unit value, we move it two places in the case of square measurements and three places in the case of cubic measurements.

Thus, take 42.365783 square meters. This consists of 42 sq. m., 36 sq. dm., 57 sq. cm., 83 sq. mm. It may be read as 42.365783 square meters, or as 4,236.5783 square decimeters, or as 423,657.83 square centimeters, or as 42,365,783 square millimeters.

Now take 75.683256 cubic meters. It is composed of 75 cu. m., 683 cu. dm., 256 cu. cm. It may be read as 75.683256 cubic meters, or as 75,683.256 cubic decimeters or as 75,683,256 cubic centimeters.

The metric system is a system of related weights and measures. The meter is the basis from which all other units are derived. The unit of weight, the gram, is the weight of a cubic volume of water (under certain conditions) measuring 1 centimeter (.01 meter) on a side. The unit of capacity, the liter, is the volume of 1 kilogram (1,000 grams) of water and thus is represented by a cube measuring 1 decimeter (10 centimeters) on a side.

The liter and its derivatives are used for both dry and liquid measure.

Practice Exercise No. 33

1 How many kilometers in 3,746.23 m.?
2 How many meters in 4.253 km.?
3 How many square kilometers in 85.46 sq. m.?
4 How many square millimeters in 47.386 sq. dm.?

5 How many cubic centimeters in 3.56 cu. m.?
6 How many cubic meters in 374,658 cu. mm.?
7 How many centiliters in 312.3765 l.?
8 How many hectoliters in 312.3765 l.?
9 How many centigrams in 7.46 kg.?
10 How many kilograms in 3,426 grams?

In the following tables wherever the metric equivalents of U. S. standard measures are given, metric equivalents of other denominations may be found by simply moving the decimal point to the right or the left as may be necessary.

EQUIVALENT VALUES

LINEAR MEASURE

1 inch	=	2.5400 centimeters
1 foot	=	.3048 meter
1 yard	=	.9144 meter
1 rod	=	5.0292 meters
1 mile	=	1.6093 kilometers
1 centimeter	=	.3937 inch
1 decimeter	=	3.9370 inches
1 decimeter	=	.3281 foot
1 meter	=	39.3700 inches
1 meter	=	3.2808 feet
1 meter	=	1.0936 yards
1 kilometer	=	3280.83 feet
1 kilometer	=	1093.611 yards
1 kilometer	=	198.838 rods
1 kilometer	=	.62137 miles

SQUARE MEASURE

1 sq. inch	=	6.4516 sq. centimeters
1 sq. foot	=	.0929 sq. meter
1 sq. yard	=	.8361 sq. meter
1 sq. rod	=	25.2930 sq. meters
1 acre	=	4046.8730 sq. meters
1 acre	=	.404687 hectare
1 sq. mile	=	258.9998 hectares
1 sq. mile	=	2.5900 kilometers
1 sq. centimeter	=	.1550 sq. inch
1 sq. decimeter	=	15.5000 sq. inches
1 sq. meter	=	1550.0000 sq. inches
1 sq. meter	=	10.7640 sq. feet
1 sq. meter	=	1.1960 sq. yards
1 hectare	=	2.4710 acres
1 hectare	=	395.3670 sq. rods
1 hectare	=	24.7104 sq. chains
1 sq. kilometer	=	247.1040 acres
1 sq. kilometer	=	.3861 sq. mile

The hectare is the unit of land measure.

CUBIC MEASURE

1 cu. inch	=	16.3872 cu. centimeters
1 cu. foot	=	28.3170 cu. decimeters

1 cu. yard	=	.7645 cu. meter
1 cord	=	3.624 cu. meters
1 cu. centimeter	=	.0610 cu. inch
1 cu. decimeter	=	.0353 cu. foot
1 cu. meter	=	1.3079 cu. yards
1 cu. meter	=	.2759 cord

The cubic meter when used for measuring wood is called a *ster*.

CAPACITY

1 minim	=	.0616 milliliters
1 fluid dram	=	3.6966 milliliters
1 fluid ounce	=	29.5730 milliliters
1 gill	=	118.2920 milliliters
1 liquid pint	=	.4732 liter
1 liquid quart	=	.9463 liter
1 gallon	=	3.7853 liters
1 milliliter	=	16.2311 minims
1 milliliter	=	.2705 fluid dram
1 milliliter	=	.0338 fluid ounce
1 liter	=	2.1134 liquid pints
1 liter	=	1.0567 liquid quarts
1 liter	=	.2642 gallon
1 dry quart	=	1.1012 liters
1 dry peck	=	.8810 dekaliter
1 bushel	=	.3523 hectoliter
1 liter	=	.9081 dry quart
1 dekaliter	=	1.1351 pecks
1 hectoliter	=	2.8378 bushels

The liter is used for both liquid and dry measure.

The milliliter is equivalent in volume to a cubic centimeter.

WEIGHT

1 grain	=	.0648 gram
1 ounce troy	=	31.103 grams
1 pound troy	=	.3732 kilogram
1 ounce avoirdupois	=	28.350 grams
1 pound avoirdupois	=	.4536 kilogram
1 short ton	=	.9072 tonneau
1 long ton	=	1.0160 tonneaus
1 gram	=	15.4324 grains
1 gram	=	.0322 ounce troy
1 gram	=	.0353 ounce avoirdupois
1 kilogram	=	2.6792 pounds troy
1 kilogram	=	2.2046 pounds avoirdupois
1 tonneau	=	1.1023 short tons
1 tonneau	=	.9842 long ton
1 tonneau	=	2204.6223 pounds avoirdupois

Practice Exercise No. 34

1 Reduce 385.25 hectares to acres.
2 How many bushels are there in 375 hectoliters?
3 How many miles in 153 kilometers?
4 How many gallons in 483 dekaliters?
5 Change 75.5 kilograms to pounds avoirdupois.
6 How many meters in 87 yards?
7 Change 157.35 acres to hectares.
8 Reduce 173 gallons to dekaliters.
9 How many grams in 3 ounces of gold?
10 How many hectoliters in 187 bushels?

CHAPTER SIX

RATIO AND PROPORTION

RATIO

A *ratio* is the relation between two like numbers or two like values. The ratio may be written as a fraction, $\frac{3}{4}$; as a division, $3 \div 4$; or with the colon or *ratio sign* (:), 3 : 4. When the last of these forms is used, it is read, 3 *to* 4; or 3 *is to* 4. Ratios may be expressed by the word *per* as in miles per hour, or revolutions per second. In arithmetic these are written miles/hour, revolutions/minute, volts/ampere. Whatever the manner of writing the ratio, its value in arithmetical computations is always the same.

Since a ratio may be regarded as a fraction, you will recognize the following principle as being true:

Rule 1: *Multiplying or dividing both terms of a ratio by the same number does not change the value of the ratio.*

Thus, 2 : 4 = 4 : 8 (multiplying both
terms by 2)

or 2 : 4 = 1 : 2 (dividing both terms
by 2)

To reduce a ratio to its lowest terms, *treat the ratio as a fraction and reduce the fraction to its lowest terms.*

EXAMPLE 1: Express $\frac{2}{3}$ to $\frac{4}{9}$ in its lowest terms.

SOLUTION: $\frac{2}{3}$ to $\frac{4}{9} = \frac{2}{3} \div \frac{4}{9} = \frac{2}{3} \times \frac{9}{4} = \frac{3}{2}$.

Hence $\frac{2}{3}$ to $\frac{4}{9}$ is the same as 3 to 2.

To separate a quantity according to a given ratio, *add the terms of the ratio to find the total number of parts. Find what fractional part each term is of the whole. Divide the total quantity into parts corresponding to the fractional parts.*

EXAMPLE 2: Three hundred tents have to be divided between two army divisions in the ratio of 1 : 2. How many does each division get?

1 + 2 = 3 (adding the terms)

$\left.\begin{array}{l}\frac{1}{3} \times 300 = 100\\ \frac{2}{3} \times 300 = 200\end{array}\right\}$ ANS. (Taking corresponding fractional parts of total quantity)

Check: 100 : 200 or $\frac{100}{200} = \frac{1}{2}$ or 1 : 2.

EXAMPLE 3: 1,600 lbs. of coffee have to be distributed to 3 wholesale dealers in the ratio of 8 : 11 : 13. How many lbs. should each dealer receive?

SOLUTION:

8 + 11 + 13 = 32

$\frac{8}{32}, \frac{11}{32}, \frac{13}{32}$ are the fractional parts

$\left.\begin{array}{l}\frac{8}{32} \times 1,600 = 400\\ \frac{11}{32} \times 1,600 = 550\\ \frac{13}{32} \times 1,600 = 650\end{array}\right\}$ ANS.

Practice Exercise No. 35

PROBLEMS

1 Reduced to its lowest terms, 24 : 32 equals what?

(A) $\frac{1}{3}$ _____   (c) $\frac{6}{8}$ _____
(B) $\frac{1}{2}$ _____   (D) $\frac{3}{4}$ _____

2 What is the value of the ratio 7 × 9 : 8 × 7?

(A) $\frac{8}{9}$ _____   (c) 8 : 9 _____
(B) $1\frac{1}{8}$ _____   (D) $1\frac{23}{49}$ _____

3 If 5 lbs. of vegetables lose 10 oz. in drying, what part of the original weight was water?

(A) $\frac{1}{6}$ _____   (c) 12% _____
(B) $\frac{1}{8}$ _____   (D) $\frac{1}{2}$ _____

4 A mixture requires 2 parts of water to 3 parts of alcohol. What percentage of the mixture is water?

(A) 40% _____   (c) 60% _____
(B) 50% _____   (D) $66\frac{2}{3}$% _____

5 Bronze consists of 6 parts tin to 19 parts copper. How many pounds of tin are there in a 500-lb. bronze statue?

(A) 100 _____   (c) 140 _____
(B) 120 _____   (D) 200 _____

6 $2,000 is to be distributed among 3 members of a family in the ratio of 5 : 14 : 21. How much greater is the largest share than the smallest share?

(A) $900 _____   (c) $500 _____
(B) $800 _____   (D) $750 _____

PROPORTION

A **proportion** is a statement of equality between two ratios. It may be written with the double colon or **proportion sign** (::), or with the sign of equality (=).

Thus, 2 : 6 :: 3 : 9 is a proportion that is read, 2 *is to* 6 *as* 3 *is to* 9; *or* $\frac{2}{6}$ *equals* $\frac{3}{9}$.

In any proportion the first and last terms are called the **extremes** and the second and third terms are called the **means.** In 2 : 6 :: 3 : 9 the *extremes* are 2 and 9; and the *means* are 6 and 3.

Multiply the two extremes and the two means of the proportion 2 : 6 :: 3 : 9 and compare the products.

Extremes: 2 × 9 = 18,
Means: 6 × 3 = 18.

This result illustrates **Rule 2:** *The product of the* means *is equal to the product of the* extremes.

If you write the proportion in the form of $\frac{2}{6} = \frac{3}{9}$, note that the means and extremes are diagonally opposite each other. This affords another way to pick out your equation.

No proportion is a true proportion unless the two ratios are equal. This is another way of saying that Rule 2 must be satisfied.

By means of this rule you can find the missing term of any proportion if the other 3 terms are given.

EXAMPLE 1: $2 : 6 = 8 : ?$ Find the value of the missing term. The letter x is traditionally used to denote a missing term or an unknown quantity. Rewriting the proportion we get

$$2 : 6 :: 8 : x.$$

(a) 2 times x = 6 times 8

$$2x = 48$$

a. Product of the extremes equals product of the means.

(b) $$\frac{2x}{2} = \frac{48}{2}$$

b. Both sides of any equation may be divided by the same number without changing the equation.

$$x = 24, \text{ Ans.}$$

The above process is the equation method of solving problems containing an unknown. This process will be treated at greater length in Chapter Eight, which deals with elementary algebra.

If you wish to use a strict arithmetic method of finding the missing term in a proportion, you may employ the following two rules.

Rule 3: *The product of the means divided by either extreme gives the other extreme as the quotient.*

$2 : 6 :: 8 : 24$;
$6 \times 8 = 48, 48 \div 2 = 24, 48 \div 24 = 2.$
Thus if given $? : 6 = 8 : 24$,
multiply the two means, $6 \times 8 = 48$,
and divide this product by the known extreme; $48 \div 24 = 2.$ The quotient here is the unknown term.

Rule 4: *The product of the extremes divided by either mean gives the other mean as a quotient.*

$2 : 6 = 8 : 24$;
$2 \times 24 = 48, 48 \div 6 = 8, 48 \div 8 = 6.$
Thus if given $2 : ? :: 8 : 24$,
multiply the two extremes, $2 \times 24 = 48$, and divide this product by the known mean; $48 \div 8 = 6.$ The quotient again is the unknown term.

Practice Exercise No. 36

Find the missing term.

1. $2 : 3 :: 4 : ?$
2. $20 : 10 :: ? : 6$
3. $2 : ? :: 8 : 24$
4. $18 : ? :: 36 : 4$
5. $12 : 4 :: ? : 7$
6. $5 : ? :: 25 : 20$
7. $? : 5 :: 12 : 20$
8. $? : 25 :: 10 : 2$
9. $9 : ? :: 24 : 8$
10. $24 : 4 :: ? : 3$

PROBLEMS IN PROPORTION

In solving problems by the ratio and proportion method it is first necessary to recognize whether a proportion exists and if so what kind it is.

A direct proportion is indicated when two quantities are so related that an increase in one causes a corresponding increase in the other or when a decrease in one causes a corresponding decrease in the other.

The following is a list of typical quantitative expressions in which the variables are directly related when other quantities remain unchanged.

a. The faster the speed, the greater the distance covered.
b. The more men working, the greater the amount of work done.
c. The faster the speed, the greater the number of revolutions.
d. The higher the temperature of gas, the greater the volume.
e. The taller the object, the longer the shadow.
f. The larger the quantity, the greater the cost.
g. The smaller the quantity, the lower the cost.
h. The greater the length, the greater the area.
j. The greater the base, the larger the discount, commission, interest and profit.

EXAMPLE 2: If 20 men assemble 8 machines in a day, how many men are needed to assemble 12 machines in a day?

SOLUTION:

8 machines need 20 men
12 machines need ? men
$8 : 12 :: 20 : x$
$8x = 240$
$x = 30, \text{ Ans.}$

EXPLANATION: Place corresponding values on the same line. Put *like numbers* together. The more machines, the more men needed. ∴ The values are a direct proportion. Solve for x.

EXAMPLE 3: If 12 drills cost $8.00, how much will 9 drills cost?

SOLUTION:

12 drills cost \$8.00   EXPLANATION: The fewer
9 drills cost   ?   the drills the lower the cost.
$12 : 9 :: 8 = x$ $\therefore$ The values are in direct
$12x = 72, x = \$6$.   proportion. Solve for x.

Examples 2 and 3 are easily recognized as direct proportions since more men can assemble more machines, and fewer drills cost less money.

CUES IN SOLVING PROPORTION PROBLEMS

In every proportion both ratios must be written in the same order of value, for instance in Example 2:

$$\frac{\text{Smaller no. of mach's}}{\text{Larger no. of mach's}} = \frac{\text{Smaller no. of men}}{\text{Larger no. of men}}$$

In Example 3:

$$\frac{\text{Larger no. of drills}}{\text{Smaller no. of drills}} = \frac{\text{Larger cost}}{\text{Smaller cost}}$$

An **inverse proportion** is indicated when two quantities are so related that an increase in one causes a corresponding decrease in the other, or vice versa.

The following are quantitative expressions in which the variables are inversely related.

a. The greater the speed, the less the time.

b. The slower the speed, the longer the time.

c. The greater the volume, the less the density.

d. The more men working, the shorter the time.

e. The fewer men working, the longer the time.

EXAMPLE 4: When two pulleys are belted together the revolutions per minute (rpm) vary inversely as the size of the pulleys. A 20-in. pulley running at 180 rpm drives an 8-in. pulley. Find the revolutions per minute of the 8-in. pulley.

SOLUTION:

20 in. makes 180 rpm
8 in. makes ? rpm

$$\frac{8}{20} = \frac{180}{x}$$

$$8x = 3,600$$

$$x = 450 \text{ rpm,   Ans.}$$

EXPLANATION: First make a table of corresponding values. Put *like numbers* together. The smaller the pulley, the greater the number of revolutions; $\therefore$ the quantities are in inverse ratio. Inverting the first ratio, write the proportion. Solve for x.

CUE: If you write your proportion in this form, $\frac{8}{20} = \frac{180}{x}$, you may note that in the inverse proportion the corresponding numbers are arranged diagonally, *i.e.*, 20 in. and 180 rpm, and 8 in. and x rpm are diagonally opposite each other.

In the direct proportion as in Example 3, $\frac{12}{9} = \frac{8}{x}$, the corresponding numbers are arranged directly on a line with each other, *i.e.*, 12 drills and \$8, 9 drills and \$x.

Practice Exercise No. 37

PROBLEMS

1   If a pole 18 ft. high casts a shadow 20 ft. long, how long a shadow would a pole 27 ft. high cast?

(A) 10 ____   (c) 30 ____
(B) 25 ____   (D) 36 ____

2   If a soldier walks 9 miles in 2 hrs. how long will it take him to walk 30 miles?

(A) 6 ____   (c) $8\frac{1}{2}$ ____
(B) $6\frac{2}{3}$ ____   (D) 9 ____

3   If an automobile runs 90 miles on 5 gal. of gas, how far will it run on a full 20-gal. tank?

(A) 300 ____   (c) 450 ____
(B) 360 ____   (D) 280 ____

4   An army camp has provisions for 240 men for 28 days; but only 112 men are sent to the camp. How long will the provisions last?

(A) 60 ____   (c) $13\frac{2}{3}$ ____
(B) 56 ____   (D) 76 ____

5   A train takes 26 hrs. at a speed of 35 miles per hr. to go from Chicago to New York. How fast must the train travel to make the trip in 20 hours?

(A) $39\frac{1}{2}$ ____   (c) $26\frac{1}{13}$ ____
(B) 40 ____   (D) $45\frac{1}{2}$ ____

6   The flywheel on an engine makes 220 revolutions in 2 seconds. How many revolutions does it make in 8 seconds?

(A) 1,760 ____   (c) 880 ____
(B) 55 ____   (D) 800 ____

CHAPTER SEVEN

SIGNED NUMBERS AND ALGEBRAIC EXPRESSIONS

Up to the present, all the numbers used here have been *positive* numbers. That is, none was less than zero (0). In solving some problems in arithmetic it is necessary to assign a *negative* value to some numbers. This is used principally for numbers with which we wish to represent opposite quantities or qualities, and can best be illustrated by use of a diagram. For example consider a thermometer, as in Fig. 1.

If temperatures *above* zero are taken as *positive*, then temperatures *below* zero are considered *negative*.

In measuring distances east and west, as in Fig. 2, if distance *east* of a certain point is taken as *positive*, then distance *west* of that point is considered *negative*.

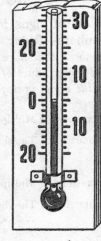

FIG. 1

FIG. 2

Another good example may be taken from commercial bookkeeping, where money in the bank and other *assets* may be considered as *positive* amounts, while money *owed* represents *negative* amounts.

Thus, in general, positive and negative numbers are used to distinguish between opposite qualities. Values above zero are considered positive and take the + sign, while values below zero are considered negative and are written with the − sign. These then become **signed numbers,** as they are called.

The + and − also continue to be used as signs of addition and subtraction. When no sign is indicated the + sign is understood.

Learning to use signed numbers is an introduction to some of the special rules for algebraic operations and also a preparation for the equation method of solving some difficult arithmetic problems in easier ways.

ADDING SIGNED NUMBERS

To add numbers of like signs, *add the numbers as in arithmetic and give to the result the common sign.*

EXAMPLE 1: −14 added to −8 = −22.

EXAMPLE 2: Add +4, +12, and +16. Ans. +32.

To add numbers of unlike signs, *combine all positive and negative quantities, subtract the smaller from the larger and give the result the sign of the larger combination.*

EXAMPLE 1: Add −4 −8 +2 +6 +10.

SOLUTION: $(-4) + (-8) = -12;$
$2 + 6 + 10 = 18$
$18 - 12 = 6,$ Ans.

EXAMPLE 2: Add 3 + 19 + 4 − 45

SOLUTION: $26 - 45 = -19,$ Ans.

What has been done above is called finding the **algebraic sum.** Similarly we can combine numbers that are represented by similar symbols.

EXAMPLE 3: Add $5b - 11b + 14b.$

SOLUTION: $19b - 11b = 8b,$ Ans.

We cannot arithmetically add terms containing unlike symbols. For instance, if we let b stand for books and p for plates we know from arithmetic that we couldn't combine books and plates as a single quantity of either. Therefore, **to add quantities containing unlike symbols,** *collect like terms and express them separately in the answer.*

EXAMPLE 4: Add $5b + 2p + 7p + 3b$.

SOLUTION: Collecting like terms,

$$5b + 3b = 8b$$
$$2p + 7p = 9p$$

Expressing unlike terms separately we get $8b + 9p$, which is an algebraic expression containing two terms, as the answer.

Practice Exercise No. 38

ADDITION OF SIGNED NUMBERS

1   $+5 + 18 =$
2   $-5 - 17 - 14 =$
3   $+7 - 12 - 6 + 4 =$
4   $-14d - 6d =$
5   $7b - 3b =$
6   $+22 - 14 - 17 - 12 + 18 =$
7   $5x - 7x + 14x =$
8   $3a + 4b + 2a - 2b =$
9   $6a + 3b + 9a - 5b =$
10 $6a + 3b + 9a - 5 =$

SUBTRACTING SIGNED NUMBERS

Subtraction means finding the difference between two numbers, or the difference between two values on a scale.

If you were asked what is the difference between $-4°$ centigrade and $+5°$, your answer would be $9°$. You would do this mentally. Now how did you arrive at the answer? First you counted from $-4°$ to zero, then added 5 to that. The rule for subtraction of signed numbers is therefore:

To subtract signed numbers, *change the sign of the subtrahend and apply the rules for addition.*

EXAMPLE 1: Subtract $+20$ from $+32$.

SOLUTION:

$+20$ is the subtrahend or number to be subtracted. Changing its sign and adding, we get $32 - 20 = 12$, ANS.

EXAMPLE 2: From -18 subtract -12.

SOLUTION:

-12 is the subtrahend. Changing its sign and adding, we get $-18 + 12 = -6$, ANS.

Practice Exercise No. 39

SUBTRACTION OF SIGNED NUMBERS

1	$+47$ $+19$	4	$+54$ -12	7	$(-5) - (-8)$
2	-26 -17	5	80 -50	8	$(-7) - (-4)$
3	-42 -18	6	$-22ab$ $+18ab$	9	$(-9) - (+16)$

MULTIPLICATION AND DIVISION OF SIGNED NUMBERS

Law of signs for multiplication of signed numbers—Rule: *The product of any two numbers that have like signs is positive* $(+)$, *and the product of any two numbers that have unlike signs is negative* $(-)$.

EXAMPLE 1: Multiply -8 by -6.

SOLUTION: The signs are the same.
$$\therefore -8 \times -6 = +48, \text{ ANS.}$$

EXAMPLE 2: Multiply $+3$ by -4.

SOLUTION: The signs are unlike.
$$\therefore 3 \times -4 = -12, \text{ ANS.}$$

EXAMPLE 3: Multiply -2 by $+5$ by -3 by $+4$.

SOLUTION: $(-2) \times (+5) = -10,$
$(-10) \times (-3) = +30,$
$+ (+30) \times (+4) = +120, \text{ ANS.}$

Division of signed numbers is carried out by the same process as division in arithmetic, but *the sign of the quotient is positive if the divisor and dividend have the same sign, and negative if the divisor and dividend have opposite signs.*

EXAMPLE 4: Divide -16 by -2.

SOLUTION: $\dfrac{-16}{-2} = +8, \text{ ANS.}$

Same signs, $\therefore$ answer is plus $(+)$.

EXAMPLE 5: Divide -35 by $+5$.

SOLUTION: $\dfrac{-35}{5} = -7, \text{ ANS.}$

Opposite signs, $\therefore$ answer is minus $(-)$.

Practice Exercise No. 40

Do the following examples:

1	$2 \times -16 =$	5	$72 \div -24 =$
2	$-18 \times -12 =$	6	$-68 \div -17 =$
3	$-4 \times -6 \times 3 =$	7	$-14 \div -5 =$
4	$4 \times 3 \times -2 \times 6 =$	8	$-24 \times 4 \div 8 =$

ALGEBRAIC EXPRESSIONS

Working with signed numbers is an introduction to using algebraic expressions. An **algebraic expression** is one in which letter symbols are used to represent numbers.

A letter symbol or other type of symbol that represents a number is called a **literal number**.

If you know the numerical values of the symbols and understand the arithmetic signs of an algebraic expression, then you can find the numerical value of any algebraic expression. *Thus:*

$a + b$ means that b is added to a.
   If $a = 2$ and $b = 3$, then $a + b = 5$.
$b - a$ means that a is subtracted from b.
   If $b = 6$ and $a = 4$, $b - a = 2$.
$a \times b$ means that b is multiplied by a.
   If $a = 7$ and $b = 3$, $a \times b = 21$.

Multiplication can be indicated in four ways in algebra. a multiplied by b can be written $a \times b$, $a \cdot b$, $(a)(b)$, or ab. That is, multiplication can be expressed by a cross $\times$, by a dot $\cdot$, by adjacent parentheses, and by directly joining a letter and its multiplier with no sign between them. *Thus* $2a$ means 2 times a, and ab means a times b.

a^2 means $a \cdot a$. You read it: a *squared*.
   If $a = 3$, then $a^2 = 3 \cdot 3$ or 9.
a^3 means $a \cdot a \cdot a$. You read it: a *cubed*.
   If $a = 3$, then $a^3 = 3 \cdot 3 \cdot 3$ or 27.
$a^2 + b^3$ means that b^3 is to be added to a^2.
   If $a = 3$ and $b = 2$, then $a^2 + b^3 = 9 + 8$, or 17.

The small 2 and 3 placed to the right and slightly above the a and the b in writing a^2 and b^3 are called **exponents**.

The number a is called the **base**. a^2 and a^3 are called **powers** of the *base a*.

$3a^2 - 2b^2$ means that $2b^2$ is subtracted from $3a^2$.

The $3a^2$ and $2b^2$ are known as **terms** in the algebraic expression.

The numbers placed before the letters are called **coefficients**. *Thus*, in $3a^2 - 2b^2$, 3 is called the *coefficient* of a^2, 2 is the *coefficient* of b^2. The coefficient so placed indicates multiplication, *i.e.*, $3a^2$ means $3 \times a^2$.

Practice Exercise No. 41

In each of the following write the algebraic expression and find its numerical value if $x = 2$, $y = 3$ and $z = 4$.

1 x added to $y =$
2 x, y and z added together =
3 Twice x added to twice $y =$
4 z subtracted from the sum of x and $y =$
5 The square of x added to the square of $y =$
6 3 less than $y =$
7 Twice the product of x and $z =$

CHAPTER EIGHT

ALGEBRAIC FORMULAS AND EQUATIONS

In the preceding chapters rules in words were used to describe methods to be followed in solving various types of problems. For example, to find the amount of a discount the rule is to multiply the base or price by the rate of discount. By the use of symbols this rule can be expressed in a brief form known as a **formula**.

Thus a short way to express the rule in question is:

    a. Discount = Base × Rate

A still shorter way is:

    b. $D = B \times R$,

in which D, B and R mean discount, base and rate respectively.

The shortest and algebraic way to express this is:

    c. $D = BR$.

DEFINITIONS

A **formula** is a shorthand method of expressing a rule by the use of symbols or letter designations (literal numbers).

At the same time it must be remembered that a formula is an equation. And what is an equation?

An **equation** is a statement that two expressions are equal.

For example, $D = BR$ states that D, the discount, is equal to B, the base, multiplied by R, the rate of discount. Before we can start working with formulas and equations there are a few things that have to be learned about them.

An equation has two equal sides or members. In the equation $D = BR$, D is the left side and BR is the right side.

Terms are made up of numbers or symbols combined by multiplication or division.

For example, $6DR$ is a term in which the factors 6, D and R are combined by *multiplication*; $\dfrac{M}{4}$ is a term in which the quantities M and 4 are combined by *division* or in which the factors M and $\frac{1}{4}$ are combined by multiplication.

An **expression** is a collection of terms combined by addition, subtraction, or both, and frequently grouped by parentheses, as in: $(3a + 2b)$, $(2c - 4c + 3b)$, $2x - 3y$.

USING PARENTHESES

Parentheses ( ) or **brackets** [ ] mean that quantities are to be grouped together, and that quantities enclosed by them are to be considered as one quantity. The line of a fraction has the same significance in this respect as a pair of parentheses.

Thus, $18 + (9 - 6)$ is read 18 *plus the quantity* $9 - 6$.

Rule: To solve examples containing parentheses, *do the work within the parentheses first; then remove the parentheses and proceed in the usual way. Within parentheses and in examples without parentheses do multiplications from left to right before doing additions and subtractions.*

It is extremely important to observe this method of procedure, since it is otherwise impossible to solve algebraic problems.

EXAMPLE 1: $94 - (12 + 18 + 20) = ?$
              $94 - 50 = 44$, ANS.

EXAMPLE 2: $12(3 + 2) = ?$
              $12 \times 5 = 60$, ANS.

EXAMPLE 3: $\dfrac{18}{2(4 - 1)} = ?$

              $\dfrac{18}{2 \times 3} = \dfrac{18}{6} = 3$, ANS.

EXAMPLE 4: $3 \times 6 - 4$
              $18 - 4 = 14$, ANS.

Note: If in this example the 4 had been subtracted from the 6 before multiplying, the answer would have been 6, but this would be wrong according to the laws of algebra. This example illustrates the absolute necessity of *doing multiplication first* in any cases similar to this.

Practice Exercise No. 42

Clear parentheses and solve.

1   $18 + (19 - 14) =$
2   $22(3 + 2) =$
3   $42 - 9 - (18 + 2) =$
4   $(6 - 4)(8 + 2) =$
5   $(18 \div 3)(9 - 7) =$
6   $(7 \times 8) - (6 \times 4) + (18 - 6) =$
7   $(6 \times 8) \div (8 \times 2) =$
8   $19 + (18 - 14 + 32) =$
9   $(7 \times 6)(6 \times 5) =$
10 $69 \div [35 - (15 - 3)] =$

TRANSLATING WORD STATEMENTS INTO FORMULAS AND ALGEBRAIC EXPRESSIONS

To express word statements as formulas or as brief algebraic expressions, letters and symbols are substituted for words.

EXAMPLE 1: Express briefly, *What number increased by 6 gives 18 as a result?*

Substituting the letter N for the unknown *what number*, we get

$$N + 6 = 18,$$
$$N = ? \quad \text{ANS.}$$

[handwritten: $N + 6 = 18$, $N = -6 + 18$, $N = 12$]

EXAMPLE 2: Express briefly, *The product of two numbers is 85. One is 5, find the other.*

$$5N = 85, N = ? \quad \text{ANS.}$$

[handwritten: $5N = 85$, $N = \frac{85}{5}$]

EXAMPLE 3: Express briefly, *Fifteen exceeds a certain number by 6. What is the number?*

$$15 - 6 = N, N = ? \quad \text{ANS.}$$

[handwritten: $N = 17$]

EXAMPLE 4: Express briefly, *Two thirds of a number is 20. Find the number.*

$$\tfrac{2}{3}N = 20, N = ? \quad \text{ANS.}$$

[handwritten: $\frac{2}{3}N = 20$, $N = 20 \times \frac{3}{2}$, $N = 30$]

In algebra, however, the regular method of writing fractions is to place all factors, as far as may be possible, above or below a single horizontal line. The form $\frac{2}{3}N$, while mathematically correct, is less regular than $\frac{2N}{3}$. Hence to express our problem in approved form we arrive at:

$$\frac{2N}{3} = 20, N = ? \quad \text{ANS.}$$

The foregoing illustrates in simple form the general method of making algebraic statements. In engineering, scientific, industrial and commercial practice, it is common to express certain kinds of facts in algebraic *formulas*. The usual way is to state the formula with symbolic letters and to follow it immediately with an explanation (starting with the words *in which*) to make intelligible to the reader any symbols that may require definition. Examples of this method of **formula statement** follow.

EXAMPLE 1: The cost equals the selling price minus the margin of profit.

FORMULA: $C = S - M$, in which C stands for cost, S for selling price and M for margin of profit.

EXAMPLE 2: The area of a rectangle equals the base times the height.

FORMULA: $A = bh$, in which A stands for area, b for base and h for height.

EXAMPLE 3: To determine the resistance in ohms of an electrical circuit, divide the number of volts by the number of amperes.

FORMULA: $O = \dfrac{V}{A}$, in which O stands for ohms, V for volts and A for amperes.

Practice Exercise No. 43

Write the following statements as equations.

Note: Most of the statements represent formulas commonly used by draftsmen, designers, carpenters, engineers and clerks.

1   The perimeter (p) of a rectangle equals twice its length (l) added to twice its width (w).

2   The distance (d) traveled by an object that moves at a given rate of speed (r) for a given time (t) equals the rate multiplied by the time.

3   To get the horsepower (H) of an electric motor multiply the number of volts (v) by the number of amperes (a) and divide by 746.

4   Interest (I) on money is figured by multiplying the principal (P) by the rate (R) by the time (T).

5   The amperage (A) of an electrical circuit is equal to the wattage (W) divided by the voltage (V).

6   Profit (P) equals the margin (M) minus the overhead (O).

7   The distance (d) that an object will fall in any given time (t) is equal to the square of the time multiplied by 16.

8   The area (A) of a square figure is equal to the square of one of its sides (S).

9   Centigrade temperature (C) is equal to Fahrenheit temperature (F) minus 32°, multiplied by $\tfrac{5}{9}$.

10   The speed (R) of a revolving wheel is proportional to the number of revolutions (N) it makes in a given time (T).

RULE FOR SOLVING EQUATIONS

When you solve an equation you are finding the value of the unknown or literal number in terms of what has been given about the other numbers in the equation. To do this you must learn the following rules of procedure for treating equations. Primarily, *what you do to one side of an equation you must also do to the other*. This might be called the golden rule of algebra. Its observance is imperative in order to preserve equality.

Rule 1. *The same number may be added to both sides of an equation without changing its equality.*

EXAMPLE 1: If $x - 4 = 6$, what does x equal?

SOLUTION:

[handwritten: $x - 4 = 6$ $x = 6 + 4$ $x = 10$]

$x - 4 + 4 = 6 + 4$. Adding 4 to both sides, $x = 10$, ANS.

To check the solution of algebraic examples, *substitute the value of the unknown quantity as determined in the answer for the corresponding symbol in the original equation. If both sides produce the same number, the answer is correct.*

EXAMPLE 1: Check the correctness of 10 as the solution of $x - 4 = 6$.

METHOD:

$\quad x - 4 = 6$, original equation,
$\quad 10 - 4 = 6$, substituting answer for symbol,
$\quad\quad 6 = 6$, proof of correctness.

Rule 2. *The same number may be subtracted from both sides of an equation.*

EXAMPLE 2: If $n + 6 = 18$, what does n equal?

SOLUTION:

$n + 6 - 6 = 18 - 6$. Subtracting 6 from both sides, $n = 12$, ANS.

Check by substituting 12 for n in the original equation. *Thus,* $n + 6 = 18$ becomes $12 + 6 = 18$ or $18 = 18$, which is correct.

Rule 3. *Both sides of an equation may be multiplied by the same number.*

EXAMPLE 3: If $\frac{1}{3}$ of a number is 10, find the number.

SOLUTION:

$\frac{1}{3} n$ or $\frac{n}{3} = 10$,

[handwritten: $\frac{1}{3} N = 10$ $\frac{N}{3} = 10$ $N = 10 \times 3$ $N = 30$]

$\frac{n}{3} \times 3 = 10 \times 3$, multiplying both sides by 3,

$\frac{n}{\cancel{3}} \times \cancel{3} = 10 \times 3$, cancelling,

$n = 30$, ANS.
Check the answer.

Rule 4. *Both sides of an equation may be divided by the same number.*

EXAMPLE 4: Two times a number is 30. What is the number?

SOLUTION:

$2n = 30$,

$\frac{2n}{2} = \frac{30}{2}$, dividing both sides by 2,

$n = 15$, ANS.
Check the answer.

TRANSPOSITION

Transposition is the process of moving a quantity from one side of an equation to the other side by changing its sign of operation. This is exactly what has been done in carrying out the rules in the four examples above.

Division is the operation opposite to multiplication.

Addition is the operation opposite to subtraction.

Transposition is performed in order to obtain an equation in which the unknown quantity is on one side and the known quantity on the other.

Rule: *A term may be transposed from one side of an equation to the other if its sign is changed from $+$ to $-$, or from $-$ to $+$.*

Rule: *A factor (multiplier) may be removed from one side of an equation by making it a divisor in the other. A divisor may be removed from one side of an equation by making it a factor (multiplier) in the other.*

Observe again the solution to Example 1.

$x - 4 = 6$,   EXPLANATION: To get x by itself
$x = 6 + 4$,   on one side of the equation, the
$x = 10$. -4 was transposed from the left to the right side and made $+4$.

Observe again the solution to Example 2.

$n + 6 = 18$,   EXPLANATION: To get n by itself
$n = 18 - 6$,   on one side of the equation, the
$n = 12$. $+6$ was transposed from the left to the right side and made -6.

Observe again the solution to Example 3.

$\frac{n}{3} = 10,$

$n = 10 \times 3,$

$n = 30.$

EXPLANATION: To get n by itself on one side of the equation, the divisor 3 on the left was changed to the multiplier $3(\frac{3}{1})$ on the right.

Observe again the solution to Example 4.

$2n = 30,$

$n = \frac{30}{2},$

$n = 15.$

EXPLANATION: To get n by itself on one side of the equation, the multiplier 2 on the left was changed to the divisor 2 on the right.

Note that transposition is essentially nothing more than a shortened method for performing like operations of addition, subtraction, multiplication or division on both sides of the equation.

Changing $x - 4 = 6$ to $x = 6 + 4$ is the same as adding 4 to both sides:

$$\begin{array}{r} x - 4 = 6 \\ +4 = +4 \\ \hline x = 10 \end{array}$$

Changing $n + 6 = 18$ to $n = 18 - 6$ is the same as subtracting 6 from both sides:

$$\begin{array}{r} n + 6 = 18 \\ -6 = -6 \\ \hline n = 12 \end{array}$$

Changing $\frac{n}{3} = 10$ to $n = 10 \times 3$ is the same as multiplying both sides by 3:

$\frac{n}{3} \times 3 = 10 \times 3$, in which the 3s on the left cancel.

Changing $2n = 30$ to $n = \frac{30}{2}$ is the same as dividing both sides by 2:

$\frac{2n}{2} = \frac{30}{2}$, in which the 2s on the left cancel.

When terms involving the unknown quantity occur on both sides of the equation, *perform such transpositions as may be necessary to collect all the unknown terms on one side (usually the left) and all the known terms on the other.*

EXAMPLE 5: If $3x - 6 = x + 8$ what does x equal?

SOLUTION:

$3x = x + 8 + 6,$ transposing -6 from left to right.

$3x - x = 14,$ transposing x from right to left.

$2x = 14,$ transposing 2 as a multiplier from left to a divisor at the right.

$x = \frac{14}{2},$

$x = 7,$ ANS.

Check:

$3x - 6 = x + 8,$

$21 - 6 = 7 + 8,$ substituting 7 for x.

$15 = 15.$ proof of correctness.

When using an algebraic formula in actual practice, it may be necessary to change its form from that in which it has been originally expressed. Such changes are effected by transposition.

EXAMPLE 6: If $R = \frac{WC}{L}$, solve for W, C and L.

SOLUTION:

$R = \frac{WC}{L}$, original formula

$\frac{LR}{C} = W.$ To separate W, C and L are transposed.

$\frac{LR}{W} = C.$ To separate C, L and W are transposed.

$L = \frac{WC}{R}$. To separate L, L and R are transposed.

Practice Exercise No. 44

Solve by transposition:

1	$p + 3 = 8$	$p = ?$
2	$2n = 25$	$n = ?$
3	$\frac{1}{2}x = 14$	$x = ?$
4	$5c - 3 = 27$	$c = ?$
5	$18 = 5y - 2$	$y = ?$
6	$\frac{2}{3}n = 24$	$n = ?$
7	$\frac{a}{2} + \frac{a}{4} = 36$	$a = ?$
8	$W = \frac{b}{c}$	$b = ?$
9	$V = \frac{W}{A}$	$A = ?$
10	$H = \frac{P}{AW}$	$W = ?$

FUNDAMENTAL OPERATIONS

Addition is performed thus:

$$3a - 4b + 2c$$
$$-8a + 6b - 3c$$
$$6a - 4b + 8c$$
$$\overline{a - 2b + 7c}$$

EXPLANATION: The terms are arranged in columns in such a way that all like terms are in the same column.

Subtraction is performed thus:

$$8a - 4b + 2c$$
$$5a - 6b + 8c$$
$$\overline{3a + 2b - 6c}$$

EXPLANATION: To subtract algebraically, whenever you cannot directly subtract a smaller from a larger quantity of like sign, mentally change the sign of the subtrahend and perform an addition. $8a - 5a = 3a$; $-4b + 6b = +2b$; $2c - 8c = -6c$.

Multiplication is performed thus:

$$a^2 - 2ab + b^2$$
$$a - b$$
$$\overline{a^3 - 2a^2b + ab^2}$$
$$ - a^2b + 2ab^2 - b^3$$
$$\overline{a^3 - 3a^2b + 3ab^2 - b^3}$$

EXPLANATION: Each term in the multiplicand is multiplied separately by a and then by b. Like terms are set under each other and the whole is added. $+ \times +$ gives $+$; $- \times -$ gives $+$; $+ \times -$ gives $-$.

Division is performed thus:

$$\frac{3a^2b + 3ab^2 + 3a}{3a} = ab + b^2 + 1, \text{ or } b^2 + ab + 1.$$

EXPLANATION: $3a$ is a factor of each term in the dividend. Separate divisions give us $ab + b^2 + 1$. This is changed to $b^2 + ab + 1$ because it is customary to place algebraic terms in the order of their highest powers.

Practice Exercise No. 45

USE OF FORMULAS AND EQUATIONS

1 Diameters of pulleys are inversely proportioned to their rpm. $\frac{D}{d} = \frac{r}{R}$. An 18″ diameter pulley turning at 100 rpm is driving a 6″ diameter pulley. **What is the rpm of the smaller pulley?**

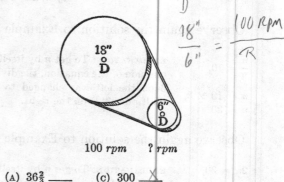

100 *rpm*   ? *rpm*

(A) $36\frac{2}{3}$ ____   (c) 300 ____
(B) 600 ____   (d) 900 ____

2 What size pulley at 144 rpm will drive a 9″ pulley at 256 rpm?
(A) 24″ ____   (c) 16″ ____
(B) $5\frac{1}{6}$″ ____   (d) 32″ ____

3 Three times a certain number plus twice the same number is 90. What is the number?
(A) 16 ____   (c) 20 ____
(B) 18 ____   (d) 24 ____

4 The larger of two numbers is seven times the smaller. What is the larger if their sum is 32?
(A) 28 ____   (c) 25 ____
(B) 36 ____   (d) 39 ____

5 Six hundred pairs of shoes are to be divided up among three army units. The second unit is to get twice as many as the first, and the third unit is to get as many as the first and second units together. How many pairs of shoes does the second unit get?
(A) 100 ____   (c) 300 ____
(B) 200 ____   (d) 400 ____

6 Two aviators are 3,000 miles apart. They start toward each other, one at a rate of 200 miles per hour and the other at 300 miles per hour. How much distance does the faster one cover up to the time they meet? $R \times T = D$.
(A) 1,200 ____   (c) 1,600 ____
(B) 1,400 ____   (d) 1,800 ____

7 Two soldiers start out from camp in opposite directions. One travels twice as fast as the other. In 10 hours they are 24 miles apart. What is the rate of the faster soldier?
(A) $\frac{4}{5}$ mi. hr. ____   (c) $1\frac{4}{5}$ mi. hr. ____
(B) 1 mi. hr. ____   (d) $1\frac{3}{5}$ mi. hr. ____

8 A man has 3 times as many nickels as quarters. How many nickels has he if the value of both together is $8.00? Hint: Let n = no. of quarters and $3n$ = no. of nickels and multiply each by their value.
(A) 20 ____   (c) 60 ____
(B) 40 ____   (d) 80 ____

9 When two gears run together the revolutions per minute vary inversely as the number of teeth. A 48-tooth gear is driving a 72-tooth gear. Find the

revolutions per minute of the larger gear if the smaller one is running at 160 rpm.

(A) $106\frac{2}{3}$ rpm ____   (c) $66\frac{2}{3}$ rpm ____
(B) 240 rpm ____   (D) 180 rpm ____

10 A teeter board is a form of lever. It is balanced when the weight times the distance on one side equals the weight times the distance on the other side. A weight of 120 lbs. is placed $4\frac{1}{2}$ feet from the fulcrum. What weight is needed to balance this at a distance of 5 feet from the fulcrum on the other end?

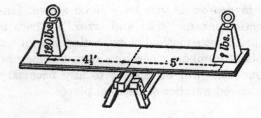

(A) 104 ____   (c) 118 ____
(B) 108 ____   (D) 128 ____

CHAPTER NINE

FACTORS AND ROOTS

A **factor** of a number is an exact divisor of that number. Thus 2 is a factor of 6 because $6 \div 2 = 3$ exactly; 3 is the other factor of 6.

For the number 9, 3 and 3 are equal factors; and for 8, 2, 2 and 2 are equal factors. These equal factors are called **roots** of the number. Thus:

The number 3 is a *root* of 9.

The number 2 is a *root* of 8.

A root of a number is therefore one of the equal factors which, if multiplied together, produce the number.

The **square root** of a number is one of TWO equal factors which, if multiplied together, produce that number.

$3 \times 3 = 9$, hence 3 is the *square root* of 9.

The **cube root** of a number is one of THREE equal factors which if multiplied together produce that number.

$3 \times 3 \times 3 = 27$, hence 3 is the *cube root* of 27.

A **fourth root** of a number is one of FOUR equal factors; the fifth root is one of five, and so on.

The square root is the one most frequently used in mathematics.

The sign indicating square root is $\sqrt{}$. It

is placed over the number whose root is to be found. $\sqrt{25}$ means the square root of 25. It is called the **square root sign** or **radical sign**.

To indicate a root other than square root a small figure called the **index** of the root is placed in the radical sign. Thus: $\sqrt[3]{8}$ means the cube root of 8.

The square root of $4 = 2$, of $36 = 6$, or $49 = 7$.

To check that you have obtained the correct square root of a number, *multiply it by itself. If the product is equal to the original number the answer is correct.*

Practice Exercise No. 46

Find the roots indicated and check.

1 $\sqrt{64}$ 7 $\sqrt[3]{1000}$
2 $\sqrt{100}$ 8 $\sqrt{1}$
3 $\sqrt{81}$ 9 $\sqrt{.04} = \sqrt{.2 \times .2} = .2$
4 $\sqrt[3]{27}$ 10 $\sqrt{.09}$
5 $\sqrt[3]{125}$ 11 $\sqrt{1.44}$
6 $\sqrt{144}$ 12 $\sqrt{.0025}$

Not all numbers have exact square roots. Nor can we always determine square root by *inspection* as you have done above. (Inspection means "trial and error.") There is an arithmetic method of extracting the square roots of numbers whereby an answer may be found that will be correct to any necessary or desired number of decimal places.

METHOD FOR FINDING SQUARE ROOTS

Find the square root of 412,164.

1. Place the square root sign over the number, and then, beginning at the right, divide it into *periods* of two figures each. Connect the digits in each period with tie-marks as shown. In the answer there will be one digit for each period.

$$\sqrt{\overline{41}\ \overline{21}\ \overline{64}}$$

2. Find the largest number which, when squared, is contained in the first left-hand period. In this case 6 is the number. Write 6 in the answer over the first period. Square it, making 36, and subtract 36 from the first period. Bring down the next period, making the new dividend 5 21.

$$\begin{array}{r} 6 \\ \sqrt{\overline{41}\ \overline{21}\ \overline{64}} \\ \underline{36} \\ 5\ 21 \end{array}$$

3. Multiply the root 6 by 2, getting 12. Place the 12 to the left of 5 21, since 12 is the new trial divisor. Allow, however, for one more digit to follow 12. The place of this missing digit may be indicated by a question mark. To find the number belonging in this place, ignore (cover over) the last number in the dividend 5 21, and see how many times 12 goes into 52. Approximately 4. Place the 4 above its period, 21, and put it in place of the ? in the divisor.

$$\begin{array}{r} 6\ \ 4 \\ \sqrt{\overline{41}\ \overline{21}\ \overline{64}} \\ \underline{36} \\ 12_{4}^{?}\ |\ 5\ 21 \end{array}$$

4. Multiply the divisor 124 by the new number in the root, 4. 124 × 4 = 496. Place this product under 521 and subtract. Bring down the next period, 64.

$$\begin{array}{r} 6\ \ 4 \\ \sqrt{\overline{41}\ \overline{21}\ \overline{64}} \\ \underline{36} \\ 124\ |\ \overline{5\ 21} \\ \underline{4\ 96} \\ 25\ 64 \end{array}$$

5. Multiply 64 by 2 to get 128 as the new trial divisor. 128 goes into 256 two times. Place the 2 above the next period in the root and also in the divisor. Then multiply the divisor 1282 by the new root 2, to get 25 64. Subtracting, the remainder is zero. 642 is therefore the exact square root.

$$\begin{array}{r} 6\ \ 4\ \ 2 \\ \sqrt{\overline{41}\ \overline{21}\ \overline{64}} \\ \underline{36} \\ 124\ |\ \overline{5\ 21} \\ \underline{4\ 96} \\ 128_{2}^{?}\ |\ \overline{25\ 64} \\ \underline{25\ 64} \\ 0 \end{array}$$

6. CHECK: 642 × 642 = 412,164.

FINDING THE SQUARE ROOT OF DECIMALS

A slight variation in method is necessary when it is required to find the square root of a decimal figure.

Mark off periods beginning at the decimal point. Count to the right for the decimal quantities and to the left for the whole numbers. If the last period of the whole numbers contains one figure, leave it by itself, but remember that in such a case the first figure in the root cannot be more than 3 because the square of any number greater than 3 is a two-place number. If the last period of the decimal numbers contains only one figure you may add a zero to it. This is because two digits are necessary to make up a period, while the addition of a zero at the right of a decimal figure does not change its value.

The square root of a decimal will contain as many decimal places as there are periods, or half as many decimal places as the given number.

The operations in obtaining the square root of a decimal number are the same as for whole numbers.

Follow the steps in the example following.

EXAMPLE 1: Find the square root of 339.2964.

1. Beginning at decimal point, mark off periods to left and right.

2. 1 is the largest whole-number square root that is contained in 3, which constitutes the first period.

3. Place decimal point in root after the 8 because the root of the next period has a decimal value.

4. Bring down 29 next to the 15, making 1529 the new dividend. Multiply the root 18 by 2, making 36 the new divisor.

$$\begin{array}{r} 1\ \ 8.\ \ 4\ \ 2 \\ \sqrt{3\ \overline{39}.\overline{29}\ \overline{64}} \\ \underline{1} \\ 2_{8}^{?}\ |\ 2\ 39 \\ \underline{2\ 24} \\ 36_{4}^{?}\ |\ 15\ 29 \\ \underline{14\ 56} \\ 368_{2}^{?}\ |\ 73\ 64 \\ \underline{73\ 64} \\ 0 \end{array}$$

5. Covering the 9 of 1529, 36 seems to be contained about 4 times in this number. Place a 4 in the root above 29, and multiply 364 by 4 to get 1456. Subtract this from 1529.

6. Bring down the 64 and repeat the previous process. Since the number is a perfect square, the remainder is zero.

When the given number is not a perfect square, *add zeros after the decimal point, or after the last figure if the original number is already in decimal form, and carry out the answer to the required or desired number of decimal places. Usually two places are sufficient.*

Note: In working a square root example, when a divisor is larger than the corresponding dividend, write zero in the trial divisor and bring down the next period. This is illustrated in the next example.

EXAMPLE 2: Find the square root of 25.63 to three decimal places.

$$
\begin{array}{r}
5.\ 0\ \ 6\ \ 2 +,\ \text{Ans.} \\
\sqrt{25.63\ 00\ 00} \\
25 \\
100^?_6|\ 0\ 63\ 00 \\
60\ 36 \\
1012^?_2|\ 2\ 64\ 00 \\
2\ 02\ 44 \\
61\ 56\ \text{remainder}
\end{array}
$$

To find the square of a fraction, determine separately the square roots of the numerator and of the denominator, and reduce to lowest terms or to a decimal.

EXAMPLE 3: $\sqrt{\dfrac{33}{67}}$.

$$\sqrt{\frac{33}{67}} = \frac{5.745}{8.185} = .701, \ \text{Ans.}$$

USE OF SQUARE ROOTS

Although in many test situations the student may be required to work out square roots as above, in actual practice it is inconvenient to stop work for such calculations. Most mathematics books therefore contain tables giving powers and roots of numbers. Table V is a simple form of such a table.

Any formula or problem containing the square of a number or factor, requires a knowledge of square roots for its solution. You will find many such problems and formulas in the material contained in Chapter Fourteen on geometry.

EXAMPLE 1: Find the length of one side of a square whose area is 225 square feet.

SOLUTION: Let x = length of one side.
Area = base × height. ∴ Area = x^2,
$x^2 = 225$,
$x = 15$, extracting the square root of both sides of the equation.

EXAMPLE 2: $d = 16t^2$ (in which d is distance and t is time) is the formula for measuring the distance an object will fall in t seconds irrespective of its weight. If an object fell 10,000 feet, how long would it take to reach the ground?

SOLUTION:
$10000 = 16t^2$,
$\dfrac{10000}{16} = t^2$, dividing both sides by 16
$625 = t^2$,
$25 = t$, extracting square root of both sides of the equation.

Practice Exercise No. 47

Work out examples 1-5. Find answers in Table V for 6-10.

1	$\sqrt{5329}$	6	$\sqrt{676}$
2	$\sqrt{1225}$	7	$\sqrt{1849}$
3	$\sqrt{2937.64}$	8	$\sqrt{3136}$
4	$\sqrt{312.649}$	9	$\sqrt{7225}$
5	$\sqrt{428}$ to 2 places	10	$\sqrt{9409}$

Table V

SQUARES AND SQUARE ROOTS, CUBES AND CUBE ROOTS OF NUMBERS FROM 1 TO 100

No. n	Sq. n^2	Cube n^3	Sq. Root $\sqrt{n}$	Cube Root $\sqrt[3]{n}$	n	n^2	n^3	$\sqrt{n}$	$\sqrt[3]{n}$
1	1	1	1.000	1.000	51	2601	132651	7.141	3.708
2	4	8	1.414	1.259	52	2704	140608	7.211	3.732
3	9	27	1.732	1.442	53	2809	148877	7.280	3.756
4	16	64	2.000	1.587	54	2916	157464	7.348	3.779
5	25	125	2.236	1.710	55	3025	166375	7.416	3.803
6	36	216	2.449	1.817	56	3136	175616	7.483	3.825
7	49	343	2.645	1.913	57	3249	185193	7.549	3.848
8	64	512	2.828	2.000	58	3364	195112	7.615	3.870
9	81	729	3.000	2.080	59	3481	205379	7.681	3.893
10	100	1000	3.162	2.154	60	3600	216000	7.746	3.914
11	121	1331	3.316	2.224	61	3721	226981	7.810	3.936
12	144	1728	3.464	2.289	62	3844	238328	7.874	3.957
13	169	2197	3.605	2.351	63	3969	250047	7.937	3.979
14	196	2744	3.741	2.410	64	4096	262144	8.000	4.000
15	225	3375	3.873	2.466	65	4225	274625	8.062	4.020
16	256	4096	4.000	2.519	66	4356	287496	8.124	4.041
17	289	4913	4.123	2.571	67	4489	300763	8.185	4.061
18	324	5832	4.242	2.620	68	4624	314432	8.246	4.081
19	361	6859	4.358	2.668	69	4761	328509	8.306	4.101
20	400	8000	4.472	2.714	70	4900	343000	8.366	4.121
21	441	9261	4.582	2.758	71	5041	357911	8.426	4.140
22	484	10648	4.690	2.802	72	5184	373248	8.485	4.160
23	529	12167	4.795	2.843	73	5329	389017	8.544	4.179
24	576	13824	4.899	2.884	74	5476	405224	8.602	4.198
25	625	15625	5.000	2.924	75	5625	421875	8.660	4.217
26	676	17576	5.099	2.962	76	5776	438976	8.717	4.235
27	729	19683	5.196	3.000	77	5929	456533	8.775	4.254
28	784	21952	5.291	3.036	78	6084	474552	8.831	4.272
29	841	24389	5.385	3.072	79	6241	493039	8.888	4.290
30	900	27000	5.477	3.107	80	6400	512000	8.944	4.308
31	961	29791	5.567	3.141	81	6561	531441	9.000	4.326
32	1024	32768	5.656	3.174	82	6724	551368	9.055	4.344
33	1089	35937	5.744	3.207	83	6889	571787	9.110	4.362
34	1156	39304	5.831	3.239	84	7056	592704	9.165	4.379
35	1225	42875	5.916	3.271	85	7225	614125	9.219	4.396
36	1296	46656	6.000	3.301	86	7396	636056	9.273	4.414
37	1369	50653	6.082	3.332	87	7569	658503	9.327	4.431
38	1444	54872	6.164	3.362	88	7744	681472	9.380	4.448
39	1521	59319	6.245	3.391	89	7921	704969	9.434	4.464
40	1600	64000	6.324	3.420	90	8100	729000	9.486	4.481
41	1681	68921	6.403	3.448	91	8281	753571	9.539	4.497
42	1764	74088	6.480	3.476	92	8464	778688	9.591	4.514
43	1849	79507	6.557	3.503	93	8649	804357	9.643	4.530
44	1936	85184	6.633	3.530	94	8836	830584	9.695	4.546
45	2025	91125	6.708	3.556	95	9025	857375	9.746	4.562
46	2116	97336	6.782	3.583	96	9216	884736	9.798	4.578
47	2209	103823	6.855	3.608	97	9409	912673	9.848	4.594
48	2304	110592	6.928	3.634	98	9604	941192	9.899	4.610
49	2401	117649	7.000	3.659	99	9801	970299	9.949	4.626
50	2500	125000	7.071	3.684	100	10000	1000000	10.000	4.641

CHAPTER TEN

POWERS

To **square** a number is to use that number as a factor twice. Thus $4 \times 4 = 16$, and 16 is said to be the **square** of 4. This is also called raising a number to its **second power.** Using a number as a factor three times (for instance, $4 \times 4 \times 4 = 64$) is called raising it to the **third power.** The given case would be written 4^3, and be read *four cubed.* 4^4 is read *four to the fourth power,* 4^5 is read *four to the fifth power,* etc.

A **power** of a number is the product obtained by multiplying the number by itself a given number of times. Raising a number to a given power is the opposite process of finding the corresponding root of a number.

To raise a given number to its indicated power, multiply the number by itself as many times as the power indicated. Thus, $3^5 = 3 \times 3 \times 3 \times 3 \times 3 = 243$. The small five used in writing 3^5 is called an *exponent,* while the number 3 is called the **base.**

An **exponent** indicates the power to which a number is to be raised. *Thus, x^3 means that x is to be raised to the third power.*

$$\text{If } x^3 = 125,$$
$$x = ?$$

To raise a **fraction** to a given power, *raise both the numerator and the denominator to the given power.*

$$\left(\tfrac{1}{3}\right)^2 = \tfrac{1}{3} \times \tfrac{1}{3} = \tfrac{1}{9},$$
$$\left(\tfrac{3}{5}\right)^2 = \tfrac{3}{5} \times \tfrac{3}{5} = \tfrac{9}{25}.$$

Any power or root of 1 is 1, because 1 multiplied or divided by 1 any number of times is 1.

Any number **without an exponent** is considered to be the first power or first root of itself. Neither the exponent nor the index 1 is written. *Thus, x means x^1.*

Any number raised to the **zero power,** such as 5^0, is equal to 1. The reason for this will appear when we consider the multiplication of powers of numbers.

When a number has a **negative exponent,** *i.e.,* when the exponent is preceded by the minus sign, as in 3^{-3}, it indicates the reciprocal of the indicated power of the number. Since $3^3 = 27$, $3^{-3} = \tfrac{1}{27}$, the reciprocal of 27. 12^{-2} means the reciprocal of 12^2, or $\tfrac{1}{144}$.

When a number has a **fractional exponent** with a numerator of 1, as has $x^{\frac{1}{2}}$, it signifies that the corresponding *root* is to be taken of the number. In other words, $16^{\frac{1}{2}} = \sqrt{16} = 4$.

When a fractional exponent has a numerator greater than one, as has $x^{\frac{3}{2}}$, the numerator indicates the power to which the number is to be raised, while the denominator indicates the root that is to be taken. Accordingly, $4^{\frac{3}{2}} = \sqrt{4^3} = \sqrt{64} = 8$. To reverse this example, $8^{\frac{2}{3}} = \sqrt[3]{8^2} = \sqrt[3]{64} = 4$.

Powers of 10

$$10^1 = 10 \qquad 10^{-1} = \frac{1}{10} \text{ or } .1$$

$$10^2 = 100 \qquad 10^{-2} = \frac{1}{100} \text{ or } .01$$

$$10^3 = 1,000 \qquad 10^{-3} = \frac{1}{1,000} \text{ or } .001$$

$$10^4 = 10,000 \qquad 10^{-4} = \frac{1}{10,000} \text{ or } .0001$$

$$10^5 = 100,000 \qquad 10^{-5} = \frac{1}{100,000} \text{ or } .00001$$

From this it is apparent that 10 raised to any positive power is equal to a multiple of 10 bearing as many zeros as are represented by the quantity of the exponent.

Also, 10 raised to any negative power is equal to a multiple of 10 containing as many decimal places as the quantity of the negative exponent.

The above forms are used for writing very large and very small numbers in an abbreviated way. *Thus,*

32,000 may be written as 32×10^3,
6,900,000 may be written as 6.9×10^6,
.000008 may be written as 8×10^{-6},
.0000000235 may be written as 2.35×10^{-8}.

A positive exponent moves the decimal point a corresponding number of places to the right. *Thus,* $8.2 \times 10^7 = 82,000,000.$

A negative exponent moves the decimal point a corresponding number of places to the left. *Thus,* $6.3 \times 10^{-5} = .000063.$

LAWS OF EXPONENTS

To multiply powers of the same base, *add their exponents.*

Thus, 2^2 times $2^3 = 2^5.$
PROOF: $2^2 = 4; 2^3 = 8; 2^5 = 32;$
$4 \times 8 = 32.$

To divide powers of the same base, *subtract the exponent of the divisor from the exponent of the dividend.*

Thus, $3^5 \div 3^3 = 3^2.$
PROOF: $3^5 = 243; 3^3 = 27; 3^2 = 9;$
$243 \div 27 = 9.$

It will now become apparent why *any* number with an exponent of zero is equal to 1. According to the laws just stated—

$$x^3 \times x^0 = x^{3-0} = x^3$$

because if equals are multiplied by equals the products are equal;

$$\text{but } x^3 \times 1 = x^3,$$
$$\therefore x^0 = 1.$$

To generalize this fact, let n denote any positive exponent whatever. Then $x^n \times x^0 = x^n$ and x^0 necessarily equals 1. The same conclusion will be reached if the process is division and the exponents are subtracted. *Thus,*

$$x^n \div x^0 = x^{n-0} = x^n, \therefore x^0 = 1.$$

Practice Exercise No. 48

Perform the indicated operations.

1	$6^2 =$	6	$8^5 =$	11	$(\frac{2}{3})^2 =$
2	$9^3 =$	7	$\sqrt{81} =$	12	$6^{\frac{3}{2}} =$
3	$25^{\frac{1}{2}} =$	8	$\sqrt[3]{125} =$	13	$2.8 \times 10^{-7} =$
4	$4^{-3} =$	9	$43 \times 10^6 =$	14	$25 \times 10^{-4} =$
5	$432^2 =$	10	$6.2 \times 10^5 =$	15	$12.2 \times 10^7 =$

METHOD FOR FINDING CUBE ROOTS

In studying the following example, read step by step the rule that follows it and note how the example illustrates the rule.

EXAMPLE: What is the cube root of 264,609,288?

$$\overset{\quad 6 \quad 4 \quad 2}{\sqrt[3]{264\ 609\ 288}}$$

	$6^3 = 216$		
1st Part. Div.	$3 \times 60^2 =$	10800	48 609
	$3 \times 60 \times 4 =$	720	
	$4^2 =$	16	
1st Comp. Div.		11536	46 144
			2 465 288
2nd Part. Div.	$3 \times 640^2 =$	1228800	
	$3 \times 640 \times 2 =$	3840	
	$2^2 =$	4	
2nd Comp. Div.		1232644	2 465 288

The following rule is more readily understood if we bear in mind the formula for the cube of the sum of two numbers:

$$(a + b)^3 = a^3 + 3a^2b + 3ab^2 + b^3$$

Rule: 1. *Separate the given number into periods of three figures each, beginning at the right, and place over it the radical sign with the proper index.*

The extreme left-hand period may contain one, two or three figures.

2. *Determine the greatest cube that is smaller than the first left-hand period, and write its cube root, in the position shown, as the first figure of the required root.*

This root corresponds to a in the formula.

3. *Subtract the cube of this root from the first period and annex the next period to the remainder.*

4. *Multiply this root mentally by ten and write three times the square of this as a partial divisor.*

5. *Make a trial division to determine what the next figure in the root will be and write it in its proper place.*

6. *Add to the partial divisor (1) the product of 3 times the first part of the root considered as tens multiplied by the second part of the root; and (2) the square of the second part of the root. The sum of these numbers is the complete divisor.*

7. *Multiply the complete divisor by the second part of the root and subtract the product from the new dividend.*

Note in the example that at this point $a = 60$ and $b = 4$. When we subtracted 216 we took 216,000 or a^3 out of the given figure. When we multiply the first complete divisor by 4, this is equivalent to multiplying $3a^2$ (10800) by b, producing $3a^2b$; $3ab$ (720) by b, producing $3ab^2$; and b^2 (16) by b, producing b^3. Hence when we write 46144 previous to performing the subtraction we have fulfilled up to this point all the requirements of the formula $(a + b)^3 = a^3 + 3a^2b + 3ab^2 + b^3$.

8. *Bring down the next period and continue the same process until all the figures of the root have been determined.*

When the third figure of the root is found in the example a becomes 640 and b becomes 2. The student should check the manner in which multiplication of the second complete divisor by 2 fulfills the requirements of the formula. The correctness of the complete extraction may of course be checked by multiplying the determined root to its third power.

APPROXIMATE ROOTS OF FRACTIONS

We have seen (page 77) that the square root of a fraction is the square root of its numerator placed over the square root of the denominator, subject to further reduction or to conversion to a decimal.

When the terms of a fraction are not perfect squares it is often desirable to approximate a square root without going to the trouble of making an exact calculation. This is done by multiplying the terms of the fraction by any number that will make the denominator a perfect square, as in the following example.

EXAMPLE: What is the approximate square root of $\frac{19}{8}$?

$\frac{19}{8} = \frac{38}{16}$, of which the approximate square root, $\frac{6}{4}$, is correct to within $\frac{1}{4}$; or
$\frac{19}{8} \times \frac{32}{32} = \frac{608}{256}$, of which the approximate square root, $\frac{25}{16}$, is correct to within $\frac{1}{16}$.

EXPLANATION: We select a factor that will make the denominator a perfect square. We then extract the square root of the denominator and the square root of the perfect square that is nearest to the numerator. If we write the fraction as $\frac{38}{16}$, the square root of the denominator is 4 and the square root of the nearest perfect square to 38 is 6. The resulting approximate square root, $\frac{6}{4}$, reducible to $\frac{3}{2}$, is correct to within $\frac{1}{4}$.

If we want a closer approximation than this, we multiply by a larger factor. Using 32 as a factor, we get $\frac{608}{256}$. The square root of the denominator is 16. The nearest perfect square to 608 is 625, the square root of which is 25. The resulting approximate square root, $\frac{25}{16}$, is correct to within $\frac{1}{16}$.

It will be noted that the larger the factor the more closely will the result approximate the correct value.

The approximate cube root of a fraction may be found by a similar process.

EXAMPLE: Find the approximate cube root of $\frac{173}{32}$.
$\frac{173}{32} = \frac{346}{64}$, of which the approximate cube root, $\frac{7}{4}$, is correct to within $\frac{1}{4}$; or
$\frac{173}{32} = \frac{2768}{512}$, of which the approximate cube root, $\frac{14}{8}$, is correct to within $\frac{1}{8}$.

EXPLANATION: The denominator has been multiplied by two different factors in order to demonstrate again that the higher factor produces the more nearly accurate answer. It will be noted that the final result in both cases has the same ultimate value since $\frac{14}{8} = \frac{7}{4}$. If, however, we had not worked out the second solution we would not know that $\frac{7}{4}$ is actually correct to within $\frac{1}{8}$.

HIGHER ROOTS

If the index of a higher root contains no other prime factors than 2 and 3, we can find the required root by repeated extraction of square or cube roots, according to the nature of the problem.

EXAMPLE 1: What is the fourth root of 923521?

SOLUTION: $\sqrt{923521} = 961$,

$\qquad \sqrt{961} = 31$,   ANS.

EXPLANATION: Since the fourth power of a number is its square multiplied by its square, we find the fourth root of a given number representing such a power by extracting the square root of the square root.

EXAMPLE 2: What is the sixth root of 191102976?

SOLUTION: $\sqrt{191102976} = 13824$,

$\qquad \sqrt[3]{13824} = 24$,   ANS.

EXPLANATION: The sixth root is found by taking the cube root of the square root. The order of making the extractions is of course immaterial.

Higher roots with indexes that are prime to 2 and 3 are found by methods based on the same general theory as that underlying the methods for extracting square and cube roots. Thus if it be required to find the fifth root of a number, we consider that $(a + b)^5 = a^5 + 5a^4b + 10a^3b^2 + 10a^2b^3 + 5ab^4 + b^5$. After subtracting a^5 from the first period we must construct a complete divisor which when multiplied by b will satisfy the whole formula. Dividing what follows a^5 in the formula by b we get as the requirement of our complete divisor, $5a^4 + 10a^3b + 10a^2b^2 + 5ab^3 + b^4$. We use the first term of this, $5a^4$, as a trial divisor, but where the complete divisor is so complex several estimates may have to be tried before finding the correct value for b. In actual practice, however, higher roots are more commonly found by the use of logarithms and the slide rule, as in Chapter Twelve.

HANDY ALGEBRAIC FORMULAS

The following formulas should be memorized.

$$(a + b)^2 = a^2 + 2ab + b^2$$
$$(a - b)^2 = a^2 - 2ab + b^2$$
$$(a + b)(a - b) = a^2 - b^2$$
$$(a + b)^3 = a^3 + 3a^2b + 3ab^2 + b^3$$

These formulas have many applications, and they are particularly applicable to doing arithmetic by short-cut methods. Compare what is said below with the methods of multiplication presented on page 19.

TRANSLATING NUMBERS INTO ALGEBRA

In the following consider that a represents a number of the tens order, like 10, 20, 30, etc., while b represents a number of the units order.

Squaring a number:

EXAMPLE 1: Multiply 63 by 63.

60×60 combined with $3 \times 3 = 3609$,

6×60, or 360, added to $3609 = 3969$,   ANS.

EXPLANATION: 60×60 represents the a^2 of the formula, to which we at once add 9 as the b^2. The $2ab$ is most quickly figured out as $2 \times 3 \times 60$.

EXAMPLE 2: What is the square of 65?

60×70 combined with $25 = 4225$,   ANS.

EXPLANATION: Doing this example by the previous method we would get $3625 + (2 \times 5 \times 60)$. But $(2 \times 5) \times 60 = 10 \times 60$. Hence we at once multiply 60 by 10 more than we otherwise would, or 70.

EXAMPLE 3: What is the square of 89?

8100 combined with $1 = 8101$,

$8101 - 180 = 7921$,   ANS.

EXPLANATION: Since the digits are large and 89 is near 90 it is preferable here to use the square of $a - b$, taking a as 90 and b as 1. $a^2 + b^2 = 8101$; $2ab = 2 \times 1 \times 90$ or 180, which in accordance with the formula is subtracted from 8101.

Multiplying a sum by a difference:

EXAMPLE 4: How much is 53×47?

$2500 - 9 = 2491$,   ANS.

EXPLANATION: $a = 50$, $b = 3$. $53 = a + b$; $47 = a - b$. $(a + b)(a - b) = a^2 - b^2 = 2500 -$ Note that this method is applicable whenever the units add up to 10 and the tens differ by 10.

Cubing a number:

EXAMPLE: What is the cube of 23?

$\qquad\qquad\quad 8027$

$(69 \times 60) \quad \underline{4140}$

$\qquad\qquad 12167$,   ANS.

EXPLANATION: $(a + b)^3 = a^3 + 3a^2b + 3ab^2 + b^3$. $a^3 + b^3$ may be quickly written down as 8027. $3a^2b + 3ab^2 = 3ab(a + b)$. $a + b$ is the given number, in this case 23. We therefore want 3×23 or 69 multiplied by ab or 3×20 or 60. In other words, to the cubes of the digits properly placed add three times the number multiplied by the product of its digits with an added 0. A little practice makes all this quite simple. For small numbers the method is very much quicker than performing separate multiplications.

In solving examples like the preceding there is of course no reason why a may not represent a number of the hundreds plus the tens order instead of one of the tens order. Consider a few examples:

EXAMPLE 1: Square 116.
$12136 + 1320 = 13456$, ANS.

EXAMPLE 2: Square 125.
130×120 combined with $25 = 15625$, ANS.

EXAMPLE 3: Multiply 127 by 113.
$14400 - 49 = 14351$, ANS. from $(a^2 - b^2)$.

Practice Exercise No. 49

Find the required roots (approximate in the case of fractions).

1	$\sqrt[3]{2460375}$	11	$\sqrt[3]{\frac{2}{3}}\,(\times \frac{7}{72})$
2	$\sqrt[3]{11089567}$	12	$\sqrt[3]{\frac{2}{3}}\,(\times \frac{15552}{15552})$
3	$\sqrt[3]{40353607}$	13	$\sqrt[3]{\frac{2}{3}}\,(\times \frac{124416}{124416})$
4	$\sqrt[3]{403583419}$	14	$\sqrt[3]{5\frac{13}{32}}\,(\times \frac{2}{2})$
5	$\sqrt[3]{115501303}$	15	$\sqrt[3]{\frac{125}{256}}\,(\times \frac{2}{2})$
6	$\sqrt{\frac{2}{3}}\,(\times \frac{48}{48})$	16	$\sqrt[4]{6561}$
7	$\sqrt{\frac{38}{5}}\,(\times \frac{5}{5})$	17	$\sqrt[6]{117649}$
8	$\sqrt{\frac{45}{7}}\,(\times \frac{343}{343})$	18	$\sqrt[4]{29\frac{52}{81}}$
9	$\sqrt{10\frac{1}{2}}\,(\times \frac{200}{200})$	19	$\sqrt[4]{104\frac{538}{625}}$
10	$\sqrt{7\frac{1}{8}}\,(\times \frac{20000}{20000})$	20	$\sqrt[6]{11\frac{25}{64}}$

Do the following mentally by algebraic methods.

21	21^2	29	105^2	36	19×21
22	23^2	30	205^2		$(a+b)(a-b)$
23	33^2	31	29^2	37	28×32
24	37^2		$(a-b)^2$	38	37×43
25	39^2	32	39^2	39	46×54
26	35^2	33	99^2	40	48×72
27	65^2	34	28^2		
28	95^2	35	38^2		

CHAPTER ELEVEN

ALGEBRAIC PROCESSES

DEFINITIONS

A **monomial** is an algebraic expression of one term. *Thus,* $8a$ and $16a^2b$ and $\sqrt{3ax}$ are monomials.

A **polynomial** is an algebraic expression of more than one term. *Thus,* $a + b$, and $a^2 + 2ab + b^2$, and $a^3 + 3a^2b + 3ab^2 + b^3$, are three different *polynomials*.

A **binomial** is a polynomial that contains *two* terms. *Thus,* $a + b$, and $a + 1$, and $\sqrt{2} + \sqrt{3}$, are *binomials*. A **trinomial** contains *three* terms.

FACTORING

Factoring is the process of separating, or resolving, a quantity into factors.

No general rule can be given for factoring. In most cases the operation is performed by inspection and trial. The methods are best explained by examples.

Principle: *If every term of a polynomial contains the same monomial factor, then that monomial is one factor of the polynomial, and the other factor is equal to the quotient of the polynomial divided by the monomial factor.*

EXAMPLE: Factor the binomial $8a^2x^2 + 4a^3x$.

SOLUTION: $8a^2x^2 + 4a^3x = 4a^2x(2x + a)$.

EXPLANATION: We see by inspection that $4a^2x$ is a factor common to both terms. Dividing by $4a^2x$ we arrive at the other factor.

Principle: *If a trinomial contains three*

terms two of which are squares and if the third term is equal to plus or minus twice the product of the square roots of the other two, the expression may be recognized as the square of a binomial.

Thus, $a^2x^2 + 2acx + c^2 = (ax + c)^2$, and $9a^2b^2 - 24a^2bc + 16a^2c^2 = (3ab - 4ac)^2$.

Principle: *If an expression represents the difference between two squares, it can be factored as the product of the sum of the roots by the difference between them.*

Thus, $4x^2 - 9y^2 = (2x + 3y)(2x - 3y)$, and $25a^4b^4x^4 - 4z^2 = (5a^2b^2x^2 + 2z)$
$$(5a^2b^2x^2 - 2z).$$

Principle: *If the factors of an expression contain like terms, these should be collected so as to present the result in the simplest form.*

EXAMPLE: Factor $(5a + 3b)^2 - (3a - 2b)^2$.

SOLUTION: $(5a + 3b)^2 - (3a - 2b)^2$
$= [(5a + 3b) + (3a - 2b)][(5a + 3b) - (3a - 2b)]$
$= (5a + 3b + 3a - 2b)(5a + 3b - 3a + 2b)$
$= (8a + b)(2a + 5b)$, ANS.

Principle: *A trinomial in the form of $a^4 + a^2b^2 + b^4$ can be written in the form of the difference between two squares.*

EXAMPLE: Resolve $9x^4 + 26x^2y^2 + 25y^4$ into factors.
SOLUTION: $9x^4 + 26x^2y^2 + 25y^4$
$$\frac{+\ 4x^2y^2 \qquad\qquad -4x^2y^2}{(9x^4 + 30x^2y^2 + 25y^4) - 4x^2y^2}$$
$= (3x^2 + 5y^2)^2 - 4x^2y^2$
$= (3x^2 + 5y^2 + 2xy)(3x^2 + 5y^2 - 2xy)$
$= (3x^2 + 2xy + 5y^2)(3x^2 - 2xy + 5y^2)$

EXPLANATION: We note that the given expression is nearly a perfect square. We therefore add $4x^2y^2$ to it to make it a square and also subtract from it the same quantity. We then write it in the form of a difference between two squares. We resolve this into factors and rewrite the result so as to make the terms follow in the order of the powers of x.

Principle: *If a trinomial has the form $x^2 + ax + b$ and is factorable into two binomial factors, the first term of each factor will be x; the second term of the binomials will be two numbers whose product is b and whose sum*

is equal to a, which is the coefficient of the middle term of the trinomial.

EXAMPLE 1: Factor $x^2 + 10x + 24$.

SOLUTION: $x^2 + 10x + 24 = (x + 6)(x + 4)$.

EXPLANATION: We are required to find two numbers whose product is 24 and whose sum is 10. The following pairs of factors will produce 24: 1 and 24, 2 and 12, 3 and 8, 4 and 6. From among these we select the pair whose sum is 10.

EXAMPLE 2: Factor $x^2 - 16x + 28$.

SOLUTION: $x^2 - 16x + 28 = (x - 14)(x - 2)$.

EXPLANATION: We are required to find two numbers whose product is 28 and whose algebraic sum is -16. Since their product is positive they must both have the same sign, and since their sum is negative they must both be negative. The negative factors that will produce 28 are -1 and -28, -2 and -14, -4 and -7. We select the pair whose algebraic sum is -16.

EXAMPLE 3: Factor $x^2 + 5x - 24$.

SOLUTION: $x^2 + 5x - 24 = (x + 8)(x - 3)$.

EXPLANATION: We are required to find two numbers whose product is -24 and whose algebraic sum is 5. Since their product is negative the numbers must have unlike signs, and since their sum is $+5x$, the larger number must be positive. The pairs of numbers that will produce 24, without considering signs, are 1 and 24, 2 and 12, 3 and 8, 4 and 6. From these we select the pair whose difference is 5. This is 3 and 8. We give the plus sign to the 8 and the minus sign to the 3.

EXAMPLE 4: Factor $x^2 - 7x - 18$.

SOLUTION: $x^2 - 7x - 18 = (x - 9)(x + 2)$.

EXPLANATION: We are required to find two numbers whose product is -18 and whose algebraic sum is -7. Since their product is negative the signs of the two numbers are unlike, and since their sum is negative, the larger number must be negative. The pairs of numbers that will produce 18, without considering signs, are 1 and 18, 2 and 9, 3 and 6. We select the pair whose difference is 7, giving the minus sign to the 9 and the plus sign to the 2.

EXAMPLE 5: Factor $x^2 - 7xy + 12y^2$.

SOLUTION: $x^2 - 7xy + 12y^2 = (x - 4y)(x - 3y)$.

EXPLANATION: We are required to find two terms whose product is $12y^2$ and whose algebraic sum is $-7y$. Since their product is positive and their sum negative they must both be negative terms. From the pairs of negative terms that will produce $+12y^2$ we select $-4y$ and $-3y$ as fulfilling the requirements.

When a trinomial factorable into two binomials has the form $ax^2 \pm bx \pm c$, it is resolved into factors by a process of trial and error which is continued until values are found that satisfy the requirements.

EXAMPLE 1: Factor $4x^2 + 26x + 22$

$4x + 11$

$\times$ $+ 11x + 8x = 19x$ (*reject*),

$x + 2$

$x + 11$

$\times$ $+ 44x + 2x = 46x$ (*reject*),

$4x + 2$

$2x + 11$

$\times$ $22x + 4x = 26x$ (*correct*).

$2x + 2$

$\therefore 4x^2 + 26x + 22 = (2x + 11)(2x + 2)$, ANS.

EXPLANATION: We use what is called the *cross multiplication* method to find the required binomials. We consider the pairs of terms that will produce the first and last terms of the trinomials. We write down the various forms of examples that can be worked out with these, and we reject one trial result after another until we find the arrangement that will give us the correct value for the middle term of the given trinomial.

Instead of making a separate example out of each of the possibilities, the process is shortened by simply listing the possible factors involved, in the following manner:

$$\begin{array}{cc|c} 1 & 4\ \ 2 & 11 \\ 4 & 1\ \ 2 & 2 \end{array}$$

Factors to the left of the vertical line represent possible coefficients of x; those to the right of the line represent possible numerical values of second terms. Each pair of x coefficients is written in two positions (1 over 4, 4 over 1, etc.). Accordingly, it is not necessary to write second-term values in more than one position in order to exhaust the possibilities. We proceed with cross multiplication of the numbers on both sides of the vertical line. $(1 \times 2) + (4 \times 11) = 46$ (*too large—reject*); $(4 \times 2) + (1 \times 11) = 19$ (*too small—reject*); $(2 \times 2) + (2 \times 11) = 26$ (*correct*.)

EXAMPLE 2: Factor $24x^2 - 2x - 15$

SOLUTION:
$$\begin{array}{cccccccc|cc} 24 & 1 & 2 & 12 & 3 & 8 & 4 & 6 & 1 & 3 \\ 1 & 24 & 12 & 2 & 8 & 3 & 6 & 4 & 15 & 5 \end{array}$$

We select $\dfrac{4}{6}$ and $\dfrac{3}{5}$ as the combination of numbers that will give us the required middle term.
$\therefore 24x^2 - 2x - 15 = (4x + 3)(6x - 5)$, ANS.

EXPLANATION: We write down the possible numerical values in the manner previously described. Inasmuch as the third term of the trinomial is negative the two second terms of its binomial factors must have unlike signs. Considering that the given middle term has a very small value, we conclude that we are more likely to find the answer quickly if we start our cross multiplication at the right of the numerical arrangement rather than at the left. In carrying out this cross multiplication we give the negative sign in each case to the larger of the two products involved. *Thus:* $6(-5) + 4(+3) = -18$ (*reject*); $4(-5) + 6(+3) = -2$ (*correct*). We have been fortunate in finding the correct values so soon. Otherwise we should have had to continue the process of trial and error with the numerical listing—though this is not as lengthy a process as may appear, since many of the wrong results are recognized at a glance without taking the trouble to calculate them. Having selected the correct combination of numbers, we write the factors as $4x + 3$ and $6x - 5$.

Practice Exercise No. 50

Resolve the following into factors

1	$7a^2bc^3 - 28abc$	9 $\quad x^2 + 10x + 21$
2	$15a^2cd + 20ac^2d - 15acd^2$	10 $\quad x^2 - 18x + 45$
3	$4x^2 + 12xy + 9y^2$	11 $\quad x^2 + 5x - 36$
4	$9a^2b^2 - 24a^2bc + 16a^2c^2$	12 $\quad x^2 - 13x - 48$
5	$9a^2x^2 - 16a^2y^2$	13 $\quad x^2 - 14xy + 33y^2$
6	$49x^4 - 16y^2$	14 $\quad 6x^2 + 21x + 9$
7	$(2x + y + z)^2$ $\quad - (x - 2y + z)^2$	15 $\quad 15x^2 - 6x - 21$
8	$a^4 + a^2 + 1$	16 $\quad 12x^2 + 27x - 39$
	(*Hint: add and subtract* a^2)	

SIMULTANEOUS EQUATIONS

Simultaneous equations are equations involving the same unknown quantities. *Thus,* $a + 2b = 11$ and $2a + b = 10$ are *simultaneous equations* since they both involve the same unknowns, namely, a and b.

Simultaneous equations involving two unknown quantities are solved as follows:

Rule 1. *Eliminate one of the unknowns.*

Rule 2. *Solve for the other unknown.*

Rule 3. *Find the value of the unknown previously eliminated.*

Elimination may be performed by any one of three different methods:

1. *By addition or subtraction.*
2. *By substitution.*
3. *By comparison.*

ELIMINATION BY ADDITION OR SUBTRACTION:

Rule 1. *Multiply one or both of the equations by such a number or numbers as will give one of the unknowns the same coefficient in both equations.*

Rule 2. *Add or subtract the equal coefficients according to the nature of their signs.*

EXAMPLE: $5x + 2y = 32, 2x - y = 2$. Find x and y.

SOLUTION:

$$5x + 2y = 32$$
$$\underline{4x - 2y = 4}, \text{ multiplying } 2x - y \text{ by 2,}$$
$$9x = 36$$
$$x = 4.$$
$$20 + 2y = 32, \text{ substituting 4 for } x \text{ in first equation,}$$
$$2y = 32 - 20, \text{ transposing}$$
$$y = 6.$$

ELIMINATION BY SUBSTITUTION:

Rule 1. *From one of the equations find the value of one of the unknowns in terms of the other.*

Rule 2. *Substitute the value thus found for the unknown in the other of the given equations.*

EXAMPLE: $2x + 4y = 50, 3x + 5y = 66$. Find x and y.

SOLUTION:

$$2x + 4y = 50,$$
$$2x = 50 - 4y, \text{ transposing,}$$
$$x = 25 - 2y.$$
$$3(25 - 2y) + 5y = 66, \text{ substituting for } x \text{ in other equation,}$$
$$75 - 6y + 5y = 66,$$
$$-y = 66 - 75 = -9, y = 9.$$
$$2x + 36 = 50, \quad \text{substituting 9 for } y \text{ in first equation,}$$
$$2x = 50 - 36 = 14, x = 7.$$

ELIMINATION BY COMPARISON:

Rule 1. *From each equation find the value of one of the unknowns in terms of the other.*

Rule 2. *Form an equation from these equal values.*

EXAMPLE: $3x + 2y = 27, 2x - 3y = 5$. Find x and y.

SOLUTION:

$$3x + 2y = 27, 3x = 27 - 2y, x = \frac{27 - 2y}{3}.$$

$$2x - 3y = 5, 2x = 5 + 3y, x = \frac{5 + 3y}{2}.$$

$$\frac{27 - 2y}{3} = \frac{5 + 3y}{2}, \text{ both being equal to } x,$$

$$27 - 2y = \frac{3(5 + 3y)}{2}, \text{ multiplying both sides by 3,}$$

$$2(27 - 2y) = 3(5 + 3y), \text{ multiplying both sides by 2,}$$

$$54 - 4y = 15 + 9y, \text{ carrying out multiplication,}$$

$$-4y - 9y = 15 - 54 = -39, y = 3.$$
$$3x + 6 = 27, 3x = 21, x = 7.$$

Of the foregoing methods, select the one which appears most likely to make the solution simple and direct.

For a more detailed discussion of this topic, and for methods of solving other types of simultaneous equations, see INTERMEDIATE ALGEBRA AND ANALYTIC GEOMETRY MADE SIMPLE in this same series of MADE SIMPLE books.

Practice Exercise No. 51

PROBLEMS

1   The hands of a clock are together at 12 o'clock. When do they next meet? (x = minute spaces passed over by minute hand; y = number passed over by hour hand.)

2   A man has \$22,000 invested and on it he earns \$1,220. Part of the money is out at 5% interest and part at 6%. How much is in each part?

3   Jack is twice as old as Joe. Twenty years ago Jack was four times as old as Joe. What are their ages?

4   There are two numbers: the first added to half the second gives 35; the second added to half the first equals 40. What are the numbers?

5   The inventory of one department of a store increased by one-third of that of a second department amounts to \$1,700; the inventory of the second in-

creased by one-fourth of that of the first amounts to $1,800. What are the inventories?

6 Find two numbers such that $\frac{1}{2}$ of the first plus $\frac{1}{3}$ of the second shall equal 45, and $\frac{1}{2}$ of the second plus $\frac{1}{5}$ of the first shall equal 40.

7 A and B invest $918 in a partnership venture and clear $153. A's share of the profit is $45 more than B's. What was the contribution of each one to the capital?

8 Two girls receive $153 for baby sitting. Ann is paid for 14 days and Mary for 15. Ann's pay for 6 days' work is $3 more than Mary gets for 4. How much does each earn per day?

9 In 80 lbs. of an alloy of copper and tin there are 7 lbs. of copper to 3 of tin. How much copper must be added so that there may be 11 lbs. of copper to 4 of tin?

10 Brown owes $1,200 and Jones $2,500, but neither has enough money to pay his debts. Brown says to Jones, "Lend me one-eighth of your bank account and I'll pay my creditors." Jones says to Brown, "Lend me one-ninth of yours and I'll pay mine." How much money has each?

FRACTIONS

To reduce a fraction to its lowest terms, *resolve the numerator and the denominator into their prime factors and cancel all the common factors, or divide the numerator and the denominator by their highest common factor.*

EXAMPLE 1: Reduce $\dfrac{12a^2b^3c^4}{9a^3bc^2}$.

SOLUTION: $\dfrac{12a^2b^3c^4}{9a^3bc^2} = \dfrac{2 \times 2 \times 3a^2bc^2(b^2c^2)}{3 \times 3a^2bc^2(a)}$

$= \dfrac{4b^2c^2}{3a}$, ANS.

EXPLANATION: The numerical parts of the fraction are separated into their prime factors, and the algebraic parts are divided by their highest common factor. The terms that cancel out are then eliminated. As a guide for determining the highest common factor of monomial terms note that such a factor is made up of the lower (or lowest) of the given powers of each letter involved.

EXAMPLE 2: Reduce $\dfrac{12x^2 + 15x - 63}{4x^2 - 31x + 42}$.

SOLUTION: $\dfrac{12x^2 + 15x - 63}{4x^2 - 31x + 42} = \dfrac{(3x + 9)(4x - 7)}{(x - 6)(4x - 7)}$

$= \dfrac{3x + 9}{x - 6}$, ANS.

EXPLANATION: Numerator and denominator are factored, and the common factor is then cancelled.

A fraction may be reduced to an integral or mixed expression if the degree (power) of its numerator equals or exceeds that of its denominator.

To reduce a fraction to an integral or mixed expression, *divide the numerator by the denominator.*

EXAMPLE 1: Reduce $\dfrac{x^2 - y^2}{x - y}$ to an integral expression.

SOLUTION: $\dfrac{x^2 - y^2}{x - y} = \dfrac{(x - y)(x + y)}{x - y} = x + y$.

EXAMPLE 2: Reduce $\dfrac{x^2 + y^2}{x + y}$ to a mixed expression.

SOLUTION: $\dfrac{x^2 + y^2}{x + y} = \dfrac{(x^2 - y^2) + 2y^2}{x + y}$

$= \dfrac{(x + y)(x - y) + 2y^2}{x + y}$

$= x - y + \dfrac{2y^2}{x + y}$, ANS.

EXPLANATION: While $x^2 + y^2$ is not evenly divisible by $x + y$, we recognize that it would be so divisible if it were $x^2 - y^2$. Hence we subtract $2y^2$ to convert it to $x^2 - y^2$ and also add to it the same amount. We divide $x^2 - y^2$ by $x + y$ and write the remainder as a fraction that has $x + y$ for its denominator.

To reduce a mixed expression to a fraction, *multiply the integral expression by the denominator of the fraction; add to this product the numerator of the fraction and write under this result the given denominator.*

EXAMPLE: Reduce $x + 1 + \dfrac{x + 1}{x - 1}$ to a fraction.

SOLUTION: $\left(x + 1 + \dfrac{x + 1}{x - 1} \right)\left(\dfrac{x - 1}{x - 1} \right)$

$= \dfrac{x^2 - 1 + x + 1}{x - 1} = \dfrac{x^2 + x}{x - 1}$, ANS.

To reduce fractions to their lowest common denominator, *find the lowest common multiple of the denominators and proceed on the same principles that govern arithmetical fractions.*

EXAMPLE: Reduce $\dfrac{1}{x^2 + 3x + 2}$, $\dfrac{2}{x^2 + 5x + 6}$ and $\dfrac{3}{x^2 + 4x + 3}$ to fractions having the lowest common denominator.

SOLUTION: $\dfrac{1}{x^2 + 3x + 2}$, $\dfrac{2}{x^2 + 5x + 6}$, $\dfrac{3}{x^2 + 4x + 3}$

$= \dfrac{1}{(x + 1)(x + 2)}$, $\dfrac{2}{(x + 2)(x + 3)}$, $\dfrac{3}{(x + 1)(x + 3)}$

The LCD is $(x + 1)(x + 2)(x + 3)$.

Dividing this by each of the denominators and multiplying each numerator by the resulting quotient we obtain

$\dfrac{x + 3}{(x + 1)(x + 2)(x + 3)}$, $\dfrac{2x + 2}{(x + 1)(x + 2)(x + 3)}$,

$\dfrac{3x + 6}{(x + 1)(x + 2)(x + 3)}$, Ans.

ADDITION AND SUBTRACTION OF FRACTIONS

EXAMPLE 1: Simplify

$$\frac{2a - 4b}{4} - \frac{a - b + c}{3} + \frac{a - b - 2c}{12}.$$

SOLUTION: $\dfrac{2a - 4b}{4} - \dfrac{a - b + c}{3} + \dfrac{a - b - 2c}{12}$

$= \dfrac{6a - 12b - 4a + 4b - 4c + a - b - 2c}{12}$

$= \dfrac{3a - 9b - 6c}{12} = \dfrac{a - 3b - 2c}{4}$, Ans.

EXAMPLE 2: Simplify $\dfrac{a + 2x}{a - 2x} - \dfrac{a - 2x}{a + 2x}$.

SOLUTION: $\dfrac{a + 2x}{a - 2x} - \dfrac{a - 2x}{a + 2x}$

$= \dfrac{(a + 2x)^2 - (a - 2x)^2}{a^2 - 4x^2}$

$= \dfrac{a^2 + 4ax + 4x^2 - a^2 + 4ax - 4x^2}{a^2 - 4x^2}$

$= \dfrac{8ax}{a^2 - 4x^2}$, Ans.

MULTIPLICATION AND DIVISION OF FRACTIONS

Principle: *The product of two or more fractions is equal to the product of the numerators multiplied together, divided by the product of the denominators multiplied together.*

EXAMPLE 1: Multiply $\dfrac{7x}{5y}$ by $\dfrac{3a}{4c}$.

SOLUTION: $\dfrac{7x}{5y} \cdot \dfrac{3a}{4c} = \dfrac{21ax}{20cy}$, Ans.

EXAMPLE 2: Multiply $\dfrac{2x}{x - y}$ by $\dfrac{x^2 - y^2}{3}$.

SOLUTION: $\left(\dfrac{2x}{x - y}\right)\left(\dfrac{x^2 - y^2}{3}\right) = \dfrac{2x(x + y)(x - y)}{3(x - y)}$

$= \dfrac{2x(x + y)}{3}$, Ans.

EXAMPLE 3: Multiply $\dfrac{2(x + y)}{x - y}$ by $\dfrac{x^2 - y^2}{x^2 + 2xy + y^2}$.

SOLUTION: $\left[\dfrac{2(x + y)}{x - y}\right]\left[\dfrac{x^2 - y^2}{x^2 + 2xy + y^2}\right]$

$= \dfrac{2(x + y)(x + y)(x - y)}{(x - y)(x + y)^2} = 2$, Ans.

Principle: *Division by a fraction is equivalent to multiplication by the reciprocal of the fraction, i.e., the fraction inverted.*

EXAMPLE: Divide $\dfrac{3a^2}{a^2 - b^2}$ by $\dfrac{a}{a + b}$.

SOLUTION: $\dfrac{3a^2}{a^2 - b^2} \div \dfrac{a}{a + b} = \dfrac{3a^2}{a^2 - b^2} \cdot \dfrac{a + b}{a}$

$= \dfrac{3a^2(a + b)}{a(a + b)(a - b)} = \dfrac{3a^2}{a(a - b)} = \dfrac{3a}{a - b}$, Ans.

Practice Exercise No. 52

1 Reduce $\dfrac{45x^3y^3z}{36abx^2y^2z}$ to its lowest terms.

2 Reduce $\dfrac{x^2 + 2ax + a^2}{3(x^2 - a^2)}$ to its lowest terms.

3 Reduce $\dfrac{x^2 + a^2 + 3 - 2ax}{x - a}$ to a mixed quantity.

4 Reduce $a + \dfrac{ax}{a - x}$ to a fraction.

5 Reduce $1 + \dfrac{c}{x - y}$ to a fraction.

6 Reduce $\dfrac{x + a}{b}$, $\dfrac{a}{b}$ and $\dfrac{a - x}{a}$ to fractions with the LCD.

7 Reduce $\dfrac{x}{1 - x}$, $\dfrac{x^2}{(1 - x)^2}$ and $\dfrac{x^3}{(1 - x)^3}$ to fractions with the LCD.

8 Add $\dfrac{x + y}{2}$ and $\dfrac{x - y}{2}$.

9 Add $\dfrac{2}{(x - 1)^3}$, $\dfrac{3}{(x - 1)^2}$ and $\dfrac{4}{x - 1}$.

10 Subtract $2a - \dfrac{a - 3b}{c}$ from $4a + \dfrac{2a}{c}$.

11 Subtract $\dfrac{x}{a + x}$ from $\dfrac{a}{a - x}$.

12 Multiply $\dfrac{2}{x - y}$ by $\dfrac{x^2 - y^2}{a}$.

13 Multiply $\dfrac{x^2 - 4}{3}$ by $\dfrac{4x}{x + 2}$.

14 Divide $\dfrac{3x}{2x - 2}$ by $\dfrac{2x}{x - 1}$.

15 Divide $\dfrac{(x + y)^2}{x - y}$ by $\dfrac{x + y}{(x - y)^2}$.

CHAPTER TWELVE

LOGARITHMS AND THE SLIDE RULE

Logarithms are a means of simplifying the manipulation of numbers containing many digits or decimal places. The system of common logarithms, which is the one in most common use, is based on powers of 10.

By this system **the logarithm of a given number** *is the exponent to which* 10 *must be raised to obtain that number. Thus:*

$10^1 = 10$; ∴ the logarithm of 10 is 1.
$10^2 = 100$; ∴ the logarithm of 100 is 2.
$10^3 = 1,000$; ∴ the logarithm of 1,000 is 3.
$10^4 = 10,000$; ∴ the logarithm of 10,000 is 4.
and so on up.

The logarithm of a number between 10 and 99 is therefore an exponent greater than 1 and less than 2.

The logarithm of a number between 100 and 200 is an exponent greater than 2 and less than 3.

The logarithm of any number other than a multiple of 10 is therefore a whole number plus a decimal.

FINDING THE LOGARITHM OF A NUMBER

The logarithm of 45 should be between 1 and 2. That is, it must be 1 plus something. To find out what this something is, we refer to what is known as a **table of logarithms,** and then we find the logarithm of 45 to be equal to 1.6532. This is written:

$$\text{Log } 45 = 1.6532.$$

The method of finding a logarithm from the table will be explained in detail later.

The **characteristic** is the whole number part of the logarithm. In the above case the *characteristic* is 1.

The **mantissa** is the decimal part of the logarithm, and is the part found in the table of logarithms. In the above case the *mantissa* is .6532.

Finding the Characteristic. *The characteristic is not found in the table but is determined by rule. It is positive for numbers equal to 1 or greater, and negative for numbers less than 1.*

By definition,

For numbers between these limits	the characteristic is
10,000 and 100,000 *minus*	4
1,000 and 10,000 *minus*	3
100 and 1,000 *minus*	2
10 and 100 *minus*	1
1 and 10 *minus*	0
.1 and 1 *minus*	−1
.01 and .1 *minus*	−2
.001 and .01 *minus*	−3
.0001 and .001 *minus*	−4

Note: The characteristic 4 would apply to numbers from 10,000 to 99,999.999999+ carried to any number of places; characteristic 3, from 1,000 to 9,999.999999 . . . etc. For the sake of simplicity the latter numbers in these groups are expressed as 100,000 minus, 10,000 minus, 1,000 minus, etc.

Rule 1. *For whole numbers the characteristic is one less than the number of figures to the left of the decimal point.*

EXAMPLE 1: What is the characteristic of 82,459.23?

SOLUTION: There are 5 figures to the left of the decimal. $5 - 1 = 4$. ∴ the characteristic is 4.

Rule 2. *The characteristic of decimal numbers is equal to minus the number of places to the right from the decimal point to the first significant figure* (number other than zero).

EXAMPLE 2: What is the characteristic of .001326?

SOLUTION: From the decimal point to 1, the first significant figure, there are 3 places. ∴ the characteristic is -3.

EXAMPLE 3: What is the characteristic of .443?

SOLUTION: There is but one place from the decimal point to the first significant figure. ∴ the characteristic is -1.

Note: If the characteristic of a number (.023) is -2, and the mantissa is 3617, the whole logarithm is written $\bar{2}.3617$. The mantissa is always considered positive, and therefore negative characteristics are denoted by the placing of the minus sign *above* the characteristic. Another notation used for negative characteristics is $8.3617 - 10$. In this the negative *characteristic* is subtracted from 10, the remainder is made the new characteristic, and the -10 is placed after the mantissa to indicate a negative characteristic.

Practice Exercise No. 53

Write the characteristics of the following.

1	17	6	67.48
2	342	7	7.4
3	78,943	8	.000571
4	4,320	9	.021
5	.42	10	1

Finding the mantissa. The mantissa is found in the table of logarithms (Table VI on pages 92–93). The mantissa is not related to the position of the decimal point in any number. For example the mantissa of 34,562 is the same as the mantissa of 3,456.2 or

345.62. But the logarithm of these numbers differs with respect to the *characteristic*, which you have learned to find by inspection of the number.

Note: The reason why the mantissa for a given set of digits does not change, no matter how they may be pointed off decimally, will appear from the following. Let us assume that m is any number and the logarithm of this number is $n + p$, in which n is the characteristic and p the mantissa. By definition $m = 10^{n+p}$. If we multiply or divide 10^{n+p} by 10, 100, 1,000, etc. we make corresponding changes in the decimal pointing of m. But by the laws of algebra multiplication or division of 10^{n+p} by 10, 100, 1,000, etc., would be performed by adding or subtracting the exponents of 10^1, 10^2, 10^3, etc. Hence to arrive at any desired decimal pointing of the number m, only the whole-number part of the exponent of 10^{n+p} is modified. This part is n, the characteristic. The mantissa, p, always remains unchanged. Similar considerations will also make it clear why the mantissa still remains positive even when the characteristic is negative.

Let us now use the table of logarithms on pages 92–93 to find the mantissa of the number 345. Find 34 in the left-hand column headed by N. Then move across to the column headed 5. The mantissa is 5378. The characteristic is 2; therefore $\log 345 = 2.5378$.

By using the same mantissa and simply changing the characteristic we arrive at the following logarithms for various decimal pointings of the digits 345:

$\log 34.5 = 1.5378$
$\log 3.45 = .5378$
$\log .345 = \bar{1}.5378$, or $9.5378 - 10$
$\log .0345 = \bar{2}.5378$, or $8.5378 - 10$

EXAMPLE 1: Find the log of .837.

SOLUTION: Find 83 in the column headed N, move across to column headed 7. The mantissa is .9227; the characteristic is -1.
∴ $\log .837 = \bar{1}.9227$ or $9.9227 - 10$, ANS.

Interpolation is an arithmetic method used to find the value of a mantissa when the original number contains more than three significant (non-zero) figures. (The table here printed gives direct answers only for numbers up to 999.)

EXAMPLE 2: Find the log of 6484.

SOLUTION:

log 6480 = 3.8116 ⎱ The difference between these
log 6490 = 3.8122 ⎰ two logs is .0006.
Difference between 6490 and 6480 is 10.
Difference between 6484 and 6480 is 4.
Difference between mantissas is .0006.
$\frac{4}{10}$ × .0006 = .00024 increment,
.8116 + .00024 = .81184.
log 6484 = 3.81184, ANS.

EXAMPLE 3: Find the log of .05368.

SOLUTION:

log .05360 = $\bar{2}$.7292,
log .05370 = $\bar{2}$.7300.
Difference between logs = .0008.
Difference between numbers is 8.
.0008 × .8 = .00064 increment,
.7292 + .00064 = .72984,
log .05368 = $\bar{2}$.72984, ANS.

Practice Exercise No. 54

Find the logarithms of the following:

1	354	6	.234
2	76	7	.00352
3	8	8	6.04
4	6346	9	.0005324
5	3.657	10	672.8

Finding the antilogarithm. The number which corresponds to a given logarithm is called its **antilogarithm.**

The antilogarithm of a logarithm is found by obtaining the number corresponding to the mantissa and determining the position of the decimal point from the characteristic.

EXAMPLE 1: Find the antilogarithm of 1.8531.

SOLUTION: Look for mantissa 8531 in the body of Table VI. In the N column to the left of the row where you have located 8531, you will find the first two figures of the number (71). The third figure (3) is found at the top of the column in which 8531 is located. Since the characteristic is 1, mark off two decimal places in the number, counting from the *left*, to give 71.3.

Usually the mantissa cannot be found exactly in the tables. It is then necessary to interpolate between the two numbers corresponding to the two nearest logarithms.

EXAMPLE 2: Find the antilog of $\bar{3}$.5484.

SOLUTION: Given mantissa 5484 is between 5478

and 5490. Hence the first three significant figures of the antilog are 353.
Diff. bet. 5490 and 5478 = 0012 ⎱ $\frac{0006}{0012}$ ⎱ = .5
Diff. bet. 5484 and 5478 = 0006 ⎰ ⎰
The first four significant figures are therefore 3535. Since the characteristic is $\bar{3}$, antilog = .003535, ANS.

HOW TO USE LOGARITHMS

To multiply by the use of logarithms, *add the logarithms of the numbers to be multiplied and find the antilogarithm corresponding to this sum.*

EXAMPLE: Multiply 25.31 by 42.18.

SOLUTION: log 25.31 = 1.4033,
log 42.18 = 1.6251.
Sum = 3.0284,
Product = antilog of 3.0284 = 1067.5, ANS.

To divide by the use of logarithms, *subtract the logarithm of the divisor from the logarithm of the dividend; the difference is the logarithm of the quotient.*

EXAMPLE 1: Divide 5,280.4 by 67.82.

SOLUTION: log 5,280.4 = 3.7226,
log 67.82 = 1.8313,
difference = 1.8913,
Quotient = antilog 1.8913 = 77.86, ANS.

EXAMPLE 2: Divide 5,280.4 by .06782.

SOLUTION:

log 5,280.4 = 13.7226 − 10
log .06782 = 8.8313 − 10
difference = 4.8913,
antilog = 77860, ANS.

EXPLANATION: log .06782 is negative with a characteristic of −2. In order to perform a subtraction with it we write it as 8.8313 − 10, but before subtraction is possible we must make a corresponding change in the minuend. This we do by both adding to it and subtracting from it the number 10, an operation that does not affect its value. The two −10s are eliminated when we subtract and the resulting logarithm has the correct characteristic.

EXAMPLE 3: Divide 52.804 by 6782.

log 52.804 = 11.7226 − 10
log 6782 = 3.8313
7.8913 − 10
= $\bar{3}$.8913
antilog = .007786, ANS.

Mathematics Made Simple

Table VI

COMMON LOGARITHMS OF NUMBERS

N	0	1	2	3	4	5	6	7	8	9
10	0000	0043	0086	0128	0170	0212	0253	0294	0334	0374
11	0414	0453	0492	0531	0569	0607	0645	0682	0719	0755
12	0792	0828	0864	0899	0934	0969	1004	1038	1072	1106
13	1139	1173	1206	1239	1271	1303	1335	1367	1399	1430
14	1461	1492	1523	1553	1584	1614	1644	1673	1703	1732
15	1761	1790	1818	1847	1875	1903	1931	1959	1987	2014
16	2041	2068	2095	2122	2148	2175	2201	2227	2253	2279
17	2304	2330	2355	2380	2405	2430	2455	2480	2504	2529
18	2553	2577	2601	2625	2648	2672	2695	2718	2742	2765
19	2788	2810	2833	2856	2878	2900	2923	2945	2967	2989
20	3010	3032	3054	3075	3096	3118	3139	3160	3181	3201
21	3222	3243	3263	3284	3304	3324	3345	3365	3385	3404
22	3424	3444	3464	3483	3502	3522	3541	3560	3579	3598
23	3617	3636	3655	3674	3692	3711	3729	3747	3766	3784
24	3802	3820	3838	3856	3874	3892	3909	3927	3945	3962
25	3979	3997	4014	4031	4048	4065	4082	4099	4116	4133
26	4150	4166	4183	4200	4216	4232	4249	4265	4281	4298
27	4314	4330	4346	4362	4378	4393	4409	4425	4440	4456
28	4472	4487	4502	4518	4533	4548	4564	4579	4594	4609
29	4624	4639	4654	4669	4683	4698	4713	4728	4742	4757
30	4771	4786	4800	4814	4829	4843	4857	4871	4886	4900
31	4914	4928	4942	4955	4969	4983	4997	5011	5024	5038
32	5051	5065	5079	5092	5105	5119	5132	5145	5159	5172
33	5185	5198	5211	5224	5237	5250	5263	5276	5289	5302
34	5315	5328	5340	5353	5366	5378	5391	5403	5416	5428
35	5441	5453	5465	5478	5490	5502	5514	5527	5539	5551
36	5563	5575	5587	5599	5611	5623	5635	5647	5658	5670
37	5682	5694	5705	5717	5729	5740	5752	5763	5775	5786
38	5798	5809	5821	5832	5843	5855	5866	5877	5888	5899
39	5911	5922	5933	5944	5955	5966	5977	5988	5999	6010
40	6021	6031	6042	6053	6064	6075	6085	6096	6107	6117
41	6128	6138	6149	6160	6170	6180	6191	6201	6212	6222
42	6232	6243	6253	6263	6274	6284	6294	6304	6314	6325
43	6335	6345	6355	6365	6375	6385	6395	6405	6415	6425
44	6435	6444	6454	6464	6474	6484	6493	6503	6513	6522
45	6532	6542	6551	6561	6571	6580	6590	6599	6609	6618
46	6628	6637	6646	6656	6665	6675	6684	6693	6702	6712
47	6721	6730	6739	6749	6758	6767	6776	6785	6794	6803
48	6812	6821	6830	6839	6848	6857	6866	6875	6884	6893
49	6902	6911	6920	6928	6937	6946	6955	6964	6972	6981
50	6990	6998	7007	7016	7024	7033	7042	7050	7059	7067
51	7076	7084	7093	7101	7110	7118	7126	7135	7143	7152
52	7160	7168	7177	7185	7193	7202	7210	7218	7226	7235
53	7243	7251	7259	7267	7275	7284	7292	7300	7308	7316
54	7324	7332	7340	7348	7356	7364	7372	7380	7388	7396

COMMON LOGARITHMS OF NUMBERS—*Continued*

N	0	1	2	3	4	5	6	7	8	9
55	7404	7412	7419	7427	7435	7443	7451	7459	7466	7474
56	7482	7490	7497	7505	7513	7520	7528	7536	7543	7551
57	7559	7566	7574	7582	7589	7597	7604	7612	7619	7627
58	7634	7642	7649	7657	7664	7672	7679	7686	7694	7701
59	7709	7716	7723	7731	7738	7745	7752	7760	7767	7774
60	7782	7789	7796	7803	7810	7818	7825	7832	7839	7846
61	7853	7860	7868	7875	7882	7889	7896	7903	7910	7917
62	7924	7931	7938	7945	7952	7959	7966	7973	7980	7987
63	7993	8000	8007	8014	8021	8028	8035	8041	8048	8055
64	8062	8069	8075	8082	8089	8096	8102	8109	8116	8122
65	8129	8136	8142	8149	8156	8162	8169	8176	8182	8189
66	8195	8202	8209	8215	8222	8228	8235	8241	8248	8254
67	8261	8267	8274	8280	8287	8293	8299	8306	8312	8319
68	8325	8331	8338	8344	8351	8357	8363	8370	8376	8382
69	8388	8395	8401	8407	8414	8420	8426	8432	8439	8445
70	8451	8457	8463	8470	8476	8482	8488	8494	8500	8506
71	8513	8519	8525	8531	8537	8543	8549	8555	8561	8567
72	8573	8579	8585	8591	8597	8603	8609	8615	8621	8627
73	8633	8639	8645	8651	8657	8663	8669	8675	8681	8686
74	8692	8698	8704	8710	8716	8722	8727	8733	8739	8745
75	8751	8756	8762	8768	8774	8779	8785	8791	8797	8802
76	8808	8814	8820	8825	8831	8837	8842	8848	8854	8859
77	8865	8871	8876	8882	8887	8893	8899	8904	8910	8915
78	8921	8927	8932	8938	8943	8949	8954	8960	8965	8971
79	8976	8982	8987	8993	8998	9004	9009	9015	9020	9025
80	9031	9036	9042	9047	9053	9058	9063	9069	9074	9079
81	9085	9090	9096	9101	9106	9112	9117	9122	9128	9133
82	9138	9143	9149	9154	9159	9165	9170	9175	9180	9186
83	9191	9196	9201	9206	9212	9217	9222	9227	9232	9238
84	9243	9248	9253	9258	9263	9269	9274	9279	9284	9289
85	9294	9299	9304	9309	9315	9320	9325	9330	9335	9340
86	9345	9350	9355	9360	9365	9370	9375	9380	9385	9390
87	9395	9400	9405	9410	9415	9420	9425	9430	9435	9440
88	9445	9450	9455	9460	9465	9469	9474	9479	9484	9489
89	9494	9499	9504	9509	9513	9518	9523	9528	9533	9538
90	9542	9547	9552	9557	9562	9566	9571	9576	9581	9586
91	9590	9595	9600	9605	9609	9614	9619	9624	9628	9633
92	9638	9643	9647	9652	9657	9661	9666	9671	9675	9680
93	9685	9689	9694	9699	9703	9708	9713	9717	9722	9727
94	9731	9736	9741	9745	9750	9754	9759	9763	9768	9773
95	9777	9782	9786	9791	9795	9800	9805	9809	9814	9818
96	9823	9827	9832	9836	9841	9845	9850	9854	9859	9863
97	9868	9872	9877	9881	9886	9890	9898	9899	9903	9908
98	9912	9917	9921	9926	9930	9934	9939	9943	9948	9952
99	9956	9961	9965	9969	9974	9978	9983	9987	9991	9996

EXPLANATION: In this case we have to increase and decrease the upper logarithm by 10 in order to perform the subtraction, but the −10 is not eliminated and hence has the effect of giving the remainder a negative characteristic.

To raise to a given power by the use of logarithms, *multiply the logarithm of the number by the given exponent of the number and find the antilogarithm.*

The reason for this may be explained as follows. Let m be a number and n its logarithm. Then—

$$m = 10^n,$$
$$m^2 = 10^n \times 10^n = 10^{n+n} = 10^{2n},$$
$$m^3 = 10^{3n}, \text{ etc.}$$

EXAMPLE 1: Find 46^4.

SOLUTION: $\log 46 = 1.6628$

$ \times 4$

$\log 46^4 = \overline{6.6512},$

$46^4 = \text{antilog } 6.6512 = 4,479,000, \quad$ ANS.

To find a given root by the use of logarithms, *divide the logarithm of the number by the index of the root and find the antilogarithm.*

This may be demonstrated thus:

$$\text{Let} \quad m = 10^n.$$
$$\text{Then} \quad \sqrt{m} = \sqrt{10^n} = 10^{\frac{n}{2}},$$
$$\sqrt[3]{m} = 10^{\frac{n}{3}}, \text{ etc.}$$

EXAMPLE 1: Find $\sqrt[3]{75}$.

SOLUTION: $\log 75 = 1.8751,$

$$\frac{1.8751}{3} = .62503,$$

Root = antilog $.62503 = 4.217,$ ANS.

EXAMPLE 2: Find $\sqrt{.251}$.

SOLUTION: $\log .251 = \overline{1}.3997$ or $9.3997 - 10,$

$$\frac{9.3997 - 10}{2} = 4.69985 - 5 = \overline{1}.69985,$$

Root = antilog $\overline{1}.69985 = .5015,$ ANS.

EXAMPLE 3: Find $\sqrt[3]{.75}$.

SOLUTION:

$\log .75 = 9.8751 - 10$
$ + 20 - 20$
$ \overline{29.8751 - 30,}$

$$\frac{29.8751 - 30}{3} = 9.9583 - 10 = \overline{1}.9583,$$

antilog $= .9084,$ ANS.

EXPLANATION: Starting in this case with a negative characteristic, we cannot make a direct division by 3 because dividing 10 by 3 would result in a fractional characteristic, which is impossible. We therefore increase and decrease the logarithm by 20 in order to make the division possible and to produce a −10 in the remainder.

Practice Exercise No. 55

Solve by logarithms.

1	3984×5.6	11	$\dfrac{5}{-7}$
2	25.316×42.18	12	$\dfrac{-17}{32}$
3	220.2×2209	13	$\dfrac{6+3}{4}$
4	$5280 \div 33.81$	14	$\dfrac{8+7}{7}$
5	$7256.2 \div 879.26$	15	$\dfrac{13-9}{3}$
6	$9783 \div .1234$	16	$\dfrac{11}{16-7}$
7	77^3	17	$\dfrac{8}{3 \times 5}$
8	$\sqrt[3]{85}$	18	$\dfrac{4 \times 6}{11}$
9	$\sqrt[5]{356.07}$	19	$\dfrac{7 \div 3}{4}$
10	2.43^5	20	$\dfrac{16}{18 \div 5}$

The principal use of logarithms is in connection with trigonometry, the branch of mathematics that has to do with the measurement of triangles.

A more advanced discussion of the topic, and an account of other kinds of logarithms, is contained in ADVANCED ALGEBRA AND CALCULUS MADE SIMPLE in this same MADE SIMPLE series of books.

THE SLIDE RULE

The slide rule represents an application of logarithmic principles. The student will find that a slide rule helps him to understand logarithms, while a knowledge of logarithms will assist him in manipulating the slide rule itself.

Slide rules are so commonly used today that there is no telling when a person in almost any kind of position may be called upon to use one.

The slide rule consists of three parts—the body of the rule, the slide which moves in the groove of the rule, and the runner or slider (omitted from the illustration). The runner is a piece of glass or celluloid marked with a vertical hairline to increase accuracy in making settings and reading scales.

Slide rules are made with various markings, including many for special purposes. The markings shown in the illustration are the most usual. Here are shown three scales on the body of the rule—A, D and K, and three on the slide—B, C and CI.

All the scales on the slide rule are measured off in logarithmic proportions. Consider the D scale on the body, which has its exact counterpart in C on the slide. At each end it is marked with 1, and between these 1's are numbers of the same size from 2 to 9. If you were to take the full length of the scale as one unit you would find that 2 is placed at a point representing .3010 of the distance, 3 at .4771 of the distance, 4 at .6021, etc., these decimals representing the logarithms of the corresponding numbers.

This being so, you get the same result by adding together portions of the slide rule that you would get by adding together the logarithms of the numbers; that is you perform a multiplication. Thus if you set the 1 on C of the slide over 2 on D and read your results on D, you will find that every number on D is twice as much as the number over it on C. Similarly, to multiply 3 by 3 you set the left-hand 1 of C over 3 on D, look for 3 on C and read 9 as your answer on D.

Upon this fundamental principle of the slide rule are based procedures for working out various kinds of calculations. But before proceeding to consider these we must pay closer attention to the manner in which the scales on the rule are arranged. Skill in using the slide rule is for the most part quickness in reading the scales, and the student should

not attempt to proceed to the actual operation of the rule until he has acquired a fair proficiency in reading the markings.

READING THE SCALE

Of the six scales on the rule there are two pairs (A–B and C–D) in which exactly the same markings are repeated. The following statements are true of all the scales but will be considered first with reference to the C or D scale, since it is the C–D pair that is used for most calculations.

1. Values on the scale are relative, depending on the magnitude of the numbers involved in the calculation in hand.
2. The scale gives readings only in whole numbers.
3. The scale gives direct readings in never more than three significant figures.
4. The values indicated by successive intervals on the scale are different in different parts of it.

1. The two 1s at the ends of the C (or D) scale may be taken as representing any two consecutive powers of 10. Thus, if the left-hand 1 is taken as 1, the right-hand 1 is read as 10. If the left-hand 1 represents 10, the right-hand becomes 100. Or the range may be from 100 to 1,000, or from 1,000 to 10,000, etc. Or the scale may represent decimal values, running from .1 to 1, or from .01 to .1, or from .001 to .01, etc.

2. In actual practice you do not attempt to make the slide rule interpret decimal values. You work with whole numbers, obtain your result as a whole number, and point this off decimally according to the decimal conditions of the problem.

3. A significant figure, it will be recalled, is a figure other than 0. The scale cannot give a direct reading of more than three significant figures. Moreover, it will give the same reading for the same significant figures irrespective of their actual value. For instance, the same point on the scale would indicate 146, 14.6, 1.46, .146, 146,000, .00146, etc.

4. The C scale is graduated in three different ways. One style of graduation extends from the extreme left-hand 1 to the large 2; the next, from 2 to 4; the third from 4 to the right-hand 1.

If, for convenience, we take the left-hand 1 as representing 100 and the right-hand 1 as representing 1,000, then the large numbers 2, 3, 4, 5, etc. between these extremes will stand for 200, 300, 400, 500, etc.

Take now the space between the left-hand 1 and the large 2—this space will cover the numbers between 100 and 200. Its major divisions, as represented by the small numbers 1, 2, 3, 4, etc. will accordingly represent 110, 120, 130, 140, etc. It will be noted that the space between these small numbers is in each case divided into ten parts, so that we get a complete reading by 1s from 100 to 110, from 110 to 120, from 120 to 130, etc. In other words, the space between 1 and 2 is divided into 100 parts enabling us to read any number from 100 to 200 directly on the scale.

If we now examine the space between 2 and 4 we see that between 2 and 3, and between 3 and 4, there are ten main divisions in each case, which accordingly read as 210, 220, 230, etc., and 310, 320, 330, etc. Each of these main divisions is divided into five parts, which thus become intervals of 2. We are thus enabled to read by 2s from 200 to 400.

The third type of marking on the rule extends from 4 to the right-hand 1, though the actual space between the markings becomes noticeably smaller as we proceed toward the right. This is because of the logarithmic character of the scale.

Between 4 and 5, 5 and 6, etc., there are in each case 10 main divisions, and these are each subdivided into two parts, so that that between 400 and 1,000 the scale reads by 5s.

Summing up this matter we have the following condensed rules for reading the C or D scales.

1. Between 1 and the large 2, read the smallest intervals by 1s—101, 102, 103, etc.
2. Between the large 2 and 4 read the smallest intervals by 2s—202, 204, 206, etc.
3. Between the large 4 and 10 read the smallest intervals by 5s—405, 410, 415, etc.

The following practice exercise is so graded that you can proceed step by step to a mastery of direct readings from the rule. When you have finished this exercise you should also set the runner haphazardly at various points on the scale and read these.

Practice Exercise No. 56

Set the C and D scales exactly above one another and indicate with the runner the following values.

200	125	200	400	200	.0019
600	195	300	600	400	.05
300	105	400	800	600	.126
700	1050	250	1000	800	.352
900	1350	350	550	250	.9650
70	16500	240	750	350	15.20
50	195	340	45	450	765
20	116	220	65	650	3.12
4000	138	260	9.5	950	94500

8000	152	380	450	150	82.50
3	197	252	460	160	11.1
5	126	232	455	260	13.6
.4	149	348	855	360	26.80
.6	163	368	865	460	5050
.07	174	20.4	475	860	640
.09	187	3.98	835	175	3020
.001	101	2.26	7.25	276	.0725
.005	111	2960	9250	376	29.8
110	1150	3420	56500	475	445
150	1170	29.80	82.50	675	18.4
180	1.960	25600	730	975	2.78
11	13.50	2600	620	112	39.80
15	18.5	3620	.0505	212	615
18	.0172	3960	.5050	312	.0875
1900	16.8	31.2	590	415	.0003
1700	18200	244	950	715	.0033
16000	1.43	2.58	905	815	.0022
1.3	1.89	.0276	.0815	163	.0222
.105	1930	.0354	.0635	262	815
.017	.123	.0318	.0855	465	310
.0012	.0194	.0308	81.50	1460	2.08
.1300	.1730	.0202	51.50	7650	.101

Reading by Interpolation

While the slide rule gives direct readings only of such numbers as have been considered in the foregoing, it is possible to find other values by *interpolation*. Thus, let us take the division of the scale that runs from 2 to 4. On this let us find the markings that indicate, say, 224 and 226. If we want the number 225, it is obvious that this would lie midway between these markings. In like manner we can find all odd numbers between 200 and 400.

On the section between 4 and the end of the scale values in three figures other than those shown directly may also be obtained by judging with the eye where their position would be. Thus 867 would lie two-fifths of the distance between 865 and 870 and 559 would be one-fifth of a space short of 560.

When it comes to reading such interpolated values in actual practice we are helped by the fact that the problem itself will indicate the third figure in many if not most cases. Thus if we had multiplied 37 by 23 and found that our answer lay a little bit past 850, we would know from the fact that 7 × 3 produces a number ending in a 1, that the required answer must be 851.

Practice Exercise No. 57a

Find the following values on the C–D scale by interpolation.

225	219	321	466	401	923
235	287	249	508	803	498
345	343	251	612	846	472
365	333	389	824	627	724
321	269	399	999	456	516

If we apply the method of interpolation which has just been described to the section of the scale between the left-hand 1 and 2 we can get readings of four significant figures. Thus, for example, the midpoint between 156 and 157 would have a value of 156.5, or if values are read in thousands, of 1565. Again if we had worked out a problem and knew that the answer required four figures ending in a 6, and if we found the solution to lie between 1810 and 1820, we should at once know the correct answer to be 1816.

On the sections beyond 2 it is also possible in many cases, but not always, to read values accurately in four significant figures.

Practice Exercise No. 57b

Find the following values on the C–D scale by interpolation.

1655	1836	4725	3155	5175	7875
1875	1542	4735	3015	6875	4325
1925	1711	2865	2865	6825	4175
1145	1347	2875	3225	5125	4225
1235	1223	3145	3875	7225	9975

In the following explanation of the operation of the slide rule the ends of the scales on the slide, marked 1, are given their usual names of the **left-hand index** and the **right-hand index.**

MULTIPLICATION

To perform a multiplication the multiplicand is found on D and either the left-hand or the right-hand index is moved to this position; the multiplier is then found on C, and in line with it on D will be found the product.

EXAMPLE 1: Multiply 2 by 3.

PROCEDURE: Set the left-hand index over 2 on the D scale. Find 3 on the C scale, and directly under it on the D scale find the required answer, 6.

EXAMPLE 2: Multiply 28 by 15.

PROCEDURE: Set the left-hand index over 28 on the D scale. Find 15 on the C scale, and directly under it on the D scale find the required answer, 420. This result is read as 420 and not 42 because it is known that the answer will lie in the hundreds.

EXAMPLE 3: Multiply 26 by 23.

PROCEDURE: Set the left-hand index over 26 on the D scale. Find 23 on the C scale and read the answer on the D scale as 598.

Why are we sure of the last digit? In this case the slide rule tells us that the answer is greater than 595 and less than 600. As we know from the given figures

that the product must end in 8, the correct answer must be 598 and not 596, 597, or 599.

EXAMPLE 4: Multiply 78 by 56.

PROCEDURE: In this case if you were to use the left-hand index to set over 78 on D, you would find that the slide projected too far to the right to make it possible to read the answer. Therefore you use the *right-hand* index to set over 78 on D. You then proceed as in the previous examples—that is, you find 56 on C, and read the value directly under it as 4370 or, more correctly, 4368.

The scale makes it very clear that the answer is nearer to 4370 than it is to either 4360 or 4380. Hence, since it must end in 8, it is easy to interpolate the correct value of 4368.

It will be noted that it makes no difference in the manner of operating the rule whether the left-hand index or the right-hand index on C is set over the multiplicand on D.

Decimal Pointing

When the numbers to be multiplied involve decimals, treat them as if they were whole numbers and determine mentally where the decimal point is to be placed in the answer. This is done by taking the whole numbers that are nearest to the given numbers and considering what their product would be.

Thus in the example that follows, which is to multiply 21.3 by 2.75, we note that $22 \times 3 = 66$ and therefore there will be two places of whole numbers in the answer.

EXAMPLE 5: Multiply 21.3 by 2.75.

PROCEDURE: Set the left-hand index over 213 on D. Find 275 on C. Determine as explained above that there will be a whole number of two places in the product and read this product as 58.6.

In this case if the given numbers are multiplied out, their product runs to five significant figures. When this occurs no more than three significant figures can be readily determined in the answer.

Continued Multiplication

When three or more factors are to be multiplied together, it is not necessary to determine any intermediate products since all we are interested in is the final answer. Therefore when we have found an intermediate product on D, we simply use this as a new multiplicand and proceed as for any other multiplication.

EXAMPLE 6: Multiply 62.5 times 43 by .0188.

PROCEDURE: Set the right-hand index over 625 on the D scale. Find 43 on the C scale, but instead of making any special note of what it indicates on the

D scale, simply move the runner so that the hairline will mark the place indicated. Then set the left-hand index under the hairline, find 188 on the C scale and find the product (505) under it on the D scale.

When it comes to pointing off the decimal places, consider that $60 \times 40 = 2400$ and that .02 of this would be 48. Therefore the correct pointing is 50.5.

By continuing the same process any number of factors may be multiplied together.

Practice Exercise No. 58

Multiply as indicated:

1	2×4	17	127×9
2	3×3	18	354×6
3	3×4	19	287×8
4	4×5	20	965×8
5	22×2	21	723×5
6	36×2	22	28.6×2.7
7	28×3	23	54.5×1.6
8	19×5	24	89.5×5.5
9	28×9	25	6.49×24
10	37×6	26	3.76×61
11	42×4	27	$72.5 \times 29 \times .0285$
12	63×5	28	$8.36 \times 4.5 \times .625$
13	28×32	29	$9.15 \times 37 \times .236$
14	42×18	30	$.955 \times 26 \times 1.235$
15	67×15	31	$.214 \times 750 \times .1875$
16	84×26		

DIVISION

Division can be performed on the slide rule in two ways. The first is simply a reversal of the process of multiplication, in which the dividend replaces the product; the divisor, the multiplier; and the quotient, the multiplicand.

EXAMPLE 1: Divide 391 by 17.

PROCEDURE: Find 391 on the D scale. Directly over this set 17 on the C scale. Look for the answer, 23, on the D scale directly under the left-hand index.

The second method of division involves the use of the CI scale. The CI scale is calibrated exactly like the C or D scale but in the opposite direction. The result of this is that numbers on the CI scale are the reciprocals of those on the C scale. This is to say that, when the proper decimal pointing is given, any number on the CI scale when multiplied by the number directly beneath it on the C scale will equal 1. Thus 5 on the CI scale is directly in line with 2 on the C scale; 3 on either scale is in line with 333 on the other; 8 with 125, etc. The numbers on the CI scale, accordingly, may be taken as the denominators of fractions that have 1 for a numerator.

When employed for division the CI scale is used in exactly the same way as the C scale is used for multiplication.

EXAMPLE 2: Divide 391 by 17.

PROCEDURE: Set the right-hand index over 391 on the D scale. Find 17 on the CI scale and directly below it on the D scale you will find the correct answer, 23.

Practice Exercise No. 59

Solve the following examples by both methods of division.

1	$36 \div 3$	6	$2.25 \div 1.5$	11	$2840 \div 45$
2	$72 \div 4$	7	$5.45 \div 54$	12	$(7400 \div 34) \div 19$
3	$88 \div 11$	8	$78.5 \div 25$	13	$(6240 \div 14) \div 13$
4	$156 \div 12$	9	$299.5 \div 11.1$	14	$(\frac{1}{2} \div \frac{1}{4}) \div \frac{1}{3}$
5	$144 \div 16$	10	$1950 \div 26$	15	$(\frac{1}{3} \div \frac{1}{5}) \div .4$

PROPORTION

However the C and D scales may be set with relation to one another all the values on the two scales are in one and the same proportion. Thus if we set 2 on the C scale in line with 3 on the D scale we note that 4 is in line with 6, 6 with 9, 12 with 18, 24 with 36, etc. In other words all values on the D scale are $1\frac{1}{2}$ times those on the C scale.

This property of the slide rule makes it very valuable in figuring the sizes that photographs or drawings will reduce to when made into plates for printing. The following example illustrates this.

EXAMPLE: I want to reduce an 8×10 photograph to make an engraving 3 inches wide. How high will the reproduction be?

PROCEDURE: Set the 8 of the C scale in line with the right-hand 1 of the D scale (representing 10). Find 3 on the C scale. Directly under it on the D scale read the answer, 3.75 or $3\frac{3}{4}$ inches.

To avoid resetting the rule for values too far to the right, the same procedure may be used with the A and B scales. Set 8 on the B scale in line with right-hand 1 on A. Answers may then be read from either of the identical halves of the A scale.

Percentage and Interest

When a number of percentages are to be figured at the same rate, the principle of proportion enables you to make successive calculations with one setting of the slide. Thus, suppose you want to calculate the interest at 6% on a number of various sums of money. You set the 6 of the C scale in line with the right-hand 1 of the D scale. Find the various principals on the D scale and read the interest on the C scale. For such examples as lie outside of the range of the setting you move the slide to bring the 6 of the C scale in line with the left-hand 1 of the D scale.

You will note that the *amount* of sums at interest (principal plus interest) can also be found in the same way. Thus if interest is at six percent the amount is 1.06. By setting 1.06 of the C scale in line with the left-hand 1 of the D scale you will find that all values on the C scale, when properly pointed, are 6 percent more than those on the D scale, thus equalling the required amount.

Denominate Numbers

The principle of proportion is used in making reductions of weights and measures, etc. Thus if you set the left-hand index in line with the 12 on the D scale, you will be able to read values in feet on the C scale and the equivalent values in inches on the D scale.

When reductions of single units would involve values difficult to find on the rule, it is more convenient to use a conversion table such as is printed here. Thus, 1 yard equals .914 meters, which is a value difficult to set. The conversion table tells you that 35 yards equal 32 meters. If you set 35 on the C scale in line with 32 on the D scale, all the values on the C scale represent yards and all the markings on the D scale represent the equivalent values reduced to meters.

CONVERSION TABLE

Inches : millimeters :: 5 : 127
Feet : meters :: 292 : 89
Yards : meters :: 35 : 32
Miles : kilometers :: 87 : 140
Sq. inches : sq. centimeters :: 31 : 20
Sq. feet : sq. meters :: 140 : 13
Sq. yards : sq. meters :: 61 : 51
Cu. inches : cu. centimeters :: 36 : 590
Cu. feet : cu. meters :: 100 : 3
Cu. inches : gallons :: 6700 : 29
Cu. feet : gallons :: 234 : 1750
Cu. feet : liters :: 3 : 85
Pounds : kilograms :: 280 : 127
Tons : metric tons :: 62 : 63

Inverse Proportion

The CI scale enables us to solve problems in inverse proportion because the values which it shows represent the denominators of fractions that have 1 for a numerator. That is to say, 2 on the CI scale represents $\frac{1}{2}$, 3 represents $\frac{1}{3}$, 4 represents $\frac{1}{4}$, etc. An inverse ratio between whole numbers is thus automatically transformed into a direct ratio between fractions. Accordingly, problems having to do with gears and pulleys as well as work problems are solved very easily.

EXAMPLE: A gear of 40 teeth is meshed with one of 64 teeth. The smaller gear is making 128 revolutions. At what rate is the larger one revolving?

PROCEDURE: As the larger gear will make the fewer revolutions, we want the fourth term of the proportion $\frac{1}{40}:\frac{1}{64}::128:?$. We set 40 on CI in line with 128 on D. As the answer lies beyond the limits of the rule, we mark with the hairline the position of the right-hand

index and move the left-hand index to this position. We then find 64 on CI and directly in line with it on D we get the answer, 80.

It should be noted that since the values on CI are the reciprocals of those on D, the two scales in their normal position give direct readings of decimal equivalents of fractions. Thus 2 on CI (representing $\frac{1}{2}$) is in line with 5 on D (representing .5); 14 on CI ($\frac{1}{14}$) is in line with 714 (.714), etc.

Practice Exercise No. 60

Solve the following proportions.

1 2:17::14:?
2 24:16::?:256
3 27:?::36:97.2
4 ?:34.1::97:106.7
5 23:4.37::105:?
6 $\frac{1}{4}:\frac{1}{5}::25:?$
7 $\frac{1}{19}:\frac{1}{17}::?:95$
8 256:64::$\frac{1}{5}$:?
9 43:?::$\frac{1}{2}:\frac{1}{8}$
10 ?:$\frac{3}{4}$::.33$\frac{1}{3}$:2

11 How many yards are in 160 meters?
12 How many kilometers are in 609 miles?
13 How many square centimeters are in 1550 square inches?
14 How many cubic feet are in a barrel of 31$\frac{1}{2}$ gallons?
15 How many kilograms are in a long ton?

COMBINED PROCESSES

When a problem involves a combination of multiplications and divisions it will usually be found more convenient to do division and multiplication alternately rather than to perform all the multiplications first and then to do all the divisions.

EXAMPLE: Simplify $\dfrac{32 \times 2.5 \times 5.4 \times 1.8}{72 \times 4 \times 4.5 \times 3}$

PROCEDURE: First divide 32 by 72 by setting 72 on the C scale in line with 32 on the D scale and moving the runner to bring the hairline over the right-hand index.

We do not need to note this value, but to multiply it by 2.5 we again move the runner so that it marks the position of 2.5 on C.

To divide by 4 the value thus indicated we bring 4 on C under the hairline and then move the runner to mark the position of the right-hand index.

To multiply this value by 5.4 we do not have to change the setting of the rule but simply move the runner to mark the position of 5.4.

We divide by 4.5 by bringing 4.5 on C under the hairline.

We multiply by 1.8 by moving the runner to mark the right-hand index, moving the slide so that the left-hand index comes into this position, and then finding 1.8 on C. We mark this position with the hairline.

We divide by 3 by bringing 3 on C under the hairline. Then in line with the left-hand index we find the final answer, 2. As for decimal pointing we note that 32 is contained in 72 approximately $2\frac{1}{2}$ times so that 32×2.5 and 72 will cancel each other. Taking what is left 5×2 or 10 divided by $4 \times 5 \times 3$ or 60 equals $\frac{1}{6}$ or .16; hence the correct answer 2 must represent .2.

Practice Exercise No. 61

Find the decimal equivalents of:

1	$\frac{1}{7}$	4	$\frac{1}{13}$	7	$\frac{1}{21}$	10	$\frac{1}{27}$
2	$\frac{1}{9}$	5	$\frac{1}{17}$	8	$\frac{1}{23}$	11	$\frac{1}{28}$
3	$\frac{1}{11}$	6	$\frac{1}{19}$	9	$\frac{1}{26}$	12	$\frac{1}{29}$

Simplify the following:

13 $\dfrac{88 \times 2 \times 9 \times 5}{15 \times 4}$　　　16 $\dfrac{2.1 \times 7 \times 5 \times 3.3}{1.1 \times 24 \times 30 \times 28}$

14 $\dfrac{3 \times 11 \times 2 \times .8}{4 \times 9 \times 3 \times 6}$　　　17 $\dfrac{6.6 \times 2.9 \times 25 \times 6}{3 \times .022 \times 12 \times 2}$

15 $\dfrac{7.9 \times 6 \times 21 \times 2}{5 \times 1.2 \times 15 \times 14}$

SQUARES AND SQUARE ROOTS

The A scale in combination with the D scale is used for calculating squares and square roots. The A scale, it will be noted, consists of two sections that exactly repeat each other.

To square a number, leave the rule in its normal position. Find the given number on the D scale, move the runner into this position and look on the A scale for the answer. Thus we find that 2 on D lines up with its square, 4, on A; 3 on D lines with 9; 4 with 16; etc.

To find a square root reverse this process, but bear in mind that the values on the second half of the A scale are ten times those on the first half. Hence this rule will apply: *if the given number has an odd number of digits before the decimal point, take it on the left half of the A scale; if the number of digits is even, take it on the right half.*

EXAMPLE: What is the square root of the perfect square 18769?

PROCEDURE: As the given number has an odd number of digits, we take it on the left half of the A scale. We set the runner to mark the first three significant figures, which we interpret as 188. We know that the root must consist of three significant figures, the last of which is either a 3 or a 7. Hence, the D scale gives a reading of 137.

Practice Exercise No. 62

1	$29^2 = ?$	6	$.72^2 = ?$	12	$\sqrt{5476} = ?$
2	$37^2 = ?$	7	$.83^2 = ?$	13	$\sqrt{20.25} = ?$
3	$48^2 = ?$	8	$.099^2 = ?$	14	$\sqrt{43.56} = ?$
4	$53^2 = ?$	9	$\sqrt{676} = ?$	15	$\sqrt{6.889} = ?$
5	$6.7^2 = ?$	10	$\sqrt{2209} = ?$	16	$\sqrt{.9216} = ?$
		11	$\sqrt{3364} = ?$		

CUBES AND CUBE ROOTS

The K scale is used with the D scale for cubes and cube roots. The K scale has three identical main divisions. To cube a number take it on D and read the answer on K.

To find the cube root of a number take it on K and read the result on D. Use the first third of K if the number of digits before the decimal point in the given number belongs in the arithmetic series 1, 4, 7, etc.; use the middle third if the number of digits conforms to 2, 5, 8, etc.; use the last third if the number of digits is 3, 6, 9, etc.

Practice Exercise No. 62a

1	$9^3 = ?$	6	$.83^3 = ?$	12	$\sqrt[3]{103823}$
2	$13^3 = ?$	7	$.91^3 = ?$	13	$\sqrt[3]{226.981}$
3	$17^3 = ?$	8	$.016^3 = ?$	14	$\sqrt[3]{300.763}$
4	$21^3 = ?$	9	$\sqrt[3]{13824}$	15	$\sqrt[3]{30.0763}$
5	$7.8^3 = ?$	10	$\sqrt[3]{46656}$	16	$\sqrt[3]{3.00763}$
		11	$\sqrt[3]{4096}$		

PROBLEMS INVOLVING THE CIRCLE

Problems having to do with circles are worked out on the A and B scales. It will be noted that both these scales indicate the exact position of π.

It should also be noted that there is a vertical mark on the right-hand A and B scales to indicate .7854, this being equal to $\dfrac{\pi}{4}$. This figure is used to determine the area of circles.

The usual formula is $A = \pi R^2$ but for the purposes of the slide rule this is converted to $A = D^2 \times \dfrac{\pi}{4}$.

To find the area of a circle 4 inches in diameter, set the right-hand index over 4 on the D scale; find .7854 on the B scale and read the answer 12.6 in line with this on the A scale. The explanation is that when the index is set on 4 on D it is also in line with the square of 4, 16, on A, and the position then of .7854 indicates the necessary multiplication.

Practice Exercise No. 63

1　Circumference = 101, diameter = ?
2　Diameter = 4.76; circumference = ?
3　Circumference = 1.71; diameter = ?
4　Diameter = 6.28; circumference = ?
5　Diameter = 25; area = ?

CHAPTER THIRTEEN

NUMBER SERIES

A **number series**, or **progression**, is a sequence of numbers arranged according to a definite pattern.

A series is **ascending** if the numbers increase from first to last, as in *1, 3, 5, 7, 9.*

A series is **descending** if the numbers decrease from first to last, as in *12, 10, 8, 6, 4.*

Three main kinds of number series, named according to the nature of the pattern, are arithmetic, geometric and miscellaneous. A series of any of these kinds may be ascending or descending.

An **arithmetic series** is one in which the successive numbers are formed by addition or subtraction. *1, 3, 5, 7, 9, 11 . . .* is an *arithmetic series* based on adding *2* to each term to make the next term.

A **geometric series** is one in which the successive numbers are formed by multiplication or division. *2, 4, 8, 16, 32, 64 . . .* is a *geometric series* in which each term is multiplied by *2* to make the next term.

A **miscellaneous series** is one in which the successive numbers are of a varied arithmetic or geometric pattern, or of a combination of patterns. *2, 4, 7, 9, 12, 14, 17 . . .* is a *miscellaneous arithmetic series* in which first *2* is added, then *3*, then *2*, then *3*, etc.

SOLVING SERIES PROBLEMS

In series problems you are generally required to add more terms to the series, to prefix numbers before the first term, to find a missing term, or to find the sum of the terms.

The secret of solving any kind of a series is to analyze the pattern—determine "how it goes"—by inspection. There are, however, rules of procedure that can be followed.

ARITHMETIC SERIES

To find missing terms in an ascending arithmetic series, *subtract any term from the next term to get the* DIFFERENCE *or* INCREMENT. *Then add the increment to the term before any missing term to obtain the latter.*

EXAMPLE 1: Supply the two missing terms in 1, 4, 7, 10, 13, —, —.

SOLUTION: The difference between successive terms is 3. Hence:

$$13 + 3 = 16$$
$$16 + 3 = 19$$ ANS.

To find the missing terms in a descending arithmetic series, *subtract any term from the preceding term to get the difference. Then subtract the difference from the term before any missing term to obtain the latter.*

EXAMPLE 2: Supply the two missing terms in 14, 11, 8, 5, —, —.

SOLUTION: $14 - 11 = 3,$
$5 - 3 = 2$
$2 - 3 = -1$ ANS.

To find a given term in an arithmetic series, *determine the difference; multiply the difference by the number of terms minus 1; add the first term to the product.*

EXAMPLE 3: Find the 10th term in this series. 3, 6, 9, 12, —

SOLUTION: Difference = 3;

No. of terms minus 1 = (10 − 1)
$9 \times 3 = 27, 27 + 3 = 30,$ ANS.

CHECK: 3, 6, 9, 12, 15, 18, 21, 24, 27, 30.

To find the sum of an arithmetic series, *divide the number of terms by 2 and multiply this by the sum of the first and last term.*

Formula: $S = \dfrac{n(a + l)}{2}$, in which S is the sum, n is the number of terms, a is the first term and l is the last term.

EXAMPLE 4: What is the sum of the numbers from 1 through 10?

SOLUTION:

Substituting for n, a and l in the formula we arrive at

$$S = \frac{10(1 + 10)}{2} = \frac{110}{2} = 55, \quad \text{Ans.}$$

CHECK:

$$1 + 2 + 3 + 4 + 5 + 6 + 7 + 8 + 9 + 10 = 55$$

GEOMETRIC SERIES

To find missing terms in a geometric series, *divide any term by the preceding term to find the multiplier or the ratio. Then multiply any term by the ratio to obtain the next term. Or, divide any term by the ratio to find the preceding term.*

EXAMPLE 5: Supply the missing terms in this series: —, 3, 6, 12, 24, 48, —.

SOLUTION: $6 \div 3 = 2$, the ratio.

$\left. \begin{array}{l} 48 \times 2 = 96, \text{ last term,} \\ 3 \div 2 = 1\frac{1}{2}, \text{ first term,} \end{array} \right\}$ Ans.

To find the sum of a geometric series, *multiply the last term by the ratio, subtract the first term from this product, and divide the remainder by the ratio minus 1.*

Formula: $S = \dfrac{rl - a}{r - 1}$, in which S is the sum, r is the ratio, a is the first term and l is the last term.

EXAMPLE: What is the sum of the series 4, 16, 64, . . . 1024?

SOLUTION: Substituting for r, l and a in the formula we arrive at

$$S = \frac{(4 \times 1024) - 4}{4 - 1} = \frac{4092}{3} = 1364, \quad \text{Ans.}$$

Practice Exercise No. 64

Write the two numbers that should follow:

1 1, 4, 7, 10, 13, 16, ____, ____.
2 2, 2, 3, 3, 4, 4, ____, ____.
3 1, 6, 2, 6, 3, 6, ____, ____.
4 1, 8, 16, 23, 31, 38, ____, ____.
5 98, 88, 79, 69, 60, 50, ____, ____.
6 34, 33, 31, 28, 24, 19, ____, ____.
7 3, 7, 4, 8, 5, 9, ____, ____.
8 7, 12, 10, 15, 13, 18, ____, ____.
9 2, 4, 8, 16, 32, 64, ____, ____.
10 96, 48, 46, 23, 21, $10\frac{1}{2}$, ____, ____.
11 4, 7, 13, 22, 34, 49, ____, ____.
12 9, 16, 25, 36, 49, 64, ____, ____.
13 256, 196, 144, 100, 64, 36, ____, ____.
14 6, 14, 7, 15, $7\frac{1}{2}$, $15\frac{1}{2}$, ____, ____.
15 2, 12, 6, 36, 18, 108, ____, ____.

Find the sums of the following series.

16 2, 4, 6, 8, 10, 12, 14
17 21, 24, 27, 30, 33, 36, 39, 42
18 4, 8, 12, 16, 20 . . . 100
19 2, 4, 8, 16, 32, 64, 128
20 3, 9, 27 . . . 6561
21 5, 5^2, 5^3 . . . 5^6

Further topics in algebra are covered in INTERMEDIATE ALGEBRA AND ANALYTIC GEOMETRY MADE SIMPLE and ADVANCED ALGEBRA AND CALCULUS MADE SIMPLE in this same MADE SIMPLE series of books.

CHAPTER FOURTEEN

GEOMETRY

DEFINITIONS AND TERMS

Elementary geometry is the branch of mathematics that deals with space relationships.

Application of the principles of geometry requires an ability to use arithmetic and elementary algebra as taught in the previous sections of this book. A knowledge of geometry in addition to simple algebra and arithmetic is basic to so many occupations (carpentry, stone-masonry, dress design, hat design, display design, sheet metal work, machine-shop work, tool-making, architecture, drafting, engineering, etc.) that no serious student should be without it.

A **geometric figure** is a point, line, surface, solid, or any combination of these.

A **point** is the *position* of the intersection of two lines. It is *not* considered to have length, breadth, or thickness.

A **line** is the intersection of two surfaces. It has *length* but neither breadth nor thickness. It may be *straight, curved,* or *broken.*

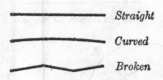

Straight

Curved

Broken

A **surface** has *two* dimensions: *length* and *breadth.* A *flat* surface may be called a **plane.**

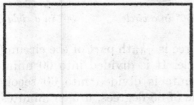

Plane Surface

A **solid** has *three* dimensions: *length, breadth,* and *thickness.*

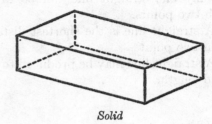

Solid

In solving geometric problems we apply certain general principles called **theorems.** These are systematically demonstrated by means of more basic principles called *axioms* and *postulates.*

Different writers use these last two terms somewhat differently. We may think of the **axioms** used in geometry, however, as *basic mathematical principles* which are so elementary that they cannot be demonstrated by means of still simpler principles. They were once widely called "self-evident truths." Note that the first seven "axioms" listed below are the principles with which you have already become familiar in performing operations upon algebraic equations (Chapter Eight).

The **postulates** used in geometry are of two different, but closely related, kinds. Some are merely restatements of more general mathematical axioms in specific geometric terms. Others are axiom-like statements which apply only to geometry. For instance, the last three "axioms" below may also be thought of as *geometric postulates.*

AXIOMS

1. Things equal to the same thing are equal to each other.

2. If equals are added to equals, the sums are equal.

3. If equals are subtracted from equals, the remainders are equal.

4. If equals are multiplied by equals, the products are equal.

5. If equals are divided by equals, the quotients are equal.

6. The whole is greater than any of its parts, and is equal to the sum of all its parts.

7. A quantity may be substituted for an equal one in an equation or in an inequality.

8. Only one straight line can be drawn through two points.

9. A straight line is the shortest distance between two points.

10. A straight line may be produced to any required length.

SYMBOLS

The following is a list of symbols used so frequently that they should be memorized.

=	equality sign	∠	angle
<	is less than	°	degree
>	is greater than	▱	parallelogram
∴	therefore	⊙	circle
‖	parallel	△	triangle
⊥	perpendicular	≠	unequal

LINES

A **horizontal** line is a straight line that is level with the horizon.

Horizontal

A **vertical** line is a straight line that is perpendicular to the horizon.

Vertical

Two lines are **perpendicular** to each other when the angles at which they intersect are all equal. Such lines are said to be at right angles to each other.

Perpendicular

An **oblique** line is neither horizontal nor vertical.

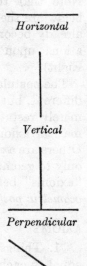

Oblique

Parallel lines are two or more straight lines which are equally distant from each other at all points and would never meet no matter how far they might be extended.

Parallel

ANGLES

An **angle** is the figure formed by two lines proceeding from a common point called the **vertex.** The lines that form an angle are called its **sides.** If three letters are used to designate an angle, the *vertex* is read between the others. Thus, Fig. 3 is written $\angle ABC$, and is read *angle ABC;* the sides are AB and BC.

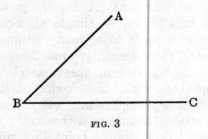

FIG. 3

In measuring an angle remember that you can think of it as composed of the spokes or radii emanating from a point (the vertex) which is at the center of a circle. As shown, there are 360 degrees around a point. The unit of measure for angles is the *degree* (°).

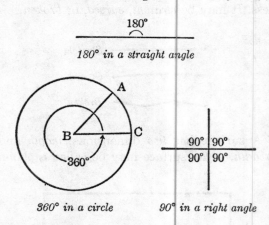

180° in a straight angle

360° in a circle   *90° in a right angle*

One degree is $\frac{1}{360}$th part of the circumference of a circle. It is divided into 60 minutes ('). The minute is divided into 60 seconds ("). An angle of 85 degrees, fifteen minutes, three seconds would be written 85° 15' 3".

A **straight angle** is one of 180°. Its two sides lie in the same straight line.

A **right angle** is one of 90°. Hence it is half a straight angle.

An **acute angle** is any angle that is less than (<) a right angle. Thus it must be less than 90°.

An **obtuse angle** is greater than (>) a right angle but less than (<) a straight angle. Hence, it must be *between 90° and 180°*.

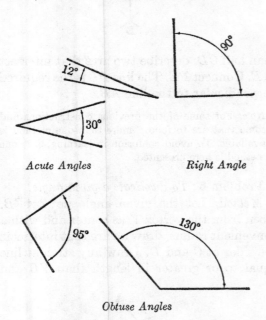

Acute Angles   *Right Angle*

Obtuse Angles

MEASURING ANGLES

Angles are measured by determining the part of a circle that the sides intersect. Therefore one measures the *opening between* the sides of an angle rather than the length of the sides. To measure or lay off angles one uses a protractor as shown in the illustration.

To measure an angle with a protractor: *Place the center of the protractor at the vertex of the angle, and the straight side on a line with one side of the angle. Read the degrees where the other side of the angle crosses the scale of the protractor.*

To draw an angle with a protractor: *Draw a straight line for one side of the angle. Place the center of the protractor at the point of the line that is to be the vertex of the angle, and make the straight side of the protractor coincide with the line. Place a dot on your paper at the*

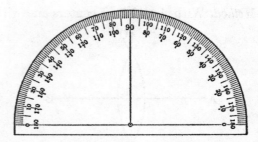

Protractor for Measuring and Laying off Angles

point on the scale of the protractor that corresponds to the size of the angle to be drawn. Connect this dot and the vertex to obtain the desired angle.

Practice Exercise No. 65

1 Draw a straight angle.
2 Draw a right angle.
3 Draw an acute angle of 30°.
4 Draw an obtuse angle of 120°.

Use the diagram for the following problems.

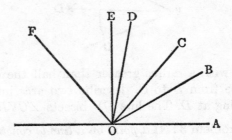

5   Measure angle *AOB*.
6   Measure angle *AOC*.
7   Measure angle *AOD*.
8   Measure ∠ *AOE*.
9   Measure ∠ *AOF*.
10 Measure ∠ *BOF*.
11 Measure ∠ *BOD*.

GEOMETRICAL CONSTRUCTIONS

Geometrical constructions, in the strict sense, involve only the use of a straight-edge (un-scaled ruler) and a pair of compasses. These are the only instruments needed to carry out the following constructions. Of course, in actual mechanical drawing the draftsman is not thus limited.

Problem 1: *To bisect a straight line.* (Bisect means to divide in half.)

Method: With *A* and *B* as centers and with

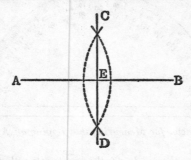

a radius greater than half the line *AB*, draw arcs intersecting at points *C* and *D*. Draw *CD*, which bisects *AB* at *E*. (It should be noted that *CD* is perpendicular to *AB*.)

Problem 2: *To bisect any angle.*

Method: With the vertex as center and any radius draw an arc cutting the sides of the angle at *B* and *C*. With *B* and *C* as centers

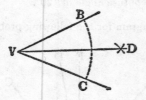

and with a radius greater than half the distance from *B* to *C*, describe two arcs intersecting at *D*. The line *DV* bisects ∠*CVB*.

Problem 3: *At a point on a line to construct a perpendicular to the line.*

Method: From point *P* as center with any radius describe an arc which cuts the line *AB* at *M* and *N*. From *M* and *N* as centers

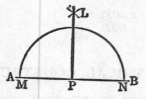

and with a radius greater than *MP*, describe arcs which intersect at *L*. Draw the line *PL*, which is the required perpendicular.

Problem 4: *From a given point away from a straight line to drop a perpendicular to the line.*

Method: From the given point *P* as center and with a large enough radius describe an

arc which cuts line *AB* at *C* and *D*. From *C* and *D* as centers and with a radius greater

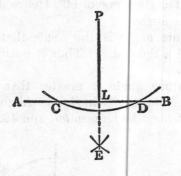

than half *CD*, describe two arcs that intersect at *E*. Connect *PE*. The line *PL* is the required perpendicular to the line *AB*.

> *Note:* For some of the previous constructions and some that are to follow, more than one method is available. To avoid confusion in learning, only one method is here presented.

Problem 5: *To duplicate a given angle.*

Method: Let the given angle be ∠*AVB*. Then from the vertex *V* as center and with a convenient radius, draw an arc that intersects the sides at *C* and *D*. Draw any straight line equal to or greater in length than *VB* and

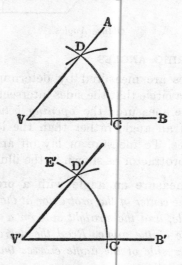

call it *V'B'*. (Read *V prime B prime*.) With *V'* as center and with the same radius, describe an arc *C'E* that cuts the line at *C'*. From *C'* as center and with a radius equal to *DC*, describe an arc intersecting arc *C'E* at *D'*. Draw *D'V'*. ∠*D'V'C'* is the required angle.

Problem 6: *To duplicate a given triangle.*
Method: Draw any straight line from any point D as center, and with a radius equal to

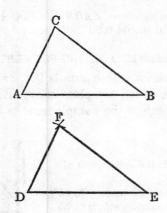

AB lay off DE equal to AB. With E as center and BC as radius, draw an arc. With D as center and AC as radius, draw an arc which intersects the other arc at F. Draw FE and FD. DEF is the required triangle.

Problem 7: *To construct a line parallel to a given line at a given distance.*
Method: If the given line is AD and the given distance is one inch, then at any two points C and D on the given line AB erect perpendiculars to AB. (See Problem 3.) With

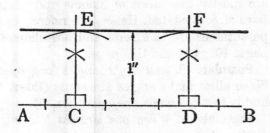

C and D as centers and with a radius equal to one inch, describe arcs cutting the perpendiculars at E and F. Draw the line EF, which is the required parallel line at a distance of one inch from AB.

Problem 8: *To divide a line into a given number of equal parts.*
Method: If AB is the given line, and if it is to be divided into six parts, then draw line AC making an angle (most conveniently an acute angle) with AB. Starting at A mark off on AC with a compass six equal divisions of

any convenient length. Connect the last point I with B. Through points D, E, F, G and H

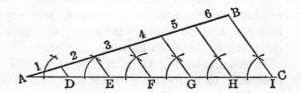

draw lines parallel to IB by making equal angles. The parallel lines divide AB into six equal parts.

Problem 9: *To find the center of a circle or arc of a circle.*
Method: Draw any two chords AB and DE. Draw the perpendicular bisectors of

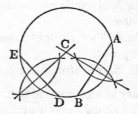

these chords. (See Problem 1.) The point C where they intersect is the center of the circle or arc.

Problem 10: *To inscribe a regular hexagon in a circle.*

Note: A regular hexagon is a polygon with six equal sides and six equal angles. The length of a side of a hexagon is equal to the radius of a circle circumscribing it.

Method: The radius of the circle is equal to AG. Starting at any point on the circle and using the length of the radius as the

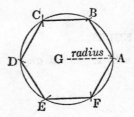

distance, lay off successive points B, C, D, E, F on the circumference of the circle. Connect the points with straight lines to obtain the required hexagon.

LINE AND ANGLE RELATIONSHIPS

Having learned some basic geometric definitions, axioms and constructions, you are now prepared to understand some important relationships between lines and angles.

In demonstrating these relationships it is necessary to introduce additional *definitions, postulates, propositions, theorems* and *corollaries*.

For example, the following are important *postulates*.

Postulate 1. *A geometric figure may be moved from one place to another without changing its size or shape.*

Postulate 2. *Two angles are equal if they can be made to coincide.*

Postulate 3. *A circle can be drawn with any point as center.*

Postulate 4. *Two straight lines can intersect in only one point.*

Postulate 5. *All straight angles are equal.*

A **corollary** is a geometric truth that follows from one previously given and needs little or no proof.

For example, from Postulate 3 above we derive the *corollary:*

Corollary 1. *An arc of a circle can be drawn with any point as center.*

Adjacent angles are angles that have a common vertex and a common side between them.

For example, ∠CPB is *adjacent* to ∠BPA but not to ∠DRC.

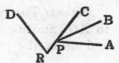

ADDING ANGLES

Postulate 6. *Adjacent angles can be added.* Thus:

∠AOB + ∠BOC
  = ∠AOC.
∠DOC + ∠COB
  + ∠BOA
  = ∠DOA.
∠EOD + ∠DOC + ∠COB = ∠EOB.

Postulate 7. *The sum of all the adjacent angles about a point on one side of a straight line is equal to one straight angle.* Thus:

If you measure ∠AOB + ∠BOC + ∠COD + ∠DOE, it should total 180°. Does it?

COMPLEMENTS AND SUPPLEMENTS

Two angles whose sum is 90°, or one right angle, are called **complementary**. Each of the angles is called the **complement** of the other. *Thus:*

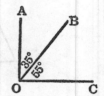

∠AOB is the *complement* of
  ∠BOC,
or 35° is *complementary* to 55°,
or 55° is *complementary* to 35°.

Two angles whose sum is 180° or a straight angle are said to be **supplementary** to each other. *Thus:*

∠AOC is the *supple-
  ment* of ∠COB,
or 150° is *supple-
  mentary* to 30°,
or 30° is *supplementary* to 150°.

The postulates that follow concerning complementary and supplementary angles are mostly corollaries of axioms and postulates already stated. Hence, the references in parentheses are to axioms and postulates on pages 103, 104 and this page.

Postulate 8. *All right angles are equal.* Since all straight angles are equal (Post. 5) and halves of equals are equal (Ax. 5).

Postulate 9. *When one straight line meets another, two supplementary angles are formed.*

∠1 + ∠2 =
∠AOB which is
a straight angle.
(Ax. 6)

Postulate 10. *Complements of the same angle or of equal angles are equal.* (Ax. 3)

Postulate 11. *Supplements of the same angle or of equal angles are equal.* (Ax. 3)

Postulate 12. *If two adjacent angles have their exterior sides in a straight line, they are supplementary.*

Postulate 13. *If two adjacent angles are supplementary, their exterior sides are in the same straight line.*

Vertical angles are the pairs of opposite angles formed by the intersection of straight lines. *Thus:*

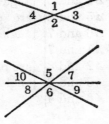

∠1 and ∠2 are *vertical angles.* ∠5 and ∠6 are *vertical angles.* What other pairs are vertical angles?

THE METHOD OF DEMONSTRATION IN GEOMETRY

A **proposition** is a statement of either a *theorem* or a *problem.*

A **theorem** is a relationship to be demonstrated.

A **problem** is a construction to be made.

In proving theorems or the correctness of constructions, the procedure is as follows.

If the proposition is a *theorem* requiring proof, you break it up into its two parts: the *hypothesis* and the *conclusion.* In the *hypothesis* certain facts are assumed. You use these given facts in conjunction with other previously accepted geometric propositions to prove the conclusion.

If the proposition is a *problem,* you make the construction and then proceed to prove that it is correct. You do this by listing the given elements and bringing forward previously established geometric facts to build up the necessary proof of correctness.*

For example, let us take the statement, *vertical angles are equal.* This theorem is given as Proposition No. 1 in many geometry textbooks, and is presented as follows.

* This is the method of procedure followed in most geometry textbooks for demonstrating the truth of established geometric principles. For the purposes of this book, however, it will not be necessary to give formal demonstrations of theorems and problems. It is our purpose to give you a working knowledge of the essential geometric principles, facts and skills that can be put to practical application in office and in shop, in following military pursuits, in indulging a hobby, or in studying higher mathematics as presented in this book and in other more advanced textbooks.

Given: Vertical angles 1 and 2 as in the diagram next to the definition of vertical angles.

To prove: ∠1 = ∠2.

Steps	*Reasons*
1. ∠2 is the supplement of ∠3.	1. Two angles are supplementary if their sum is a straight ∠.
2. ∠1 is the supplement of ∠3.	2. Same as Reason 1.
3. ∠1 = ∠2.	3. Supplements of the same ∠ are equal. (Post. 4)

ABBREVIATIONS

The following abbreviations are used:

adj.	adjacent	def.	definition
alt.	alternate	ext.	exterior
	altitude	hyp.	hypotenuse
ax.	axiom	iden.	identity
comp.	complementary	int.	interior
cong.	congruent	rt.	right
const.	construction	st.	straight
cor.	corollary	supp.	supplementary
corr.	corresponding	vert.	vertical

It should also be noted that the plurals of a number of the symbols listed on page 104 are formed by inserting an *s* in the symbol. Thus, ∠ means angles; ⧍, triangles; |S|, parallels; ⊙, circles; ▱, parallelograms, etc.

Practice Exercise No. 66

1 ∠1 coincides with ∠2. ∠1 = 30°. Find ∠2.

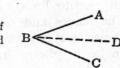

2 *BD* is the bisector of ∠*ABC*, which is 45°. Find ∠*ABD*.

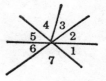

3 ∠1 = ∠5, ∠2 = ∠1 and ∠3 = ∠5. What is the relationship between:

(a) ∠1 and ∠3
(b) ∠2 and ∠5
(c) ∠4 and ∠7

4 In the same figure list the pairs of adj. ∠.

5 In the same figure list the pairs of vertical angles.

6 In the accompanying figure the opposite ∡ are vertical ∡; ∠1 = 30° and ∠3 = 100°. Find the remaining four angles.

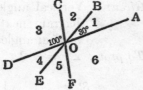

7 In the same figure find the values of ∠AOC, ∠AOD, ∠BOE and ∠FOB.

8 How many degrees are there in (a) ¾ of a rt. ∠, (b) ⅔ rt. ∠, (c) ½ rt. ∠, (d) ⅓ rt. ∠, (e) ¼ rt. ∠?

9 Find the complement of (a) 68°, (b) 45°, (c) 55°, (d) 32°, (e) 5°, (f) 33° 30′.

10 What is the supplement of (a) 25°, (b) 125°, (c) 44°, (d) 88°, (e) 74° 30′, (f) 78° 30′?

PARALLEL LINES

Postulates Concerning Parallels

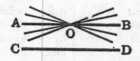

1. Through a given point only one line can be drawn parallel to a given line.

In the diagram, the only line that can be drawn ∥ to *CD* through point *O* is *AB*.

2. Two intersecting lines cannot both be parallel to a third straight line.

3. Two straight lines in the same plane, if produced, either will intersect or else are parallel.

Definitions

A **transversal** is a line that intersects two or more other lines.

When a **transversal** cuts two parallel or intersecting lines, various angles are formed. The names and relative positions of these angles are important. The relationship of angles as shown in the following diagram should be memorized.

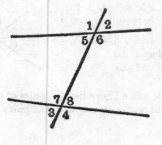

∡1, 2, 3, 4 are termed **exterior** angles.

∡5, 6, 7, 8 are termed **interior** angles.

∡1 and 4 | are pairs of **alternate exterior**
∡2 and 3 | angles.

∡5 and 8 | are pairs of **alternate interior**
∡6 and 7 | angles.

∡1 and 7 |
∡2 and 8 | are pairs of **corresponding**
∡5 and 3 | angles.
∡6 and 4 |

Theorem 1. If two straight lines are parallel to a third straight line, they are parallel to each other.

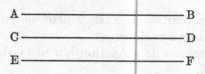

Given: *AB* and *EF* ∥ to *CD*.
To prove: *AB* ∥ *EF*.

If *AB* is not ∥ to *EF* the two lines would intersect and they would then be two intersecting lines parallel to a third straight line. But this is impossible according to Parallel Postulate 2. Hence *AB* must be parallel to *EF*.

Relationships Formed by Parallels and a Transversal

If two parallel lines are cut by a transversal, certain definite relationships will always be found to exist among the angles that are formed by the parallel lines and the transversal.

If we take the rectangle *ABCD*, we know that the opposite sides are parallel and equal and that all the angles are right angles. If we then draw the diagonal *DB* we have formed two triangles, △*DAB* and △*DCB*.

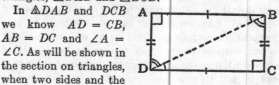

In △*DAB* and *DCB* we know *AD* = *CB*, *AB* = *DC* and ∠*A* = ∠*C*. As will be shown in the section on triangles, when two sides and the included ∠ of one △ are equal to two sides and the included ∠ of another, the two triangles are said to be congruent. This means that all their corresponding sides and angles are equal. (In the diagram the corresponding sides and angles of each triangle are marked with matched check marks.)

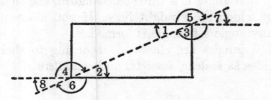

If we extend lines AB and CD, we have two ∥ lines cut by a transversal. We number the related angles for convenience, and the following relationships become evident.

∠1 = ∠2 (Corr. ⊿ of cong. ⧍.)
∠1 = ∠7 and ∠2 = ∠8 (Vert. ⊿ are equal.)
∴ ∠7 = ∠8 = ∠1 = ∠2 (Things = to the same thing are = to each other.)

∠5 is supp. ∠7 (Ext. sides form a st. ∠.)
∴ ∠6 = ∠4 and ∠3 = ∠5 (Vert. ⊿ are equal.)
∴ ∠3 = ∠6, ∠5 = ∠6 and ∠3 = ∠4 (Things = to the same thing are = to each other. Ax. 1.)

Presenting the above conclusions verbally, the angle relationships that occur when two parallel lines are cut by a transversal may be stated as follows.

1. The alternate interior angles are equal.

∠1 = ∠2, and ∠3 = ∠4

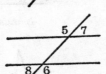

2. The alternate exterior angles are equal.

∠5 = ∠6, and ∠7 = ∠8

3. The corresponding angles are equal.

∠4 = ∠5, ∠3 = ∠6,   ∠2 = ∠7, ∠1 = ∠8

4. The two interior angles on the same side of a transversal are supplementary.

∠1 supp. ∠4, and ∠3 supp. ∠2

5. The two exterior angles on the same side of a transversal are supplementary.

∠5 supp. ∠8, and ∠7 supp. ∠6

These angle relationships may now be employed to prove that certain straight lines are parallel. Such proofs are represented by the *converses* of statements 1 to 5, in the form of the following theorems.

Theorems on Parallel Lines

Two lines are parallel if:

Theorem 2. *A transversal to the lines makes a pair of alternate interior angles equal.*

Theorem 3. *A transversal to the lines makes a pair of alternate exterior angles equal.*

Theorem 4. *A transversal to the lines makes a pair of corresponding angles equal.*

Theorem 5. *A transversal to the lines makes a pair of interior angles on the same side of the transversal supplementary.*

Theorem 6. *A transversal to the lines makes a pair of exterior angles of the same side of the transversal supplementary.*

A *corollary* that follows from these theorems is the following.

Corollary 1. *If two lines are perpendicular to a third line they are parallel.*

This can be easily proved by showing alt. int. ⊿ equal as ∠1 = ∠2, or corr. ⊿ equal, as ∠1 = ∠2, etc.

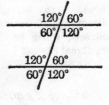

We may summarize the relationships of the angles formed by parallel lines cut by a transversal as follows:

(a) *The four acute angles formed are equal.*
(b) *The four obtuse angles formed are equal.*
(c) *Any one of the acute angles is the supplement of any one of the obtuse angles; that is, their sum equals 180°.*

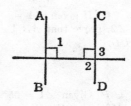

Practice Exercise No. 67

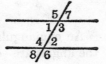

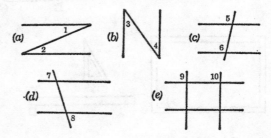

1 In the above diagram identify the kinds of angles indicated.

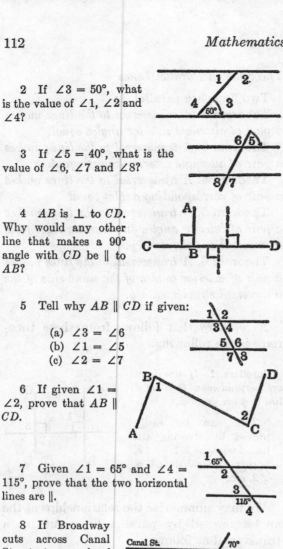

2   If $\angle 3 = 50°$, what is the value of $\angle 1$, $\angle 2$ and $\angle 4$?

3   If $\angle 5 = 40°$, what is the value of $\angle 6$, $\angle 7$ and $\angle 8$?

4   AB is $\perp$ to CD. Why would any other line that makes a 90° angle with CD be $\parallel$ to AB?

5   Tell why $AB \parallel CD$ if given:

    (a) $\angle 3 = \angle 6$
    (b) $\angle 1 = \angle 5$
    (c) $\angle 2 = \angle 7$

6   If given $\angle 1 = \angle 2$, prove that $AB \parallel CD$.

7   Given $\angle 1 = 65°$ and $\angle 4 = 115°$, prove that the two horizontal lines are $\parallel$.

8   If Broadway cuts across Canal Street at an angle of 70°, at what angle does it cut across Broome and Spring Streets, which are $\parallel$ to Canal Street?

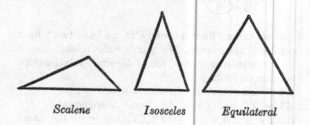

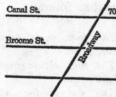

9   Given $\angle ABC = 60°$, construct a line $\parallel$ to BC using the principle of corresponding angles being equal.

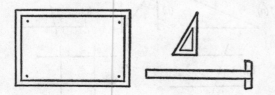

10   Using the drawing-board, T-square and triangle pictured, how would you construct two angles the sides of which are $\parallel$ to each other?

TRIANGLES

A **triangle** is a three-sided figure, the sides of which are straight lines. If you close off any angle a triangle is formed.

Triangles are classified according to their sides as *scalene, isosceles* and *equilateral.*

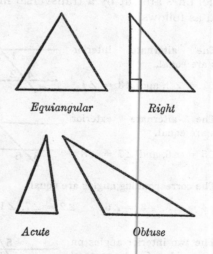

Scalene   *Isosceles*   *Equilateral*

A **scalene triangle** is one in which no two sides are equal. An **isosceles triangle** is one in which two sides are equal. An **equilateral triangle** is one with three sides equal.

Triangles may also be classified with respect to their angles as *equiangular, right, acute* and *obtuse.*

Equiangular   *Right*

Acute   *Obtuse*

An **equiangular triangle** is one in which all the angles are equal (each measuring 60°).

A **right triangle** (or *right-angled triangle*) contains one right angle (often indicated by placing a small square in the 90° angle).

An **acute triangle** is one in which all angles are less than right angles.

An **obtuse triangle** has one angle greater than a right angle.

Note that an *equiangular* triangle is always *equilateral;* a *right* triangle may be *scalene* or *isosceles;* an *acute* triangle may be *scalene, isosceles,* or *equilateral* (equiangular is merely a special case of acute); an *obtuse* triangle may be *scalene* or *isosceles.*

Note also that either the scalene or the isosceles triangle may be right, acute or obtuse. The scalene cannot be *equiangular,* but the isosceles can, since the equilateral may be considered a special type of the isosceles.

It is a basic theorem that the sum of the angles of any triangle is equal to 180°. (See Theorem 14, page 116.)

TRIANGULAR MEASUREMENT

The **height** or **altitude** of a triangle is the perpendicular distance from the base to the vertex of the opposite angle. In Fig. 4, *AC* represents height or altitude of the triangles.

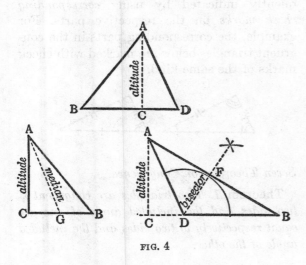

FIG. 4

A **median** is a line drawn from any vertex of a triangle to the middle of the opposite side. *AG* in Fig. 4.

The **bisector** of an angle is the line which divides it into two equal angles. *DF* bisects ∠*BDA* in Fig. 4.

The **perimeter** of any figure is *the entire distance around the figure.*

Rule: *The area of a triangle equals one half the product of the base and the height.*

Expressed as a **formula:**

$$A = \tfrac{1}{2} bh \text{ or } A = \frac{bh}{2}.$$

EXAMPLE 1: Find the area of the triangle shown.

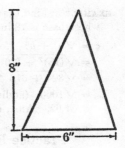

SOLUTION: $A = \dfrac{bh}{2}$

$= \dfrac{6 \times 8}{2}$

$= 24$ sq. in., ANS.

EXAMPLE 2: What is the height of a triangle if its area is 1 sq. ft. and its base 16 in.?

SOLUTION: $A = \dfrac{bh}{2}$. ∴ $h = \dfrac{2A}{b}$

$= \dfrac{2 \times 144}{16} = 18$ in., ANS.

FACTS ABOUT RIGHT TRIANGLES

The **hypotenuse** of a right triangle is the side opposite the right angle.

In the figure below it is shown that the square drawn on the hypotenuse of a right triangle is equal in area to the sum of the areas of the squares drawn on the other two sides.

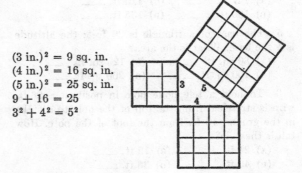

(3 in.)² = 9 sq. in.
(4 in.)² = 16 sq. in.
(5 in.)² = 25 sq. in.
9 + 16 = 25
3² + 4² = 5²

Rule: *The square of the hypotenuse of a right triangle is equal to the sum of the squares of the other two sides.*

From this there arise several self-evident formulas with reference to the right triangle.

Let *c* = hypotenuse, *a* = altitude, *b* = base; then:

Formula 1: $c^2 = a^2 + b^2$

Formula 2: $c = \sqrt{a^2 + b^2}$. (Taking the square root of both sides of the first equation.)

Formula 3: $a^2 = c^2 - b^2$; or, by transposition, $b^2 = c^2 - a^2$.

EXAMPLE 3: Find the hypotenuse of a right triangle whose base is 18 inches and altitude 26 inches.

$$c = \sqrt{a^2 + b^2} \quad \text{(formula)}$$
$$= \sqrt{(18)^2 + (26)^2} \quad \text{(substituting)}$$
$$= \sqrt{324 + 676} \quad \text{(squaring)}$$
$$= \sqrt{1000} \quad \text{(adding)}$$
$$= 31.62, \quad \text{ANS., extracting the square root.}$$

Practice Exercise No. 68

1   A derrick standing perpendicular to the ground is 45 ft. high, and is tied to a stake in the ground by a cable 51 ft. long. How far is the foot of the derrick from the stake?

(A) 68 ft. ____   (C) 24 ft. ✓
(B) 6 ft. ____   (D) 96 ft. ____

2   The base of a triangle is 18 in.; the altitude is $3\frac{1}{2}$ times the base. What is the area?

(A) 1,296 sq. in. ____   (C) 567 sq. in. ✓
(B) 600 sq. in. ____   (D) 648 sq. in. ____

3   How much will it cost to fence off an isosceles shaped lot if one side is 75 ft. and the base is 50 ft.? Fencing costs $2.00 a foot.

(A) $40.00 ____   (C) $25.00 ____
(B) $400.00 ✓   (D) $50.00 ____

4   In a square baseball field it is 90 ft. from home to first base. How far in a straight line is it from home to second base?

(A) 127 ft. ✓   (C) 120 ft. ____
(B) 180 ft. ____   (D) 135 ft. ____

5   The base of a triangle is 20 feet; the altitude is $\frac{1}{2}$ the base. What is the area?

(A) 80 sq. ft. ____   (C) 120 sq. ft. ____
(B) 100 sq. ft. ✓   (D) 200 sq. ft. ____

6   To hold a telephone pole in position a 26-ft. wire is stretched from the top of the pole to a stake in the ground 10 ft. from the foot of the pole. How tall is the pole? $\sqrt{26^2 - 10^2}$

(A) 24 ft. ✓   (C) 12 ft. ____
(B) 40 ft. ____   (D) 36 ft. ____

7   What must be the length of a ladder to reach to the top of a house 40 ft. high, if the bottom of the ladder is placed 9 ft. from the house?

(A) 36 ft. ____   (C) 41 ft. ✓ $\sqrt{40^2 + 9^2}$
(B) 45 ft. ____   (D) 54 ft. ____

8   A tree is 100 ft. in a horizontal line from a river and its base is 20 ft. above the river. It is 160 ft. high. A line from its top to the opposite shore of the river measures 500 ft. How wide is the river?

(A) 250.93 ft. ____   (C) 342.89 ft. ____
(B) 366.47 ft. ✓   (D) 329.65 ft. ____

$$(\sqrt{500^2 - 180^2}) - 100$$

DEMONSTRATING THE CONGRUENCE OF TRIANGLES

In demonstrating some fundamental re-lationships between lines and angles of tri-angles, a method of proving triangles to be *congruent* is employed.

Congruent figures are those which can be made to coincide or fit on one another. Thus if two triangles can be made to coincide in all their parts, they are said to be congruent.

The symbol for congruence is $\cong$.

In triangles that are congruent the re-spective equal angles and equal sides that would coincide if one figure were placed on top of the other, are termed **corresponding** angles and *corresponding* sides.

Corresponding parts are also called *ho-mologous* parts. From what has been said it follows that corresponding parts of congruent figures are equal.

In geometry the corresponding or homolo-gous parts of corresponding figures are fre-quently indicated by using *corresponding check marks* on the respective parts. For example, the corresponding parts in the con-gruent triangles below are marked with check marks of the same kind.

Seven Theorems on Congruence

Theorem 7. *Two triangles are congruent if two sides and the included angle of one are equal respectively to two sides and the included angle of the other.*

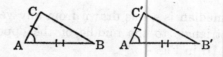

According to this theorem you are given $\angle ABC \cong \triangle A'B'C'$, with $AC = A'C'$, $AB = A'B'$ and $\angle A = \angle A'$.

If you construct the figures with the given equal parts and then place $\triangle ABC$ on $\triangle A'B'C'$ so that the given equal parts correspond, it will be seen that the third line, CB, coincides with $C'B'$, making the triangles congruent at all points. Thus all the corresponding parts not given may also be assumed to be respectively equal.

For example, construct AC and $A'C'$ to equal $\frac{3}{8}''$; $\angle A$ and $\angle A' = 60°$; AB and $A'B' = \frac{3}{4}''$.

Then measure the distances between *CB* and *C'B'*, and you will find them to be equal. If you measure ∡*C* and *C'* and ∡*B* and *B'*, you will find these pairs to be equal as well.

Proving congruence by this theorem is known as the *side angle side* method. It is abbreviated *s.a.s. = s.a.s.*

By employing a similar approach you can readily verify the following theorems on the correspondence of triangles.*

Theorem 8. *Two triangles are congruent if two angles and the included side of one are equal respectively to two angles and the included side of the other.*

This is known as the *angle side angle* theorem, and is abbreviated *a.s.a. = a.s.a.*

Theorem 9. *Two triangles are congruent if the sides of one are respectively equal to the sides of the other.*

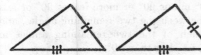

This is known as the *side side side* theorem, and is abbreviated *s.s.s. = s.s.s.*

Theorem 10. *Two triangles are congruent if a side and any two angles of one are equal to the corresponding side and two angles of the other.*

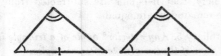

This is known as the *side angle angle* theorem, and is abbreviated *s.a.a. = s.a.a.*

Theorem 11. *Two right triangles are equal if the sides of the right angles are equal respectively.*

*Formal proofs employing geometric axioms, postulates and theorems to illustrate these cases of congruent triangles are given in regular school text-books on geometry. The student interested in academic study should refer to such books.

Since the included right angles are equal, this theorem is really a special case of *s.a.s. = s.a.s.*

Theorem 12. *Two right triangles are equal if the hypotenuse and an acute angle of one are equal to the hypotenuse and an acute angle of the other.*

Since the right angles are equal, this theorem is a special case of *s.a.a. = s.a.a.*

Theorem 13. *Two right triangles are congruent if a side and an acute angle of one are equal to a side and corresponding acute angle of the other.*

Since the right angles are equal, this is again a special case of *s.a.a. = s.a.a.*

Practice Exercise No. 69

Note: Mark corresponding parts with corresponding check marks as previously explained. Use the method of demonstration shown under Theorem 14, following lines of reasoning similar to that used in connection with Theorem 7.

1 *Given* *AB = AD*
        ∠1 = ∠2
   Prove
   △*ABC* ≅ △*ADC*

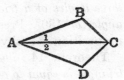

2 *Given* *BD* ⊥ *AC*
        D is the
        mid-point
        of *AC*
   Prove
   △*ABD* ≅ △*CBD*

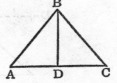

3 *Given* ∠3 = ∠5
AE is the bisector of BD

Prove
△ABC ≅ △EDC

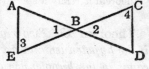

4 *Given* AD and CE bisect each other

Prove AE ∥ CD

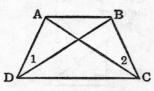

5 *Given* AD = BC
AC = BD

Prove
△BAD ≅ △ABC
and ∠1 = ∠2

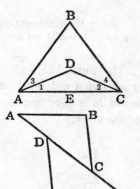

6 *Given* AB = CB
AD = CD

Prove ∠1 = ∠2
Hint: Draw BD and then extend it to meet AC at E.

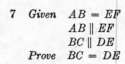

7 *Given* AB = EF
AB ∥ EF
BC ∥ DE

Prove BC = DE

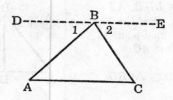

FACTS ABOUT TRIANGLES IN GENERAL

The general properties of the triangle not only form the foundation of trigonometry, but also find a wide application in the analysis and measurement of straight-sided plane figures of every kind.

One of the most important facts about triangles in general is that, regardless of the shape or size of any triangle, *the sum of the three angles of a triangle is equal to a straight angle, or 180°.* Presented as a theorem this proposition is easily proved.

Theorem 14. *The sum of the angles of a triangle is equal to a straight angle.*

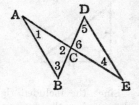

Given: △ABC.
To prove: ∠A + ∠B + ∠C = a straight angle.

Steps	Reasons
1. Through B draw DE ∥ AC.	1. Parallel postulate No. 1.
2. ∠1 = ∠A.	2. Alt. int. ⱷ of ∥ lines are =.
3. ∠2 = ∠C.	3. Same reason as 2.
4. ∠1 + ∠B + ∠2 = a straight angle.	4. By definition, since the exterior sides lie in a straight line.
5. ∴ ∠A + ∠B + ∠C = a straight angle.	5. Substituting ∠A and ∠C for ∠1 and ∠2 in step 4 by Axiom 7.

From this knowledge of the sum of the angles of a triangle the following corollaries concerning triangles in general become self-evident.

Corollary 1. *Each angle of an equiangular triangle is 60°.*

Since the angles of an equiangular triangle are equal, each angle = 180° ÷ 3, or 60°.

Corollary 2. *No triangle may have more than one obtuse angle or right angle.*

180° minus 90° or more leaves 90° or less, to be split between the two remaining angles, and therefore each of the two remaining angles must be acute, *i.e.,* less than 90°.

Corollary 3. *The acute angles of a right triangle are complementary.*

180° minus 90° leaves two angles whose sum equals 90°.

Corollary 4. *If two angles of one triangle are equal respectively to two angles of another, the third angles are equal.*

This truth is supported by Ax. 3 (page 104), namely, that if equals are subtracted from equals the remainders are equal.

Corollary 5. *Any exterior* angle of a triangle is equal to the sum of the two remote interior angles.*

* An exterior angle of a triangle is the angle formed by a side and the extension of its adjacent side. Every triangle has six exterior angles as shown in the diagram.

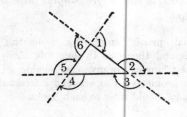

Thus in $\triangle ABC$ if you extend AC to D and draw $CE \parallel AB$, you have the two $\parallel$ lines AB and CE cut by the transversal AD. $\therefore \angle 1 = \angle B$ and $\angle 2 = \angle A$, so that $\angle 1 + \angle 2$, or $\angle BCD = \angle A + \angle B$.

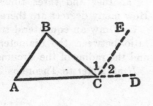

A few characteristic properties of special triangles frequently used are worth noting at this point.

Theorem 15. *The base angles of an isosceles triangle are equal.*

By definition the sides of an isosceles triangle are equal.

$\therefore$ if you draw the bisector BD of $\angle B$ it is readily seen that $\triangle ABD \cong \triangle CBD$ by s.a.s. = s.a.s. Hence $\angle A = \angle C$.

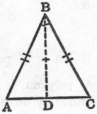

This theorem may be stated in another way, namely:

Theorem 16. *If two sides of a triangle are equal, the angles opposite those sides are equal.*

The following corollaries may readily be seen to follow from this theorem.

Corollary 1. *If two sides of a triangle are equal, the angles opposite these sides are equal and the triangle is isosceles.*

Corollary 2. *The bisector of the apex angle of an isosceles triangle is perpendicular to the base, bisects the base and is the altitude of the triangle.*

Corollary 3. *An equilateral triangle is equiangular.*

Theorem 17. *If one acute angle of a right triangle is double the other, the hypotenuse is double the shorter side.* Or

In a 30°-60° right triangle the hypotenuse equals twice the shorter side.

The following properties of bisectors, altitudes and medians of triangles are frequently applied in the practical problems of geometric design and construction that arise in shop and office.

Theorem 18. *Every point in the perpendicular bisector of a line is equidistant from the ends of that line.*

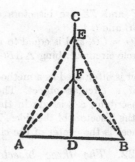

If CD is $\perp$ bisector of AB
Then $DA = DB$
       $FA = FB$, etc.

Theorem 19. *Every point in the bisector of an angle is equidistant from the sides of the angle.*

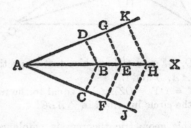

If AX is the bisector of $\angle A$
Then $BC = BD$, $EF = EG$, $HJ = HK$, etc.

Theorem 20. *The perpendicular is the shortest line that can be drawn from a point to a given line.*

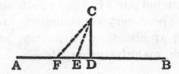

If $CD \perp AB$
Then $CD < CE$, $CD < CF$, etc.

Theorem 21. *The three bisectors of the sides of a triangle meet in one point which is equidistant from the three vertices of the triangle.*

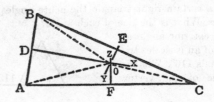

If   *DX, EY* and *FZ* are bisectors of the sides
       AB, BC and *CA*

Then   *AO = BO = CO*, and is equal to the radius of
       the circle circumscribing △*ABC*

Note: This fact is often used as a method for finding the center of a circular object. The procedure consists in inscribing a triangle in the circle and constructing the bisectors of the sides. The point at which they meet is the center of the circle.

Theorem 22. *The three bisectors of the angles of a triangle meet in one point which is equidistant from the three sides of the triangle.*

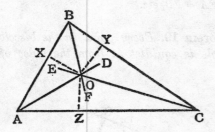

If   *AD, BF* and *CE* are bisectors respectively of
       ∡*A, B* and *C*

Then   *OX = OY = OZ*, and is equal to the radius of
       the circle inscribed in △*ABC*.

Note: This geometric theorem is employed as a method for determining the largest circular pattern that can be cut out of a triangular piece of material.

For practical purposes you should carry out the constructions involved in the theorems of this section. Check the accuracy of your constructions by determining whether the constructed parts fit the hypothesis of the theorem. These very constructions are daily applied in architecture, carpentry, art, machine work, manufacturing, etc.

Practice Exercise No. 70

1 Two angles of a triangle are 62° and 73°. What does the third angle equal?

2 How many degrees are there in the sum of the angles of a quadrilateral?

Hint: Draw the figure and then construct a diagonal.

3 What is the value of an exterior angle of an equilateral triangle?

4 In a certain right triangle the acute angles are $2x$ and $7x$. What is the size of each angle?

5 An exterior angle at the base of an isosceles triangle equals 116°. What is the value of the vertex angle?

6 In a certain triangle one angle is twice as large as another and three times as large as the third. How many degrees are there in each angle?

7 Draw an equilateral triangle and by it find the ratio between the diameter of the inscribed circle and the radius of the circumscribed circle.

Hint: Refer to Theorems 20 and 22.

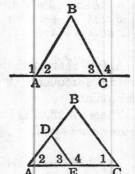

8 Given ∠1 = ∠4, prove that △*ABC* is isosceles.

9 Given *BA = BC* and *DE* ∥ *BC*, prove that *DE = DA*.

POLYGONS

A **polygon** is a plane geometric figure bounded by three or more sides. Any triangle, for instance, is a polygon.

The **vertices** of a polygon are the angle points where two sides meet.

A **diagonal** of a polygon joins two nonconsecutive vertices. How many diagonals has a triangle? None. How many diagonals can a four-sided figure have? Two.

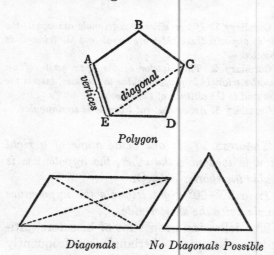

Polygon

Diagonals   *No Diagonals Possible*

Polygons derive their names from the number of and nature of the sides and the types of angles included.

Quadrilaterals are polygons with four sides. There are six types of quadrilaterals: the *rectangle*, the *square* (a special form of rectangle), the *rhomboid*, the *rhombus*, the *trapezoid* and the *trapezium*.

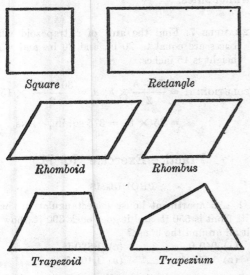

Square   Rectangle

Rhomboid   Rhombus

Trapezoid   Trapezium

TYPES OF QUADRILATERALS

A **parallelogram** is a quadrilateral in which the opposite sides are parallel and the opposite angles are equal.

A **square** is a parallelogram in which the angles are all right angles and the sides are all equal.

A **rectangle** is a parallelogram that has 4 right angles and in which opposite sides are equal.

A **rhomboid** has opposite sides parallel but no right angles.

A **rhombus** is a parallelogram having four equal sides but no right angles.

A **trapezoid** is a quadrilateral having one pair of parallel sides.

A **trapezium** is a quadrilateral in which no two sides are parallel.

(*Note:* In England these last two definitions are interchanged.)

SURFACE MEASUREMENT OF QUADRILATERALS

The **height** or **altitude** of a **parallelogram** is the distance perpendicular from the base to the opposite side.

Rule: *The area of a rectangle equals the base multiplied by the height.*
Formula: $A = bh$.

EXAMPLE 1: Find the area of a rectangle that is 3 inches high with a 4-inch base.

SOLUTION:
$A = bh$, formula.
$A = 4 \times 3 = 12$.
12 sq. inches, ANS.

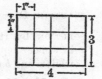

Note: The diagram has been drawn to scale on a $\frac{3}{16}$ basis. There are 4 columns and 3 rows of sq. in. units. The number of sq. in. by count is seen to be 12. The area is thus 12 sq. in.

EXAMPLE 2: Find the height of a rectangle with a 16 ft. base and an area of 80 sq. ft.

SOLUTION: $A = bh. \therefore h = \dfrac{A}{b}$
$$= \tfrac{80}{16} = 5 \text{ ft., ANS.}$$

Rule: *The area of a square is equal to the square of one of its sides.*
Formula: $A = S^2$.

EXAMPLE 3: Find the side of a square whose area is 121 sq. in.

SOLUTION: $A = S^2. \therefore \sqrt{A} = S$
$$= \sqrt{121} = 11 \text{ ft., ANS.}$$

Rule: *The perimeter of a square is equal to four times the square root of the area.*
Formula: $P = 4\sqrt{A}$ or $P = 4S$, where P = perimeter, A = area, and S = side of a square.

EXAMPLE 4: Find the perimeter of a square whose area is 144 sq. in.

SOLUTION: $P = 4\sqrt{A}, P = 4 \times 12 = 48 \text{ in., ANS.}$

Rule: *The diagonal of a square equals the square root of twice the area.*

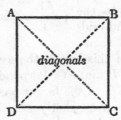

diagonals

Formula: $D = \sqrt{2A}$

Note: Check back on your right triangle formula.

EXAMPLE 5: Find the diagonal of a square if the area is 49 sq. inches.

SOLUTION: $D = \sqrt{2A}$, $D = \sqrt{98} = 9.899$, ANS.

SOLUTION by rt. triangle formula: $c^2 = a^2 + b^2$, in which c represents the diagonal or hypotenuse while a and b are the sides. Then

$$c^2 = 7^2 + 7^2, c^2 = 98$$
$$c = \sqrt{98} = 9.899, \text{ ANS.}$$

Any parallelogram can be converted to a rectangle without changing its area. This is shown in the following diagram.

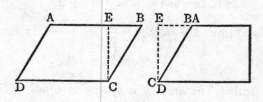

By taking the triangle *EBC* from the figure at the left and changing its position as shown in the figure at the right, we create a rectangle without adding to or deducting from the total area. Hence—

Rule: *The area of a parallelogram is equal to the product of the base times the height.*

EXAMPLE 6: Find the area of a rhomboid whose base is 12 inches and whose height is 8 inches.

SOLUTION: $A = bh$. $\therefore A = 12 \times 8 = 96$ sq. in.

Rule: *The area of a trapezoid equals half the sum of the parallel sides multiplied by the height.*

PROOF:

Make a rectangle of the trapezoid *ABCF* by drawing a line *GH* ∥ to the two ∥ sides and midway between them.

The length of this line is the average of the two ∥ sides *AB* and *FC*. Perpendiculars from the midline *GH* to the larger base *FC* cut off triangles that are exactly equal to the triangles needed above the midline to form a rectangle of the new figure.

Formula: A of trapezoid $= \dfrac{B + b}{2} \times h$, in which h is the ⊥ height and B, b are the parallel sides.

EXAMPLE 7: Find the area of a trapezoid whose bases are equal to 20 in. and 30 in. and whose height is 15 inches.

SOLUTION: $A = \dfrac{B + b}{2} \times h$; $A = \dfrac{30 + 20}{2} \times 15$

$$= 25 \times 15 = 375 \text{ sq. in., ANS.}$$

Practice Exercise No. 71

PROBLEMS

1 An apartment house is rectangular in shape. If its front is 550 ft. and it goes back 390 ft., how far is it all around the house?
(A) 940 ft. _____   (c) 1,880 ft. ✓
(B) 1,800 ft. _____   (D) 1,100 ft. _____

2 A rectangular hangar is to house an airplane. What must its area be if you desire a 20-foot allowance on all sides and if the plane is 110 feet wide by 64 feet long?
(A) 23,200 sq. ft. _____
(B) 14,420 sq. ft. _____
(c) 15,600 sq. ft. ✓
(D) 14,000 sq. ft. _____

3 How much would it cost to resurface a square plot 75 ft. long at a cost of 20¢ a sq. foot?
(A) $6,000 _____   (c) $1,000 _____
(B) $1,600 _____   (D) $1,125 ✓

4 A square field whose area is 1,024 sq. feet is to be completely covered by flagstones 4 ft. square. How many flags will be needed to cover the field?
(A) 32 _____   (c) 64 ✓
(B) 56 _____   (D) 84 _____   1024/16

5 How much barbed wire would be needed to go diagonally across a rectangular piece of land that is 66 ft. wide by 88 ft. long?
(A) 90 ft. _____   (c) 110 ft. ✓ $\sqrt{88^2 + 66^2}$
(B) 100 ft. _____   (D) 120 ft. _____

6 If you had a square frame for the floor of a tent and if it contained 288 sq. ft., how long a piece of lumber would be needed to brace the frame from one corner to the other?   DIAG
(A) 12 ft. _____   (c) 21 ft. _____
(B) 17 ft. _____   (D) 24 ft. ✓

7 If molding cost 6 cents a ft., how much would it cost to put a border of molding around a square window that had an area of 81 sq. ft.?
(A) $4.86 _____   (c) $1.08 ✓ $(4\sqrt{81}) \times .06$
(B) $.54 _____   (D) $2.16 ✓

8 What is the area of the figure shown below?

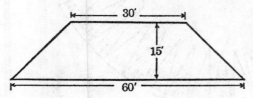

(A) 450 sq. ft. ____   (c) 750 sq. ft. ____
(B) 675 sq. ft. ✓   (D) 2,700 sq. ft. ____

9 What is the area of the figure below?

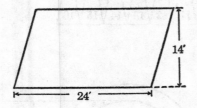

(A) 168 sq. ft. ____   (c) 76 sq. ft. ____
(B) 336 sq. ft. ✓   (D) 206 sq. ft. ____

10 What is the area of the figure to the right?

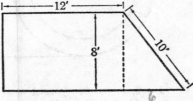

(A) 120 sq. ft. ✓   (c) 160 sq. ft. ____
(B) 140 sq. ft. ____   (D) 180 sq. ft. ____

$$\left(\frac{12 + 18}{2}\right) \times 8 = 120$$

CIRCLES

A **circle** is a curved line on which every point is equally distant from a point within called the **center**.

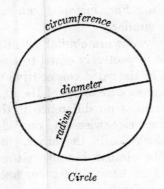

Circle

A **radius** of a circle is a line drawn from the center to the outer edge.

The **diameter** of a circle is a straight line drawn from any point on the outer edge through the center to the outer edge on the opposite side. It is equal to twice any radius.

The **circumference** of a circle is the line representing its outer edge and is equal to the complete distance around the circle. It is analogous to perimeter.

Pi, written π, is the name given to the ratio expressed by dividing the circumference of any circle by its diameter. In quantity it is a constant approximately equal to $3\frac{1}{7}$ or 3.1416. If you measure the distance around any circle, and its diameter, and then divide the distance by the diameter you will always get a result of approximately $3\frac{1}{7}$.

Formula: $\pi = \dfrac{C}{d}$, where C = circumference and d = diameter; or $\pi = \dfrac{C}{2r}$, where r = radius.

Rule: *To find the circumference of a circle multiply the diameter by π.*

Formula: $C = \pi d$; or $C = 2\pi r$.

EXAMPLE 1: The spoke of a wheel is 21 inches. Find its circumference.

SOLUTION: $C = 2\pi r$

$$= 2 \times \frac{22}{7} \times \overset{3}{2\!\!\!/1} = 132 \text{ in.,} \quad \text{ANS.}$$

EXAMPLE 2: The circumference of a pulley is 33 inches. What is its diameter?

SOLUTION: $C = \pi d, \ \therefore \ d = \dfrac{C}{\pi}$.

$$d = \frac{33}{\frac{22}{7}} = \overset{3}{3\!\!\!/3} \times \frac{7}{\underset{2}{2\!\!\!/2}} = \frac{21}{2} = 10\tfrac{1}{2} \text{ in.,} \quad \text{ANS.}$$

AREA OF A CIRCLE

Rule: *The area of a circle equals one-half the product of the circumference and the radius.*

This can be reasoned informally as follows. Any circle can be cut to form many narrow triangles as shown in Fig. 5. The altitude of each triangle would be equal to a radius r. The base would be a part of the circumference C. We know the area of each triangle

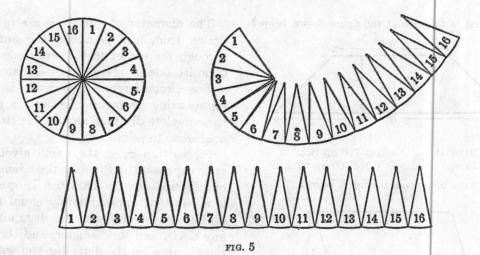

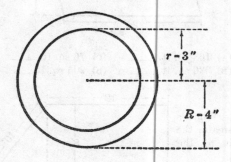

FIG. 5

to be equal to $\frac{1}{2}$ the base times the altitude. Since r is the altitude, and the sum of the bases equals the circumference, the area = $\frac{1}{2}r \times C$. Since $C = 2\pi r$, $A = \frac{1}{2}r \times 2\pi r$. $\therefore A = r \times \pi r = \pi r^2$.

Rule: *The area of a circle in terms of the radius is π times the radius squared.*

Formula: $A = \pi r^2$.

EXAMPLE 3: Find the area of a circle that has a 6-in. radius.

SOLUTION: $A = \pi r^2 = 3.1416 \times (6)^2$
$= 113.10$ sq. in., Ans.

EXAMPLE 4: The area of a circle is 396 sq. in. Find its radius.

SOLUTION:

$$A = \pi r^2, \qquad \frac{A}{\pi} = r^2, \qquad \sqrt{\frac{A}{\pi}} = r,$$

$$r = \sqrt{\frac{396}{\frac{22}{7}}} = \sqrt{396 \times \frac{7}{22}} = \sqrt{126} = 11.18 \text{ in.}$$

11.22

Rule: *The area of a circular ring equals the area of the outside circle minus the area of the inside circle.*

Formula: $A = \pi R^2 - \pi r^2$, where $R =$ radius of larger circle and $r =$ radius of smaller circle.

EXAMPLE: In a circular ring the outside diameter is 8″ and the inside diameter is 6″. What is the area of a cross-section of the ring?

R 4   *R 3*

SOLUTION:

$A = \pi R^2 - \pi r^2$. $D = 8, \therefore R = 4$.

$d = 6, \therefore r = 3$. $\therefore A = \pi(4^2 - 3^2)$.
$A = \frac{22}{7}(4^2 - 3^2) = \frac{22}{7}(16 - 9)$
$= \frac{22}{7} \times 7 = 22$ sq. in., Ans.

SIMILAR PLANE FIGURES

In ordinary language plane figures are similar when they are alike in all respects except size. For instance, all circles are obviously similar.

Two polygons are **similar** when the angles of one are respectively equal to the angles of the other in the same consecutive order.

If the *consecutive* order of the angles is the same, it makes no difference if they follow each other clockwise in one figure and counter-clockwise in the other. Such figures will still be similar because either may be considered as having been reversed like an image in a mirror.

In the case of triangles it is impossible *not* to arrange the angles in the same consecutive order, so that two triangles are similar if only their angles are equal.

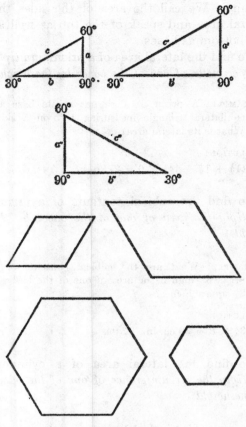

Similar Polygons

In the preceding diagram all three triangles are similar because they all have the same angles.

The two rhombuses are similar, though the direction of the lines in one reverses that in the other.

All *regular* polygons with a given number of sides are similar.

Rule 1: *If two figures are similar, the ratio of any line in one to the corresponding line in the other applies to all the lines that correspond in the two figures.*

Rule 2: *If two figures are similar, the ratio of their areas is that of the squares of corresponding lines.*

These rules apply not only to simple geometric figures but to drawings, photographs, engravings, blueprints, etc. presenting the greatest complexity of lines. Because of the broad applicability of the rules governing similar polygons, we have generalized the whole subject.

To find the length of any line in a plane figure that is similar to another plane figure, *apply the ratio that exists between any other two corresponding lines.*

EXAMPLE: In a rhombus measuring 4 inches on a side the longer diagonal is $5\frac{1}{2}$ inches. How long would this diagonal be in a similar rhombus measuring 7 inches on a side?

SOLUTION:

$$D : d :: S : s,$$

$$\frac{D}{5\frac{1}{2}} = \frac{7}{4},$$

$$D = \frac{7 \times 5\frac{1}{2}}{4} = \frac{38\frac{1}{2}}{4} = \frac{77}{2 \times 4} = 9\frac{5}{8} \text{ in., } \text{Ans.}$$

To find the area of a plane figure that is similar to another plane figure having a known area, *determine the ratio of any two corresponding lines in the two figures and make the required area proportional to the squares of these lines.*

EXAMPLE: A trapezium in which one of the sides measures 6 inches has an area of 54 square inches. What would be the area of a similar trapezium in which a corresponding side measured 15 inches?

SOLUTION:

$$A' : A :: S^2 : s^2,$$

$$\frac{A'}{54} = \frac{15^2}{6^2},$$

$$A' = \frac{225 \times 54}{36} = \frac{225 \times 3}{2} = 337\frac{1}{2} \text{ in., } \text{Ans.}$$

SOLID GEOMETRY

Plane geometry treats of surfaces or of figures having *two* dimensions, namely *length* and *breadth*. **Solid geometry** treats of **solids** or of **bodies** having *three* dimensions, namely *length*, *breadth*, and *thickness*.

RECTANGULAR SOLIDS

A **rectangular solid** is one in which all the faces are rectangles. The **cube** is a special type of rectangular solid in which all the faces are equal.

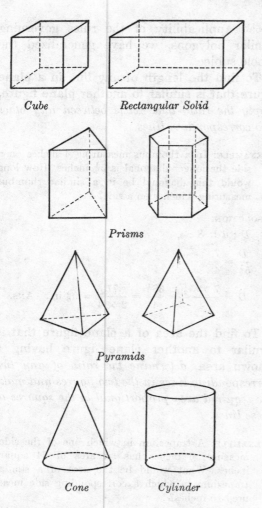

Cube   *Rectangular Solid*

Prisms

Pyramids

Cone   *Cylinder*

To find the area of the faces of a rectangular solid, *add the areas of the three different forms of face and multiply by 2.*

EXAMPLE: A rectangular solid measures 6″ × 4″ × 3″. What is the total area of its faces?

SOLUTION: It has two faces measuring 6″ × 4″, two measuring 6″ × 3″ and two measuring 4″ × 3″.

$(6 \times 4) + (6 \times 3) + (4 \times 3) = 54$ sq. in.

$2 \times 54 = 108$ sq. in., ANS.

To find the area of the faces of a cube, *multiply the area of one face by six.*

To find the cubical contents of a rectangular solid, *multiply together the three dimensions.*

EXAMPLE: What are the cubical contents of a box measuring 11″ × 6″ × 4½″?

$11 \times 6 \times 4\frac{1}{2} = 297$ cu. in., ANS.

With solids other than rectangular ones we consider the surfaces and areas of the sides as distinct from those of the bottom and top (if any). We call the area of the sides the **lateral area** and speak of the top as well as the bottom as **bases**.

To find the lateral area of a prism, *multiply the perimeter of one of the bases by the height.*

EXAMPLE: A prism 6″ high has as its base an equilateral triangle measuring 1½″ on a side. What is its lateral area?

SOLUTION:

$(1\frac{1}{2} + 1\frac{1}{2} + 1\frac{1}{2}) \times 6 = 27$ sq. in., ANS.

To find the cubical contents of a prism, *multiply the area of one of the bases by the height.*

EXAMPLE: What are the cubical contents of a prism 8″ high if the area of one of the bases is $3\frac{3}{4}$ square inches?

SOLUTION:

$3\frac{3}{4} \times 8 = 30$ cu. in., ANS.

To find the lateral area of a cylinder, *multiply the circumference of one of the bases by the height.*

EXAMPLE: What is the lateral surface of a cylinder with a base 6″ in diameter if its height is 7″?

SOLUTION:

$6 \times \frac{22}{7} \times 7 = 132$ sq. in., ANS.

To find the cubical contents of a cylinder, *multiply the area of one of the bases by the height.*

EXAMPLE: What are the cubical contents of the cylinder in the preceding example?

SOLUTION:

$3^2 \times \frac{22}{7} \times 7 = 9 \times 22 = 198$ cu. in., ANS.

To find the lateral area of a pyramid, *multiply its slant height by the perimeter and divide by two.*

EXAMPLE: What is the lateral area of a triangular pyramid having a base measuring 2″ on a side and a slant height of 9″?

SOLUTION:

$(2 + 2 + 2) \times 9 \div 2 = 27$ sq. in.,   ANS.

To find the cubical contents of a pyramid,
multiply the area of the base by the altitude (not slant height) *and divide by three.*

EXAMPLE: A square pyramid 10 inches high has a base measuring 4 inches on a side. What are its cubical contents?

SOLUTION:

$$\frac{4 \times 4 \times 10}{3} = \frac{160}{3} = 53\frac{1}{3} \text{ cu. in.,} \quad \text{ANS.}$$

To find the lateral area of a cone, *multiply its slant height by the circumference of the base and divide by two.* (Compare this with the rule for finding the lateral area of a pyramid as given above.)

To find the cubical contents of a cone, *multiply the area of the base by the altitude and divide by three.* (Compare this with the rule for finding the cubical contents of a pyramid as given above.)

To find the area of the surface of a sphere, *multiply the square of the radius by 4π.*

EXAMPLE: What is the surface area of a sphere one foot in diameter?

SOLUTION:

$$6^2 \times 4\pi = 36 \times 4 \times \frac{22}{7}$$
$$= \frac{3168}{7} = 452\frac{4}{7} \text{ sq. in.,} \quad \text{ANS.}$$

To find the cubical contents of a sphere, *multiply the cube of the radius by $\frac{4\pi}{3}$.*

EXAMPLE: What are the cubical contents of a sphere one foot in diameter?

SOLUTION:

$$6^3 \times \frac{4\pi}{3} = \frac{216 \times 4 \times 22}{3 \times 7} = \frac{6336}{7}$$
$$= 905\frac{1}{7} \text{ cu. in.,} \quad \text{ANS.}$$

Practice Exercise No. 72
PROBLEMS

1   The diameter of an automobile tire is 28″. What is its circumference?
- (A) 66″ ____
- (B) 77″ ____
- (C) 88″ ✓
- (D) 99″ ____

2   The circumference of a wheel is 110 inches. How long is one of its spokes?
- (A) 35″ ____
- (B) $17\frac{1}{2}$″ ✓
- (C) 15″ ____
- (D) $12\frac{1}{2}$″ ____

3   To make a circular coil for a magnet you need 49 turns of wire. How much wire will you need if the diameter of the coil is 4″?
- (A) $12\frac{4}{7}$ in. ____
- (B) $84\frac{2}{7}$ in. ____
- (C) 324 in. ____
- (D) 616 in. ✓

4   How many square inches of tin are needed for the top of a can that is 14 inches in diameter?
- (A) 616 sq. in. ____
- (B) 308 sq. in. ____
- (C) 462 sq. in. ____
- (D) 154 sq. in. ✓

5   You have a circular grazing field 96 ft. in diameter, which is roped around. Concentric with that you have a circular trotting track 128 ft. in diameter. How much will it cost to regravel the trotting track at a price of 10¢ per sq. ft.?
- (A) $426.00
- (B) $563.20 ✓
- (C) $826.40
- (D) $968.20

6   The area of canvas needed to just cover the muzzle of a cannon is $50\frac{1}{4}$ sq. in. What is the diameter of the muzzle?
- (A) 12 in. ____
- (B) 8 in. ✓
- (C) 6 in. ____
- (D) 5 in. ____

7   If the radius of a circle is twice as great as the radius of a smaller circle, how many times as large will the area of the greater circle be than the area of the smaller circle?
- (A) 2 ____
- (B) 4 ✓
- (C) 6 ____
- (D) 8 ____

8   You have 4 circular garden plots, each having a 14-foot radius. What must the radius be of one large circular plot that will have as much area as the four combined?
- (A) 28 ft. ✓
- (B) 21 ft. ____
- (C) 20 ft. ____
- (D) 64 ft. ____

9   How much will it cost to re-surface a circular swimming tank that has a diameter of 56 ft. if surfacing costs 25 cents a sq. ft.?
- (A) $154.00 ____
- (B) $308.00 ____
- (C) $462.00 ____
- (D) $616.00 ✓

10   If you wish to convert a circular field that has a diameter of 56 feet to a square field with the same area, how long will a side of the square be?
- (A) 28 ft. ____
- (B) 36.8 ft. ____
- (C) 49.6 ft. ✓
- (D) 46.0 ft. ____

NOTE: For other methods of solving geometric problems, see the section on **analytic geometry** in INTERMEDIATE ALGEBRA AND ANALYTIC GEOMETRY MADE SIMPLE, and the sections on **vector analysis** and on **calculus** in ADVANCED ALGEBRA AND CALCULUS MADE SIMPLE.

CHAPTER FIFTEEN

TRIGONOMETRY

Trigonometry is the branch of mathematics that deals with the measurement of triangles. (The word *trigonometry* comes from the Greek and means *to measure a triangle*.) Trigonometry enables us to find the unknown parts of triangles by arithmetical processes. For this reason it is constantly used in surveying, mechanics, navigation, engineering, physics and astronomy.

From geometry you learned that there are many shapes of triangles. For our purpose we can start with the simple case of a right triangle. Starting from this, you will eventually be able to work with all types of triangles because any triangle can be broken down into two right triangles.

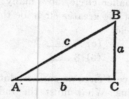

In the right triangle BAC you know from geometry that

(a) $\angle A + \angle B = 90$,

(b) $c^2 = a^2 + b^2$.

From equation (a) you can find one of the acute angles if the other is given, and from equation (b) you can determine the length of any side if the other two are given. But as yet you do not have a method for finding angle A if given the two sides a and b, even though by geometry you could construct the triangle with this information. And this is where trigonometry makes its contribution. It gives you a method for calculating the angles if you know the sides or for calculating the sides if you know the angles.

TRIGONOMETRIC FUNCTIONS OF AN ANGLE

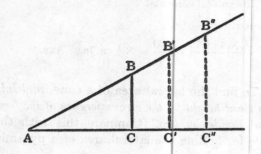

If we take the triangle in the previous figure and extend lines AB and AC, and then drop perpendiculars from points B' and B'' to AC, we form three similar triangles:

$$\triangle CAB, \triangle C'AB' \text{ and } \triangle C''AB''$$

When two triangles are similar, the ratio of any two sides of one triangle equals the ratio of corresponding sides of the second triangle. Thus in the three triangles of the figure,

$$\frac{BC}{AC} = \frac{B'C'}{AC'} = \frac{B''C''}{AC''}, \text{ or}$$

$$\frac{BC}{AB} = \frac{B'C'}{AB'} = \frac{B''C''}{AB''}.$$

Similar equalities hold for the ratios between the other sides of the triangles.

These equalities between the ratios of the corresponding sides of similar triangles illustrate the fact that *no matter how the size of a right triangle may vary, the values of the ratios of the sides remain the same so long as the acute angles are unchanged.* In other words each of the above ratios is a **function** of angle A.

From algebra and geometry we learn that a variable quantity which depends upon another quantity for its value is called a **function** of the latter value.

Therefore in the above figure the value of

the ratio $\dfrac{BC}{AC}$ is a function of the magnitude of angle A; and as long as the magnitude of angle A remains the same, the value of the ratio $\dfrac{BC}{AC}$ will be the same.

DESCRIPTION OF THE TANGENT FUNCTION

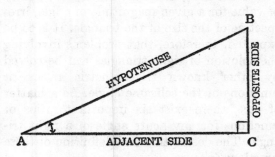

The constant ratio or function, $\dfrac{BC}{AC}$, is termed the **tangent** of angle A. It will be noted that this function represents the ratio of the side *opposite* angle A divided by the side next to angle A, called the *adjacent* side —that is, the side next to it other than the hypotenuse. Accordingly,

$$\text{tangent } \angle A = \frac{\text{opposite side}}{\text{adjacent side}},$$

or

$$\tan A = \frac{\text{opp}}{\text{adj}}.$$

MAKING A TABLE OF TRIGONOMETRIC FUNCTIONS

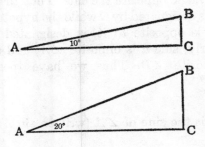

If you construct $\angle A$ equal to 10° and measure BC and AC and then compute the value of $\dfrac{BC}{AC}$, you will find it to be .176. Then if you construct $\angle A$ to equal 20°, you

will find $\dfrac{BC}{AC}$ equal to .364. For $\angle A$ at 30° you will find $\dfrac{BC}{AC}$ equal to .577. This means that thereafter you will know that the *tangent* of any angle of 10° in a right triangle is equal to .176, and the tangent of any angle of 20° is equal to .364. Thus by computing the values of the ratios of $\dfrac{BC}{AC}$ for all angles from 1° to 90° you would obtain a complete table of tangent values. A sample of such a table is shown below.

SAMPLE TABLE OF TRIGONOMETRIC FUNCTIONS

Angle	Sine	Cosine	Tangent
68	.9272	.3746	2.4751
69	.9336	.3584	2.6051
70	.9397	.3420	2.7475
71	.9455	.3256	2.9042
72	.9511	.3090	3.0777

This sample table and the more complete table on pages 141–45 give the tangents of angles to four decimal places. For instance in the table above, to find the value of the tangent of an angle of 69° you first look in the column head *Angle* and find 69°. Then on the same horizontal line in the column headed *Tangent* you find the value 2.6051. This means that tan 69° = 2.6051.

The following example will show how you can solve problems in trigonometry by the use of the table of tangents.

EXAMPLE: An airplane is sighted by two observers. One observer at A indicates it to be directly overhead. The other observer at B, 3,000 feet due west of A, measures its angle of elevation (*see below*) at 70°. What is the altitude of the airplane?

SOLUTION:

$$\tan \angle B = \frac{\text{(opp side)}}{\text{(adj side)}} = \frac{CA}{BA}$$

Since $\quad \angle B = 70°$,
$\tan \angle B = 2.7475$.
$\qquad$ (*see table above*)

Substituting, $2.7475 = \dfrac{CA}{3000}$.

Transposing, $CA = 3000 \times 2.7475$
$= 8242.5$ ft.

Altitude of airplane is 8242.5 ft.,
Ans.

PRACTICAL OBSERVATION OF ANGLES

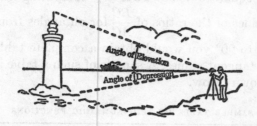

The *angle of elevation or depression* of an object is the angle made between a line from the eye to the object and a horizontal line in the same vertical plane. If the object is above the horizontal line it makes an *angle of elevation;* if below the horizontal line it makes an *angle of depression.*

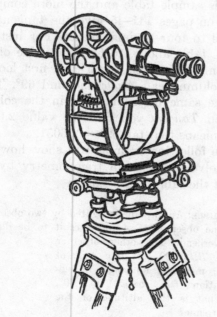

Courtesy of Keuffel & Esser Co., New York

For measuring both vertical and horizontal angles out of doors an engineer's *transit* or *theodolite* is used. As may be seen from the illustration, the instrument combines a telescope with a horizontal and a vertical plate, each of which is graduated by degrees, minutes and seconds. By moving the telescope to right or left, horizontal angles can be measured on the horizontal plate. Vertical angles are measured on the vertical disc by moving the telescope up and down.

THE SIX TRIGONOMETRIC FUNCTIONS

As has been previously pointed out, ratios other than those involved in the *tangent function* exist between the sides of the triangle, and have, like the tangent, an equality of value for a given magnitude of angle, irrespective of the size of the triangle. It is to be expected, therefore, that problems involving the solution of right triangles can be solved by other known trigonometric ratios or functions of the selfsame angle. As a matter of fact, there exist six important ratios or functions for any acute angle of a right triangle. The description and definition of these functions follows.

The sides and angles of triangle CAB in the following diagram have been marked in the manner traditionally employed in trigonometry. It is the custom to have the angles represented by capital letters and the sides

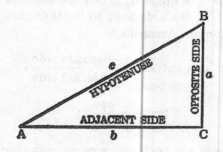

indicated by the small letter corresponding to the angle opposite the side. Thus the right angle is designated by C while the hypotenuse, which is opposite to it, is designated by c. Similarly, side a is opposite $\angle A$, and side b is opposite $\angle B$. Thus we have these six ratios:*

$\dfrac{a}{c}$ is the **sine** of $\angle A$ (written **sin** A).

$\dfrac{b}{c}$ is the **cosine** of $\angle A$ (written **cos** A).

* Two additional functions which are little used are: **versed sine** $\angle A = 1 - \cos A$ (written **vers** A), and **coversed sine** $\angle A = 1 - \sin A$ (written **covers** A).

$\dfrac{a}{b}$ is the **tangent** of $\angle A$ (written **tan** A).

$\dfrac{b}{a}$ is the **cotangent** of $\angle A$ (written **cot** A).

$\dfrac{c}{b}$ is the **secant** of $\angle A$ (written **sec** A).

$\dfrac{c}{a}$ is the **cosecant** of $\angle A$ (written **csc** A).

Using self-explanatory abbreviations, we thus have by definition:

$$\sin A = \frac{\text{opp}}{\text{hyp}} = \frac{a}{c}, \qquad \cos A = \frac{\text{adj}}{\text{hyp}} = \frac{b}{c},$$

$$\tan A = \frac{\text{opp}}{\text{adj}} = \frac{a}{b}, \qquad \cot A = \frac{\text{adj}}{\text{opp}} = \frac{b}{a},$$

$$\sec A = \frac{\text{hyp}}{\text{adj}} = \frac{c}{b}, \qquad \csc A = \frac{\text{hyp}}{\text{opp}} = \frac{c}{a}.$$

This table of definitions of the trigonometric functions should be committed to memory.

Practice Exercise No. 73

1 In the preceding figure, $\tan B = \dfrac{b}{a}$. Write the other five functions of $\angle B$.

2 Which is greater, $\sin A$ or $\tan A$?

3 Which is greater, $\cos A$ or $\cot A$?

4 Which is greater, $\sec A$ or $\tan A$?

5 Which is greater, $\csc A$ or $\cot A$?

6 Sin $A = \frac{3}{5}$. What is the value of $\cos A$?
Hint: Use rt. $\triangle$ formula $c^2 = a^2 + b^2$ to find side b.

7 Tan $A = \frac{3}{4}$. What is the value of $\sin A$?

8 Sin $A = \frac{8}{17}$. Find $\cos A$.

9 Cot $A = \frac{15}{8}$. Find $\sec A$.

10 Find the value of the other five functions of A if $\sin A = \frac{5}{13}$.

RELATIONS BETWEEN FUNCTIONS OF COMPLEMENTARY ANGLES

If you observe the relations between the functions of the two acute angles of the same right triangle, you will note that every function of each of the two acute angles is equal to a different function of the other acute angle. These correspondences of value are demonstrated in the following.

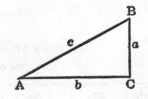

$$\sin A = \frac{a}{c} \quad \text{and} \quad \cos B = \frac{a}{c},$$

$$\cos A = \frac{b}{c} \quad \text{and} \quad \sin B = \frac{b}{c},$$

$$\tan A = \frac{a}{b} \quad \text{and} \quad \cot B = \frac{a}{b}, \text{ etc.}$$

Thus we have:

$$\sin A = \cos B, \qquad \cot A = \tan B$$
$$\cos A = \sin B, \qquad \sec A = \csc B$$
$$\tan A = \cot B, \qquad \csc A = \sec B$$

From these equalities it will be evident that any function of an acute angle of a right triangle equals the co-function of the complement of that angle.*

For example, $\tan 40° = \cot 50°$; $\sin 70° = \cos 20°$; $\csc 41° 20' = \sec 48° 40'$.

Since angles A and B are complementary, another way of writing these equations is as follows:

$$\sin (90° - A) = \cos A, \qquad \cot (90° - A) = \tan A$$
$$\cos (90° - A) = \sin A, \qquad \sec (90° - A) = \csc A$$
$$\tan (90° - A) = \cot A, \qquad \csc (90° - A) = \sec A$$

Practice Exercise No. 74

Fill in the blanks in examples 1–6 with the equivalent co-functions

1 $\sin 26° =$

2 $\tan 43° =$

3 $\cos 24° 28' =$

4 $\cot 88° 50' =$

5 $\sec 6° 10' =$

6 $\csc 77\frac{1}{2}° =$

7 How many degrees must $\angle A$ be if $90° - A = 5A$?

8 What is the value of $\angle A$ if $\tan A = \cot A$?

9 Find A if $90° - A = A$.

10 Find A if $\cos A = \sin 2A$.

* The name *cosine* means *complement's sine*. It is a contraction from the Latin *complementi sinus*. The words *cotangent* and *cosecant* were derived in the same manner.

Table VII

TABLE OF NATURAL TRIGONOMETRIC FUNCTIONS

For explanation of the use of this table see following page.

Angle	Sin	Cos	Tan	Cot	Sec	Csc	
0°	.0000	1.0000	.0000	∞	1.0000	∞	90°
1	.0175	.9998	.0175	57.2900	1.0002	57.2987	89
2	.0349	.9994	.0349	28.6363	1.0006	28.6537	88
3	.0523	.9986	.0524	19.0811	1.0014	19.1073	87
4	.0698	.9976	.0699	14.3007	1.0024	14.3356	86
5°	.0872	.9962	.0875	11.4301	1.0038	11.4737	85°
6	.1045	.9945	.1051	9.5144	1.0055	9.5668	84
7	.1219	.9925	.1228	8.1443	1.0075	8.2055	83
8	.1392	.9903	.1405	7.1154	1.0098	7.1853	82
9	.1564	.9877	.1584	6.3138	1.0125	6.3925	81
10°	.1736	.9848	.1763	5.6713	1.0154	5.7588	80°
11	.1908	.9816	.1944	5.1446	1.0187	5.2408	79
12	.2079	.9781	.2126	4.7046	1.0223	4.8097	78
13	.2250	.9744	.2309	4.3315	1.0263	4.4454	77
14	.2419	.9703	.2493	4.0108	1.0306	4.1336	76
15°	.2588	.9659	.2679	3.7321	1.0353	3.8637	75°
16	.2756	.9613	.2867	3.4874	1.0403	3.6280	74
17	.2924	.9563	.3057	3.2709	1.0457	3.4203	73
18	.3090	.9511	.3249	3.0777	1.0515	3.2361	72
19	.3256	.9455	.3443	2.9042	1.0576	3.0716	71
20°	.3420	.9397	.3640	2.7475	1.0642	2.9238	70°
21	.3584	.9336	.3839	2.6051	1.0711	2.7904	69
22	.3746	.9272	.4040	2.4751	1.0785	2.6695	68
23	.3907	.9205	.4245	2.3559	1.0864	2.5593	67
24	.4067	.9135	.4452	2.2460	1.0946	2.4586	66
25°	.4226	.9063	.4663	2.1445	1.1034	2.3662	65°
26	.4384	.8988	.4877	2.0503	1.1126	2.2812	64
27	.4540	.8910	.5095	1.9626	1.1223	2.2027	63
28	.4695	.8829	.5317	1.8807	1.1326	2.1301	62
29	.4848	.8746	.5543	1.8040	1.1434	2.0627	61
30°	.5000	.8660	.5774	1.7321	1.1547	2.0000	60°
31	.5150	.8572	.6009	1.6643	1.1666	1.9416	59
32	.5299	.8480	.6249	1.6003	1.1792	1.8871	58
33	.5446	.8387	.6494	1.5399	1.1924	1.8361	57
34	.5592	.8290	.6745	1.4826	1.2062	1.7883	56
35°	.5736	.8192	.7002	1.4281	1.2208	1.7434	55°
36	.5878	.8090	.7265	1.3764	1.2361	1.7013	54
37	.6018	.7986	.7536	1.3270	1.2521	1.6616	53
38	.6157	.7880	.7813	1.2799	1.2690	1.6243	52
39	.6293	.7771	.8098	1.2349	1.2868	1.5890	51
40°	.6428	.7660	.8391	1.1918	1.3054	1.5557	50°
41	.6561	.7547	.8693	1.1504	1.3250	1.5243	49
42	.6691	.7431	.9004	1.1106	1.3456	1.4945	48
43	.6820	.7314	.9325	1.0724	1.3673	1.4663	47
44	.6947	.7193	.9657	1.0355	1.3902	1.4396	46
45°	.7071	.7071	1.0000	1.0000	1.4142	1.4142	45°
	Cos	Sin	Cot	Tan	Csc	Sec	Angle

HOW TO USE A TABLE OF TRIGONOMETRIC FUNCTIONS

From the foregoing it becomes apparent that you can easily compute the functions of any angle greater than 45° if you know the functions of all angles between 0° and 45°. Therefore in a table of trigonometric functions, such as appears on the preceding page, it is only necessary to have a direct table of functions for angles from 0° to 45°, since the function of any angle above 45° is equal to the co-function of its complement.

To find the functions of angles from 0° to 45° read the table from the top down, using the values of angles at the left and the headings at the top of the table. To find the functions of angles from 45° to 90° read from the bottom up, using the values of angles at the right and the function designations at the bottom of the table.

If you know the value of the function of an angle and wish to find the angle, look in the body of the table in the proper column and then read the magnitude of the angle in the corresponding row of one or the other of the angle columns.

For example, you are told that the sine of a certain angle is .5000 and wish to find the angle. Look in the *Sin* column, locate .5000 and read the angle value (30°) from the left *Angle* column. If this value had been given to you as a cosine, you would have noted that it does not appear in the column headed *Cos* at the top but does appear in the column that has *Cos* at the bottom. Hence you would then use the *Angle* column at the right and find .5000 to be the cosine of 60°.

You should become thoroughly familiar with the use of the table. To this end you can supplement the following exercise by making up your own examples.

Practice Exercise No. 75

From the table of trigonometric functions find the values required in examples 1–15:

1	sin 8°	6	cos 25°	11	cos 62°
2	sin 42°	7	csc 14°	12	tan 56°
3	tan 40°	8	sin 78°	13	sin 58°
4	cot 63°	9	cot 69°	14	cos 45°
5	sec 22°	10	sec 81°	15	sin 30°

16 Find the angle whose sine is .2588.
17 Find the angle whose tangent is .7002.
18 Find the angle whose cosine is .5000.
19 Find the angle whose secant is 2.9238.
20 Find the angle whose cotangent is 5.6713.

FUNCTIONS OF 45°, 30°, AND 60° ANGLES

For some rather common angles the exact values of their functions can be easily found by the application of elementary principles of geometry.

Functions of a 45° Angle

In the isosceles right triangle *ACB*, if $\angle A = 45°$, then $\angle B = 45°$, and therefore side a = side b. Now if we let side a equal 1 or unity, then from the right triangle formula of

$$a^2 + b^2 = c^2$$

we get

$$c = \sqrt{1+1} \text{ or } \sqrt{2}$$

(taking the square

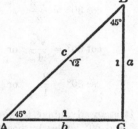

root of both sides of the equation). Now since any trigonometric function of an acute angle is equal to the corresponding co-function of its complement, therefore

$$\sin 45° = \frac{1}{\sqrt{2}} \text{ or } \tfrac{1}{2}\sqrt{2} = \cos 45°,$$

$$\tan 45° = \frac{1}{1} \text{ or } 1 = \cot 45°,$$

$$\sec 45° = \frac{\sqrt{2}}{1} \text{ or } \sqrt{2} = \csc 45°.$$

Functions of 30° and 60° Angles

In the equilateral triangle *ABD* the three sides are equal and the three angles each equal 60°. If we drop a perpendicular from *B* to *AD*, it bisects $\angle B$ and the base *AD* at *C*.

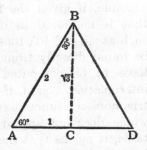

If we let the length of each of the sides equal 2 units, then $AC = CD = 1$; and in the right triangle ACB

$$\angle B = 30°, \ \angle C = 90°, \ \angle A = 60°$$

$$AC = 1, \ AB = 2$$

Then, since $(AB)^2 = (AC)^2 + (BC)^2$, it follows that $(BC)^2 = 3$ and $BC = \sqrt{3}$.

Thus in the right triangle ACB

$$\sin 30° = \tfrac{1}{2} \qquad\qquad = \cos 60°,$$

$$\tan 30° = \frac{1}{\sqrt{3}} \quad \text{or} \quad \tfrac{1}{3}\sqrt{3} = \cot 60°,$$

$$\sec 30° = \frac{2}{\sqrt{3}} \quad \text{or} \quad \tfrac{2}{3}\sqrt{3} = \csc 60°,$$

$$\cos 30° = \frac{\sqrt{3}}{2} \qquad\qquad = \sin 60°,$$

$$\cot 30° = \frac{\sqrt{3}}{1} \quad \text{or} \quad \sqrt{3} = \tan 60°,$$

$$\csc 30° = \frac{2}{1} \quad \text{or} \quad 2 \quad = \sec 60°.$$

It is an advantage to know the values of the 30°, 45° and 60° angles by heart. To help yourself memorize them, fill in the outline of the table below with the proper values of the functions.

Function	30°	60°	45°
Sine			
Cosine			
Tangent			
Cotangent			
Secant			
Cosecant			

INTERPOLATION

Interpolation is used in trigonometry in connection with the table of functions. For example, if given the function of an angle that is measured in degrees and minutes, such as sin 30° 40′, its exact value could not be found directly from the table but would have to be computed by the method of interpolation. Again, if given the value of a trigonometric function such as tan A = .7400, which does not appear in the body of the table, it means that the corresponding angle is expressed in units more exact than the nearest degree and must be found by interpo-

lation. The following examples will illustrate the method of performing interpolations with reference to the table of trigonometric functions.

EXAMPLE 1: Find sin 30° 40′.

SOLUTION: sin 30° 40′ is between sin 30° and sin 31°. Since there are 60′ in 1°, 40′ = $\tfrac{2}{3}$ of 1°

From the table
$$\sin 30° = .5000$$
$$\sin 31° = .5150$$
$$\text{Difference} = .0150$$

$$\sin 30° = .5000$$
$$\tfrac{2}{3} \text{ of } .0150 = .0100$$
$$\sin 30° \ 40′ = .5100, \quad \text{Ans.}$$

Note: In this case we added the proportional part of the difference (.0100) to the value of sin 30° because the sine of an angle *increases* as the angle increases.

EXAMPLE 2: Find cos 59° 48′.

SOLUTION: cos 59° 48′ is between cos 59° and cos 60°. 48′ is $\tfrac{4}{5}$ of 1°.

From the table
$$\cos 59° = .5150$$
$$\cos 60° = .5000$$
$$\text{Difference} = .0150$$

$$\cos 59° = .5150$$
$$\tfrac{4}{5} \text{ of } .0150 = .0120$$
$$\cos 59° \ 48′ = .5030, \quad \text{Ans.}$$

Note: In this case we subtracted the proportional part of the difference (.0120) from the value of cos 59° because the cosine of an angle *decreases* as the angle increases.

EXAMPLE 3: Find $\angle A$ if tan A = .7400.

SOLUTION:
From the table, in the tan column, we see that .7400 is between tan 36° and tan 37°.
$$\tan 37° = .7536$$
$$\tan 36° = .7265$$
$$\text{Difference} = .0271$$

$$\tan A = .7400$$
$$\tan 36° = .7265$$
$$\text{Difference} = .0135$$

The proportional difference between tan A and tan 36° is .0135. The difference between tan 36° and tan 37° is .0271.

$$\frac{.0135}{.0271} \text{ of } 1° \text{ or } 60′ \text{ equals } \tfrac{1}{2}° \text{ or } 30′$$

$$\therefore \tan A = 36° + 30′ = 36° \ 30′, \quad \text{Ans.}$$

Further familiarity with the table of functions will indicate the following about variations of the trigonometric functions.

As an angle increases from 0° to 90°, its:

sine   *increases* from 0 to 1,
cosine   *decreases* from 1 to 0,
tangent   *increases* from 0 to ∞,
cotangent   *decreases* from ∞ to 0,
secant   *increases* from 1 to ∞,
cosecant   *decreases* from ∞ to 1.

Also note that:

sines and cosines are never > 1,
secants and cosecants are never < 1,
tangents and cotangents may have any value from 0 to ∞.*

Practice Exercise No. 76

Find by interpolation the values of the functions in examples 1–5:

1 sin 15° 30′
2 cos 25° 40′
3 tan 47° 10′
4 cot 52° 30′
5 sec 40° 30′

Find by the interpolation method the value of ∠A to the nearest minute in examples 6–10:

6 $\sin A = .0901$
7 $\tan A = .3411$
8 $\cos A = .4173$
9 $\cot A = .8491$
10 $\csc A = 1.4804$

RECIPROCALS AMONG THE FUNCTIONS

If you inspect the ratios of the six functions of ∠A, you will readily note that they are not independent of each other. In fact, if you line them up as follows:

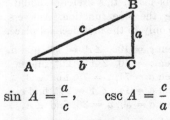

$$\sin A = \frac{a}{c}, \qquad \csc A = \frac{c}{a}$$

---

* The symbol ∞ denotes "infinity" and is used in mathematics to represent a number that is indefinitely large, or larger than any preassignable quantity. This is discussed in detail in INTERMEDIATE ALGEBRA AND ANALYTIC GEOMETRY MADE SIMPLE. The sign > means greater than, and < means less than.

$$\cos A = \frac{b}{c}, \qquad \sec A = \frac{c}{b}$$

$$\tan A = \frac{a}{b}, \qquad \cot A = \frac{b}{a}$$

it becomes obvious that *the sine is the reciprocal of the cosecant, the cosine is the reciprocal of the secant, and the tangent is the reciprocal of the cotangent.* Accordingly,

$$\sin A = \frac{1}{\csc A} \qquad \cos A = \frac{1}{\sec A}$$

$$\tan A = \frac{1}{\cot A} \qquad \csc A = \frac{1}{\sin A}$$

$$\sec A = \frac{1}{\cos A} \qquad \cot A = \frac{1}{\tan A}$$

Therefore:

$$\sin A \times \csc A = 1, \quad \cos A \times \sec A = 1$$

$$\tan A \times \cot A = 1$$

In accordance with the usual algebraic method of notation (by which ab is equivalent to $a \times b$) these relationships are usually written:

$$\sin A \csc A = 1, \quad \cos A \sec A = 1$$

$$\tan A \cot A = 1$$

To illustrate such a relation, find, for example, in the table of functions the tangent and the cotangent of 30°.

$$\tan 30° = .5774, \quad \cot 30° = 1.7321$$

$$\tan 30° \cot 30° = .5774 \times 1.7321$$
$$= 1.00011454$$

INTERRELATIONS AMONG THE FUNCTIONS

Since $\tan A = \frac{a}{b}$, $\sin A = \frac{a}{c}$, and $\cos A = \frac{b}{c}$, it follows that

$$\tan A = \frac{\sin A}{\cos A}, \quad \text{and} \quad \sin A = \tan A \cos A.$$

The student will the more readily grasp these interrelations if instead of considering only abstract values, he translates these into actual numbers. The 3–4–5 right triangle in the diagram will serve this purpose.

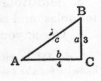

From the interrelations of sine, cosine and tangent it follows that if we know two of these values, we can always find the third.

From the Pythagorean theorem of the right triangle we know that $a^2 + b^2 = c^2$. If we divide both sides of this equation by c^2, we get

$$\frac{a^2}{c^2} + \frac{b^2}{c^2} = 1.$$

Since $\frac{a}{c} = \sin A$ and $\frac{b}{c} = \cos A$, it follows that

(1) $\sin^2 A + \cos^2 A = 1$*

Therefore

(2) $\sin A = \sqrt{1 - \cos^2 A}$ and

(3) $\cos A = \sqrt{1 - \sin^2 A}$

MAKING PRACTICAL USE OF THE FUNCTIONS

With the information on trigonometry outlined in the previous pages you will be able to solve many triangles if you know three parts one of which is a side. And in the case of the right triangle, since the right angle is a part of it, you need only to know two other parts one of which must be a side.

As will be brought out in the practice exercises that follow, these trigonometric methods of solving triangles are used daily in handling problems that arise in military operations, engineering, navigation, shopwork, physics, surveying, etc.

You should adopt a planned method of procedure in solving problems. One such method is as follows.

1. After reading the problem, draw a figure to a convenient scale, and in it show those lines and angles which are given and those which are to be found.

2. Write down all the formulas that apply to the particular problem.

3. Substitute the given data in the proper formulas, and solve for the unknowns.

4. Check your results.

*(sin A)² is customarily written as sin² A, and likewise for the other functions.

Incidentally we would suggest that you work with a hard lead pencil or a fine-pointed pen. Nothing is of greater help to accuracy in mathematics than neatness of work, and neatness is next to impossible if you use writing instruments that make thick lines and sprawly figures.

Applying the Sine Function,

$$\sin A = \frac{\text{opp}}{\text{hyp}} = \frac{a}{c}.$$

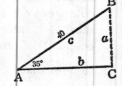

EXAMPLE 1: In the accompanying figure $c = 40$ and $\angle A = 35°$. Find a.

SOLUTION: $\frac{a}{c} = \sin A$, $a = c \sin A$

$\sin 35° = .5736$, $c = 40$
$c \sin A = 40 \times .5736 = 22.944$
$a = 22.944$, ANS.

CHECK: $\frac{a}{c} = \sin A$

$\frac{22.944}{40} = .5736$ which is $\sin 35°$.

EXAMPLE 2: Given $c = 48$ and $\angle B = 22°$, find a by means of the sine formula.

SOLUTION: $\frac{a}{c} = \sin A$, $a = c \sin A$,

$\angle A = 90° - \angle B$, $\angle A = 90° - 22° = 68°$,
$\sin 68° = .9272$, $c = 48$,
$c \sin A = 48 \times .9272 = 44.5056$,
$a = 44.50+$, ANS.

CHECK: $\frac{a}{c} = \sin A$.

$\frac{44.5056}{48} = .9272$ which is $\sin 68°$.

Practice Exercise No. 77

The problems in this exercise should be solved by using the sine function. Answers need be accurate only to the first decimal place.

1 Given $c = 100$, $\angle A = 33°$, find a.
2 Given $c = 10$, $\angle A = 20°$, find a.
3 Given $a = 71$, $c = 78$, find $\angle A$.
4 Given $a = 14$, $\angle A = 28°$, find c.
5 Given $c = 50$, $a = 36$, find $\angle A$.

6 An airplane is 405 feet above a landing field when the pilot cuts out his motor. He glides to a landing at an angle of 13° with the field. How far will he glide in reaching the field?

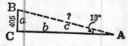

(A) 300 ft. ____   (c) 1,800 ft. ____
(B) 1,248 ft. ____   (D) 1,641 ft. ____

7 An ascension balloon is moored by a rope 150 ft. long. A wind blowing in an easterly direction keeps the rope taut and causes it to make an angle of 50° with the ground. What is the vertical height of the balloon from the ground?

(A) 180 ft. ____   (c) 177.5 ft. ____
(B) 114.9 ft. ____   (D) 189.4 ft. ____

8 A carpenter has to build a ramp to be used as a loading platform for a carrier airplane. The height of the loading door is 12 ft., and the required slope or gradient of the ramp is to be 18°. How long must the ramp be?

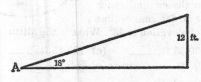

(A) 24 ft. ____   (c) 48.42 ft. ____
(B) 38.83 ft. ____   (D) 10.14 ft. ____

9 The fire department has a new 200-ft. ladder. The greatest angle at which it can be placed against a building with safety is at 71° with the ground. What is the maximum vertical height that the ladder can reach?

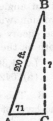

(A) 189.1 ft. ____   (c) 300 ft. ____
(B) 209.4 ft. ____   (D) 162.3 ft. ____

10 A road running from the bottom of a hill to the top is 625 ft. long. If the hill is $54\frac{1}{2}$ ft. high, what is the angle of elevation of the road?

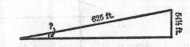

(A) 25° ____   (c) 5° ____
(B) 15° ____   (D) 2° ____

Applying the Cosine Function,

$$\cos A = \frac{\text{adj}}{\text{hyp}} = \frac{b}{c}.$$

EXAMPLE 1: In the accompanying figure $c = 36$ and $\angle A = 40°$. Find b.

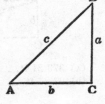

SOLUTION: $\frac{b}{c} = \cos A$, $b = c \cos A$.

$\cos 40° = .7660$
$c = 36$
$c \cos A = 36 \times .7660 = 27.576$
$b = 27.58$,   ANS.

CHECK: $\frac{b}{c} = \cos A$, $\frac{27.576}{36} = .7660$ or $\cos 40°$.

EXAMPLE 2: Given $b = 26$ and $\angle A = 22°$; find c.

SOLUTION: $\frac{b}{c} = \cos A$, $c = \frac{b}{\cos A}$,

$b = 26$
$\cos 22° = .9272$

$\frac{b}{\cos A} = 26 \div .9272 = 28.04$

$c = 28.04$,   ANS.

CHECK: $\frac{b}{c} = \cos A$

$\frac{26}{28.04} = .9272$ which is $\cos 22°$.

Practice Exercise No. 78

Use the cosine function in solving the problems in this exercise.

1 Given $c = 400$, $b = 240$; find $\angle A$.
2 Given $c = 41$, $\angle A = 39°$; find b.
3 Given $c = 67.7$, $\angle A = 23° 30'$; find b.
4 Given $c = 187$, $b = 93\frac{1}{2}$; find $\angle A$.
5 Given $b = 40$, $\angle A = 18°$; find c.

6 A carpenter has to build a triangular roof to a house. The roof is to be 30 feet wide. If the rafters are 17 feet long, at what angle will the rafters be laid at the eaves?

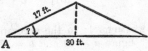

(A) 34° ____   (c) 28° 05' ____
(B) 19° 30' ____   (D) 42° 10' ____

7 Desiring to measure distance across a pond, a surveyor standing at point A sighted on a point B across the pond. From A he ran a line AC, making an angle of 27° with AB. From B he ran a line perpendicular to AC. He measured the line AC to be 681 feet. What is the distance across the pond from A to B?

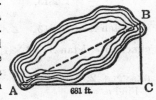

(A) 100 ft. ____   (c) 681 ft. ____
(B) 764.3 ft. ____   (D) 862.8 ft. ____

8 A scout on a hill 125 feet above a lake sights

a boat on the water at an angle of depression of 10° as shown. What is the exact distance from the scout to the boat?

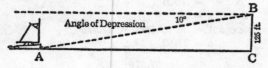

(A) 240.5 ft. ____   (c) 468.4 ft. ____
(B) 720 ft. ____   (D) 1020 ft. ____

9 A mountain climber stretches a cord from the rocky ledge of a sheer cliff to a point on a horizontal plane, making an angle of 50° with the ledge. The cord is 84 feet long. What is the vertical height of the rocky ledge from its base?

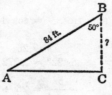

(A) 45 ft. ____   (c) 76.8 ft. ____
(B) 82 ft. ____   (D) 54 ft. ____

10 A 100-foot ladder is placed against the side of a house with the foot of the ladder 16½ feet away from the building. What angle does the ladder make with the ground?

(A) 65° ____
(B) 25° 40′ ____
(c) 80° 30′ ____
(D) 72° 20′ ____

Applying the Tangent Function,

$$\tan A = \frac{\text{opp}}{\text{adj}} = \frac{a}{b}.$$

EXAMPLE 1: In the accompanying figure $a = 40$ and $b = 27$. Find $\angle A$.

SOLUTION: $\frac{a}{b} = \tan A$, $a = 40$, $b = 27$,

$$\frac{40}{27} = 1.4815,$$

$\tan A = 1.4815$, $\angle A = 55° 59′$,   ANS.

CHECK: $a = b \tan A$; $27 \times 1.4815 = 40$ which is a.

EXAMPLE 2: Given angle $A = 28°$ and $a = 29$. Find b.

SOLUTION: $\frac{a}{b} = \tan A$, $b = \frac{a}{\tan A}$,

$a = 29$, $\tan 28° = .5317$, $\frac{29}{.5317} = 54.54$,

$b = 54.54$,   ANS.

CHECK: $\frac{a}{b} = \tan A$,

$$\frac{29}{54.54} = .5317 \text{ which is } \tan A.$$

Practice Exercise No. 79

Use the tangent function in solving the problems in this exercise.

1 Given $a = 18$, $b = 24$; find $\angle A$.
2 Given $b = 64$, $\angle A = 45°$; find a.
3 Given $b = 62$, $\angle A = 36°$; find a.
4 Given $\angle A = 70°$, $a = 50$; find b.
5 Given $\angle A = 19° 36′$, $b = 42$; find a.

6 An engineer desires to learn the height of a cone-shaped hill. He measures its diameter to be 280 feet. From a point on the circumference of the base he determines that the angle of elevation is 43°. What is the altitude?

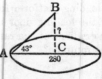

(A) 130.55 ft. ____   (c) 125.45 ft. ____
(B) 260 ft. ____   (D) 560 ft. ____

7 From a lookout tower 240 feet high an enemy tank division is sighted at an angle of depression which is measured to be 10°. How far is the enemy away from the lookout tower if they are both on the same level?

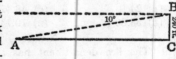

(A) 1,361.11 ft. ____   (c) 866 ft. ____
(B) 642.25 ft. ____   (D) 2,434.16 ft. ____

8 The upper deck of a ship stands 30 feet above the level of its dock. A runway to the deck is to be built having an angle of inclination of 20°. How far from the boat should it start?

(A) 60 ft. ____
(B) 76.25 ft. ____
(c) 82.42 ft. ____
(D) 42.30 ft. ____

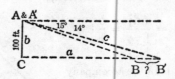

9 From a boathouse 100 feet above the level of a lake two rowing crews were sighted racing in the direction of the boathouse. The boats were directly in a line with each other. The leading boat was sighted at an angle of depression equal to 15°, and the other at 14°. How far apart were the boats?

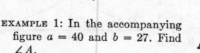

(A) 373.21 ft. ____   (c) 64.14 ft. ____
(B) 27.87 ft. ____   (D) 401.08 ft. ____

10 A clock on the tower of a building is observed from two points which are on the same level and in the same straight line with the foot of the tower. At the nearer point the angle of elevation to the clock is 60°, and at the farther point it is 30°. If the two points are 300 feet apart, what is the height of the clock?

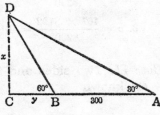

(A) 130.8 ft. ____   (C) 259.8 ft. ____
(B) 400 ft. ____   (D) 360.4 ft. ____

THE OBLIQUE TRIANGLE

As previously stated, you can use right triangle methods to solve most oblique triangles by introducing perpendiculars and resolving the oblique triangle into two right triangles.

For example:

1. Triangle *ABC* can be resolved into right triangles *ADC* and *BDC* by introducing the perpendicular *CD*.

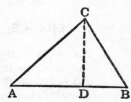

2. Triangle *DEF* can be resolved into right triangles *DGF* and *EGF* by extending *DE* and dropping the perpendicular *FG*.

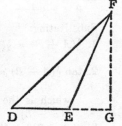

3. Triangle *HJK* can be resolved into right triangles *HLJ* and *KLJ* by introducing the perpendicular *JL*.

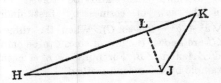

In practical problems, however, it is often impossible or too cumbersome to use a right triangle, and in such cases formulas for oblique angles are needed.*

There are three important formulas that may be used in the solution of triangles of any shape. They are known as the *law of sines*, the *law of cosines* and the *law of tangents*.

For our purposes it will be sufficient to state the law, give the corresponding formulas and show the application of the law to the solution of problems involving oblique triangles.†

The law of sines: *The sides of a triangle are proportional to the sines of their opposite angles:*

$$\frac{a}{\sin A} = \frac{b}{\sin B} = \frac{c}{\sin C}, \quad \text{or}$$

$$\frac{a}{b} = \frac{\sin A}{\sin B}, \quad \frac{b}{c} = \frac{\sin B}{\sin C}, \quad \frac{a}{c} = \frac{\sin A}{\sin C}.$$

The law of cosines: *The square of any side of a triangle is equal to the sum of the squares of the other two sides minus twice their product times the cosine of the included angle.*

$$a^2 = b^2 + c^2 - 2bc \cos A,$$
$$b^2 = a^2 + c^2 - 2ac \cos B,$$
$$c^2 = a^2 + b^2 - 2ab \cos C, \quad \text{or}$$

$$a = \sqrt{b^2 + c^2 - 2bc \cos A},$$
$$b = \sqrt{a^2 + c^2 - 2ac \cos B},$$
$$c = \sqrt{a^2 + b^2 - 2ab \cos C}.$$

The law of tangents: *The difference between any two sides of a triangle is to their sum as the tangent of half the difference between their opposite angles is to tangent of half their sum.*

$$\frac{a - b}{a + b} = \frac{\tan \frac{1}{2}(A - B)}{\tan \frac{1}{2}(A + B)},$$

$$\frac{a - c}{a + c} = \frac{\tan \frac{1}{2}(A - C)}{\tan \frac{1}{2}(A + C)},$$

* For work with oblique triangles a more detailed table of functions graduated by tenths of degrees appears at the end of this section. Use of this table will obviate much of the extra arithmetic ordinarily employed in interpolation procedures.

† The interested reader can obtain from any standard textbook on trigonometry a detailed description of the mathematics involved in deriving these formulas.

$$\frac{b - c}{b + c} = \frac{\tan \frac{1}{2}(B - C)}{\tan \frac{1}{2}(B + C)},$$

or if $b > a$, then

$$\frac{b - a}{b + a} = \frac{\tan \frac{1}{2}(B - A)}{\tan \frac{1}{2}(B + A)}.$$

SOLVING OBLIQUE TRIANGLES

Any triangle has six parts, namely, three angles and the sides opposite the angles.

In order to solve a triangle three independent parts must be known in addition to the fact that the sum of the angles of any triangle equals 180°.

In problems involving triangles there occur the following four combinations of parts which if known will determine the size and form of the triangle.

    I. *One side and two angles are known*
   II. *Two sides and the included angle are known*
  III. *Three sides are known*
  IV. *Two sides and the angle opposite one of them is known.**

Applying the Laws of Sine, Tangent and Cosine to Oblique Triangles

Case I: One side and two angles are known

EXAMPLE: Given $\angle A = 56°$, $\angle B = 69°$ and $a = 467$; find b and c.

SOLUTION: We use the law of sines.

Formulas needed:

1. $C = 180° - (\angle A + \angle B)$

2. $\dfrac{b}{a} = \dfrac{\sin B}{\sin A},$

$\therefore b = \dfrac{a \sin B}{\sin A},$

3. $\dfrac{c}{a} = \dfrac{\sin C}{\sin A},$

$\therefore c = \dfrac{a \sin C}{\sin A}.$

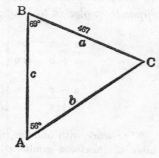

Substituting:

1. $\angle C = 180° - (56° + 69°) = 55°$

* This combination is considered an ambiguous case because it is often possible to form more than one triangle to satisfy the given conditions.

2. $b = \dfrac{467 \times .9336}{.8290} = 525.9$ ⎫
3. $c = \dfrac{467 \times .8192}{.8290} = 461.5$ ⎬ ANS.

Case II: Two sides and the included angle are known

EXAMPLE: Given $a = 17$, $b = 12$ and $\angle C = 58°$; find $\angle A$, $\angle B$ and c.

SOLUTION: We use the law of tangents to obtain $\angle A$ and $\angle B$ and the law of sines to obtain c.

Formulas needed:

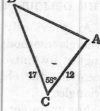

1. $A + B = 180° - C$ and $\frac{1}{2}(A + B) = \frac{1}{2}(180° - C)$
When $\frac{1}{2}(A + B)$ has been determined $\frac{1}{2}(A - B)$ is found by the following

2. $\dfrac{a - b}{a + b} = \dfrac{\tan \frac{1}{2}(A - B)}{\tan \frac{1}{2}(A + B)}$

$\therefore \tan \frac{1}{2}(A - B) = \dfrac{a - b}{a + b} \times \tan \frac{1}{2}(A + B)$

3. $\angle A = \frac{1}{2}(A + B) + \frac{1}{2}(A - B)$
in which the Bs cancel out
4. $\angle B = \frac{1}{2}(A + B) - \frac{1}{2}(A - B)$,
in which the As cancel out

5. $\dfrac{c}{a} = \dfrac{\sin C}{\sin A},$ $\therefore c = \dfrac{a \sin C}{\sin A}.$

Substituting:

1. $\frac{1}{2}(A + B) = \frac{1}{2}(180° - 58°) = 61°$

2. $\tan \frac{1}{2}(A - B) = \dfrac{17 - 12}{17 + 12} \times \tan 61° = .3110,$

which is the tan of 17° 16′ and equal to $\frac{1}{2}(A - B)$

3. $\angle A = 61° + 17° 16′ = 78° 16′$ ⎫
4. $\angle B = 61° - 17° 16′ = 43° 44′$ ⎬ ANS.
5. $c = \dfrac{17 \times \sin 58°}{\sin 78° 16′} = 14.7$ ⎭

This example could also be solved by the use of the law of cosines by first finding c ($c = \sqrt{a^2 + b^2 - 2ab \cos C}$). When the three sides and $\angle C$ are known the law of sines can be employed to find $\angle A$ and $\angle B$. For purposes of a check, do this example by the second method.

Case III: Three sides are known

EXAMPLE: Given $a = 5$, $b = 6$ and $c = 7$; find $\angle A$, $\angle B$ and $\angle C$.

SOLUTION: We use the law of cosines and the law of sines.

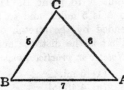

Formulas needed:

1. $a^2 = b^2 + c^2 - 2bc \cos A$

$$\therefore \cos A = \frac{b^2 + c^2 - a^2}{2bc}$$

2. $\dfrac{a}{b} = \dfrac{\sin A}{\sin B}$, $\qquad \therefore \sin B = \dfrac{b \sin A}{a}$

3. $\angle C = 180° - (A + B)$

Substituting:

$$\cos A = \frac{36 + 49 - 25}{2(6 \times 7)} = .7143$$

which is the cos of 44° 25′

$$\sin B = \frac{6 \times .69995}{5} = .8399,$$

which is the sin of 57° 45′

$\angle C = 180° - (44° 25′ + 57° 45′) = 77° 50′$

$\left.\begin{array}{l} \angle A = 44° 25′ \\ \angle B = 57° 45′ \\ \angle C = 77° 50′ \end{array}\right\}$ Ans.

Case IV (*the ambiguous case*): **Two sides and the angle opposite one of them are known**

When given two sides of a triangle and the angle opposite one of them, there is often a possibility of two solutions unless one of the solutions is excluded by the statement of the problem.

This fact may be clarified by the next figure. It will be seen in the triangle ABC

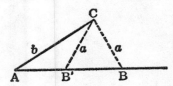

that if $\angle A$ and sides a and b are given, either of the triangles ABC or $AB'C$ meet the given conditions.

By varying the relative lengths of a and b and the magnitude of $\angle A$, the following possibilities can be recognized.

If $a > b$, $\angle A > \angle B$, which makes $\angle B$ less than 90°, and allows for only one solution.

If $a = b$, $\angle A = \angle B$; both angles are less than 90° and only an isosceles triangle can be formed.

If $a < b$ and $\angle A$ is acute, two triangles are possible.

If $a = b \sin A$, the figure is a right triangle and only one solution is possible.

If $a < b \sin A$, no triangle is possible.

Before doing a problem of this type you can generally determine the number of possible solutions by making an approximate small-scale drawing of the given parts.

In the cases where there are two possible solutions and the unknown parts are $\angle B$, $\angle C$ and side c, the second set of unknown parts should be designated as $\angle B'$, $\angle C'$ and side c'. They will then be found as follows:

$B' = 180° - B$, because when an angle is determined by its sine, it has two possible values that are supplementary to each other.

$C' = 180° - (A + B')$.

$$c' = \frac{a \sin C'}{\sin A}.$$

EXAMPLE: Given $a = 5$, $b = 8$ and $\angle A = 30°$; find $\angle B$, $\angle C$ and side c.

Here $a < b$ and $\angle A$ is acute. $\therefore$ two triangles are possible.

Formulas needed for $\triangle ABC$:

1. $\dfrac{b}{a} = \dfrac{\sin B}{\sin A}$, $\qquad \therefore \sin B = \dfrac{b \sin A}{a}$.

2. $\angle C = 180° - (A + B)$.

3. $\dfrac{c}{a} = \dfrac{\sin C}{\sin A}$, $\qquad \therefore c = \dfrac{a \sin C}{\sin A}$.

Substituting:

1. $\sin B = \dfrac{8 \times .5000}{5} = .8000,$

which is the sin of 53° 8′

2. $\angle C = 180° - (30° + 53° 8′) = 96° 52′$

3. $c = \dfrac{5 \times .9928}{.5000} = 9.928$

$\left.\begin{array}{l} \angle B = 53° 8′ \\ \angle C = 96° 52′ \\ c = 9.928 \end{array}\right\}$ Ans.

To find $\angle B'$, $\angle C'$ and c':

$\angle B' = 180° - B = 126° 52′$, Ans.

$\angle C' = 180° - (A + B') = 23° 8′$, Ans.

$$c' = \frac{a \sin C'}{\sin A} = \frac{5 \times 3.929}{5} = 3.929, \quad \text{Ans.}$$

Practice Exercise No. 80

In working out the problems in this exercise apply the principles for solving oblique triangles.

1 Given $\angle A = 45°$, $\angle B = 60°$ and $c = 9.562$; find a and b.

2 Given $a = 43$, $\angle A = 43°$ and $\angle B = 68°$; find $\angle C$, b and c.

3 Given $a = 22$, $b = 13$ and $\angle C = 68°$; find $\angle A$, $\angle B$ and c.

4 Given $a = 27$, $b = 26$, $c = 34$; find $\angle A$, $\angle B$ and $\angle C$.

5 Given $a = 8$, $b = 5$ and $\angle A = 21$; find c, $\angle A$ and $\angle B$.

6 Two airplane spotters, A and B, are 1.83 miles apart on the same level of ground. B is due north of A. At the same instant they both spot an airplane to the north, which makes an angle of elevation of 67° 31′ at A and 82° 16′ at B. What is the altitude of the airplane from the ground?

(A) 2.5 mi. _____   (c) 4 mi. _____
(B) 6.6 mi. _____   (D) 3.2 mi. _____

7 An observer on a boat anchored offshore sights on two points, A and B, on the shore. He determines the distance from himself to point A to be 985 feet, and the distance between A and B as 1,460 feet. The angle to the observer subtended by the points on shore is 64° 20′. How far is it from the observer to point B?

(A) 1,585.6 ft. _____   (c) 1,760 ft. _____
(B) 1,242.6 ft. _____   (D) 927.7 ft. _____

8 An observer at a fire tower spots a fire in a forest area extending across a stretch of land from point A to point B. The distance from the tower to A is 5 miles, and to B, 5½ miles. The angle subtended by the stretch of land to the tower is 50°. What is the distance across which the fire extends? (*Note: For practice purposes solve by the tangent law.*)

(A) 6 mi. _____   (c) 3.42 mi. _____
(B) 4.46 mi. _____   (D) 8.5 mi. _____

9 Two scouts start from a point C at the same time and branch out at an angle of 33° to each other. If one scout travels at the rate of 1 mile per hour while the other travels at the rate of 3 miles per hour, how far apart will they be at the end of 2 hours? (*Note: Solve by cosine law.*)

(A) 3 mi. _____   (c) 4.46 mi. _____
(B) 5.42 mi. _____   (D) 8.56 mi. _____

10 A cannon is placed in position at point A to fire upon an enemy fort located on a mountain. The airline distance from the gun to the fort has been determined as 5 miles. The distance on a horizontal plane from the gun to a point C at the base of the mountain is 3½ miles. From this point at the base to the fort itself the distance is 1.8 miles. (a) At what angle of elevation will the cannon have to be set in order to score a direct hit upon the fort? (b) What is the angle of depression from the fort to the cannon?

(a) (A) 27° 21′ _____   (c) 13° 40′ _____
    (B) 38° 59′ _____   (D) 16° 8′ _____

(b) (A) 38° 59′ _____   (c) 22° 16′ _____
    (B) 27° 21′ _____   (D) 13° 40′ _____

NOTE: For a more general discussion of trigonometric functions and trigonometric equations, see Chapter Eight of INTERMEDIATE ALGEBRA AND ANALYTIC GEOMETRY MADE SIMPLE.

Table VIII

TABLE OF NATURAL TRIGONOMETRIC FUNCTIONS

Degrees	Sin	Cos	Tan	Cot	Sec	Csc	
0° 00′	.0000	1.0000	.0000	——	1.000	——	90° 00′
10	029	000	029	343.8	000	343.8	50
20	058	000	058	171.9	000	171.9	40
30	.0087	1.0000	.0087	114.6	1.000	114.6	30
40	116	9999	116	85.94	000	85.95	20
50	145	999	145	68.75	000	68.76	10
1° 00′	.0175	.9998	.0175	57.29	1.000	57.30	89° 00′
10	204	998	204	49.10	000	49.11	50
20	233	997	233	42.96	000	42.98	40
30	.0262	.9997	.0262	38.19	1.000	38.20	30
40	291	996	291	34.37	000	34.38	20
50	320	995	320	31.24	001	31.26	10
2° 00′	.0349	.9994	.0349	28.64	1.001	28.65	88° 00′
10	378	993	378	26.43	001	26.45	50
20	407	992	407	24.54	001	24.56	40
30	.0436	.9990	.0437	22.90	1.001	22.93	30
40	465	989	466	21.47	001	21.49	20
50	494	988	495	20.21	001	20.23	10
3° 00′	.0523	.9986	.0524	19.08	1.001	19.11	87° 00′
10	552	985	553	18.07	002	18.10	50
20	581	983	582	17.17	002	17.20	40
30	.0610	.9981	.0612	16.35	1.002	16.38	30
40	640	980	641	15.60	002	15.64	20
50	669	978	670	14.92	002	14.96	10
4° 00′	.0698	.9976	.0699	14.30	1.002	14.34	86° 00′
10	727	974	729	13.73	003	13.76	50
20	756	971	758	13.20	003	13.23	40
30	.0785	.9969	.0787	12.71	1.003	12.75	30
40	814	967	816	12.25	003	12.29	20
50	843	964	846	11.83	004	11.87	10
5° 00′	.0872	.9962	.0875	11.43	1.004	11.47	85° 00′
10	901	959	904	11.06	004	11.10	50
20	929	957	934	10.71	004	10.76	40
30	.0958	.9954	.0963	10.39	1.005	10.43	30
40	987	951	992	10.08	005	10.13	20
50	.1016	948	.1022	9.788	005	9.839	10
6° 00′	.1045	.9945	.1051	9.514	1.006	9.567	84° 00′
10	074	942	080	9.255	006	9.309	50
20	103	939	110	9.010	006	9.065	40
30	.1132	.9936	.1139	8.777	1.006	8.834	30
40	161	932	169	8.556	007	8.614	20
50	190	929	198	8.345	007	8.405	10
7° 00′	.1219	.9925	.1228	8.144	1.008	8.206	83° 00′
10	248	922	257	7.953	008	8.016	50
20	276	918	287	7.770	008	7.834	40
30	.1305	.9914	.1317	7.596	1.009	7.661	30
40	334	911	346	7.429	009	7.496	20
50	363	907	376	7.269	009	7.337	10
8° 00′	.1392	.9903	.1405	7.115	1.010	7.185	82° 00′
10	421	899	435	6.968	010	7.040	50
20	449	894	465	6.827	011	6.900	40
30	.1478	.9890	.1495	6.691	1.011	6.765	30
40	507	886	524	6.561	012	6.636	20
50	536	881	554	6.435	012	6.512	10
9° 00′	.1564	.9877	.1584	6.314	1.012	6.392	81° 00′
	Cos	Sin	Cot	Tan	Csc	Sec	Degrees

Mathematics Made Simple

TABLE OF NATURAL TRIGONOMETRIC FUNCTIONS (*Continued*)

Degrees	Sin	Cos	Tan	Cot	Sec	Csc	
9° 00′	.1564	.9877	.1584	6.314	1.012	6.392	81° 00′
10	593	872	614	197	013	277	50
20	622	868	644	084	013	166	40
30	.1650	.9863	.1673	5.976	1.014	6.059	30
40	679	858	703	871	014	5.955	20
50	708	853	733	769	015	855	10
10° 00′	.1736	.9848	.1763	5.671	1.015	5.759	80° 00′
10	765	843	793	576	016	665	50
20	794	838	823	485	016	575	40
30	.1822	.9833	.1853	5.396	1.017	5.487	30
40	851	827	883	309	018	403	20
50	880	822	914	226	018	320	10
11° 00′	.1908	.9816	.1944	5.145	1.019	5.241	79° 00′
10	937	811	974	066	019	164	50
20	965	805	.2004	4.989	020	089	40
30	.1994	.9799	.2035	4.915	1.020	5.016	30
40	.2022	793	065	843	021	4.945	20
50	051	787	095	773	022	876	10
12° 00′	.2079	.9781	.2126	4.705	1.022	4.810	78° 00′
10	108	775	156	638	023	745	50
20	136	769	186	574	024	682	40
30	.2164	.9763	.2217	4.511	1.024	4.620	30
40	193	757	247	449	025	560	20
50	221	750	278	390	026	502	10
13° 00′	.2250	.9744	.2309	4.331	1.026	4.445	77° 00′
10	278	737	339	275	027	390	50
20	306	730	370	219	028	336	40
30	.2334	.9724	.2401	4.165	1.028	4.284	30
40	363	717	432	113	029	232	20
50	391	710	462	061	030	182	10
14° 00′	.2419	.9703	.2493	4.011	1.031	4.134	76° 00′
10	447	696	524	3.962	031	086	50
20	476	689	555	914	032	039	40
30	.2504	.9681	.2586	3.867	1.033	3.994	30
40	532	674	617	821	034	950	20
50	560	667	648	776	034	906	10
15° 00′	.2588	.9659	.2679	3.732	1.035	3.864	75° 00′
10	616	652	711	689	036	822	50
20	644	644	742	647	037	782	40
30	.2672	.9636	.2773	3.606	1.038	3.742	30
40	700	628	805	566	039	703	20
50	728	621	836	526	039	665	10
16° 00′	.2756	.9613	.2867	3.487	1.040	3.628	74° 00′
10	784	605	899	450	041	592	50
20	812	596	931	412	042	556	40
30	.2840	.9588	.2962	3.376	1.043	3.521	30
40	868	580	994	340	044	487	20
50	896	572	.3026	305	045	453	10
17° 00′	.2924	.9563	.3057	3.271	1.046	3.420	73° 00′
10	952	555	089	237	047	388	50
20	979	546	121	204	048	356	40
30	.3007	.9537	.3153	3.172	1.049	3.326	30
40	035	528	185	140	049	295	20
50	062	520	217	108	050	265	10
18° 00′	.3090	.9511	.3249	3.078	1.051	3.236	72° 00′
	Cos	Sin	Cot	Tan	Csc	Sec	Degrees

TABLE OF NATURAL TRIGONOMETRIC FUNCTIONS (*Continued*)

Degrees	Sin	Cos	Tan	Cot	Sec	Csc	
18° 00′	.3090	.9511	.3249	3.078	1.051	3.236	72° 00′
10	118	502	281	047	052	207	50
20	145	492	314	018	053	179	40
30	.3173	.9483	.3346	2.989	1.054	3.152	30
40	201	474	378	960	056	124	20
50	228	465	411	932	057	098	10
19° 00′	.3256	.9455	.3443	2.904	1.058	3.072	71° 00′
10	283	446	476	877	059	046	50
20	311	436	508	850	060	021	40
30	.3338	.9426	.3541	2.824	1.061	2.996	30
40	365	417	574	798	062	971	20
50	393	407	607	773	063	947	10
20° 00′	.3420	.9397	.3640	2.747	1.064	2.924	70° 00′
10	448	387	673	723	065	901	50
20	475	377	706	699	066	878	40
30	.3502	.9367	.3739	2.675	1.068	2.855	30
40	529	356	772	651	069	833	20
50	557	346	805	628	070	812	10
21° 00′	.3584	.9336	.3839	2.605	1.071	2.790	69° 00′
10	611	325	872	583	072	769	50
20	638	315	906	560	074	749	40
30	.3665	.9304	.3939	2.539	1.075	2.729	30
40	692	293	973	517	076	709	20
50	719	283	.4006	496	077	689	10
22° 00′	.3746	.9272	.4040	2.475	1.079	2.669	68° 00′
10	773	261	074	455	080	650	50
20	800	250	108	434	081	632	40
30	.3827	.9239	.4142	2.414	1.082	2.613	30
40	854	228	176	394	084	595	20
50	881	216	210	375	085	577	10
23° 00′	.3907	.9205	.4245	2.356	1.086	2.559	67° 00′
10	934	194	279	337	088	542	50
20	961	182	314	318	089	525	40
30	.3987	.9171	.4348	2.300	1.090	2.508	30
40	.4014	159	383	282	092	491	20
50	041	147	417	264	093	475	10
24° 00′	.4067	.9135	.4452	2.246	1.095	2.459	66° 00′
10	094	124	487	229	096	443	50
20	120	112	522	211	097	427	40
30	.4147	.9100	.4557	2.194	1.099	2.411	30
40	173	088	592	177	100	396	20
50	200	075	628	161	102	381	10
25° 00′	.4226	.9063	.4663	2.145	1.103	2.366	65° 00′
10	253	051	699	128	105	352	50
20	279	038	734	112	106	337	40
30	.4305	.9026	.4770	2.097	1.108	2.323	30
40	331	013	806	081	109	309	20
50	358	001	841	066	111	295	10
26° 00′	.4384	.8988	.4877	2.050	1.113	2.281	64° 00′
10	410	975	913	035	114	268	50
20	436	962	950	020	116	254	40
30	.4462	.8949	.4986	2.006	1.117	2.241	30
40	488	936	.5022	1.991	119	228	20
50	514	923	059	977	121	215	10
27° 00′	.4540	.8910	.5095	1.963	1.122	2.203	63° 00′
	Cos	Sin	Cot	Tan	Csc	Sec	Degrees

Mathematics Made Simple

TABLE OF NATURAL TRIGONOMETRIC FUNCTIONS (*Continued*)

Degrees	Sin	Cos	Tan	Cot	Sec	Csc	
27° 00′	.4540	.8910	.5095	1.963	1.122	2.203	63° 00′
10	566	897	132	949	124	190	50
20	592	884	169	935	126	178	40
30	.4617	.8870	.5206	1.921	1.127	2.166	30
40	643	857	243	907	129	154	20
50	669	843	280	894	131	142	10
28° 00′	.4695	.8829	.5317	1.881	1.133	2.130	62° 00′
10	720	816	354	868	134	118	50
20	746	802	392	855	136	107	40
30	.4772	.8788	.5430	1.842	1.138	2.096	30
40	797	774	467	829	140	085	20
50	823	760	505	816	142	074	10
29° 00′	.4848	.8746	.5543	1.804	1.143	2.063	61° 00′
10	874	732	581	792	145	052	50
20	899	718	619	780	147	041	40
30	.4924	.8704	.5658	1.767	1.149	2.031	30
40	950	689	696	756	151	020	20
50	975	675	735	744	153	010	10
30° 00′	.5000	.8660	.5774	1.732	1.155	2.000	60° 00′
10	025	646	812	720	157	1.990	50
20	050	631	851	709	159	980	40
30	.5075	.8616	.5890	1.698	1.161	1.970	30
40	100	601	930	686	163	961	20
50	125	587	969	675	165	951	10
31° 00′	.5150	.8572	.6009	1.664	1.167	1.942	59° 00′
10	175	557	048	653	169	932	50
20	200	542	088	643	171	923	40
30	.5225	.8526	.6128	1.632	1.173	1.914	30
40	250	511	168	621	175	905	20
50	275	496	208	611	177	896	10
32° 00′	.5299	.8480	.6249	1.600	1.179	1.887	58° 00′
10	324	465	289	590	181	878	50
20	348	450	330	580	184	870	40
30	.5373	.8434	.6371	1.570	1.186	1.861	30
40	398	418	412	560	188	853	20
50	422	403	453	550	190	844	10
33° 00′	.5446	.8387	.6494	1.540	1.192	1.836	57° 00′
10	471	371	536	530	195	828	50
20	495	355	577	520	197	820	40
30	.5519	.8339	.6619	1.511	1.199	1.812	30
40	544	323	661	501	202	804	20
50	568	307	703	1.492	204	796	10
34° 00′	.5592	.8290	.6745	1.483	1.206	1.788	56° 00′
10	616	274	787	473	209	781	50
20	640	258	830	464	211	773	40
30	.5664	.8241	.6873	1.455	1.213	1.766	30
40	688	225	916	446	216	758	20
50	712	208	959	437	218	751	10
35° 00′	.5736	.8192	.7002	1.428	1.221	1.743	55° 00′
10	760	175	046	419	223	736	50
20	783	158	089	411	226	729	40
30	.5807	.8141	.7133	1.402	1.228	1.722	30
40	831	124	177	393	231	715	20
50	854	107	221	385	233	708	10
36° 00′	.5878	.8090	.7265	1.376	1.236	1.701	54° 00′
	Cos	Sin	Cot	Tan	Csc	Sec	Degrees

TABLE OF NATURAL TRIGONOMETRIC FUNCTIONS (*Continued*)

Degrees	Sin	Cos	Tan	Cot	Sec	Csc	
36° 00′	.5878	.8090	.7265	1.376	1.236	1.701	54° 00′
10	901	073	310	368	239	695	50
20	925	056	355	360	241	688	40
30	.5948	.8039	.7400	1.351	1.244	1.681	30
40	972	021	445	343	247	675	20
50	995	004	490	335	249	668	10
37° 00′	.6018	.7986	.7536	1.327	1.252	1.662	53° 00′
10	041	969	581	319	255	655	50
20	065	951	627	311	258	649	40
30	.6088	.7934	.7673	1.303	1.260	1.643	30
40	111	916	720	295	263	636	20
50	134	898	766	288	266	630	10
38° 00′	.6157	.7880	.7813	1.280	1.269	1.624	52° 00′
10	180	862	860	272	272	618	50
20	202	844	907	265	275	612	40
30	.6225	.7826	.7954	1.257	1.278	1.606	30
40	248	808	.8002	250	281	601	20
50	271	790	050	242	284	595	10
39° 00′	.6293	.7771	.8098	1.235	1.287	1.589	51° 00′
10	316	753	146	228	290	583	50
20	338	735	195	220	293	578	40
30	.6361	.7716	.8243	1.213	1.296	1.572	30
40	383	698	292	206	299	567	20
50	406	679	342	199	302	561	10
40° 00′	.6428	.7660	.8391	1.192	1.305	1.556	50° 00′
10	450	642	441	185	309	550	50
20	472	623	491	178	312	545	40
30	.6494	.7604	.8541	1.171	1.315	1.540	30
40	517	585	591	164	318	535	20
50	539	566	642	157	322	529	10
41° 00′	.6561	.7547	.8693	1.150	1.325	1.524	49° 00′
10	583	528	744	144	328	519	50
20	604	509	796	137	332	514	40
30	.6626	.7490	.8847	1.130	1.335	1.509	30
40	648	470	899	124	339	504	20
50	670	451	952	117	342	499	10
42° 00′	.6691	.7431	.9004	1.111	1.346	1.494	48° 00′
10	713	412	057	104	349	490	50
20	734	392	110	098	353	485	40
30	.6756	.7373	.9163	1.091	1.356	1.480	30
40	777	353	217	085	360	476	20
50	799	333	271	079	364	471	10
43° 00′	.6820	.7314	.9325	1.072	1.367	1.466	47° 00′
10	841	294	380	066	371	462	50
20	862	274	435	060	375	457	40
30	.6884	.7254	.9490	1.054	1.379	1.453	30
40	905	234	545	048	382	448	20
50	926	214	601	042	386	444	10
44° 00′	.6947	.7193	.9657	1.036	1.390	1.440	46° 00′
10	967	173	713	030	394	435	50
20	988	153	770	024	398	431	40
30	.7009	.7133	.9827	1.018	1.402	1.427	30
40	030	112	884	012	406	423	20
50	050	092	942	006	410	418	10
45° 00′	.7071	.7071	1.0000	1.000	1.414	1.414	45° 00′
	Cos	Sin	Cot	Tan	Csc	Sec	Degrees

CHAPTER SIXTEEN

SCALES AND GRAPHS

SCALES

A **scale** is a convenient representation of one quantity or magnitude in terms of another. A scale thus expresses a ratio.

For instance, what covers miles in reality, occupies only inches on a map. Hence, a map has a scale based on the ratio between distances *mapped* and distances *on* the map. This scale is usually shown on the map by a diagram, as here illustrated.

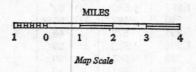

MILES

Map Scale

The *speedometer* in an automobile has a scale based on the ratio between circular displacements on its dial and the speed at which the car is traveling.

EXAMPLE: In making a speedometer, if a displacement equivalent to a 10° angle represented a speed of 5 miles per hour, what angle would be needed to represent a speed of 30 miles an hour?

SOLUTION: If 10° = 5 miles per hour, then 2° = 1 mile per hour, and 30 miles per hour = 30 × 2 or 60°, Ans.

A *thermometer* has a scale based on the ratio between the height of a column of mercury and the temperature of air or of some other medium or material, as measured in centigrade or Fahrenheit degrees.

A *blueprint* is "drawn to scale." This means that the drawing on the blueprint represents a scale ratio. For instance in the blueprint of the hull of a ship, if the scale is $\frac{1}{4}''$ to $1'$, then every line 1 inch in length on the blueprint represents 4 ft. of the hull.

EXAMPLE: If a beam of the hull is to be 100 ft., how long a line would be needed on the blue-

print just described in order to represent this beam?

SOLUTION: If $\frac{1}{4}'' = 1$ ft., then $1'' = 4$ ft., then $1' = 48$ ft. $100 \div 4 = 2'\ 1''$, Ans.

GRAPHS

A *graph* is a diagram showing relationships between two or more factors. Most graphs have two scales, as the following population graph indicates:

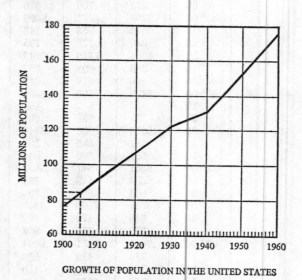

GROWTH OF POPULATION IN THE UNITED STATES

PARTS OF A GRAPH

In the preceding example the graph has a vertical scale, in which a unit of space on the paper represents 20 million population, and a horizontal scale, in which the same unit represents a period of 10 years. The **vertical scale** is sometimes called the **vertical axis** or **ordinate,** while the **horizontal scale** is called the **horizontal axis** or **abscissa.**

READING THE GRAPH

The graph just presented shows the population of the United States in millions from

1900 to 1960. If you could assume that the population growth was fairly uniform for any ten-year period, then you could estimate from the graph the population for the years 1905, 1906, 1907, etc. For example, 1905 is midway between 1900 and 1910. At this point move up vertically until you reach the graph line. From this point follow the broken line horizontally. It intersects the population scale about one-fifth of the way between 80 and 100. The population estimate would therefore be about 84 million in 1905.

TYPES OF GRAPHS

The **broken line graph** next shown illustrates the variations in deaths due to automobile accidents between the years 1925 and 1955. It is called a line graph because a line is used to represent the factors in the two scales.

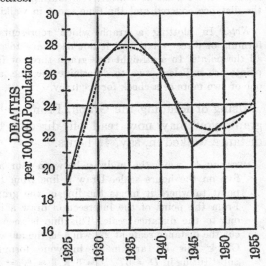

AUTOMOBILE DEATHS PER 100,000 POPULATION

The broken line in this graph is plotted from the actual number of accidents. The light dotted line averages the path of the broken line.

Broken line graphs are especially suitable for recording so-called *historical* data involving a factor subject to constant and severe fluctuation. This type of graph, accordingly, is preferred for presenting price records of stocks, commodities, etc.

The **bar graph** illustrated in the right-hand column gives the number of persons examined in a certain city during the years 1935 to 1960. The height of the black bar, indicating the number of cases, represents the vertical scale, while its base position, indicating the specific year, represents the horizontal scale.

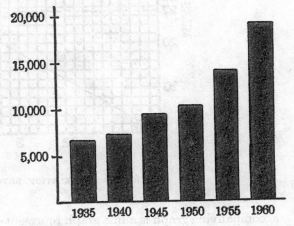

CASES EXAMINED BY A MEDICAL ADVISORY SERVICE

The **circle graph** is usually on a percentage basis: the whole circle represents 100%, while fractional percentages are indicated by proportionate segments of the circle. The following figure illustrates such a graph.

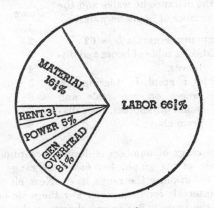

HOW A MANUFACTURER'S EXPENSES ARE APPORTIONED BEFORE TAXES

MATHEMATICAL GRAPHS

The graphs presented up to this point were merely graphic representations of statistical facts about items that are related but not according to any well-defined rules or formulas. The items were not causally related, that is, a change in one did not always produce a change in the other. However, the

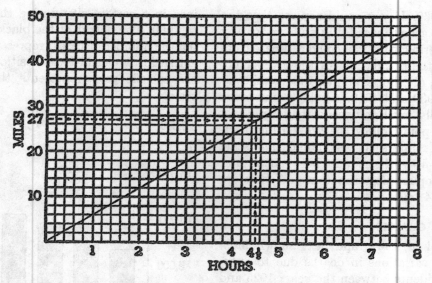

GRAPH SHOWING RELATION BETWEEN WALKER'S TIME AND DISTANCE

accompanying graph is a line graph representing quantities that change together. Such graphs may be made from formulas or equations and vice versa. These may be called mathematical graphs.

EXAMPLE: A man walks at a rate of 6 miles an hour. Show graphically the relation between the distance he walks and the number of hours he walks.

SOLUTION: Formula $D = 6T$.

Make a table of hours and distances.

Plot a graph by placing distances on one scale and hours on another. (See diagram above.)

Hours	Distance
1	6
2	12
3	18
4	24
5	30
6	36
7	42
8	48

The range of numbers is decided according to the purpose of the graph. For *hours* the range selected is 8; for *distance* the range is 48. Next choose your unit intervals for each scale. For the scale of hours, since the range is 8, you can choose one large or unit box on the graph paper as equal to one hour. For the scale of distance this would not be practical, since you would need too much space. Therefore you choose a convenient interval. In this case let one small unit or square equal a distance of two miles. Then proceed to plot each point according to the pairs of items in the table. Thus the first point on the graph represents 1 hour and a distance of 6 miles, the second point represents 2 hours and a distance of 12 miles, etc. These points are called coordinates. When all the points are plotted draw your line, which in this case proves to be a straight line, show-

ing that there must be a direct relationship between the distance covered and the time spent in walking.

Note: In plotting a graph which represents a formula or direct relation it is not necessary to plot all the points. In a straight line graph three or four points are sufficient, two to determine the line, and one or two more as a check for accuracy.

Using or Reading the Graph. From such a graph you may now read off directly the distance walked in, say, $4\frac{1}{2}$ hours.

METHOD: $4\frac{1}{2}$ would be midway between four and five on the hours scale. Draw a line from this point to where it meets the line of the graph. From the point of the intersection draw a line out to the distance scale. This line is seen to cut the distance scale at 27, which is the answer. Check this by arithmetic in your formula. Substituting in $D = 6T$, $D = 6 \times \frac{9}{2} = \frac{54}{2} = 27$.

Picture graphs are used to illustrate statistical information, but the unit is not a distance measure on a page as in the line and bar graphs, but rather a symbol of the fact being illustrated. The next figure illustrates such a graph in which several symbols are used.

THE MAN-POWER SITUATION IN "COUNTRY X"

Practice Exercise No. 81

PROBLEMS

1 Construct a broken line graph from the data given in the bar graph on page 147.

2 From the data given in the broken line graph construct a bar graph giving the number of deaths due to automobile accidents during the years 1925, 1930, 1935, 1940, 1945, 1950 and 1955.

3 If a certain type of lumber cost 8 cents a foot, make a table and graph showing the relationship between the cost and the number of feet of lumber bought. The range in feet should be from 15 ft. to 55 ft. Use intervals of 10 ft. and 80 cents. By arithmetic compute the price of $36\frac{1}{2}$ feet of lumber. Now find the price of $36\frac{1}{2}$ feet of lumber from the graph by the method indicated for graphic reading.

4 From the graph on the preceding page find out how long it would take to walk 39 miles and check by arithmetic.

5 From your graph in Problem 3 above, find out how many feet of lumber you can buy for $256. Check by arithmetic.

6 A young man's day is divided as follows: work, 7 hrs.; eating and dressing, $3\frac{1}{2}$ hrs.; study, 3 hrs.; travel, $1\frac{1}{2}$ hrs.; recreation and miscellaneous, 1 hr.; sleep, 8 hrs. Figure out the percentages for these divisions and draw a circular graph to illustrate.

NOTE: For the use of graphing devices to interpret and solve algebraic and geometric problems, see INTERMEDIATE ALGEBRA AND ANALYTIC GEOMETRY MADE SIMPLE.

CHAPTER SEVENTEEN

COMBINATIONS AND PERMUTATIONS

PRELIMINARY EXPLANATIONS

When a baseball coach picks *9* men out of a *squad* of *20* to form a team, mathematically he may be said to be making a *combination* of *20* "*things*" taken *9 at a time*. When the coach assigns the members of such a team the *sequence* of a particular batting *order*, mathematically he may be said to be making a *permutation* of the *same* 20 "things" 9 at a time.

Combinations, we thus see, are *groupings* of things *without* regard to their order. *Permutations* are *arrangements* of the same in the *sequences* of *particular orders*. And the numerical aspects of both topics are important since our workaday world is obviously one of much grouping and arranging.

Common symbols for the *total number* of *all possible combinations* of *n* *things taken t at a time* are

$$C(n, t), \quad C_t^n, \quad {}_nC_t, \quad \text{or} \quad \binom{n}{t}.$$

Of these we shall here use only the first two, as when we designate all the possible combi-

nations of 20 things taken 9 at a time, by the symbols $C(20, 9)$ or C_9^{20}.

The corresponding *symbols* for the *total number* of *all possible permutations* of *n* things taken *t* at a time are

$$P(n, t), \quad P_t^n, \quad \text{or} \quad {}_nP_t.$$

Of these we shall here use only the first, as when we designate *all* the possible permutations of 20 things, taken 9 at a time, by the symbol $P(20, 9)$.

For any given pair of numerical values of *n* and *t* in these formulas, there are in general many *more* possible *permutations* than there are possible *combinations*.

As a simple illustration, suppose that we have any *3* objects—such as a set of three paintings designated *A*, *B*, *C*. The only possible *grouping* of all *3* of these which we can select at a time *without* regard to sequence is the *combination*,

$$C(3, 3) = 1: \quad \overparen{A \text{ and } B \text{ and } C.}$$

But we can *arrange* this one combination—

by hanging the paintings on adjacent wall panels, for instance—in any of the *sequences* of the possible *permutations* of 3 things taken all 3 at a time,

$$P(3, 3) = 6: \quad ABC, \quad BAC, \quad CAB,$$
$$ACB, \quad BCA, \quad CBA.$$

Moreover, we can select *groupings* from these same 3 objects, *2* at a time without regard to sequence, in any of the *combinations*,

$$C(3, 2) = 3: \quad \overparen{A \text{ and } B},$$
$$\overparen{B \text{ and } C},$$
$$\overparen{C \text{ and } A}.$$

But we can *arrange* these *combinations* in the *sequences* of the possible *permutations* of 3 things taken 2 at a time,

$$P(3, 2) = 6: \quad AB, \quad BA, \quad CA,$$
$$AC, \quad BC, \quad CB.$$

However, in the *special case* that we select *only 1* of these 3 objects at a time, we *cannot* permute any single grouping from its original order of *1 thing standing by itself*. In other words, the numbers of possible combinations and permutations are *the same*,

$$C(3, 1) = P(3, 1) = 3: \quad A \text{ (alone)},$$
$$B \text{ (alone)},$$
$$C \text{ (alone)}.$$

This illustrates the *general fact* that, for *any number* of objects, n,

$$P(n, 1) = C(n, 1) = n.$$

EXAMPLE 1: By forming arrays of all the possibilities, as above, find $C(5, 2)$ and $P(5, 2)$.

SOLUTION: Letting A, B, C, D, E represent the *5 things*, we can systematically *combine* them 2 at a time in any of the ways,

$$C(5, 2): \quad \overparen{A \& B},$$
$$\overparen{A \& C}, \quad \overparen{B \& C},$$
$$\overparen{A \& D}, \quad \overparen{B \& D}, \quad \overparen{C \& D},$$
$$\overparen{A \& E}, \quad \overparen{B \& E}, \quad \overparen{C \& E}, \quad \overparen{D \& E}.$$

And we can systematically *permute* these combinations in the ways,

$$P(5, 2): \quad \begin{array}{ccccc} AB, & BA, & CA, & DA, & EA, \\ AC, & BC, & CB, & DB, & EB, \\ AD, & BD, & CD, & DC, & EC, \\ AE, & BE, & CE, & DE, & ED. \end{array}$$

By actual count of these arrays, as in the preceding illustrations, we now find that

$$C(5, 2) = 10, \quad P(5, 2) = 20, \quad \text{Ans.}$$

In other words: there are 10 possible *combinations* of 5 things taken 2 at a time; and there are 20 possible *permutations* of 5 things taken 2 at a time.

Unless n and t have very small values, it is tedious to find $C(n, t)$ and $P(n, t)$ by the method of the above illustrations in which all the separate possibilities are written out in an *array* and then counted. Hence, in actual practice, *short-method formulas* are used.

One might, perhaps, expect the derivation of these formulas to begin with the simpler concept of a combination, which does not involve the idea of arrangement in different sequences. Nevertheless, in most instances, it is mathematically simpler to compute $P(n, t)$ than to compute $C(n, t)$; and for this reason we begin with permutations formulas.

PERMUTATIONS FORMULAS

Returning to the above illustration of $P(3, 3) = 6$, the 6 possible permutations of 3 things taken 3 at a time—ABC, ACB, etc.— note now that each arrangement in the array begins with one of the *3* possibilities, A, B, C. But once this first permutational position has been filled, only the *2* remaining possibilities can be assigned to the second permutational position (B or C after A, and A or C after B, etc.). And once both of the first 2 permutational positions have been filled, only the *one* remaining possibility can be assigned to the third permutational position (C after A and B, etc.).

Thus we see that $P(3, 3)$ must be the *product* of *3* possible entries for the *first* permutational position, times $3 - 1 = 2$ possible entries for the *second* permutational position, times $3 - 2 = 1$ possible entry for the *third* permutational position; or $3(2)(1) = 6$, which was the actual count.

The product in this form is called **factorial three.** The symbol for it is **3!,** meaning **3** times **2** times **1,** which is a special case of

$$n! = n(n-1)(n-2) \cdots (2)(1).$$

Return next to the illustration in Example 1 of $P(5, 2) = 20,$ the 20 possible permutations of 5 things taken 2 at a time—*AB, AC, AD,* etc. We can similarly see that $P(5, 2)$ must be the product of *5* possible entries for the *first* permutational position, times $5 - 1 = 4$ possible entries for the *second* permutational position; or $5(4) = 20,$ which again was the actual count.

Note in this last case, however, that $5(4) = 5!/3! = 5!/(5 - 2)!,$ since $3! = (5 - 2)!$ in the denominator of this fraction cancels out the $(3)(2)(1)$ of *5!* in its numerator. Therefore, *generalizing* the reasoning of the two above examples to the case of *all the possible permutations* of any *n* things taken *t* at a time, we arrive at the *formula,*

$$P(n, t) = \frac{n!}{(n-t)!} \cdot$$

In the **special case** where $t = n,$ this becomes

$$P(n, n) = n!,$$

since the denominator of the $P(n, t)$ formula is then *eliminated.* [NOTE especially here that when $t = n,$ then $(n - n)!$ or $(0)!$ in the denominator is, by definition, *no number at all.* Therefore, it is NOT equal to *zero,* which would make the first permutation formula *meaningless!*]

Permutations formulas are applicable to the solution of many different types of problems involving arrangements in different sequences.

EXAMPLE 2: In how many different orders may 5 of 7 different wires from one piece of electrical equipment be attached to 5 different posts on another?

SOLUTION: Since the question of *sequence* (order) is involved in this problem, it is one of *permutations* with $n = 7$ and $t = 5.$ Hence

$$P(7, 5) = \frac{7!}{(7-5)!} = \frac{7!}{2!}$$

$$= \frac{7 \cdot 6 \cdot 5 \cdot 4 \cdot 3 \cdot 2 \cdot 1}{2 \cdot 1} = 2,520, \quad \text{ANS.}$$

Since it is obvious from the arithmetic of this solution that the *1* (*one*) factor of *n!* never affects the result, we shall hereafter leave it implied (not written) in numerical computations.

EXAMPLE 3: In how many different arrangements may 5 persons be seated along the head of a banquet table?

SOLUTION: Here $n = t = 5,$ and

$$P(5, 5) = 5! = 5 \cdot 4 \cdot 3 \cdot 2 = 120, \quad \text{ANS.}$$

When *special conditions* are attached to permutation problems, the *same formulas* may often still be used, but they must be *adapted* to the problems' different requirements.

EXAMPLE 4: How many different arrangements are there possible in the preceding example if one particular pair of persons must always be seated next to each other?

SOLUTION: Temporarily considering the special pair as *a unit,* we may think of the first part of our problem as one of permuting *this unit* with the other three persons. *Then* $n = t = 4,$ and

$$P(4, 4) = 4! = 4 \cdot 3 \cdot 2 = 24, \quad \text{PARTIAL ANS.}$$

But in *each* such permutation, the 2 members of the special pair may sit next to each other in *either* of the *2* possible orders, *AB* or *BA.* Hence, the total number of possible permutations is really *twice* $P(4, 4),$ or

$$2P(4, 4) = 2(24) = 48, \quad \text{ANS.}$$

EXAMPLE 5: Answer the same question if the special pair must always be seated *separated from* each other.

SOLUTION: The entire group can be seated with no special conditions in $P(5, 5)$ different ways (*Example 2*), and with the special pair together in $2P(4, 4)$ different ways (*Example 3*). Hence, the number of ways in which they can be seated with the special pair separated must be the *difference* between these two figures, or

$$P(5, 5) - 2P(4, 4) = 120 - 48 = 72, \quad \text{ANS.}$$

EXAMPLE 6: Recompute the answer to Example 2 if the 5 persons are to be seated, with no others, about a *round* table.

SOLUTION: Now no one person is actually "first," "last," or "centered," in a linear ("lined up") arrangement. However, we may arbitrarily think of any *one* person's position as "fixed" for purposes of reference and then permute the positions of the other *4* with respect to each other, clockwise or counter-clockwise from this point of reference. Thus $n = 5 - 1 = 4$, and as further above,

$$P(4, 4) = 4! = 24, \quad \text{ANS.}$$

Arrangements of things in a *closed chain* or *ring*, as in the last example, are called *circular permutations*. Generalizing the method of reasoning just illustrated, therefore, we derive for P_c, the *total number of circular permutations* possible for any *n* things taken *n* at a time, the *formula*

$$P_c(n, n) = (n - 1)!$$

Thus the preceding solution could have been arrived at directly, by substitution in this formula, as

$$P_c(5, 5) = (5 - 1)! = 4!, \text{ etc.}$$

EXAMPLE 7: In Example 3 suppose 3 of the 5 persons to be men (represented by M's) and 2 to be women (represented by W's). In how many different arrangements can they be seated *according to gender* rather than as individuals?

SOLUTION: Let our answer be P_a, the total number of permutations possible for 3 (indistinguishable) M's and 2 (indistinguishable) W's, taken all 5 at a time as in the typical case of $MMMWW$. Then in order to express $P(5, 5)$ in terms of P_a, we would have to multiply the latter by $P(3, 3) = 3!$ to obtain the number of permutations in which the 3 M's are distinguishable as M_1, M_2, M_3, and by $P(2, 2) = 2!$ to obtain the number of cases in which the 2 W's are also distinguishable as W_1 and W_2. But we already know that $P(5, 5) = 5!$ Hence, by substitution

$$3!2!P_a = P(5, 5) = 5!$$

And therefore

$$P_a = \frac{5!}{3!2!} = \frac{\overset{2 \cdot 1 \cdot 1}{5 \cdot 4 \cdot 3 \cdot 2}}{\underset{1 \cdot 1 \cdot 1}{3 \cdot 2 \cdot 2}} = 10, \quad \text{ANS.}$$

These 10 possible ways, 6 beginning with a man and 4 with a woman, are illustrated as follows:

$$6 \begin{cases} MMMWW, \\ MMWMW, \\ MMWWM, \\ MWMMW, \\ MWMWM, \\ MWWMM, \end{cases} \left. \begin{matrix} WMMMW, \\ WMMWM, \\ WMWMM, \\ WWMMM. \end{matrix} \right\} 4$$

Note that the preceding problem requires us to treat its "men" as M's "all alike" and its "women" as W's "all alike." This is doubtless sociologically superstitious and matrimonially foolish. But the accompanying mathematical procedure is nevertheless sound. Generalizing the solution's method of reasoning, we derive for P_a, the *total number of indistinguishable permutations* possible for *n* things taken *n* at a time when n_1 are all alike, and n_2 are all alike, etc., the *formula*,

$$P_a = \frac{n!}{n_1! n_2! \cdots}$$

EXAMPLE 8: As for purposes of cryptography, how many indistinguishable 9-letter words can be formed by permutations of the letters in the code word, "TENNESSEE"?

SOLUTION: Here $n = 9$, $n_1 = 4$ for the E letters, and $n_2 = n_3 = 2$ for the N and S letters. Hence,

$$P_a = \frac{9!}{4!2!2!} = \frac{\overset{2}{9} \cdot 8 \cdot 7 \cdot 6 \cdot 5 \cdot \overset{1 \cdot 1 \cdot 1}{4 \cdot 3 \cdot 2}}{\underset{1 \cdot 1 \cdot 1 \cdot 1 \cdot 1}{4 \cdot 3 \cdot 2 \cdot 2 \cdot 2}} = 3{,}780, \quad \text{ANS.}$$

EXAMPLE 9: In how many different ways can a coach assign speakers to the first and second positions of a 2-man debating team from a squad of 12 candidates?

SOLUTION: Here $N = 12$, $t = 2$, and

$$P(12, 2) = \frac{12!}{(12 - 2)!} = \frac{12!}{10!}$$

$$= \frac{12 \cdot 11 \cdot \overset{1\,1\,1\,1\,1\,1\,1\,1\,1\,1}{10 \cdot 9 \cdot 8 \cdot 7 \cdot 6 \cdot 5 \cdot 4 \cdot 3 \cdot 2}}{\underset{1\,1\,1\,1\,1\,1\,1\,1\,1}{10 \cdot 9 \cdot 8 \cdot 7 \cdot 6 \cdot 5 \cdot 4 \cdot 3 \cdot 2}}$$

$$= 132, \quad \text{ANS.}$$

Or, with the second line written more briefly,

$$= 12 \cdot 11 \cdot \frac{10!}{10!} = 132, \quad \text{THE SAME ANS.}$$

since $10!/10! = 1$.

From this example we see that *it is always*

correct, and often arithmetically more convenient, to treat

$$\frac{n!}{(n-t)!} = n(n-1)(n-2) \cdots (n-t+1)$$

in the *basic formula* for $P(n, t)$. From now on, therefore, we shall write $12!/(12 - 10)!$ or $12!/10!$ directly as $12 \cdot 11$, etc., whenever we do not wish to use the other factors of the numerator for cancellations with other denominator factors in the same term.

COMBINATIONS FORMULAS

From the very beginning of this chapter we have seen that *permutations are simply different arrangements of the things grouped in corresponding combinations.* More particularly, each *set* of *permutations* of any given t things in $P(n, t)$ consists simply of *different arrangements* of the *same* t things in a *corresponding combination* of $C(n, t)$.

But now we know from our basic permutations formula that *each combination* of t things in $C(n, t)$ can have $P(t, t) = t!$ possible *permutations*. Hence,

$$t! C(n, t) = P(n, t).$$

Dividing by $t! = t!$, we then obtain the second important *basic relationship*,

$$C(n, t) = \frac{P(n, t)}{t!},$$

and by substitution for $P(n, t)$ from our basic permutations formula, this gives us for the **number of all possible combinations of n things taken t at a time**, the *basic formula*,

$$C(n, t) = \frac{n!}{t!(n-t)!}.$$

In the *special case* where $t = n$, the denominator factor, $(t - t)!$ or $(0)!$ is again *eliminated* (see NOTE on page 151), and the above formula takes the anticipated form,

$$C(n, n) = n!/n! = 1.$$

Combinations formulas can be applied to the solution of many different types of problems in which selections are to be made without regard to the possible permutations of arrangement.

EXAMPLE 10: (a) In how many different ways may a coach assign players, from a squad of 12, to the 9 *positions* on a baseball line-up? (b) In how many different ways can he select a team of 9 from the same squad *without regard to the positions they are to play?*

SOLUTION: Here $n = 12$ and $t = 9$. Since question (a) involves positions, we must again use the previously derived *permutations* formula,

$$P(12, 9) = \frac{12!}{(12 - 9)!} = \frac{12!}{3!}$$
$$= 12 \cdot 11 \cdot 10 \cdot 9 \cdot 8 \cdot 7 \cdot 6 \cdot 5 \cdot 4$$
$$= 79,833,600, \quad \text{Ans. (a)}$$

But since question (b) concerns *selection without regard to position played*, we must now use our new *combinations* formula,

$$C(12, 9) = \frac{12!}{9!(12 - 9)!} = \frac{12!}{9!3!}.$$

Then, dividing numerator and denominator by $9!$ rather than by $3!$, this gives us most simply,

$$\frac{\overset{4}{1\!\!\!/2} \cdot 11 \cdot \overset{5}{1\!\!\!/0}}{\underset{1}{3} \cdot \underset{1}{2}} = 220, \quad \text{Ans. (b)}$$

Note in this numerical instance how very large a number of possible permutations may be as compared to the corresponding number of possible combinations. The latter may also be surprisingly large, however; and then it is important to shorten the computation by the arithmetic device of the above solution.

EXAMPLE 11: In how many different ways can one poker hand of 5 cards be dealt from a 52-card deck?

SOLUTION: Since the final grouping of the cards, rather than the order in which they are dealt, is important here, the problem is again one of combinations rather than of permutations. Hence, $n = 52$, $t = 5$, and

$$C(52, 5) = \frac{52!}{5!(52 - 5)!} = \frac{52!}{5!47!}$$
$$= \frac{52 \cdot 51 \cdot \overset{10}{5\!\!\!/0} \cdot 49 \cdot \overset{2}{4\!\!\!/8}}{\underset{1}{5} \cdot \underset{1}{4} \cdot \underset{1}{3} \cdot \underset{1}{2}} = 2,598,960, \quad \text{Ans.}$$

INTER-GROUP COMBINATIONS

Thus far we have meant by "combinations" only "*sub-group* combinations"—those of t

things taken from the *same* group of n things. But many related problems concern **inter-group** combinations. These may be defined as selections of t_1 things at a time from a *first* group of n_1 things, *along with* t_2 things at a time from a *second* group of n_2 things, *along with* t_3 things at a time from a *third* group of n_3 things, *etc.*

Suppose, for instance, that we wish to combine 1 of 2 photographs, R and S, with 2 of the 3 paintings, A, B, and C, mentioned at the beginning of this chapter (page 149). Here $n_1 = 2$ (photographs), $t_1 = 1$; $n_2 = 3$ (paintings), $t_2 = 2$; and *the total number of possible inter-group combinations*, $N = 6$, is illustrated by the array:

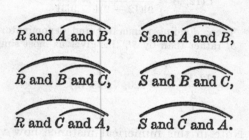

R and A and B, S and A and B,

R and B and C, S and B and C,

R and C and A, S and C and A.

Evidently, here, we may make our *first* choice (of 1 of the 2 photographs, R and S) in either of the *2* ways,

$$C(2, 1) = \frac{2!}{1!(2-1)!} = \frac{2!}{1!1!} = \frac{2}{1 \cdot 1} = 2.$$

Also, we may make our *second* choice (of 2 of the 3 paintings, A, B, and C) in any of the *3* ways,

$$C(3, 2) = \frac{3!}{2!(3-2)!} = \frac{3!}{2!1!} = \frac{3 \cdot 2}{2} = 3.$$

Hence, the total number, N, of possible ways in which we may combine *both* of these choices (to make up a selection of 1 photograph *and* 2 paintings) is

$$N = C(2, 1)C(3, 2) = 2(3) = 6.$$

Applying the same method of reasoning to the general case defined above, therefore, we derive the **basic inter-group combinations** formula,

$$N = C(n_1, t_1)C(n_2, t_2) \cdots C(n_k, t_k),$$

for *the total number of joint selections possible from k different sets of n_1, n_2, $\cdots$ n_k, things taken t_1, t_2, $\cdots$, t_k at a time, respectively.* In the *special case* where $t_1 = t_2 = \cdots t_k = 1$, this becomes

$$N = n_1 n_2 \cdots n_k,$$

since $C(n, 1) = n$ for *all* possible values of n.

The k different *kinds of things* from which choices are to be *combined* in applications of these formulas may be *objects, events, placements,* or whatever. They may also occur or be selected in the actual time sequence, $1, 2, 3, \cdots k$, or simultaneously. In the latter case, however, it is convenient to assign some *one arbitrarily selected order* to them. This is to avoid the sort of duplicated count we would get if we were (mistakenly) to regard the combination of photograph R with paintings A and B, in the above instance, as different from the combination of paintings A and B with photograph R (the latter being a different *permutation,* but *not* a different *combination*).

EXAMPLE 12: In planning a plane trip from Boston to San Diego with stops at Chicago and St. Louis, a travel agent finds he can book a seat for his customer on 5 different flights to Chicago, on 4 different flights from there to St. Louis, and on 7 different flights from there on. How many different complete itineraries can he book?

SOLUTION: Here $k = 3$ (different stages of the trip), and it is *common-sense routine* to let $n_1 = 5$ (possible choices for the first stage), $n_2 = 4$ (possible choices for the second stage), and $n_k = n_3 = 7$ (possible choices for the third stage), all in their *actual time sequence.* Then the total number of possible itineraries is

$$N = n_1 n_2 n_3 = 5(4)(7) = 140, \quad \text{ANS.}$$

EXAMPLE 13: An international scientific conference is attended by 5 representatives from North America, 4 from South America, 7 from Europe, 6 from Asia, and 3 from Africa. How many different committees can be chosen from this assemblage with three representatives from each area?

SOLUTION: Here there is no natural time sequence of choice, but we may *arbitrarily* let $n_1 = 5$

(possibilities of choice from North America), $n_2 = 4$ (from South America), etc. Then $t_1 = t_2 = \cdots t_5 = 3$, and

$$N = C(5, 3)C(4, 3)C(7, 3)C(6, 3)C(3, 3)$$

$$= \frac{\overset{2}{\underset{1}{5}} \cdot \overset{1}{\underset{1}{4}} \cdot \overset{1}{\underset{3}{3}}}{\underset{1}{3} \cdot \underset{1}{2}} \cdot \frac{\overset{1}{\underset{1}{4}} \cdot \overset{1}{\underset{1}{3}} \cdot 2}{\underset{1}{3} \cdot \underset{1}{2}} \cdot \frac{\overset{1}{\underset{1}{7}} \cdot \overset{1}{\underset{1}{6}} \cdot 5}{\underset{1}{3} \cdot \underset{1}{2}} \cdot \frac{\overset{1}{\underset{1}{6}} \cdot \overset{1}{\underset{1}{5}} \cdot 4}{\underset{1}{3} \cdot \underset{1}{2}} \cdot \frac{\overset{1}{\underset{1}{3}} \cdot 2}{\underset{1}{3} \cdot \underset{1}{2}}$$

$$= (10)(4)(35)(20)(1) = 28{,}000, \quad \text{Ans.}$$

EXAMPLE 14: Designate the "head" and "tail" faces of 3 coins in any arbitrary order as H_1 and T_1, H_2 and T_2, H_3 and T_3, respectively. If we count $H_1T_2T_3$ as *different* from $T_1H_2T_3$ or $T_1T_2H_3$, etc., in how many different patterns, of their head or tail faces up, can the 3 coins land when tossed?

SOLUTION: Here the 3 coins and their corresponding faces may be identical. However, when we consider them in the proposed *arbitrary* order, $n_1 = 2$ (possibilities of H_1 or T_1 for the *first* coin), $n_2 = 2$ (possibilities of H_2 or T_2 for the *second* coin), etc.; then $k = 3$, and the total number of different possible ways in which the 3 coins can land is

$$N = n_1 n_2 n_3 = 2(2)(2) = 2^3 = 8, \quad \text{Ans.}$$

EXAMPLE 15: Each die of a pair has its faces numbered from 1 to 6. In how many different patterns of their numbered faces up—"different" being defined as in the preceding problem—can the pair come to rest when rolled?

SOLUTION: By the method of the preceding solution, $k = 2$, and $n_1 = n_2 = 6$. Hence,

$$N = n_1 n_2 = 6^2 = 36, \quad \text{Ans.}$$

From the last two examples we see that, in the further special case where $n_1 = n_2 = \cdots n_k = n$, the preceding formula becomes:

$$N = n^k.$$

In Example 14, for instance, $k = 3$, $n = 2$, and

$$N = n^k = 2^3 = 8, \text{ as before.}$$

In Example 15, also, $k = 2$, $n = 6$, and

$$N = n^k = 6^2 = 36, \text{ as before.}$$

But a more general result now follows. . . .

In a fairly common type of combinations problem we are required to find M, the *sum of all the possible combinations* of k things taken *1, 2, 3, . . . and any other number up to, and including, k at a time.* This can always

be done "the long way" by substitution in the defining formula,

$$M = C_1^k + C_2^k + \cdots + C_k^k.$$

Note, however, that we can think of the k things in this formula as the same k as in the preceding formula for $N = n^k$. Also, we can think of $n = 2$ in the latter as the *two possibilities* of each of the same k things being either (a) *included* in possible combinations, or (b) *excluded* from such combinations. Then

$$N = M + 1, \quad \text{or} \quad M = N - 1,$$

with the *1* in these equations being the number of the *one* possibility in which *all* k things are *excluded* from any possible combination. Hence, by substitution, we obtain the formula

$$M = C_1^k + C_2^k + \cdots + C_k^k = 2^k - 1.$$

(NOTE: Most textbooks derive this formula by a longer method which applies a special case of quite a different principle called *the binomial theorem.* But this method is recommended as shorter, more direct, and less dependent upon other principles or the special device of ingenious substitution.)

EXAMPLE 16: In how many different combinations can we replace 1 or more electronic tubes in a set of 8?

SOLUTION: Since these replacements may be made for any 1, *or* 2, *or* 3, *or* more tubes *up to and including* all 8, our M formula applies with $n = 8$. Hence,

$$M = 2^8 - 1 = 256 - 1 = 255, \quad \text{Ans.}$$

Obviously, the *minus one* in this computation *adjusts* the total for the *rejected* possibility that *no* tube be replaced.

As when we apply permutations formulas (page 150) we may sometimes have to *adapt* the above *combination formulas* to the *special conditions* of particular problems.

Care must be taken, however, not to *insinuate duplications of arrangement in this procedure,* for then we shall obtain *numerical results* which are *too large by some factor of a corresponding permutations formula.* The very real danger of this becomes immediately evident when we recognize that the reasoning by which we originally arrived at our basic permutations formula (page 151) was itself but an application of our basic inter-group combinations formula (page 154) to the systematic filling of successive positions in a permutational arrangement!

EXAMPLE 17: Of all the possible poker hands computed in the solution of Example 11, how many contain "4 of a kind"—defined as 4 cards of 1 rank (all *sevens*, or all *jacks*, etc.)?

SOLUTION: Since there are only 4 cards in each of the 13 ranks (*ace, king, queen, jack, 10, 9, 8, 7, 6, 5, 4, 3, 2*) of a bridge or poker deck, *4* cards of the *same rank* can be dealt from such a deck in only

$$13C_4^4 = 13 \cdot 1 = 13 \text{ different ways.}$$

But each such combination can be further combined with any one of the remaining $12C_1^4 = 12 \cdot 4 = 48$ cards of 12 *other* ranks in the deck. Hence, the number of 5-card hands with "4 of a kind" is

$$13C_4^4 12C_1^4 = 13 \cdot 12 \cdot 4 = 624, \text{ ANS.}$$

EXAMPLE 18: In how many different ways can a poker hand be dealt containing only "one pair"—defined as *2* cards of *1* rank and *3* other cards of ranks *different* from each other and from that of the pair?

SOLUTION: Obviously a pair can be formed in *each* rank in C_2^4 ways, and hence in *all* 13 ranks of the deck in

$$13C_2^4 = 13 \cdot \frac{4 \cdot 3}{2} = 78 \text{ ways.}$$

There is a *danger* we may now make the *mistake* of reasoning (erroneously) that each such combination can be further combined with 1 card from each of 3 remaining ranks in

$$12C_1^4 11C_1^4 10C_1^4 = 14 \cdot 4 \cdot 11 \cdot 4 \cdot 10 \cdot 4$$
$$= 84,480 \text{ different ways.}$$

Multiplied by *78*, this would give us a product of *6,589,440 ways*, which is *impossible* since it is more than twice as great as the total of *all* possible poker hands, including those with no pairs or with other sub-combinations than pairs (see Example 11)!

The error of the preceding reasoning is that it *permutes*, rather than *combines*, selections from three of the remaining suits. Hence, the product at which it arrives is *too great* by a factor of *3! = 3·2 = 6*.

To correct the error, we could divide the obtained product by a compensating factor of

3! = 6. Or, *to avoid the error altogether*, we can reason that 3 ranks different from the pair's rank can be combined in

$$C_3^{12} = \frac{12 \cdot 11 \cdot 10}{3 \cdot 2} = 220 \text{ ways.}$$

Then from each of the latter we can make an inter-group combination of one of *n = 4* cards from each of *k = 3* ranks in

$$n^k = 4^3 = 64 \text{ ways.}$$

Hence a 5-card hand with only "1 pair" can be dealt in

$$13C_2^4 64 C_3^{12} = 78 \cdot 64 \cdot 220$$
$$= 1,098,240 \text{ ways, ANS.}$$

Further illustrations of how to apply permutations and combinations formulas are given in the following chapter on *Probability Theory*.

Practice Exercise No. 82

1 Illustrate in array form, and then count, $C(4, 3)$ and $P(4, 3)$.

2 Compute the same by formula.

3 How many different selections can we make of 5 flags from among 12 different flags?

4 How many different signals can we form by hoisting in a line to a ship's masthead: (a) 5 different flags? (b) 5 of 12 different flags?

5 (a) Derive the formula,

$$P(n, t) = C(n, t) P(t, t).$$

(b) By substitution in this formula, check your answers to questions 3 and 4 above.

6 In how many different ways can 8 people be seated at a round table if one particular couple is never to be separated?

7 How many 5-letter words can there be formed, like "crate," in which no letter is repeated, the third and fifth are from the 5 vowels, *a, e, i, o, u,* and the other 3 are from the other 21 letters of the alphabet?

8 In how many different indistinguishable sequences can 3 pennies, 6 nickels, and 4 dimes be arranged?

9 (a) How many 2-piece suits can a man select from a wardrobe of 4 jackets and 6 pairs of trousers?

(b) How many 3-piece suits if the same wardrobe also includes 3 vests?

10 If 5 coins are tossed, in how many different patterns can they land heads or tails?

11 Answer the corresponding question if 4 dice are rolled.

12 A manufacturer offers automobiles, with or without automatic transmission, in 6 different

body styles, 4 different interior finishes, and 9 different colors. How many models would a dealer have to stock in order to display all possible combinations?

13 The Braille system of writing for the blind is based on raised dots in 6 possible positions. How many different characters are there possible in this system?

14 How many different signals can we form by hoisting, in a line to the masthead of a ship, any 5 of 5 different *kinds* of flags?

15 How many different selections can there be made of 1 or more books from a shelf of 16?

16 In how many different ways can each of the following poker hands be dealt:

(a) a "full house"—defined as a pair from 1 rank and 3 of a kind from another?
(b) any "flush"—defined as 5 cards from one suit?
(c) any "straight"—defined as 5 cards of consecutive ranks with ace either high or low?
(d) a "straight flush"?
(e) a "flush" other than a *straight* flush"?
(f) a "straight" other than a "straight *flush*"?

NOTE: Authors such as Hoyle in *The Official Rules of Card Games* usually mean by "straights" and "flushes" only those which are not "straight flushes." The latter they give a separate, higher listing—above "full houses" and "fours of a kind"—because of their relative rarity.

SUMMARY

Combinations are *groupings* of things *without* regard to their sequence. **Permutations** are *arrangements* of the same in *different sequences*.

In theory, at least, we can always find how many combinations and permutations are possible under any stated set of conditions by systematically constructing *arrays* of the separate possibilities and then *counting* their numbers.

In most instances, however, it is more practicable to apply *formulas* such as those recapitulated here for convenient reference:

Formula	Application
$P(n, t) = \dfrac{n!}{(n - t)!}$	The number P of all possible *permutations* of any n things taken t at a time.
$P(n, n) = n!$	The same in the special case when $t = n$.
$P_c(n, n) = (n - 1)!$	The number P_c of all possible *circular permutations* of n things arranged in a *circle* or *closed chain*.
$P_a = \dfrac{n!}{n_1! n_2! \cdots}$	The number P_a of all possible *indistinguishable permutations* of n things when n_1 are all alike, n_2 are all alike, etc.
$C(n, t) = \dfrac{n!}{t!(n - t)!}$	The number of all possible *combinations* of n things taken t at a time.
$C(n, n) = 1$	The same for the special case of $t = n$.
$C(n, t) = \dfrac{P(n, t)}{t!}$ $\quad$ $P(n, t) = C(n, t)P(t, t)$	Basic relationships between P and C.
$N = C(n_1, t_1)C(n_2, t_2)$ $\cdots C(n_k, t_k)$	The number of all possible *inter-group combinations* of n_1 things taken t_1 at a time, etc., up to n_k things taken t_k at a time.
$N = n_1 n_2 \cdots n_k$	The same for the special case of $t_1 = t_2 = \cdots = t_k = 1$.
$N = n^k$	The same for the further special case of $n_1 = n_2 = \cdots n_k = n$.
$M = C_1^k + C_2^k +$ $\cdots C_k^k$ $= 2^k - 1$	The number of all possible combinations of k things taken *1*, or *2*, or $\cdots k$ at a time.

The principal danger to avoid in applying these formulas is that of (erroneously) insinuating *permutation* factors into calculations of numbers of *combinations*.

CHAPTER EIGHTEEN

THEORY OF PROBABILITY

PRELIMINARY EXPLANATIONS

In *everyday* language we call something "probable" if we believe it *likely to happen*, "improbable" if we believe it *unlikely to happen*, or "certain" if we believe it *sure to happen*. In **the mathematical theory of probability** we try to *define* such concepts *more precisely* so as to assign them *measures*, or *numerical indices*, which can be computed, and therefore compared, arithmetically.

As may be expected from its title, the theory deals with the likelihood of things which happen *by chance* or are selected *at random*. By definition, these are *events* which are not influenced to happen one way rather than another by *known* causes. Simple instances are: the landing of a tossed coin heads or tails, or the "blindfolded" selection of "any card" from a shuffled deck.

At first approach, this sort of subject matter may seem to upset all our previous ideas of what mathematics is about. Previously in this subject we have not made such statements, for instance, as "the base angles of an isosceles triangle are *probably* equal," or "the *odds* are *in favor of* the sine of 30° being 0.500"!

When we understand the nature of mathematics, however, we realize that the more precise statements usually made about such matters are just short forms of "*If* . . . , *then* . . ." hypothetical generalizations. What we really mean, when we take the trouble to repeat it all over again each time, is that "*if* a triangle is isosceles, *then* its base angles are equal," or "*if* an angle is 30°, *then* its sine is 0.500." These *hypothetical generalizations* follow from the *theoretical assumptions* upon which they are based *even though* there may be *no* actual physical structure in the entire material universe which is *exactly* isosceles or which has an angle of *precisely* 30°.

The corresponding *theoretical assumption* by which we can put even *uncertainties* on *an exact mathematical* basis is that of something happening in a *definite number* of *equally likely ways*. Instances are: the assumption of a "well balanced" coin being *equally likely* to land with *either* heads *or* tails face up, or the assumption of an "unloaded" die being *equally likely* to stop rolling with *any one* of its 6 faces up.

BASIC DEFINITIONS

If *on any given trial,* we say, an *event E* can *happen in h ways,* and *fail to happen in f ways,* out of $w = h + f$ *equally likely ways,* then the *mathematical measure* of *the probability of E happening* is, by definition,

$$p = h/w, \text{ or } h \text{ chances out of } w;$$

and the *mathematical measure* of *the probability of E failing to happen* (or of the *im*probability of E happening) is, **also by definition,**

$$q = f/w, \text{ or } f \text{ chances out of } w.$$

In other words, p and q are simply *numerical indices* assigned to the *likelihood* and *unlikelihood*, respectively, that E will happen *under the assumed theoretical conditions*.

From these definitions it follows at once that, in the *special case* when $h = 0$, then $h/w = 0/w = 0$, and

$$p = 0, \text{ the } measure \text{ of } \textbf{impossibility.}$$

Also, in the *special case* when $h = w$, then $h/w = w/w = 1$, and

$$p = 1, \text{ the } measure \text{ of } \textbf{certainty.}$$

For instance, let our *trial* be the tossing of a "well balanced coin"—by assumption, a coin which can land heads *or* tails with *equal*

158

likelihood but *cannot* stand on edge. And let three *events* be defined as follows:

E—the coin lands heads,
E_1—the coin stands on edge,
E_2—the coin lands heads or tails.

Then for event E, that the coins land heads,

$$h = 1, \quad f = 1, \quad w = h + f = 1 + 1 = 2,$$

and we obtain the probability measures,

$$p = h/w = 1/2 \text{ for } E \text{ happening,}$$

$$q = f/w = 1/2 \text{ for } E \text{ failing to happen.}$$

These *express numerically* the fact that the coin is *equally likely* to land heads *or* not to land heads.

Likewise for event E_1, that the coin stands on edge,

$$h_1 = 0, \quad f_1 = 2,$$

$$w_1 = h_1 + f_1 = 0 + 2 = 2,$$

and we obtain the *probability measures*,

$$p_1 = h_1/w_1 = 0/2 = 0 \text{ for } E_1 \text{ happening,}$$

$$q_1 = f_1/w_1 = 2/2 = 1 \text{ for } E_1 \text{ failing.}$$

These *express numerically* the fact that the coin *cannot* stand on edge.

Finally, for event E_2,

$$h_2 = 2, \quad f_2 = 0,$$

$$w_2 = h_2 + f_2 = 2 + 0 = 2,$$

and we obtain the *probability measures*,

$$p_2 = h_2/w_2 = 2/2 = 1 \text{ for } E_2 \text{ happening,}$$

$$q_2 = f_2/w_2 = 0/2 = 0 \text{ for } E_2 \text{ failing.}$$

These *express numerically* the fact that the coin *must* certainly land *either* heads *or* tails (not heads) *under the given assumptions.*

From the above definitions it is also clear that *the probability measures, p and q, must always have values from 0 to 1 inclusive:*

$$0 \leq p \leq 1, \text{ and } 0 \leq q \leq 1.$$

This is only reasonable since we should not expect a measure of probability to be less than that of impossibility (*0*) or greater than that of certainty (*1*).

Finally, since $w = h + f$ by definition, we see that

$$\frac{h}{w} + \frac{f}{w} = \frac{h + f}{w} = \frac{w}{w} = 1.$$

Hence, by substitution of $p = h/w$ etc.,

$$p + q = 1, \quad p = 1 - q, \quad q = 1 - p.$$

Any one of these last three relationships may serve as a partial check upon the accuracy of work in calculating p and q. (The "check" works unless pairs of errors have been made exactly compensating for each other.) The last two relationships may also serve for finding either p or q once the other has been computed.

In the preceding illustration of event E, for instance,

$$p + q = \tfrac{1}{2} + \tfrac{1}{2} = 1. \text{ \textit{Partial check.}}$$

Also, if we had not separately computed q, we could have found it by substitution, as

$$q = 1 - p = 1 - \tfrac{1}{2} = \tfrac{1}{2}, \text{ as before.}$$

Values of the probability fractions, p and q, may also be expressed in *decimal* or in percentage form. In the latter case they are called *percentage chances*. From the above illustration again, for instance,

$$p = \tfrac{1}{2} = 0.5, \text{ or \textit{a 50\% chance of E}}$$
$$\textit{happening,}$$

$$q = \tfrac{1}{2} = 0.5, \text{ or \textit{a 50\% chance of E}}$$
$$\textit{failing.}$$

In this special case, the "chances" may be said to be "50-50"; or, if betting is involved, it can be said to be based on "even money" terms.

A different, but equivalent, way of expressing the ideas of probability and improbability is in terms of "odds." By definition, *the ratio,*

$$h{:}f, \text{ or } h \text{ to } f,$$

states the *odds for E* happening; and the *inverse ratio*

$$f{:}h, \text{ or } f \text{ to } h,$$

states the *odds against E* happening. In the case of the preceding illustration, for instance, the odds are:

> $h:f$, or *1 to 1 for* E *happening*, and
> $f:h$, or *1 to 1 against* E *happening*.

In this special case where both ratios are the same, we say "the odds are even."

When the *odds for* E *happening* are *greater than 1:1*, they may also be called the odds *in favor of* E.

If the statement of a probability problem is such that you can determine h, f, *and* w *by actual count, you can always solve the problem directly by the method of the above illustrations.*

The most important **applications of probability** theory which you are likely to encounter later are in *economics, genetics, thermodynamics, nuclear physics, information theory,* and other highly technical sciences which require special backgrounds for an adequate understanding of their problems. However, most essential principles of the probability theory involved in such applications can be more simply illustrated in elementary experiments like the tossing of coins, or in common games of chance. Hence, we shall here make greatest use of examples from the latter sources.

EXAMPLE 1: If 2 well balanced coins are tossed, what are the probabilities of, and the odds on, the following events:

> E_1—both land heads,
> E_2—1 lands heads and 1 tails,
> E_3—neither lands heads,
> E—at least 1 lands heads?

SOLUTION: Designate the respective heads and tails sides of the 2 coins in some arbitrary order as H_1, T_1, and H_2, T_2 (see the preceding chapter, page 152). Then the assumption that the coins are well balanced means that they are equally likely to land with any 1 of the 4 possible intergroup combinations of their faces up,

$$H_1H_2, \quad H_1T_2, \quad T_1H_2, \quad T_1T_2.$$

For event E_1, then, $w_1 = 4$, $h_1 = 1$ (the count of the H_1H_2 possibility), and *the probability of E_1 happening* is

$$p_1 = h_1/w_1 = 1/4, \text{ or } 1 \text{ chance out of } 4,$$

which may also be expressed as

$$p_1 = 0.25, \text{ or } a \text{ } 25\% \text{ chance.}$$

Alternatively, since $f_1 = w_1 - h_1 = 4 - 1 = 3$, *the odds on E_1 happening* are

$$h_1:f_1 = 1:3, \text{ or } 1 \text{ to } 3 \text{ for, and}$$

$$f_1:h_1 = 3:1, \text{ or } 3 \text{ to } 1 \text{ against.}$$

For event E_2, next, $w_2 = 4$ as before, but $h_2 = 2$ (the count of the H_1T_2 and T_1H_2 possibilities). Hence, the *probability of E_2 happening* is

$$p_2 = h_2/w_2 = 2/4, \text{ or } 2 \text{ chances out of } 4.$$

Equivalently, by reduction of the fraction to lowest terms, etc., this is

$$p_2 = 1/2, \text{ or } 1 \text{ chance out of } 2,$$
$$= 0.5, \text{ or } a \text{ } 50\% \text{ chance.}$$

And since $f_2 = w_2 - h_2 = 4 - 2 = 2$, the *odds on E_2 happening* are

$$h_2:f_2 = 2:2 = 1:1, \text{ or } even \text{ (for } or \text{ against).}$$

For event E_3, again $w_3 = 4$, but (as for E_1) $h_3 = 1$ (this time the count of the T_1T_2 possibility). Hence, the *probability of, and the odds on, E_3 happening* are exactly *the same as for E_1 happening.*

For event E, however, although $w = 4$ again, now $h = 3$ (the count of the H_1H_2, H_1T_2, and T_1H_2 possibilities).

Hence, *the probability of E happening* is

$$p = h/w = 3/4, \text{ or } 3 \text{ chances out of } 4,$$
$$= 0.75, \text{ or } a \text{ } 75\% \text{ chance.}$$

Alternatively, since $f = w - h = 4 - 3 = 1$, the *odds on E happening* are

$$h:f = 3:1, \text{ or } 3 \text{ to } 1 \text{ for, and}$$

$$f:h = 1:3, \text{ or } 1 \text{ to } 3 \text{ against.}$$

EXAMPLE 2: A deck of bridge cards is shuffled and split at random. What is the probability that the card thus exposed is: (a) of a red suit—hearts or diamonds? (b) a diamond? (c) a queen? (d) the queen of diamonds?

SOLUTION: Since there are $w = 52$ cards in the deck and $h_a = 26$ of these are of the 2 red suits, the probability of the exposed card having a red face is

$$p_a = h_a/w = 26/52 = 1/2, \quad \text{ANS. (a).}$$

Since $h_b = 13$ of the cards are diamonds, the probability of the exposed card being a diamond is

$$p_b = h_b/w = 13/52 = 1/4, \quad \text{ANS. (b).}$$

Since $h_c = 4$ of the cards are queens, the probability of the exposed card being a queen is

$$p_c = h_c/w = 4/52 = 1/13, \quad \text{ANS. (c)}.$$

But since there is only $h_d = 1$ queen of diamonds in the deck, the probability of the exposed card being this one is

$$p_d = h_d/w = 1/52, \quad \text{ANS. (d)}.$$

RELATIVE PROBABILITIES

If the *probabilities* of *events* E_1 and E_2 are p_1 and p_2 respectively, then by definition *event* E_1 is p_1/p_2 **times as probable** (likely to happen) *as event* E_2. From the findings in the solution of Example 2, for instance, we may say that when a card is drawn at random from a shuffled bridge deck, the event of its being a diamond is $(13/52)/(4/52) = 13/4 = 3\frac{1}{4}$ times as probable as the event of its being a queen; or, more briefly, such a card is $3\frac{1}{4}$ times more likely to be a diamond than it is to be a queen (although, of course, it may be both in the special case of the queen of diamonds).

To illustrate the *relative likelihoods of all the possible outcomes of a game*, it is sometimes convenient to prepare a table of all its basic events and their consequent probabilities.

In the game of dice, for instance, each of 2 (cubical) dice has its faces numbered from 1 to 6 by a corresponding number of spots, and when the dice come to rest after being rolled, the players add the 2 of these numbers faced upward. We have already seen that the total number of possible combinations of the faces of 2 dice is $6^2 = 36$ (see the preceding chapter, Example 15, page 155). But the corresponding game events (sums of 2 numbers each from 1 to 6) can also be catalogued in a table constructed as follows: all the possible face numbers from 1 to 6 for an arbitrarily selected first die are written on successive lines down the left side; the same numbers for the other die are written at the heads of columns along the top; and the 36 different possible sums of one number from each are written at corresponding intersections of lines and columns, thus:

		(Face numbers of second die)					
+		1	2	3	4	5	6
(Face numbers of first die)	1	2	3	4	5	6	7
	2	3	4	5	6	7	8
	3	4	5	6	7	8	9
	4	5	6	7	8	9	10
	5	6	7	8	9	10	11
	6	7	8	9	10	11	12

(Sums of both face numbers)

By counting identical entries in the body of this table, we can now see at a glance in how many ways, out of $w = 36$, a pair of die faces can add up to each possible total. Hence, assuming that all $w = 36$ ways are *equally likely*—that the dice are not "loaded," that is—to compute the corresponding probabilities we have only to substitute these values of h in the definition formulas.

EXAMPLE 3: What is the sum (of 2 face numbers) most likely to be rolled on a pair of dice? How does the probability of this sum being rolled compare with the probabilities of others?

SOLUTION: Let $h_1, h_2 \cdots h_{13}$ and $p_1, p_2, \cdots p_{13}$ be respectively the number of favorable happenings and the probabilities for the sums, 1, 2, $\cdots$ 13. Then by inspection of the above table and actual count we find

$$h_1 = h_{13} = 0, \quad h_2 = h_{12} = 1,$$
$$h_3 = h_{11} = 2, \quad h_4 = h_{10} = 3, \text{ etc.}$$

And,

$$p_1 = p_{13} = 0/36, \text{ (or } 0),$$
$$p_2 = p_{12} = 1/36,$$
$$p_3 = p_{11} = 2/36, \text{ (or } 1/18),$$
$$p_4 = p_{10} = 3/36, \text{ (or } 1/12),$$
$$p_5 = p_9 = 4/36, \text{ (or } 1/9),$$
$$p_6 = p_8 = 5/36,$$
$$p_7 = \qquad 6/36, \text{ (or } 1/6).$$

Thus we see that the most likely number to be rolled is *7*, with a probability of *6 chances out of 36*, or of *1 out of 6*. By comparison, *6* and *8* are only $(5/36)/(6/36) = 5/6$ as likely to be rolled; *5* and *9* are only $4/6 = 2/3$ as likely; *4* and *10* are only

$3/6 = 1/2$ *as likely; 3* and *11* are only $2/6 = 1/3$ *as likely; 2* and *12* are only *1/6 as likely;* and *1* and *13* are *impossible* (as are all numbers higher than 13). Ans.

EXAMPLE 4: On his first cast a dice player rolls a 10, which he regards as his "lucky number." To win, he must again roll this number, called "his point," before he rolls a 7 instead. Another player now offers a "side bet" on "even money" terms that he will not make his point. Is this a fair wager?

SOLUTION: Definitely not! As we have already seen from the preceding solution, a *10* is only *half as likely* to be rolled as a *7*. Hence, a *fair bet would require the holder of the dice to be given 2-to-1 odds.* If he takes the bet on the superstitious theory that 10 is his "lucky number," then so much the worse for him in the long run of several trials!

WARNING: If event E_1 is h_1/h_2 *times as probable* as event E_2, this means only that the *odds* are h_1/h_2 for E_1 happening *before* E_2. To compute the *probability* of event E, that E_1 will happen before E_2, we must recognize that E can happen in only $h = h_1$ out of

$$w = h_1 + h_2 \text{ possible ways.}$$

Hence the *probability* that E_1 will happen before E_2 is only

$$p = \frac{h_1}{h_1 + h_2}.$$

In the preceding case, for instance, the probability that a *4* will be rolled before a *7* is NOT $3/6 = 1/2$, BUT . . .

$$p = \frac{3}{3 + 6} = \frac{3}{9} = \frac{1}{3},$$

or equivalently

$$p = \frac{1}{1 + 2} = \frac{1}{3}.$$

Likewise, the probability of a *7* being rolled before a *4* is

$$q = \frac{2}{2 + 1} = \frac{2}{3}.$$

Partial check:

$$p + q = \frac{1}{3} + \frac{2}{3} = \frac{3}{3} = 1.$$

ADDITION OF PROBABILITIES

Any 2 events are by definition *mutually exclusive* if the happening of either *excludes* the possible happening of the other *on the same trial.*

For instance, the event e of a coin landing heads is *mutually exclusive* with the event e' of the *same* coin landing tails on the same trial (toss). Similarly, the 11 events $E_2, E_3 \cdots E_{12}$, of a pair of dice rolling sums of *2, 3 $\cdots$ 12*, respectively, are all *mutually exclusive with respect to each other* on the same trial (roll).

In other words, *mutually exclusive events* are *alternative possible outcomes* of the *same trial.*

From this definition, it follows that *if E_1 and E_2 are any two mutually exclusive events,* then E_1 can happen in h_1 *ways* and E_2 in h_2 *ways* out of the *same* w equally likely ways, but the h_1 ways of E_1 happening must all be *different from* the h_2 ways of E_2 happening. (This has been illustrated at length in the dice-sum table on page 161.)

Suppose, then, that E is the event of any one of n mutually exclusive events, E_1, or E_2, or E_2 or $\cdots E_n$. Then E can happen in any of the ways,

$$h = h_1 + h_2 + \cdots + h_n,$$

out of the *same* w equally likely ways.

Hence,

$$\frac{h}{w} = \frac{h_1 + h_2 + \cdots h_n}{w}$$

$$= \frac{h_1}{w} + \frac{h_2}{w} + \cdots + \frac{h_n}{w}.$$

But, by definition,

$$p = \frac{h}{w}, \quad p_1 = \frac{h_1}{w}, \quad \cdots p_n = \frac{h_n}{w}.$$

Therefore, by substitution,

$$p = p_1 + p_2 + \cdots p_n.$$

Stated verbally, this means that if $E_1, E_2 \cdots E_n$ are n *mutually exclusive events,* then the *probability of E_1 or E_2 or $\cdots E_n$ happening is equal to the sum of the probabilities of each of these events happening separately.*

In Example 1 above, for instance, the events E_1 (that two tossed coins land heads) and E_2 (that one lands heads and one tails) are *mutually exclusive*. Also, E (that at least one lands heads) is the event that *either* E_1 or E_2 happens. In the direct solution of that problem we found, moreover, that

$$p_1 = \tfrac{1}{4}, \quad p_2 = \tfrac{1}{2}, \quad p = \tfrac{3}{4}.$$

This solution is now confirmed by the above formula, as follows:

$$p_1 + p_2 = \tfrac{1}{4} + \tfrac{1}{2} = \tfrac{3}{4} = p, \text{ as}$$
anticipated.

In the special case where $E_1, E_2 \cdots E_n$ are *all* the *mutually exclusive events which can possibly happen in the given w equally likely outcomes of the same trial*, then by the same reasoning,

$$p = p_1 + p_2 + \cdots p_n = 1.$$

From Example 1 again, for instance, we also have the event E_3 (that 2 tossed coins both land tails). With E_1 and E_2, this completes the mutually exclusive possibilities for the outcome of the trial of tossing 2 coins. Also, $p_3 = \tfrac{1}{4}$, and

$$p = \tfrac{1}{4} + \tfrac{1}{2} + \tfrac{1}{4} = 1, \text{ as anticipated.}$$

Or, from Example 3 concerning cast dice:

$$p = (1 + 2 + 3 + 4 + 5 + 6 + 5 +$$
$$4 + 3 + 2 + 1)/36$$
$$= 36/36 = 1, \text{ as anticipated.}$$

The above probability **addition formulas** *can often be applied to shorten* the computation of probabilities, *or to find further probabilities in terms of those already computed.*

EXAMPLE 5: Using the data in the solution of Example 3, find the probability that a player will roll a *7 or an 11* on his first cast of the dice.

SOLUTION: The probability is

$$p = p_7 + p_{11} = 6/36 + 2/36 = 8/36$$
$$= 2/9, \text{ or } 2 \text{ chances out of 9}, \quad \text{Ans.}$$

EXAMPLE 6: Find the corresponding probability that he will roll a *2 or a 3 or a 12* on his first cast.

SOLUTION: The probability is

$$p = p_2 + p_3 + p_{12} = 1/36 + 2/36 + 1/36$$
$$= 4/36 = 1/9, \text{ or } 1 \text{ chance out of 9}, \quad \text{Ans.}$$

Two events which are *not mutually exclusive* may be so because they are (partially) overlapping. In Example 2 above, for instance, the event E_b (that a card drawn from a deck at random be a *diamond*) and the event E_c (that the card be a *queen*) are not mutually exclusive, but are *(partially) overlapping* in the case of the event E_d (that the card be the *queen of diamonds*).

By the methods of reasoning already illustrated, we may show that if **E_1 and E_2 are any 2 (*partially*) overlapping events with probabilities p_1 and p_2 respectively**, and if $p(E_1 \text{ and } E_2)$ is the probability that *both* E_1 and E_2 happen, then **the *probability* that *either* E_1 or E_2 happen** is

$$p(E_1 \text{ or } E_2) = p_1 + p_2 - p(E_1 \text{ and } E_2).$$

EXAMPLE 7: What is the probability that a card drawn at random from a bridge deck is *either* a diamond *or* a queen?

SOLUTION: From the solution of Example 2 we already know that the probability of such a card's being a diamond is *13/52 = 1/4*, that the probability of its being a queen is *4/52 = 1/13*, and that the probability of its being *both* a queen *and* a diamond is 1/52. Hence, the probability of its being *either* a queen *or* a diamond is

$$p = \frac{13}{52} + \frac{4}{52} - \frac{1}{52} = \frac{13 + 4 - 1}{52}$$

$$= \frac{16}{52} = \frac{4}{13}, \quad \text{Ans.}$$

EXAMPLE 8: The probability that a poker hand be "any straight" (including a "straight flush") is $p_1 = 0.003940$. The probability that it be "any flush" (including a "straight flush") is $p_2 = 0.001970$. The probability that it be a "straight flush" is $p_{12} = 0.000014$. (For descriptions of these hands, recall page 157 above.) What is the probability that a poker hand be *either* a "straight" *or* a "flush"?

SOLUTION: As in the preceding solution,

$$
\begin{array}{rl}
p_1 = & 0.003940 \\
+p_2 = & +0.001970 \\
\hline
p_1 + p_2 = & 0.005910 \\
-p_{12} = & -0.000014 \\
\hline
p = & 0.005896, \quad \text{Ans.}
\end{array}
$$

MULTIPLICATION OF PROBABILITIES

Events which are *neither mutually exclusive* nor *(partially) overlapping* are separate events.

By definition, **any 2 events e_1 and e_2 are separate if the set of w_1 ways in which e_1 can happen or fail to happen are completely distinct from the w_2 ways in which e_2 can happen or fail to happen.** For instance, the event e_1 that a *first* coin land heads is separate from the event e_2 that a (different) *second* coin land heads, because the $w_1 = 2$ ways in which the *first* can land either heads or tails are *completely distinct from* the $w_2 = 2$ ways in which the *second* coin can land either heads or tails.

Also by definition, **if e_1, e_2 $\cdots$ e_n are n separate events and E is the event that e_1, and e_2, $\cdots$ and e_n all happen (either concurrently or in succession) on the same trial, then E is a multiple event with e_1, e_2 $\cdots$ e_n as its (separate) constituent events.** For instance, the event E (that 2 coins land heads) is a *multiple* event consisting of the 2 separate *constituent* events, e_1 (that the *first* coin lands heads) and e_2 (that the *second* coin lands heads).

Now let E be the *multiple event* that n separate constituent events, e_1 and e_2, and $\cdots$ e_n all happen on the same trial, and let h_1 be the number of ways in which e_1 can happen out of a total of w_1 possible ways *distinct from* the w_2, w_3 $\cdots$ w_n distinct ways of e_2, e_3 $\cdots$ e_n happening or failing to happen, etc. Then, by inter-group combinations of the possibilities, E can happen in

$$h = h_1 h_2 \cdots h_n \text{ ways}$$

out of a total of

$$w = w_1 w_2 \cdots w_n \text{ ways.}$$

Hence,

$$\frac{h}{w} = \frac{h_1 h_2 \cdots h_n}{w_1 w_2 \cdots w_n} = \frac{h_1}{w_1} \cdot \frac{h_2}{w_2} \cdots \frac{h_n}{w_n}.$$

And so, if all these ways are equally likely, then by substitution of $p = h/w$, etc.,

$$p = p_1 p_2 \cdots p_n.$$

Stated verbally, this means that **the *probability* of the happening of a *multiple event* on *any given trial* is equal to the *product* of *separate probabilities* of its n separate constituent events.**

Along with the preceding *addition formulas* for the probabilities of *mutually exclusive events* (E_1 or E_2 or $\cdots$ E_n), this *multiplication formula* for the probabilities of *separate events* (e_1 and e_2 and $\cdots$ e_n) can shorten the work of computing many probabilities.

EXAMPLE 9: What are the odds against a coin landing heads 8 times in a row?

SOLUTION: The landings of the *same* coin 8 different times (or of *different* coins at the *same* time) are *separate* trials. Moreover, for each the probability of the coin landing heads is *1/2* as we have already seen. Hence, the probability of the *multiple event* of the coin landing heads all 8 times is, by the *multiplication theorem*,

$$p = (\tfrac{1}{2})^8 = 1/256.$$

Accordingly,

$$h = 1, \quad w = 256,$$
$$f = w - h = 256 - 1 = 255$$

and the odds on the multiple event are

$$f : h = 255 \text{ to } 1 \text{ } against \text{ its happening,} \quad \text{ANS.}$$

EXAMPLE 10: A coin has been tossed and fallen heads seven times in a row. An excited spectator, aware of the result of the previous solution, offers to bet 100 to 1 that it will not come heads again! What is the wisdom of his wager?

SOLUTION: The man is a fool who completely misses the point about separate events. His bet would have been a very advantageous one if made *before* the series of tosses began. But the solution of Example 7 is valid only because the *separate* probability of *each separate constituent event* is *exactly 1 chance out of 2*. And this holds for the eighth trial, the first trial, or the millionth trial, considered *separately* from the series in which it occurs.

Two separate events are said to be **independent** if the *happening* of *neither* affects the *probability* of the *happening* of the *other*. But 2 separate events are said to be **dependent** if the *happening* of *either* does *affect* the *probability* of the *happening* of the *other*. Numerical consequences of this distinction are illustrated in the following two examples.

EXAMPLE 11: One card is drawn from each of 2 different decks (or else a card is drawn from one deck and *returned* to it after which another card is drawn from the *same* deck). What is the probability that both cards are aces?

SOLUTION: The 2 separate events, E_1 and E_2, of drawing an ace are here independent because the probability of each,

$$p_1 = p_2 = 4/52 = 1/13,$$

is not affected by the occurrence of the other. Hence, the probability of both cards being aces is

$$p = p_1 p_2 = \tfrac{1}{13} \cdot \tfrac{1}{13} = 1/169, \quad \text{ANS.}$$

EXAMPLE 12: Two cards are drawn *in succession* from the *same* deck *without* the first being returned to it. What is the probability that both are aces?

SOLUTION: As before, the probability of event E_1, that the first card be an ace, is $p_1 = 1/13$. But now the event E_3, that the second card also be an ace, is *dependent upon* event E_1 having happened. For if an ace has already been drawn from the deck, then there are only $h_3 = 3$ aces left in a "short deck": of $w_3 = 51$ cards. Hence, the probability of E_3 is

$$p_3 = h_3/w_3 = 3/51 = 1/17,$$

and therefore the probability of both cards being aces is now only

$$p = p_1 p_3 = \tfrac{1}{13} \cdot \tfrac{1}{17} = 1/221, \quad \text{ANS.}$$

MISCONCEPTIONS AND SUPERSTITIONS

The *uncertainties of chance*, which is the subject matter of probability theory, is also the object of many hopes and fears. Understandably, therefore, the field is one in which wishful thinking often leads to *misconceptions*, or to *superstitions* based on misconceptions.

Two simple instances have already been pointed out in Examples 4 and 10 (pages 162 and 164) above. Another now follows.

EXAMPLE 13: By the rules in the game of dice, the player who rolls the dice must match bets placed against him on an "even money" basis. He can win either (a) by rolling a "natural"—*7* or *11*—on his first cast; or else (b) by rolling a "point"—*4, 5, 6, 8, 9,* or *10*—on his first cast and then "making his point" by rolling the same number again before a *7* or *11*. On the other hand, he can lose either (c) by rolling "craps"—*2, 3,* or *12*—on his first cast; or else (d) by rolling *7* or *11* before his "point" if that is what he has rolled on his first cast.

Against the background of these rules, amateur dice players are known to "feel" that it is "luckier" to roll the dice themselves, even when they have no question about the honesty of their fellow players. But *professional* gambling-house operators always require the "customer" to roll the dice rather than their own employee. Which policy is *mathematically* more advantageous?

SOLUTION: By applying the probability addition and multiplication formulas to the data of Examples 3 and 4 above (pages 161), we can now compute the probabilities of all the possible outcomes of this game—both favorable and unfavorable to the one who cast the dice. For instance, in the case with a 1/12 probability that the player rolls a *4* as his point, we know that he has only $1/(1 + 2) = 1/3$ chance thereafter of making this point (recall the WARNING on probabilities versus odds, page 162). Hence, the probability of his winning in this instance is the *product* of the probabilities of *2 separate constituent events*,

$$\tfrac{1}{12} \cdot \tfrac{1}{3} = \tfrac{1}{36} = 2.77\%.$$

Moreover, his probability of winning in the *mutually* exclusive event of his rolling a *10* as his point is the same. Hence, the probability of his winning in either of these cases is the *sum* of the probabilities of these two *mutually exclusive events*,

$$\tfrac{1}{36} + \tfrac{1}{36} = 2 \cdot \tfrac{1}{36} = \tfrac{1}{18} = 5.55\%.$$

On the other hand, the probability of his *losing* in the cases of these same two mutually exclusive "point" possibilities is the corresponding sum of two products,

$$2 \cdot \tfrac{1}{12} \cdot \tfrac{2}{2 + 1} = \tfrac{4}{36} = \tfrac{1}{9} = 11.11\%.$$

Analyzing all other possibilities in the same way, we obtain the table at the top of page 166. There we see that the one who rolls the dice has a *49.29% chance of winning* as opposed to a *50.71% chance of losing*. This means that, for a fair game, turns to roll the dice should be alternated among *all* the players. It also means that, even if there is no "admission fee" or "percentage charge for cashing chips," the *professional* gambling house *always wins in the long run*—for, in this case, the "house" literally has the customer who rolls the dice working for it!

TABLE OF PROBABILITIES FOR
GAME EVENTS IN DICE

Possible Casts by Player	Probability Calculations	Percentage Chances	
		to Win	to Lose
"Craps": 2, 3, or 12	$\dfrac{1+2+1}{36} = \dfrac{4}{36} = \dfrac{1}{9} =$		11.111
"Point" 4 or 10, made	$2 \cdot \dfrac{1}{12} \cdot \dfrac{1}{1+2} = \dfrac{2}{36} = \dfrac{1}{18} =$	5.555	
"Point" 4 or 10, lost	$2 \cdot \dfrac{1}{12} \cdot \dfrac{2}{2+1} = \dfrac{4}{36} = \dfrac{1}{9} =$		11.111
"Point" 5 or 9, made	$2 \cdot \dfrac{1}{9} \cdot \dfrac{4}{4+6} = \dfrac{8}{90} = \dfrac{4}{45} =$	8.889	
"Point" 5 or 9, lost	$2 \cdot \dfrac{1}{9} \cdot \dfrac{6}{6+4} = \dfrac{12}{90} = \dfrac{2}{15} =$		13.333
"Point" 6 or 8, made	$2 \cdot \dfrac{5}{36} \cdot \dfrac{5}{5+6} = \dfrac{50}{396} = \dfrac{25}{198} =$	12.626	
"Point" 6 or 8, lost	$2 \cdot \dfrac{5}{36} \cdot \dfrac{6}{6+5} = \dfrac{60}{396} = \dfrac{5}{33} =$		15.151
A "natural": 7 or 11	$\dfrac{6+2}{36} = \dfrac{8}{36} = \dfrac{2}{9} =$	22.222	
Total percentage chances:		49.29	50.71
Partial Check: 49.29% + 50.71% =		100%	

MATHEMATICAL EXPECTATION

As distinguished from *psychological* or *subjective* expectation, **mathematical expectation** is defined as the product, $p \cdot A$, of the probability p that a particular event will happen, and the amount A one will receive if it does happen.

Suppose, for instance, that a dice player has bet $5.00. When this amount is "matched," it results in a "pot" of $A = \$10.00$ which the player will receive if he wins. From the preceding table we know that the probability of his winning is $p = 49.29\%$. Hence, his mathematical expectation is:

$$p \cdot A = 0.4929(\$10.00) = \$4.93$$

to the nearest cent. However, if he should roll a *4* or a *10* as his "point," then the probability of his winning drops to $p = \frac{1}{2}$ and his mathematical expectation thereafter is only

$$\$10.00/3 = \$3.33$$

to the nearest cent, whereas that of the "house" then increases from $5.07 to $6.67 to the nearest cent.

This concept, to be applied later to the computation of insurance rates, may also help to analyze certain further misconceptions in the area of probability theory.

EXAMPLE 14: In a lottery, 20,000 tickets are to be sold at 25¢ each, and the one prize is an automobile valued at $2,500. In another lottery, 200,000 tickets are to be sold at $1.00 each, and the prizes are one of $50,000 and 25 of $1,000. Mr. Sloe, who has never even heard of Adam Smith's comment that lotteries are the greatest single device ever invented by the ingenuity of man to separate a fool from his money, is thinking of making a $1.00 "investment" in either. He is tempted by the first lottery because he thinks it will give him "4 times as many *chances* (by which he means *tickets*) for the same money." But he is also tempted by the second lottery because he thinks "there is so much more prize money." Compare his actual mathematical expectations in the two cases.

SOLUTION: In the first lottery, Sloe would have a $4/20,000 = 0.0002$ probability of winning $2,500. Hence, for his *$1.00 cost* of 4 tickets he would receive a *mathematical expectation* worth

$$V_1 = 0.0002(\$2,500) = 50 \cent.$$

In the second lottery he would have a $1/200,000 = 0.000005$ probability of winning $50,000, plus a $25/200,000 = 0.000125$ probability of winning $1,000. Hence for the *same $1.00 cost* he would receive a *mathematical expectation* worth

$$V_2 = 0.000005(\$50,000) + 0.000125(\$1,000)$$
$$= 25\cent + 12\tfrac{1}{2}\cent = 37\tfrac{1}{2}\cent.$$

Consequently, we might advise Sloe that neither purchase is an "investment," and the second is by 25% an even worse "speculation" than the first.

APPLYING COMBINATIONS FORMULAS

In the probability problems considered thus far it has been possible to *count* values of h, f, and w directly. In more complicated problems, however, these quantities are better *computed* by *formula* as in the preceding chapter.

EXAMPLE 15: What are the odds against the event of a poker player being dealt a 2-pair hand—defined as one having a pair in each of 2 different ranks plus a fifth card in a still different rank?

SOLUTION: From Example 11 (page 153) of the preceding chapter we know that a poker hand can be dealt in a total of $w = 2,598,960$ different ways. To compute h we can now reason that two different *ranks* may be combined in $C(13, 2)$ different ways; that in *each* of these cases *2 pairs* of *different ranks* can occur in $C(4, 2)$ times $C(4, 2) = 6 \cdot 6 = 36$ different ways; and that a *fifth* card from a *still different rank* can occur in *44* different ways, for a product of

$$h = C_2^{13}C_2^4C_2^4 44 = 78 \cdot 36 \cdot 44 = 123,552.$$

Hence,

$$f = w - h = 2,598,960 - 123,552$$
$$= 2,471,040,$$

and the *odds against* dealing a 2-pair hand are

$$f{:}h = 2,471,040{:}123,552 = 20 \text{ to } 1, \quad \text{ANS.,}$$

rounded off to the nearest whole number.

Since the various patterns of "poker hands" illustrate very simply the most common types of combinations which are likely to occur in more technical probability

TABLE OF *MATHEMATICAL ODDS* FOR HANDS DRAWN IN POKER

Hand	Computation of h	Value of h	Odds Against (*, approximate)
Straight Flush	$10C_1^4 = 10 \cdot 4 =$	40	64,973 to 1
Four of a kind	$C_1^{13}C_4^4C_1^{12}C_1^4 = 13 \cdot 1 \cdot 12 \cdot 4 =$	624	4,164 to 1
Full house	$C^{13}2C_2^4C_3^4 = 78 \cdot 2 \cdot 6 \cdot 4 =$	3,744	693 to 1
Flush (non-straight)	$C_5^{13}C_1^4 - 40 = 5,148 - 40 =$	5,108	508 to 1*
Straight (non-flush)	$10(4^5) - 40 = 10,248 - 40 =$	10,208	254 to 1*
Three of a kind	$C_1^{13}C_3^4C_2^{12}4^2 = 13 \cdot 4 \cdot 66 \cdot 16 =$	54,912	46 to 1*
Two pairs	$C_2^{13}C_2^4C_2^4 44 = 78 \cdot 6 \cdot 6 \cdot 44 =$	123,552	20 to 1*
One pair	$C_1^{13}C_2^4C_3^{12}4^3 = 13 \cdot 6 \cdot 220 \cdot 64 =$	1,098,240	1.4 to 1*
Other	$w - \text{(all the above)} =$	1,302,540	1 to 1*
Any five cards	$w = C_5^{52} = 52!/5!47! =$	2,598,960	0.0 to 1

problems, a *comparative table* of their *computations* is appended on page 167. For definitions of the patterns and more detailed explanations of the computations, also recall the solutions of Example 17 and Practice Exercise No. 82, problems 16 (a) through (f) of the preceding chapter.

EXAMPLE 16: What is the probability of dealing (a) a bridge hand consisting of 13 cards all of the same suit? (b) 4 such hands from the same deck? (c) a bridge hand with a *4, 4, 3, 2* suit distribution?

SOLUTION: (a) One bridge hand of 13 cards can be dealt from a 52-card deck in any of

$$w_a = C_{13}^{52} = \frac{52!}{13!39!} = 635{,}013{,}559{,}600 \text{ ways.}$$

Of these, only $h_a = 4$ have all 13 cards in the same suit. Hence, the probability of such a deal is

$$p_a = 4/w_a = 1/158{,}753{,}389{,}900, \quad \text{ANS. (a).}$$

(b) Since it makes no difference whether each of 4 hands is dealt, from a shuffled deck, 1 card at a time or all 13 cards at a time, let us for convenience assume the deal to be the latter. Then the 4 hands can be dealt consecutively to 4 players in

$$C_{13}^{52}, \ C_{13}^{39}, \ C_{13}^{26}, \ \text{and } C_{13}^{13}, \text{ ways}$$

respectively, and the product of these 4 quantities would give the number of ways in which bridge hands can be *permuted* among 4 players. Dividing this product by *factorial 4*, therefore, we find the total number of *combinations* of such hands to be

$$w_b = C_{13}^{52}C_{13}^{39}C_{13}^{26}C_{13}^{13}/4!$$

$$= \frac{52!}{13!39!} \cdot \frac{39!}{13!26!} \cdot \frac{26!}{13!13!} \cdot \frac{13!}{13!} \cdot \frac{1}{4!}$$

$$= \frac{52!}{(13!)^4 4!}$$

when like factors are canceled from numerator and denominator. This last quantity has been machine computed to be *2,235 followed by 24 additional* digits. Since $h_b = 1$, therefore, the required probability is

$$p_b = h_b/w_b$$
$$= 1/2{,}235 \text{ trillions of billions,} \quad \text{ANS. (b).}$$

(c) There are $C(4, 2) = 6$ ways of choosing the 2 suits in which (the same numbers of) 4 cards are to be dealt, and $2C_2^2 = 2 \cdot 1 = 2$ different ways of next choosing the 2 suits in which (the *different* numbers of) *3* and *2* cards are to be dealt. Hence,

$$h_c = 6C_4^{13}C_4^{13}2C_3^{13}C_2^{13}$$

$$= 12 \cdot \frac{13!}{4!9!} \cdot \frac{13!}{4!9!} \cdot \frac{13!}{3!10!} \cdot \frac{13!}{2!11!}$$

$$= \frac{(13!)^4}{11!10!(9!)^2(4!)^2} = \frac{13^4 12^4 11^3 10^2}{4^2 3^2 2^2}$$

$$= 13^4 12^2 11^3 5^2 = 136{,}852{,}875{,}100.$$

Divided by w_a (rounded off to 635 billion) from above, this gives us the required probability as

$$p_c = h_c/w = 0.2155,$$

or *somewhat better than 1 chance in 5,* ANS. (c).

"CONTINUOUS PROBABILITY"

In all preceding parts of this chapter we have thus far considered only events E for which it was possible *to count* or *to compute* a definite number of ways h in which E could happen out of an equally definite number of ways w in which E could either happen or fail to happen. These are variously called **discontinuous, arithmetic,** or *finite events.* And, by a somewhat inappropriate transfer of adjectives, the corresponding measures of the likelihoods of their happening are called **discontinuous, arithmetic,** or *finite probabilities.*

But suppose we are told that a "stick" is broken "anywhere at random," and we are asked to compute the probability of its being broken closer to its mid-point than to either end. Since the stick can be broken in an *infinite (indefinitely large) number* of points, we cannot count, or otherwise compute, any *definite* values for either h or w. In such a case, the possibilities are said to be *continuous, geometric,* or *infinite* events. And obviously our previously stated definitions of probability and improbability do not, in their original form, apply to such events.

However, for convenience in referring to its points and to segments of its length, let us suppose the "stick" in the preceding instance to be a common *12-inch* ruler. Obviously such a stick will be broken closer to the *6-inch* mark of its mid-point anywhere between its *3-inch* and *9-inch* marks. If, temporarily to *simplify* the problem therefore, we were to consider it breakable only at its *full-inch* marks, then we should have $w = 11$

(the count of the *1-inch*, *2-inch* ··· *11-inch* marks), and $h = 5$ (the count of the *4-inch*, *5-inch* ··· *8-inch* marks). Hence, in this simplified case,

$$p = h/w = 5/11 = 0.4545 \cdots.$$

Or if, coming a little closer to the original problem's condition, we were to consider the ruler to be breakable at any of its *eighth-of-an-inch marks*, then we should have $w = 95$, $h = 47$,

$$p = h/w = 47/95 = 0.4947 \cdots.$$

And by continuing this process of considering the ruler to be breakable in more and more points, we begin to suspect that, as can actually be proven in *calculus* (see ADVANCED ALGEBRA AND CALCULUS MADE SIMPLE), the value of $p = h/w$ comes closer and closer to $\frac{1}{2} = 0.5$, which is the *ratio* of the *length* of the middle 6 inches of the ruler (between the *3-inch* mark and *9-inch* marks) to its entire length.

In such a case, therefore, we define the—so-called—*continuous, geometric,* or *infinite probability* of the *continuous, geometric,* or *infinitely varied event* as the *limit p* to which the *ratio h/w* comes closer and closer as the number of possible cases increases indefinitely. You will find this reasoning more fully developed later in *calculus*. But in a *literally geometric case* such as that just considered, we may take this *limit* to be *the ratio of the corresponding geometric lengths, areas, volumes, angles, or even time intervals,* involved in the statement of the problem. In the present illustration, for instance,

$$p = (6 \text{ inches})/(12 \text{ inches}) = \tfrac{1}{2}, \quad \text{Ans.}$$

EXAMPLE 17: If a stick of length L is broken anywhere at random, what is the probability that one piece is more than twice as long as the other?

SOLUTION: One piece will be more than twice as long as the other only if the break occurs at a point less than $L/3$ distant from either end—that is, in one of the two segments marked more heavily in the accompanying diagram. Hence,

$$p = (L/3 + L/3)/L = \tfrac{2}{3}L/L = 2/3, \quad \text{Ans.}$$

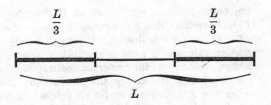

EXAMPLE 18: If a 12-inch ruler is broken in any 2 points at random, what is the probability that a triangle can be formed with the 3 segments?

SOLUTION: Let x be the length of the left-hand segment, and let y be the length of the middle segment, so that $12 - x - y$ is the length of the third segment. Then, since any side of a triangle must be less than the sum of the other 2 sides (page 116), the condition of this problem will be satisfied only if x, y, and $12 - x - y$ are *all less than 6*:

$$x < 6, \quad y < 6, \quad 12 - x - y < 6.$$

Now, to construct a *geometric diagram* which expresses these algebraic requirements, measure all possible lengths of x along a *horizontal 12-inch scale* from O to L, and measure corresponding lengths of y and of $12 - x$ along a *vertical 12-inch scale* from O to M, perpendicular to OL at O, as in the accompanying Figure 6. Then, corre-

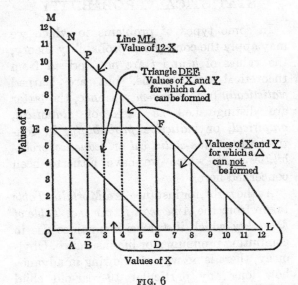

FIG. 6

sponding to the point A for $x = 1$ inch on OL, we have an *11-inch* vertical line AN representing $12 - x = 12 - 1 = 11$, perpendicular to OL at A; and beginning from A we can find points on AN corresponding to any possible values of y. Of the latter, however, only those between $y = 5$ and $y = 6$, dotted in Figure 6, satisfy the above inequalities. Likewise, corresponding to the point B for $x = 2$ inches on OL, we have 10-inch vertical line BP representing $12 - x = 12 - 2$; but on this line only those points representing values of y from $y = 4$ inches to $y = 6$ inches, dotted in the diagram, correspond to values of y which satisfy the above equalities when $x = 2$, etc. Moreover, for all values of x on OL from D for $x = 6$ inches, to L for $x = 12$ inches, there is *no* corresponding value of y which satisfies the above inequalities, since x already violates the first inequality.

Thus we see that for each possible pair of values of x and y there corresponds *some* point in the *large* triangle OLM with an *area* $= 12 \cdot 12/2 = 72$, and that for those values of x and y which satisfy the conditions of our problem the *points* all lie within the *smaller* triangle DEF with an *area* $= 6 \cdot 6/2 = 18$. Hence, our required probability is

$$p = 18/72$$
$$= 1/4, \text{ or one chance in four, ANS.}$$

The same reasoning would apply, of course, to a stick of any length. The only difference is that we should find it more awkward to refer repeatedly to different fractional parts of its length L.

STATISTICAL PROBABILITY

In some types of problems to which we may apply the concepts of probability theory, the values of h and f are not derived from theoretical assumptions, but are learned *statistically* from *experience*. Hence, the latter are distinguished as cases of **statistical, empirical,** or **inductive probability,** in contrast to the *non-statistical* or *deductive probabilities* with which we have hitherto been concerned here.

At the right, for instance, is a *Mortality Table* taken from the *American Experience Table of Mortality* which insurance companies use in computing premiums for life insurance. Obviously, there is no way of knowing in advance how long any particular 10-year-old child will live, and it is reasonable to assume that those who have serious organic defects, or who grow up to pursue dangerous occupations, may very well, on the average, die sooner than others. Nevertheless, this table has been compiled, and reduced to a *common denominator of 100,000*, from actual statistics concerning how long people do live. By it we

see, for instance, that of $w = 100,000$ people alive at age 10, only $h = 14,474$ are still alive at age 80. Hence, we may say, in this *statistical sense*, that *the probability of a child of 10 living to attain the age of 80 is*, on the average,

$$p = h/w = 14,474/100,000$$
$$= 14.5\% \text{ approximately.}$$

MORTALITY TABLE

Age	Number Living	Age	Number Living
10	100,000	60	57,917
20	92,637	70	38,569
30	85,441	80	14,474
40	78,106	90	847
50	69,804	100	0

Of course, the last entry in this table means only that, corresponding to each person still alive at age 100, there were more than 200,000 alive at age 10. Otherwise, the entry would have rounded off to *1* or more, instead of to *zero*, as the nearest whole number.

EXAMPLE 19: To the nearest tenth of 1 percent, what is the *statistical probability* that a child living at the age of 10 (a) will *still* be living at age 60? (b) will *not* be living at age 60? (c) will die *between* the ages of 60 and 70?

SOLUTION: (a) From the above *Mortality Table*, of $w = 100,000$ children living at age 10, only $h = 57,917$ are still living at age 60. Hence, the probability of the latter event is

$$p = h/w$$
$$= 57,917/100,000 = 57.9\%, \text{ ANS. (a).}$$

(b) From the same figures, the number not living at age 60 is

$$f = w - h = 100,000 - 57,917 = 42,083.$$

Hence, the probability of such a child not living at age 60 is

$$q = f/w$$
$$= 42,083/100,000 = 42.1\%, \text{ ANS. (b).}$$

Or, alternatively from answer (a),

$$q = 1 - p = 1 - 57.9 = 42.1\%. \text{ same ANS.}$$

(c) From the same *Table*, the number who die between ages 60 and 70 is

$$h = 57{,}917 - 38{,}569 = 19{,}345.$$

Hence, the required statistical probability is

$$\begin{aligned}p &= h/w \\ &= 19{,}345/100{,}000 = 19.3\%, \quad \text{ANS. (c).}\end{aligned}$$

The amounts of most *insurance premiums* are *based* on *statistically determined mathematical expectations* (see page 170 above) plus prorated overhead costs and reserve or profit margins. Of this, the following is a greatly simplified illustration.

EXAMPLE 20: An insurance company knows from statistical studies that 45 out of every 10,000 houses in a particular area are destroyed annually by fire. A man in this area applies for a $20,000 fire-insurance policy on his home. What must the company charge him annually for this *risk* in addition to its prorated other costs?

SOLUTION: The company should charge the man, for this part of its premium, the *mathematical expectation* which he would be purchasing. The amount is *A = $20,000*, and the *statistical probability* of *loss* in any year is

$$p = 45/10{,}000 = 0.0045.$$

Hence, the proper annual charge (for risk only) is the *mathematical expectation,*

$$V = p \cdot A = 0.0045(\$20{,}000) = \$90.00, \quad \text{ANS.}$$

NOTE: If your own fire-insurance premiums differ greatly from this rate, you probably live in a very different statistical fire-experience area or are covered by a company with high overhead costs.

Practice Exercise No. 83

1 Letting the heads and tails faces of 3 coins be designated H_1T_1, H_2T_2, H_3T_3, make a systematic array of the $w = n^k = 2^3 = 8$ possible combinations in which they can fall face up when tossed. Then find the corresponding values of h and f for the following events:

E_1—all 3 land heads.
E_2—only 2 land heads.
E_3—only 1 lands heads.
E_4—none lands heads.
E_5—at least 2 land heads.

2 Using your answers to Question 1, find the probabilities p and q of these same events happening and not happening.

3 Which of the events defined in Question 1 are mutually exclusive? Verify your answer by applying probability addition formulas.

4 For events E_1, E_2, and E_5, defined as in Question 1, compute p_5 in terms of p_1 and p_2.

5 For the events in Question 1, what are the odds

(a) for E_1 to happen?
(b) against E_2 to happen?
(c) for E_5 to happen?

6 If a shuffled deck of cards is split at random, what is the probability that the exposed card is: (a) a "face card"—*king, queen,* or *jack,* in any suit? (b) a "black card"—*spades* or *clubs?* (c) a "black face card"? (d) *either* a "face card" *or* a "black card"?

7 What is the probability that, if 5 coins are tossed, all will land with the same face—heads or tails—up?

8 Each of 2 boxes contains 10 balls which are identical except that, in each case, 4 are red and 6 are white. What is the probability that, if 2 balls are selected at random from each box, all 4 turn out to be red?

9 What is the probability in the preceding question if all 4 balls are drawn from the *same* box without any being returned?

10 Referring to the *Table* on page 167, what is the probability of a player's being dealt an "opening hand"—defined as one which has a pair of jacks or any higher combination?

11 A common (Monte Carlo) type of roulette wheel has 37 sectors numbered from *0* to *36,* the *zero* being a "free house number." A player receives $36.00 for each dollar he bets on any given number if the wheel stops spinning with a small ball coming to rest on that number. On the sound, but here irrelevant, theory that "the house always wins," Mr. Sloe decides to place a $10.00 bet on the "house number" *zero,* rather than on *13* which he regards as "unlucky." Discuss his mathematical expectations in both cases.

12 From the solution of Example 16 (page 168) of the text, we know that the probability of a *4, 4, 3, 2* bridge-hand distribution is $p_1 = 0.2155$. The corresponding probabilities of *4, 3, 3, 3* and *4, 4, 4, 1* bridge-hand distributions are $p_2 = 0.1054$ and $p_3 = 0.0299$, respectively. What is the probability of drawing a hand with a distribution of at least 5 cards in at least one suit?

13 One or more balls are drawn at random from a bag containing 7. What is the probability that an *even* number are drawn?

14 Due to a purely accidental failure of its power source, an electric clock has stopped. What is the (continuous) probability (a) that the hour hand has stopped between the 12- and 1-hour marks? (b) that both hands have stopped there?

15 What is the (statistical) probability, to the nearest tenth of one percent, that of any 2 given persons alive at age 10 both will be alive at age 50?

SUMMARY

In the **theory of probability** we give *exact numerical measures* to our common-sense notions of *likelihood, unlikelihood, certainty,* and *impossibility.*

Approaching the subject first from a *non-statistical, deductive point of view,* we begin with the *hypothetical assumption* that a particular occurrence can happen in a definite number w *of equally likely ways.* This corresponds to such postulates in geometry, for instance, as the assumption that a straight line segment, or an angle, can be duplicated any definite number of times.

Then, if an *event E* can *happen* in h of these ways and fail to happen in $f = w - h$ of these ways, we define 4 *basic ratios* as follows:

$p = h/w$ — the *probability* of E happening.

$q = f/w$ — the *probability* of E *not* happening.

$h{:}f$ — the *odds for E* to happen.

$f{:}h$ — the *odds against E* to happen.

From these it follows that:

$0 \leqq p \leqq 1,\ \ 0 \leqq q \leqq 1,\ \ p + q = 1,$

0 is the *measure* of **impossibility,**

1 is the *measure* of **certainty,**

$h + f = w,\ \ h = w - f,\ \ f = w - h.$

Of the above ratios, p and q may also be stated in terms of h *or* f chances out of w, in terms of **decimal fractions,** or in terms of equivalent **percentage chances.**

If the probability of event E_1 is h_1/w and the probability of event E_2 is h_2/w, then the **odds** for E_1 to happen before E_2 are $h_1{:}h_2$; and the probability of E_1 happening *before* E_2 is $h_1/(h_1 + h_2)$.

This last statement implies the concept of *mutually exclusive events.* By definition, events E_1 and E_2 are *mutually exclusive* if they are *alternative possible outcomes of the same trial;* or they are *partially overlapping events* if *some* of the ways in which E_1 can happen are *identical with some* of the ways in which E_2 can happen *as outcomes of the same trial.*

Let $p(E_1$ or $E_2)$ be the probability that *either* of *two mutually exclusive or partially overlapping* events E_1 or E_2 happen, and let $p(E_1$ and $E_2)$ be the probability that *both of the two partially overlapping events* E_1 and E_2 happen. Then the **basic probability addition formula** is

$$p(E_1 \text{ or } E_2) = p_1 + p_2 - p(E_1 \text{ and } E_2),$$

with the last term $= 0$ in the case when E_1 and E_2 are not *overlapping* but *mutually exclusive.*

In the *special case* when $E_1, E_2 \cdots E_n$ are *all the possible alternative outcomes of the same trial,* then the preceding formula becomes

$$p(E_1, \text{ or } E_2, \text{ or } \cdots E_n)$$
$$= p_1 + p_2 + \cdots p_n = 1.$$

On the other hand, events E_1 and E_2 are **separate** events if they are **possible outcomes of different trials** — **independent** if the outcome of *neither* affects the *probability* of the outcome of the *other,* or **dependent** if the outcome of *either* does *affect* the *probability* of the outcome of the *other.*

Also, when $E_1, E_2 \cdots E_n$ are n *independent events,* then E is by definition the **multiple event** that E_1, and E_2, and $\cdots E_n$ *all* happen —its *probability* being given by the *multiplication formula,*

$$p(E_1, \text{ and } E_2, \text{ and } \cdots E_n) = p_1 p_2 \cdots p_n$$

In *simple* probability problems, h, f, and w may be *counted.* In more *complicated* probability problems they are better *computed* by the combinations and permutations formulas summarized at the end of the preceding chapter.

When it is *not possible* either to *count* or to *compute* values of h, f, and w, because they are *infinite (indefinitely large),* the methods of *calculus* (see ADVANCED ALGEBRA AND CALCULUS MADE SIMPLE) are needed for a complete analysis. But in simple cases we can regard the *so-called* "continuous," "infinite," or "geometric" probabilities of corresponding events as equal to the *ratios* of certain geometric quantities or time intervals.

Finally, when values of h, f, and w are found *empirically* by *statistical surveys* rather than deductively by theoretical assumptions and computations based upon such assumptions, then we *define the same ratios* of these quantities as **statistical** or **empirical probabilities** and **odds,** applying to them all the same addition and multiplication theorems.

Whether the probability of an event is deductive and discontinuous, deductive and continuous, or statistical, however, we define one's **mathematical expectation V** with regard to it by the formula

$$V = p \cdot A$$

in which *p* is *the event's probability* and *A* is *the amount one may expect to receive if it happens.*

Finally, since the *uncertainties of chance* give rise to much *wishful thinking* in this area, certain resulting **superstitions** and **misconceptions** have also been analyzed in this chapter.

NOTE: To provide you with a *transition to more advanced studies,* the mathematical topics of these last two chapters have been treated more in the manner of INTERMEDIATE ALGEBRA AND ANALYTIC GEOMETRY MADE SIMPLE and ADVANCED ALGEBRA AND CALCULUS MADE SIMPLE in this same MADE SIMPLE series.

TEST NO. 3

FINAL TEST

1 A brick wall tumbled down, leaving a height of 24 inches standing. You were told that $\frac{5}{8}$ of the wall had fallen. How many inches of brick would you have to add to rebuild the wall?

(A) 15 in. ____   (c) 36 in. ____
(B) 30 in. ____   (D) 40 in. ____

2 Two cargoes together weigh 1,800 lbs. The lighter cargo weighs $\frac{1}{2}$ as much as the heavier. What is the weight of the heavier cargo?

(A) 1,000 lbs. ____   (c) 1,400 lbs. ____
(B) 1,200 lbs. ____   (D) 1,600 lbs. ____

3 12% of one man's money equals 18% of the amount another man has. The poorer of the two men has $300. How much does the richer man have?

(A) $350 ____   (c) $400 ____
(B) $374 ____   (D) $450 ____

4 How much would you have to lend for $1\frac{1}{2}$ years at 4% to get back $424 in all?

(A) $328.56 ____   (c) $400.00 ____
(B) $407.04 ____   (D) $390.00 ____

5 A retailer wishes to make 20% on shoes. At what price must he buy them in order to sell them at $4.50 a pair?

(A) $2.50 ____   (c) $3.50 ____
(B) $4.25 ____   (D) $3.75 ____

6 A supply pipe with a capacity of 8 gals. per minute can fill a reservoir in 18 hrs. What capacity pipe would be needed to fill the reservoir in 10 hrs.?

(A) $4\frac{4}{5}$ ____   (c) $22\frac{1}{2}$ ____
(B) $14\frac{2}{5}$ ____   (D) 24 ____

7 The formula for the length of the sides of a right triangle is $c^2 = a^2 + b^2$. If $c = 15$ and $a = 12$, what does *b* equal?

(A) 9 ____   (c) 11 ____
(B) 10 ____   (D) 12 ____

8   What will be the diameter of a wheel whose area is 264 sq. in.?

    (A) 15.25 in. _____   (c) 21.66 in. _____

    (B) 18.33 in. _____   (D) 24.50 in. _____

9   The radius of a circular room having a tile floor is 21 ft. You wish to use the tiling in a rectangular room of the same area. The latter room is to be 14 ft. wide. What will be its length?

    (A) 21 ft. _____   (c) 99 ft. _____

    (B) 63 ft. _____   (D) 120 ft. _____

10   A man has six times as many nickels as he has dimes. The value of his total money is $4.80. How many nickels has he?

    (A) 60 _____   (c) 72 _____

    (B) 68 _____   (D) 80 _____

11   What is the cube root of 262,144?

    (A) 512 _____   (c) 256 _____

    (B) 64 _____   (D) 32 _____

12   What is the capacity of a can 4 inches in diameter and 6 inches high?

    (A) $301\frac{5}{7}$ cu. in. _____   (c) $75\frac{3}{7}$ cu. in. _____

    (B) $150\frac{6}{7}$ cu. in. _____   (D) $13\frac{5}{7}$ cu. in. _____

13   Which of the following is one of the factors of $15x^2 - 21xy - 18y^2$?

    (A) $5x - 3y$ _____   (c) $3x - 3y$ _____

    (B) $5x + 6y$ _____   (D) $3x - 6y$ _____

14   What is the sum of the angles of a hexagon?

    (A) 360° _____   (c) 540° _____

    (B) 720° _____   (D) 180° _____

15   If sin 22° = .3745, tan 32° = .6249, sin 39° = .6293 and sec 52° = 1.6243, at what angle of depression would a plane one mile high sight a target that was $1\frac{3}{5}$ miles from a point directly below?

    (A) 22° _____   (c) 39° _____

    (B) 32° _____   (D) 52° _____

ANSWERS

TEST NO. 1

1   If $\frac{2}{5}$ broke, then $\frac{3}{5}$ was left; 6 ft. = $\frac{3}{5}$. ∴ $\frac{1}{5}$ = 2 ft; and $\frac{2}{5}$ = 4 ft.

2   $\frac{7}{7} + \frac{2}{7} = 117$. If $\frac{9}{7} = 117$ then $\frac{1}{7} = 13$, and $\frac{7}{7} = 7 \times 13$ or 91.

3   132% = 99. ∴ 1% = 99 ÷ 132 = .75, and 100% = .75 × 100 or 75.

4   Since boat is slower it takes $2\frac{1}{2} \times 10$ or $\frac{50}{2}$ = 25 hrs.

5   At 2 drums daily we use 40 drums for 20 days. To make 40 drums last 30 days you must use 40 ÷ 30 or $1\frac{1}{3}$ drums daily. $2 - 1\frac{1}{3} = \frac{2}{3}$.

6   $1.00 at 6% for $1\frac{1}{3}$ years would cost $1.08. ∴ the number of dollars that would cost $432 is 432 ÷ 1.08 = 400.

7   $C = \frac{5}{9}(113 - 32) = \frac{5}{9} \times 81 = 45$.

8   Let x = number of dimes. ∴ $36 - x$ = number of quarters.

.10(x) + .25(36 − x) = $6.60

.10x + 9.00 − .25x = 6.60.

9.00 − 6.60 = .15x, .15x = 2.40, $x = \dfrac{2.40}{.15}$,

x = 16, number of dimes,

36 − 16 = 20, number of quarters.

9   9 : 5 :: x : 15, 5x = 135, $x = \frac{135}{5} = 27$.

10   Let B = body and T = tail.

$T = 6 + \frac{1}{4}B$

$B = 6 + T$ or $T = B - 6$

$6 + \frac{1}{4}B = B - 6$ for $T = T$

$B - \frac{1}{4}B = 6 + 6$

$\frac{3}{4}B = 12$

$B = 12 \times \frac{4}{3} = 16$

6 + 16 + (6 + 4) = 32

TEST NO. 2

A

1	15	8	39	14	103	20	460
2	20	9	29	15	166	21	674
3	18	10	51	16	185	22	964
4	29	11	66	17	235	23	1241
5	32	12	92	18	363	24	1473
6	42	13	76	19	533	25	2251
7	83						

B

26	15	33	37	39	113	45	480
27	18	34	32	40	176	46	674
28	19	35	61	41	185	47	944
29	28	36	79	42	245	48	1271
30	33	37	92	43	343	49	1473
31	41	38	96	44	533	50	2192
32	73						

C

51	18	58	49	64	133	70	591
52	38	59	32	65	154	71	694
53	47	60	81	66	185	72	914
54	58	61	81	67	215	73	1251
55	42	62	102	68	343	74	1473
56	54	63	106	69	420	75	2281
57	83						

TEST NO. 3

1. If $\frac{5}{8}$ fell, $\frac{3}{8}$ was left, and that was equal to 24 inches. $\therefore \frac{1}{8} = 24 \div 3 = 8$, and $\frac{5}{8} = 5 \times 8$ or 40 inches.

2. Let $x = $ wt. of heavier. $\therefore$ lighter $= \frac{1}{2}x$, $x + \frac{1}{2}x = 1\frac{1}{2}x = 1,800$.
   $x = \frac{1800}{\frac{3}{2}} = 1,800 \times \frac{2}{3} = 1,200$.

3. $100\% = 300$, then $18\% = \$54$. If $12\% = 54$, $100\% = \frac{100}{12} \times 54 = 450$.

4. \$1 at 4% for $1\frac{1}{2}$ years amounts to \$.06. $\therefore$ the sum that will amount to \$424 is $424 \div 1.06$ or \$400.

5. Let $x = $ cost. $\therefore x + \frac{1}{5}x = \frac{6}{5}x = 4.50$,
   $6x = 4.50 \times 5$, $6x = 22.50$, $x = \frac{22.50}{6} = \$3.75$.

6. $\frac{18}{10} = \frac{x}{8}$ (inverse proportion), $10x = 144$,
   $x = \frac{144}{10} = 14\frac{2}{5}$

7. If $c^2 = a^2 + b^2$, $b^2 = c^2 - a^2$, and $b = \sqrt{c^2 - a^2} = \sqrt{225 - 144} = \sqrt{81} = 9$

8. $A = \pi r^2$. $\therefore r^2 = \frac{A}{\pi}$, and $r = \sqrt{\frac{A}{\pi}} = \sqrt{264 \times \frac{7}{22}} = \sqrt{84} = 9.165$
   $D = 2r = 18.33$

9. Area $\bigcirc = \pi r^2$, $A = \frac{22}{7} \times 441 = 1,386$ sq. in.
   Area rectangle $= b \times h$. $\therefore \frac{1386}{14} = 99$

10. Let $n = $ number of dimes. $\therefore 6n = $ number of nickels. $.10n + .05(6n) = 4.80$
    $.10n + .30n = 4.80$, $.40n = 4.80$, $n = \frac{4.80}{.40} = 12$
    If $n = 12$, then $6n = 72$

11. $64 \times 64 \times 64 = 262,144$.

12. $2^2 \times 3\frac{1}{7} \times 6 = 75\frac{3}{7}$ cu. in.

13. $(5x + 3y)(3x - 6y) = 15x^2 - 21xy - 18y^2$.

14. Divide into 6 equilateral $\triangle$. Each of the 6 $\angle$ of the hexagon equals 2 $\angle$ of an equilateral $\triangle$. $6 \times 2 \times 60° = 720°$. Or add all the angles of the $\triangle$ formed (12 rt. $\angle$) and subtract the 4 rt. $\angle$ at the center: 12 rt. $\angle$ − 4 rt. $\angle$ = 8 rt. $\angle$ = 720°.

15. Form a $\triangle$ with side $a \perp$ from plane to ground, b thence to target, and c thence to plane. Then $\angle$ at target = angle of depression at plane (alt. int. $\angle$ of $\parallel$ lines). Tan of $\angle$ at target = $a : b$ = $1 : 1\frac{3}{5} = .625 = \tan 32°$ within .0001.

Exercise No. 1

	Col. I	Col. II	Col. III	Col. IV
A-B	37,249	57,365	41,757	22,728
B-C	45,262	39,969	48,211	19,858
C-D	37,339	38,753	43,447	21,680
D-E	38,886	41,657	38,601	35,667
A-C	82,511	97,334	89,968	42,586
B-D	82,601	78,722	91,658	41,538
C-E	76,225	80,410	82,048	57,347
A-D	119,850	136,087	133,415	64,266
B-E	121,487	120,379	130,259	77,205
A-E	158,736	177,744	172,016	99,933

Exercise No. 2

1	389	4	41,482
2	4,968	5	37,789
3	3,484	6	452,884

Exercise No. 3

1. 1,504

2. 5,289

3. 9,464

4. 4,557

5. 3,264

6. 993,016. To solve this, reverse the example, multiplying 893 by 12 and then by 11.

7. 537,633. Note that $36 = 4 \times 9$. $1457 \times 9 = 13113$. This $\times 4 = 52,452$.

8. 2,304. 4×4 combined with $8 \times 8 = 1664$. To this add twice 8×40.

9. 4,399. 8×5 combined with $3 \times 3 = 4009$. To this add $3 \times (8 + 5)$ with 0 after it.

10. 13,225. Note ending in 5. Combine 11×12 with 5×5.

11. 5,524,582. Use 11 and 12 as multipliers.

12   2,439,720. 64 = 8 × 8. After multiplying by 8, multiply this figure by 8.

13   7,569. 8 × 8 combined with 7 × 7 = 6449. To this add twice 7 × 80.

14   4,416. 9 × 4 combined with 6 × 6 = 3636. To this add 6 × (9 + 4) with 0 after it.

15   326,019. 997 is near 1000. 327000 − 3 × 327 gives the answer.

Exercise No. 4

1	382	4	534	7	$917\frac{19}{48}$
2	384	5	645	8	903
3	$405\frac{27}{53}$	6	843	9	593

Exercise No. 5

1	8	5	1	9	6	13	0
2	6	6	0	10	0	14	8
3	0	7	8	11	3	15	3
4	5	8	2	12	4		

Exercise No. 6

1	Right	9	Wrong	17	Right
2	Right	10	Wrong	18	Wrong
3	Wrong	11	Right	19	Right. $\frac{1}{4}=\frac{24}{96}$.
4	Right	12	Wrong	20	Wrong
5	Wrong	13	Right	21	Right
6	Right	14	Right	22	Right
7	Right	15	Right	23	Right
8	Right	16	Wrong	24	Wrong

Exercise No. 7

1   178,322. You should use the horizontal method and make only one addition for the numbers in the thousands.

2   12 mos. in 1 yr. ∴ 12 × 152 = $1,824. *Note:* the sign ∴ means *therefore.*

3   Distance marched last day is 48 minus 12 + 9 + 7 + 9 = 48 − 37 = 11 mi.

4   If 2 cost 60 cents, one cost 30 cents; 300 ÷ 30 = 10.

5   450 ÷ 15 = 30 yds. as the distance traveled in 1 second. 30 × 3 = 90 ft., distance traveled in 1 second. 90 ÷ 3 = 30 ft., or distance traveled in $\frac{1}{3}$ of a second.

6   80 + 90 + 70 + 60 + 50 = 350. 350 ÷ 5 = 70

7   Total capacity of barracks is 100 × 50 × 10 = 50,000 cu. ft. If 1,000 cu. ft. cost $25.00 per season, 50,000 cu. ft. costs 50 ($25) = $1,250.

8   If 5 lbs. covers 10 sq. ft., then 10 ÷ 5 = 2 sq. ft. or the amount 1 lb. will cover. Area of the rectangle is 25 × 10 or 250 sq. ft. 250 ÷ 2 = 125 lbs.

9   Acreage left over is 142 minus 22 + 30 + 14 + 16 = 142 − 82 = 60

10   Difference per hr. = 200. Diff. per day = 10 × 200 = 2,000. Diff. for 30 days = 30 × 2,000 = 60,000.

11   200 × 6 = 1,200 mi. covered in 6 days + 2 days delay. 12 − 8 = 4 days left to cover remainder of distance, or 2,400 − 1,200 = 1,200 mi. 1,200 ÷ 4 = 300 mi. per day average needed.

12   52 weeks' payment on car = 52 × $20 = $1,040. Home remittances = 52 × $10 = $520. Insurance = 12 × $20 = $240. $1,040 + $520 + $240 = $1,800. ($4,800 − $1,800)/12 = $250.

Exercise No. 8

1	4	5	16	9	33	13	24
2	12	6	12	10	32	14	16
3	7	7	9	11	8	15	3
4	3	8	18	12	9		

Exercise No. 9

1	$\frac{2}{3}$	5	$\frac{3}{8}$	9	$\frac{5}{6}$	13	$\frac{5}{6}$
2	$\frac{2}{5}$	6	$\frac{4}{11}$	10	$\frac{9}{28}$	14	$\frac{36}{61}$
3	$\frac{2}{5}$	7	$\frac{5}{6}$	11	$\frac{5}{9}$	15	$\frac{1}{7}$
4	$\frac{3}{8}$	8	$\frac{1}{4}$	12	$\frac{1}{3}$		

Exercise No. 10

1	$\frac{2}{8}$	5	$\frac{24}{48}$	9	$\frac{9}{24}$	13	$\frac{42}{75}$
2	$\frac{4}{12}$	6	$\frac{14}{49}$	10	$\frac{27}{45}$	14	$\frac{72}{88}$
3	$\frac{8}{20}$	7	$\frac{8}{64}$	11	$\frac{8}{36}$	15	$\frac{40}{98}$
4	$\frac{36}{81}$	8	$\frac{30}{78}$	12	$\frac{44}{60}$	16	$\frac{28}{63}$

Exercise No. 11

1	$2\frac{2}{5}$	4	$8\frac{3}{5}$	7	$2\frac{2}{7}$	10	3
2	2	5	$6\frac{1}{2}$	8	$4\frac{2}{3}$	11	2
3	$1\frac{7}{12}$	6	$1\frac{1}{3}$	9	$4\frac{3}{4}$	12	16

Exercise No. 12

1	$\frac{11}{4}$	4	$\frac{28}{5}$	7	$\frac{139}{7}$	10	$\frac{94}{7}$
2	$\frac{13}{4}$	5	$\frac{38}{3}$	8	$\frac{97}{7}$	11	$\frac{71}{5}$
3	$\frac{24}{5}$	6	$\frac{75}{4}$	9	$\frac{86}{7}$	12	$\frac{112}{5}$

Exercise No. 13

1	$1\frac{5}{8}$	4	$1\frac{13}{18}$	7	$9\frac{1}{4}$	10	$6\frac{13}{24}$
2	$\frac{2}{9}$	5	$\frac{1}{2}$	8	$7\frac{3}{4}$	11	$1\frac{7}{12}$
3	$\frac{11}{40}$	6	$\frac{1}{8}$	9	$23\frac{11}{18}$	12	$6\frac{13}{24}$

Exercise No. 14

1	$\frac{9}{35}$	7	$\frac{25}{54}$	13	$1\frac{1}{4}$	19	$1\frac{1}{4}$
2	$\frac{1}{4}$	8	$\frac{1}{6}$	14	$4\frac{3}{8}$	20	$\frac{4}{5}$
3	$\frac{1}{9}$	9	36	15	14	21	28
4	$\frac{3}{10}$	10	9	16	6	22	$2\frac{1}{5}$
5	$4\frac{1}{2}$	11	$1\frac{1}{3}$	17	$6\frac{1}{4}$		
6	$\frac{7}{64}$	12	$4\frac{4}{5}$	18	40		

Exercise No. 15

1	$46\frac{7}{8}$	6	$37\frac{8}{11}$	11	$2\frac{18}{35}$	16	$3\frac{51}{79}$
2	$88\frac{1}{2}$	7	$141\frac{1}{2}$	12	$2\frac{17}{25}$	17	$6\frac{162}{167}$
3	$80\frac{1}{4}$	8	$41\frac{7}{8}$	13	$3\frac{11}{105}$	18	$23\frac{9}{11}$
4	$71\frac{1}{3}$	9	$57\frac{3}{8}$	14	$2\frac{91}{110}$	19	$5\frac{51}{148}$
5	$94\frac{4}{7}$	10	7650	15	$6\frac{17}{30}$	20	$7\frac{14}{17}$

Exercise No. 15a

1	$\frac{8}{11}$	3	$\frac{16}{21}$	5	200	7	154
2	$\frac{3}{80}$	4	$\frac{9}{14}$	6	160	8	$1\frac{5}{16}$

Exercise No. 16

1 $25\frac{1}{2}$ divided by $\frac{1}{32} = \frac{51}{2} \times \frac{32}{1} = 816$.

2 $\frac{1}{16}$ = the amount he can do in 1 day. ∴ the amount of work he can do in $\frac{1}{2}$ day = $\frac{1}{2} \times \frac{1}{16} = \frac{1}{32}$.

3 The top and bottom wings placed together measure $\frac{5}{8}''$ in height. $\frac{5}{8} \times \frac{3}{4} + \frac{5}{8} \times 1\frac{3}{4} = \frac{5}{8} \times \frac{5}{2} = \frac{25}{16} = 1\frac{9}{16}$.

4 If $\frac{1}{3}$ = 10, then 1 whole = $\frac{3}{3}$ or 3 times 10, which is 30. Or invert and multiply: if $\frac{1}{3}$ = 10, then $\frac{3}{1} \times 10 = 30$.

5 If the output of the faster machine is 1, then the slower machine produces $2 \times \frac{1}{3}$ or $\frac{2}{3}$. The combined output is $1 + \frac{2}{3}$ or $\frac{5}{3}$. If $\frac{5}{3}$ = 600, $\frac{3}{3}$ = $600 \times \frac{3}{5} = 360$.

6 If $\frac{2}{3}$ takes 5 hours, $\frac{1}{3}$ will take half that time or $2\frac{1}{2}$ hours, and $\frac{3}{3}$ or the whole job will take 3 times $2\frac{1}{2}$ or $7\frac{1}{2}$ hrs. Or—by inverting and multiplying: if $\frac{2}{3}$ = 5, then $\frac{3}{3} = \frac{3}{2} \times 5 = \frac{15}{2}$ or $7\frac{1}{2}$.

7 If second turns out $\frac{5}{6}$, then he loses $\frac{1}{6}$. If first turns out $\frac{1}{2}$ of $\frac{5}{6}$ he turns out $\frac{5}{12}$ and loses $\frac{7}{12}$. ∴ $\frac{1}{6} + \frac{7}{12}$ or $\frac{9}{12} = \frac{3}{4}$. $\frac{3}{4}$ of the output of one machine equals $\frac{3}{8}$ of the combined output.

8 2nd flight = $\frac{1}{2}$ of 432 or 216, 3rd flight = $\frac{1}{3}$ of 432 or 144, 4th flight = $\frac{1}{2}$ of 216 + 144 = 180 miles.

9 $\frac{1}{4} + \frac{3}{8} = \frac{5}{8}$ of the job completed in 24 + 31 days or 55 days. If $\frac{5}{8}$ = 55 days, then $\frac{1}{8} = \frac{1}{5}$ of 55 or 11 days, and $\frac{8}{8}$ = 88 days. Or—by inverting, if $\frac{5}{8}$ = 55, then $\frac{8}{8} = \frac{8}{5} \times 55 = 88$ days.

10 Both travel for 5 hours. ∴ $62\frac{3}{5} \times 5 = 313$, and $69\frac{4}{5} \times 5 = 349$. $3,000 - (313 + 349) = 2,338$ miles, the distance apart at the end of 5 hrs.

Note: Easier methods for doing examples of this type are explained in the chapters on ratios and equations.

Exercise No. 17

1	$\frac{1}{100}$	6	$\frac{1}{1250}$	11	.3	16	18.7
2	$\frac{1}{2}$	7	$\frac{38}{625}$	12	.05	17	.3
3	$\frac{5}{8}$	8	$\frac{2341}{10000}$	13	.312	18	1.45
4	$2\frac{1}{10}$	9	$\frac{4329}{100000}$	14	12.01	19	22.3
5	$23\frac{2}{5}$	10	$18\frac{1}{50}$	15	124.0003	20	4.33

Exercise No. 18

1	.5	5	.563	8	.875
2	.75	6	.531	9	.688
3	.375	7	.875	10	.875
4	.313				

Exercise No. 19

1	.77	7	.0045	12	10.439
2	25.03	8	.869	13	51.292
3	641.099	9	.802	14	44.3456
4	22.165	10	.08	15	57.3583
5	38.89	11	63.554	16	4.51235
6	12.42				

Exercise No. 20

1	74	11	32.67	21	.94
2	9.36	12	.3267	22	92
3	32.40	13	2.86268	23	749
4	30.602	14	.4077	24	5.3479
5	.4144	15	6.0088	25	.492568
6	.067648	16	87	26	.0249653
7	.98076	17	.069	27	.05908
8	.004284	18	9560	28	.00007156
9	.001803	19	4.53	29	.495674
10	.0000896	20	4069	30	.00000038649

Exercise No. 21

1	.17	5	420	8	.67
2	.05	6	3.7	9	404.286
3	.6	7	.047	10	36.818
4	4.73				

Exercise No. 22

1	$46	5	$14,665	8	$1,333\frac{1}{3}$
2	$215	6	800	9	120
3	$222.50	7	750	10	$1\frac{1}{8}$
4	$2,385				

Exercise No. 23

1 Amount of sand is .84 of the quantity of mortar. ∴ $.84 \times 250 = 210$ lbs.

2 Since each side is $2 \times .04''$ less than the outside length, the total difference in length for the four sides is $4 \times .08'' = .32''$; $8.32'' - .32'' = 8''$.

3 $$.675 \\ +.0007 \over .6757''$$

4 If 52 cents is amount received for one dozen, then $44.20 divided by .52 = 85 dozen.

5 Height of one story = $158.72 \div 16$ or $9.92'$, 6 stories = 9.92×6 or 59.52.

6 The average of the 4 readings or $.641'' + .647'' + .642'' + .646'' = 2576 \div 4 = .644''$.

7 $3\frac{3}{8} = 3.375$, $.0045 \times 2 = .009$, $3.375 - .009 = 3.366$.

Exercise No. 24

1 $\frac{1}{100}$	4 $\frac{7}{100}$	7 $\frac{1}{15}$	10 $\frac{3}{400}$
2 $\frac{1}{50}$	5 $\frac{1}{200}$	8 $\frac{3}{40}$	11 $\frac{3}{200}$
3 $\frac{1}{25}$	6 $\frac{1}{16}$	9 $\frac{1}{300}$	12 $\frac{1}{30}$

Exercise No. 25

1 186	6 25%	11 48
2 12	7 50	12 50
3 10	8 7%	13 320
4 $50	9 50%	14 800
5 $\frac{13}{20}$	10 75%	15 96

16 $20,000 \times \frac{4}{5} = 16,000$, $20,000 - 16,000 = 4,000$

17 $.08 \times 275 = 22$

18 $45\% = \frac{9}{20}$, $75 \times \frac{9}{20} = 33\frac{3}{4}$, $75 - 33\frac{3}{4} = 41\frac{1}{4}$

19 The number = 100%. ∴ 175% = 140, and 1% = 140 ÷ 175 or .8, and 100% = 100 × .8 or 80.

20 If 5.25 = 17.5%, 1% = 5.25 ÷ 17.5 or .3, and 100% = 100 × .3 = $30.

21 9,000 − 6,750 = 2,250 lbs., wt. of truck. $\frac{2250}{9000} = \frac{1}{4}$ or 25%.

22 $28 - 3\frac{1}{2} = 24\frac{1}{2}$, $\frac{24\frac{1}{2}}{28} = \frac{49}{2} \times \frac{1}{28} = \frac{7}{8}$ or $87\frac{1}{2}\%$.

23 If 8% = 144, then 1% = 144 ÷ 8 or 18, and 100% = 18 × 100 or 1,800.

24 $140 \times \frac{1}{20} = 7,140 - 7 = 133$ volts.

25 100% or total output of slower man equals 1,500. ∴ 50% = 750. Since $33\frac{1}{3}\%$ of faster man = 50% of slower man, his $33\frac{1}{3}\%$ = 750. ∴ his total output is 100% or 3 times 750 or 2,250.

Exercise No. 26

1 $129.00 \times .25 = 32.25$, amount of discount. ∴ selling price = $129.00 − $32.25 or $96.75.

2 $66\frac{2}{3}\% = \frac{2}{3}$, $58.50 \times \frac{2}{3} = \frac{117.00}{3} = \$39.00$.

3 $3.50 \times 60 = \$210$, total cost. $210 \times .08 = \$16.80$, amt. of 8% discount. $210 − $16.80 = $193.20. $193.20 \times .02 = \$3.86$, amt. of 2% discount; $193.20 − $3.86 = $189.34.

4 $40 \times .40 = \$16.00$, $40 − $16 = $24.00 $24.00 \times .10 = \$2.40$, $24.00 − $2.40 = $21.60 $21.60 \times .05 = \$1.08$, $21.60 − $1.08 = $20.52 or 100% − 40% = .60, 100% − 10% = .9, 100% − 5% = .95 $.6 \times .9 \times .95 = .513$, $40 \times .513 = \$20.52$ net.

5 $300 \times .25 = \$75$, $300 − $75 = $225 $225 \times .08 = \$18$, $225 − $18 = $207 $207 \times .05 = \$10.35$, $207 − $10.35 = $196.65 $75 + $18 + $10.35 = $103.35 discounts.

Exercise No. 27

1 $25,000 \times .015 = \$375$.

2 $165 \times 100 = \$16,500$, selling price of 100 sets; $16,500 \times .16 = \$2,640$, total commission.

3 If 5% = $400, then 100% equals $\frac{100}{5} \times 400 = \frac{40,000}{5} = \$8,000$.

4 $37\frac{1}{2}\% = \$600$. Since $37\frac{1}{2} = \frac{3}{8}$, then $\frac{8}{3} \times 600 = \frac{4,800}{3} = \$1,600$.

Exercise No. 28

1 Interest for one year on $188.60 at $4\frac{1}{2}\% = \$188.60 \times .045 = \$8.49$.

2 Interest on $1,850 at 4% for 1 yr. = $1,850 \times .04 = \$74.00$; for $2\frac{1}{2}$ yrs. interest = $74 \times \frac{5}{2} = \$185$.

3 For one year $275 \times .045 = \$12.375$. For 3 months interest = $12.375 \times \frac{1}{4} = \$3.09$.

4 $\frac{2}{3}$ of $60,000 = $40,000; $40,000 \times .04 = \$1,600$; $1,600 \times 2 = \$3,200$; $\frac{1}{3}$ of $60,000 = $20,000; $20,000 \times .05 = \$1,000$; $1,000 \times 2 = \$2,000$; $3,200 + $2,000 = $5,200.

5 If $67.50 = interest for $4\frac{1}{2}$ yrs., then $67.50 \div \frac{9}{2} = \$15$ of interest for 1 yr.; $15 on $300 is 15 ÷ 300 or .05 = 5%.

6 This means what rate of interest will yield $150 in 14 years. $150 ÷ 14 = $10.714, amt. interest in 1 yr. $\frac{10.714}{150} = 7\frac{1}{7}\%$

7 $480 \times .05 = \$24.00$, amt. of interest for 1 year. $\frac{\$56}{24} = 2\frac{1}{3}$.

8 $36 for 3 months would be 4×36 or $144 for 1 yr. If $144 equals 3%, 100% = $144 \times \frac{100}{3} = \frac{\$14,400}{3} = \$4,800$.

9 $800 at 6% for 1 yr. yields $48; $\frac{80}{48} = 1\frac{32}{48} = 1\frac{2}{3}$.

Exercise No. 29

1 $20\% = \frac{1}{5}$, $\frac{1}{5} \times 5 = 1¢$ profit on one. $5¢ + 1¢ = 6$ cents, selling price of one. $6 \times 12 = 72$ cents, selling price per doz.

2 $10,000 \times 2.50 = \$25,000$, total cost. $25,000 \times .06 = \$1,500$ profit. $25,000 + $1,500 = $26,500, total selling price.

3 $\frac{2}{5}$ of 10 = 4. $30 \times 4 = \$120$, selling price of 4 books. 10 − 4 = 6. $25 \times 6 = \$150$, selling price of 6 books. $150 + $120 = $270. $270 − $200 = $70; $\frac{\$70}{\$200} = 35\%$.

4 100% = cost of the boat; ∴ 125% or $\frac{5}{4}$ = selling price or $500; if $\frac{5}{4}$ = 500, $\frac{1}{4}$ = $500 ÷ 5 or $100, and $\frac{4}{4}$ = $400.

5 If 15% = $75, then 100% = $\frac{100}{15}$ × $75 = $500.

6 If $\frac{3}{8}$ = $90, then $\frac{8}{8}$ = $\frac{8}{3}$ × 90 or $240, total cost. Loss of $90 makes $150, selling price.

7 If loss = $12\frac{1}{2}$%, then $259 = 100% − $12\frac{1}{2}$ or $87\frac{1}{2}$% = $\frac{7}{8}$.
If $259 = $\frac{7}{8}$, then $\frac{8}{8}$ = $\frac{8}{7}$ × 259 = $296.

8 If mark-up was 24%, then 124% = $806, and 100% = $\frac{100}{124}$ × $806 = $650, cost.

9 $10,000 × .18 = $1,800 profit; $10,000 × .18 = $1,800 loss. $1,800 minus $1,800 = 0.

10 If rate of profit is 20%, and selling price is $3,600, then $3,600 = 120% or $\frac{6}{5}$, and $\frac{5}{5}$ = $\frac{5}{6}$ × $3,600 or $3,000. $3,600 − $3,000 = $600 profit. If rate of loss is 20% and selling price is $3,600, then $3,600 = 80% or $\frac{4}{5}$, and $\frac{5}{5}$ = $\frac{5}{4}$ × $3,600 or $4,500; $4,500 − $3,600 = $900 loss. $900 − $600 = $300 total loss.

11 If the selling price includes $37\frac{1}{2}$% profit, the cost must represent $62\frac{1}{2}$% of the selling price. $62\frac{1}{2}$% is $\frac{5}{8}$; $\frac{5}{8}$ of $4 is $2.50.

12 $1,000 represents 100%, of which $12\frac{1}{2}$% is profit and $87\frac{1}{2}$% is cost. $87\frac{1}{2}$% of $1,000 is $875.

13 Since there is a profit, this represents a smaller proportion of the selling price than it does of the cost. Hence we divide 15% by 100% + 15%.
$\frac{.15}{1.15}$ = .1304 = 13.04%

14 Where there is a loss it represents a larger percent of the selling price than it does of the cost. Hence we divide 15% loss on selling price by 100% + 15%. $\frac{.15}{1.15}$ = .1304 = 13.04%

15 A's house is assessed at $\frac{5}{6}$ of $11,000, or $9,166.67. The taxes on this at the rate of $28 per $1,000 amount to $256.67. B's house is assessed at $\frac{4}{5}$ of $11,000, or $8,800. At $28.50 per $1,000 the taxes on this amount to $250.80. Hence A pays $5.87 more than B.

Exercise No. 30

1	418	7	1,920	13	3,097,600
2	17,806	8	27,102	14	40
3	2,904	9	6	15	126
4	633,600	10	12	16	1,792
5	55,464	11	22,400	17	120
6	234	12	$60\frac{1}{3}$	18	1.22 or $1\frac{31}{144}$

Exercise No. 30a

1	148 yd. 1 ft. 6 in.	6	3 bu. 2 pk. 6 qt.
2	$\frac{3}{8}$	7	20 tons 500 lb.
3	10 lb. 8 oz. 7 pwt.	8	41 gal. 1 pt.
4	109° 23′ 58″	9	1 mi. 5 fur. 23 rd.
5	10 bbl. 25 gal. 2 qt.	10	2 bbl. 27 gal. 1 qt.

Exercise No. 30b

1	6° 41′ 21″	4	70° 15′ 15″
2	149° 14′ 13″		Maine
3	2 hr. 9 min. 37 sec.	5	212

Exercise No. 30c

1	$11.20	2	$20.00	3	$13.70

Exercise No. 31

1 A space 8 ft. square contains 8 × 8 or 64 sq. ft. The difference between this and 8 sq. ft. is 56 sq. ft.

2 The fence is 880 yd. long by $2\frac{2}{3}$ yd. high. 880 × $2\frac{2}{3}$ = 2,346$\frac{2}{3}$ sq. yd.

3 If we lay the carpet the long way of the room we get 9 strips each $11\frac{1}{6}$ yd. long. These make $100\frac{1}{2}$ sq. yd. If we lay the carpet the other way we get 12 strips each $8\frac{1}{3}$ yd. long, making 100 sq. yd. Hence we choose the latter way, and the carpet comes to $9.50 × 100 or $950.

4 The acreage is $\frac{360 × 189}{160}$ = $\frac{9}{4}$ × 189 = $\frac{1701}{4}$ = $425\frac{1}{4}$ acres. At $36 per acre this comes to $15,309.

5 The bricks would naturally run the long way of the walk. 8″ is contained in 50′, $\frac{50}{\frac{2}{3}}$ or 75 times.

4″ is contained in 5′, $\frac{5}{\frac{1}{3}}$ or 15 times. 75 × 15 = 1,125 bricks.

6 In 65 × 35 ft. there are 22.75 squares of 100 sq. ft. each. Multiplying by the cost per square gives $45 × 22.75 or $1,023.75.

Exercise No. 32

1	22,464	5	9	8	46,656
2	513,216	6	10	9	10,368
3	243,648	7	$411\frac{1}{3}$	10	$\frac{2}{9}$
4	3,645				

Exercise No. 32a

1	26.24 imp. gal.	3	216 bu.	5	15,750.288 lbs.
2	16,875 lbs.	4	12,960 lbs.	6	4.77 lbs.

Exercise No. 33

1	3.74623	5	3,560,000	8	3.123765
2	4,253	6	.000374658	9	746,000
3	.00008546	7	31,237.65	10	3.426
4	473,860				

Exercise No. 34

1	951.9528 A.	5	166.4473 lb.	8	65.4857 Dl.
2	1064.175 bu.	6	79.5528 M.	9	93.309 g.
3	95.0696 mi.	7	63.6775 Ha.	10	65.8801 Hl.
4	1276.086 gal.				

Exercise No. 35

1 $\frac{24}{32} = \frac{3}{4}$

2 $63 : 56 = \frac{63}{56} = 1\frac{7}{56} = 1\frac{1}{8}$

3 1 lb. = 16 oz., 5 lb. = 80 oz., $\frac{10}{80} = \frac{1}{8}$.

4 2 parts + 3 parts = 5 parts. Since 2 parts are water, then $\frac{2}{5}$ of total is water, or 40%.

5 6 parts tin + 19 parts copper = 25 parts to make bronze. The amount of tin in 500 lbs. of bronze is $\frac{6}{25} \times 500$ or 120.

6 5 + 14 + 21 = 40 parts = the total of $2,000. $\frac{21}{40} \times 2,000 = \$1,050$ as the largest share; $\frac{5}{40} \times 2,000 = \$250$ as the smallest share; $\$1,050 - 250 = \$800$ difference.

Exercise No. 36

1	6	3	6	5	21	7	3	9	3
2	12	4	2	6	4	8	125	10	18

Exercise No. 37

1 $\frac{18}{27} = \frac{20}{x}$ Direct prop. $18x = 540$, $x = \frac{540}{18} = 30$

2 $\frac{9}{30} = \frac{2}{x}$ Direct prop. $9x = 60$, $x = \frac{60}{9} = 6\frac{2}{3}$

3 $\frac{5}{20} = \frac{90}{x}$ Direct prop. $5x = 1,800$, $x = \frac{1,800}{5} = 360$

4 $\frac{112}{240} = \frac{28}{x}$ Inverse prop. $112x = 6,720$, $x = \frac{6,720}{112} = 60$

5 $\frac{26}{20} = \frac{x}{35}$ Inverse prop. $20x = 910$, $x = \frac{910}{20} = 45\frac{1}{2}$

6 $\frac{220}{x} = \frac{2}{8}$ Direct prop. $2x = 1,760$, $x = \frac{1,760}{2} = 880$

Exercise No. 38

1	23	5	$4b$	8	$5a + 2b$
2	−36	6	−3	9	$15a − 2b$
3	−7	7	$12x$	10	$15a + 3b − 5$
4	−20d				

Exercise No. 39

1	28	4	66	7	3
2	−9	5	130	8	−3
3	−24	6	$−40ab$	9	−25

Exercise No. 40

1	−32	3	72	5	−3	7	$2\frac{4}{5}$
2	216	4	−144	6	4	8	−12

Exercise No. 41

1 $x + y = 5$

2 $x + y + z = 9$

3 $2x + 2y = 10$

4 $x + y − x = 1$

5 $x^2 + y^2 = 13$

6 $y − 3 = 0$

7 $2xz = 16$

Exercise No. 42

1	23	4	20	7	3	9	1,260
2	110	5	12	8	55	10	3
3	13	6	44				

Exercise No. 43

1 $p = 2l + 2w$

2 $d = rt$

3 $H = \frac{av}{746}$

4 $I = PRT$

5 $A = \frac{W}{V}$

6 $P = M − O$

7 $d = 16t^2$

8 $A = S^2$

9 $C = \frac{5}{9}(F − 32°)$

10 $R = \frac{N}{T}$

Exercise No. 44

1 $p = 5$

2 $n = 12\frac{1}{2}$

3 $x = 28$

4 $c = 6$

5 $y = 4$

6 $n = 36$

7 $a = 48$

8 $b = Wc$

9 $A = \frac{W}{V}$

10 $W = \frac{P}{AH}$

Exercise No. 45

1 Since $\frac{D}{d} = \frac{r}{R}$ then $rd = DR$, and $r = \frac{DR}{d}$; substituting, $r = \frac{18 \times 100}{6} = \frac{1,800}{6} = 300$.

2 Since $DR = dr$, and D is the unknown, then $D = \frac{dr}{R}$; substituting, $D = \frac{9 \times 256}{144} = \frac{2,304}{144} = 16$.

3 Let n represent the number. Then $3n + 2n = 90$, $5n = 90$, $n = \frac{90}{5} = 18$

4 Let n represent the smaller number. Then $n + 7n = 32$, $8n = 32$, $n = \frac{32}{8} = 4$, and $7n = 7 \times 4$ or 28.

5 Let $x =$ the amount the first unit gets. Then the second unit receives $2x$, and the third unit receives $x + 2x$ or $3x$. The total $x + 2x + 3x = 6x = 600$, $x = 100$, and $2x = 200$.

6 Rate $\times$ Time = Distance; $R \times t = D$. They both travel the same amount of time. Let t equal the time they travel. Then $300t + 200t = 3,000$ mi., $500t = 3,000$, $t = \frac{3,000}{500} = 6$ hrs. $300 \times 6 = 1,800$ mi.

7 $R \times t = D$. Let $R =$ rate of slower soldier. Then $2R =$ rate of faster one. $10R + 20R = 24$ mi., $30R = 24$, $R = \frac{24}{30}$ or $\frac{4}{5}$, and $2R = \frac{8}{5}$ or $1\frac{3}{5}$ mi. per hr.

8 Let n = number of quarters the man has. Then $3n$ = number of nickels, and $.25(n) + .05(3n) =$ 8.00 or his total money.

$$.25n + .15n = .40n = 8.00, \ n = \frac{8.00}{.40} = 20$$

CHECK: $3n = 60$. $20 \times .25 = \$5.00$, and $60 \times .05 = \$3.00$, $\$5.00 + \$3.00 = \$8.00$.

9 Let T and t represent no. of teeth in large and small gears and let R and r represent rpm. Then $\frac{T}{t} = \frac{r}{R}$, and $\frac{72}{48} = \frac{160}{R}$, $72R = 7,680$,

$$R = \frac{7,680}{72} = 106\tfrac{2}{3}.$$

10 Weight $\times$ Distance = Weight $\times$ Distance. $\therefore 120 \times \frac{9}{2} = x \times 5$. $5x = 540$, $x = 108$.

Exercise No. 46

1	8	4	3	7	10	10	.3
2	10	5	5	8	1	11	1.2
3	9	6	12	9	.2	12	.05

Exercise No. 47

1	73	4	17.68	7	43	9	85
2	35	5	20.69	8	56	10	97
3	54.2	6	26				

Exercise No. 48

1	36	6	32,768	11	$\frac{4}{9}$
2	729	7	9	12	14.6969
3	5	8	5	13	.00000028
4	$\frac{1}{64}$	9	43,000,000	14	.0025
5	186,624	10	620,000	15	122,000,000

Exercise No. 49

1	135	11	$\frac{5}{6}$	21	441	31	841
2	223	12	$\frac{31}{36}$	22	529	32	1521
3	343	13	$\frac{63}{72}$	23	1089	33	9801
4	739	14	$\frac{7}{4}$	24	1369	34	784
5	487	15	$\frac{6}{8}$	25	1521	35	1444
6	$\frac{10}{12}$	16	9	26	1225	36	399
7	$\frac{14}{5}$	17	7	27	4225	37	896
8	$\frac{124}{49}$	18	$2\frac{1}{3}$	28	9025	38	1591
9	$\frac{65}{20}$	19	$3\frac{1}{5}$	29	11025	39	2484
10	$\frac{1068}{400}$	20	$1\frac{1}{2}$	30	42025	40	3456

Exercise No. 50

1	$7abc(ac^2 - 4)$	9	$(x + 7)(x + 3)$
2	$5acd(3a + 4c - 3d)$	10	$(x - 15)(x - 3)$
3	$(2x + 3y)(2x + 3y)$	11	$(x + 9)(x - 4)$
4	$(3ab - 4ac)(3ab - 4ac)$	12	$(x - 16)(x + 3)$
5	$(3ax + 4ay)(3ax - 4ay)$	13	$(x - 11y)(x - 3y)$
6	$(7x^2 + 4y)(7x^2 - 4y)$	14	$(3x + 9)(2x + 1)$
7	$(3x - y + 2z)(x + 3y)$	15	$(5x - 7)(3x + 3)$
8	$(a^2 + a + 1)(a^2 - a + 1)$	16	$(4x + 13)(3x - 3)$

Exercise No. 51

1 Let x = no. of min. spaces passed over by min. hand; y = no. passed by hr. hand. $12y = x$; $y = x - 60$. Subtracting, $11y = x - (x - 60) = 60$; $y = 5\frac{5}{11}$. $5\frac{5}{11}$ min. spaces past 12 o'clock gives $1.05\frac{5}{11}$ o'clock.

2 Try elimination by substitution. x = part inv. at 5%; y = part inv. at 6%. $.05x + .06y = \$1,220$; $x + y = \$22,000$. Multiplying $.05x$ etc. by 20 we get $x + 1.20y = \$24,400$, from which $x = \$24,400 - 1.20y$. Substituting this value in other equation, $\$24,400 - 1.20y + y = \$22,000$; $-.20y = -\$2,400$; $y = \$12,000$; hence $x = \$10,000$.

3 Try elimination by comparison. a = Jack's age; b = Joe's age. $a = 2b$; $a - 20 = 4(b - 20)$; $a = 4(b - 20) + 20$; hence $2b = 4b - 80 + 20$; $2b - 4b = -60$; $b = 30$ years for Joe; $2 \times 30 = 60$ years for Jack.

4 a = first; b = second. $a + \frac{b}{2} = 35$; $\frac{a}{2} + b = 40$. Multiply first equation by 2, $2a + b = 70$. Subtracting second equation from this $1\frac{1}{2}a = 30$; $a = 20$; $a + \frac{b}{2} = 35$; $\frac{b}{2} = 35 - 20$; $\frac{b}{2} = 15$; $b = 30$.

5 $a + \frac{b}{3} = \$1700$; $\frac{a}{4} + b = \$1800$. Multiplying first equation by 3, $3a + b = \$5100$. Subtracting second equation, $2\frac{3}{4}a = \$3300$; $a = \$1200$. Substituting in first equation $\$1200 + \frac{b}{3} = \$1700$; $\frac{b}{3} = \$1700 - \$1200 = \$500$; $b = \$1500$.

6 $\frac{a}{2} + \frac{b}{3} = 45$; $\frac{a}{5} + \frac{b}{2} = 40$. Multiplying both equations, $a + \frac{2b}{3} = 90$; $a + \frac{5b}{2} = 200$. Subtracting the first from the second $\frac{11b}{6} = 110$; $b = 60$. Substituting in first equation, $\frac{a}{2} + 20 = 45$; $\frac{a}{2} = 25$; $a = 50$.

7 a = A's profit; b = B's profit. $a + b = \$153$; $a - b = \$45$. Adding, $2a = \$198$; $a = \$99$; $b = 54$. Dividing \$918 in the proportions of 99 and 54, $\$918 \div 153 = 6$; $\$99 \times 6 = \$594$ for A; $\$54 \times 6 = \$324$ for B.

8 Try substitution. $14A + 15M = \$153$; $6A - 4M = \$3$; $6A = \$3 + 4M$, whence $A = \$.50 + \frac{2M}{3}$. Substituting in other equation $\$7 + \frac{28M}{3} + 15M = \$153$; $9\frac{1}{3}M + 15M = \$153 - \$7$. $\frac{73M}{3} = \$146$; $M = \$6$. Substituting in original equation, $6A - \$24 = \$3$; $6A = \$27$; $A = \$4.50$.

9 There are several ways to solve problems like this. The method by simultaneous equations might be as follows. Select letters to represent values that do not change. a = wt. of copper *to be added;* b = wt. of tin. $b = 80 - \dfrac{7b}{3} = 24$. $a = \dfrac{11b}{4} - \dfrac{7b}{3} = 66 - 56 = 10$ lbs.

10 Eliminate by comparison. $B + \dfrac{J}{8} = \$1200$; $\dfrac{B}{9} + J = \$2500$. $B = \$1200 - \dfrac{J}{8}$; $B = \$22,500 - 9J$; $\$1200 - \dfrac{J}{8} = \$22,500 - 9J$; $9J - \dfrac{J}{8} = \$22,500 - \$1200$; $\dfrac{71J}{8} = \$21,300$; $J = \$2400$; $B + \dfrac{J}{8} = \$1200$; $B + \$300 = \$1200$; $B = \$900$.

Exercise No. 52

1 $\dfrac{5xy}{4ab}$

2 $\dfrac{x + a}{3(x - a)}$

3 $x - a + \dfrac{3}{x - a}$

4 $\dfrac{a^3}{a - x}$

5 $\dfrac{x - y + c}{x - y}$

6 $\dfrac{a(x + a)}{ab}, \dfrac{a^2}{ab}, \dfrac{b(a - x)}{ab}$

7 $\dfrac{x(1 - x)^2}{(1 - x)^3}, \dfrac{x^2(1 - x)}{(1 - x)^3}, \dfrac{x^3}{(1 - x)^3}$

8 x

9 $\dfrac{4x^2 - 5x + 3}{(x - 1)^3}$

10 $2a + \dfrac{3(a - b)}{c}$

11 $\dfrac{a^2 + x^2}{a^2 - x^2}$

12 $\dfrac{2(x + y)}{a}$

13 $\dfrac{4x(x - 2)}{3}$

14 $\frac{3}{4}$

15 $x^2 - y^2$

Exercise No. 53

1 1   4 3   7 0   9 −2
2 2   5 −1   8 −4   10 0
3 4   6 1

Exercise No. 54

1 2.5490   4 3.8025   7 $\bar{3}$.5465   9 $\bar{4}$.7262
2 1.8808   5 .56312   8 .7810   10 2.8279
3 .9031   6 $\bar{1}$.3692

Exercise No. 55

1 22,310   4 156.2   7 456,500   9 3.238
2 1,068   5 8.252   8 4.396   10 84.72
3 486,400   6 79,280

11 Log 5 = .6990, log 7 = .8451, antilog 1.8539 = .71. Prefix minus sign.

12 Log 17 = 1.2304, log 32 = 1.5051, antilog $\bar{1}$.7253 = .53. Prefix minus sign.

13 First perform addition. Log 9 = .9542, log 4 = .6021, antilog .3521 = 2.25.

14 First perform addition. Log 15 = 1.1761, log 7 = .8451, antilog .3310 = 2.14.

15 First perform subtraction. Log 4 = .6021, log 3 = .4771, antilog .1250 = 1.33.

16 First perform subtraction. Log 11 = 1.0414, log 9 = .9542, antilog .0872 = 1.22.

17 First multiply. Log 8 = .9031, log 15 = 1.1761, antilog $\bar{1}$.7270 = .53.

18 First multiply. Log 24 = 1.3802, log 11 = 1.0414, antilog .3388 = 2.18.

19 $\dfrac{7 \div 3}{4} = \dfrac{7}{12}$. Log 7 = .8451, log 12 = 1.0792, antilog $\bar{1}$.7659 = .58.

20 $\dfrac{16}{18 \div 5} = \dfrac{80}{18} = \dfrac{40}{9}$. Log 40 = 1.6021, log 9 = .9542, antilog .6479 = 4.44.

Exercise No. 58

9 252   15 1005   21 3615   27 59.9
10 222   16 2184   22 77.2   28 23.5
11 168   17 1143   23 87.2   29 80.0
12 315   18 2124   24 492   30 30.5
13 896   19 2296   25 155   31 30.1
14 756   20 7720   26 229

Exercise No. 59

7 .101   10 75   13 34.4
8 3.14   11 631   14 16
9 27   12 11.4   15 4.17

Exercise No. 60

1 119   5 19.95   9 10.75   13 1000
2 384   6 20   10 .125 or $\frac{1}{8}$ 14 4.21
3 72.9   7 85   11 175   15 1016
4 31.0   8 $\frac{1}{36}$ 12 980

Exercise No. 61

1 .143   6 .0526   10 .037   14 .0815
2 .111   7 .0476   11 .0357   15 1.58
3 .091   8 .0435   12 .0345   16 .0109
4 .0769   9 .0384   13 132   17 1813
5 .0588

Exercise No. 62

1 841   5 44.89   9 26   13 4.5
2 1369   6 .5184   10 47   14 6.6
3 2304   7 .6889   11 58   15 2.62
4 2809   8 .009801 12 74   16 .96

Exercise No. 62a

1	729	5	47.5	9	24	13	6.1
2	2197	6	.572	10	36	14	6.7
3	4913	7	.754	11	16	15	3.11
4	9261	8	.0000041	12	47	16	1.44

Exercise No. 63

1	32.1	3	.544	5	491
2	14.95	4	19.7		

Exercise No. 64

1	19 and 22	8	16 and 21	15	54 and 324
2	5 and 5	9	128 and 256	16	56
3	4 and 6	10	$8\frac{1}{2}$ and $4\frac{1}{4}$	17	252
4	46 and 53	11	67 and 88	18	1,300
5	41 and 31	12	81 and 100	19	254
6	13 and 6	13	16 and 4	20	9,840
7	6 and 10	14	$7\frac{3}{4}$ and $15\frac{3}{4}$	21	19,530

Exercise No. 65

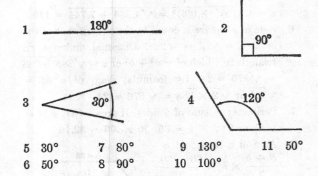

1 180°
2 90°
3 30°
4 120°

5	30°	7	80°	9	130°	11	50°
6	50°	8	90°	10	100°		

Exercise No. 66

1 $\angle 2 = 30°$. $\angle$ that coincide are =.

2 $\angle ABD = 22° 30'$. A bisector divides an $\angle$ in half.

3 (a) $\left.\begin{array}{l}\angle 1 = \angle 3\\ \text{(b) } \angle 2 = \angle 5\end{array}\right\}$ Ax. 1, p. 103
   (c) Relationship unknown

4 $\angle 1$ and $\angle 2$, $\angle 2$ and $\angle 3$, $\angle 3$ and $\angle 4$, $\angle 4$ and $\angle 5$, $\angle 5$ and $\angle 6$, $\angle 6$ and $\angle 7$, $\angle 7$ and $\angle 1$

5 $\angle 1$ and $\angle 5$, $\angle 2$ and $\angle 6$

6 $\angle 2 = 50°$, $\angle 4 = 30°$, $\angle 5 = 50°$, $\angle 6 = 100°$

7 $\angle AOC = 80°$, $\angle AOD = 180°$, $\angle BOE = 180°$, $\angle FOB = 130°$

8 (a) 67° 30', (b) 60°, (c) 45°, (d) 30°, (e) 22° 30'

9 (a) 22°, (b) 45°, (c) 35°, (d) 58°, (e) 85°, (f) 56° 30'

10 (a) 155°, (b) 55°, (c) 136°, (d) 92°, (e) 105° 30', (f) 101° 30'

Exercise No. 67

1 (a) alt. int., (b) alt. int., (c) corr., (d) alt. ext., (e) corr.

2 $\angle 1 = 50°$, $\angle 2 = 130°$, $\angle 4 = 130°$

3 $\angle 6 = 140°$, $\angle 7 = 140°$, $\angle 8 = 40°$

4 Two lines $\perp$ to a third line are $\parallel$

5 (a) alt. int. $\angle$ are =
   (b) corr. $\angle$ are =
   (c) alt. ext. $\angle$ are =

6 If a pair of alt. int. $\angle$ are = the lines are $\parallel$.

7 $\angle 3$ is sup. to 115°. $\therefore$ $\angle 3 = 65°$, making corr. $\angle$ =.

8 70°

9 Extend AB to D and construct $\angle BDE$ = to 60°. Then $DE \parallel BC$ because corr. $\angle$ are =.

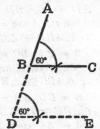

10 If the triangle is moved along the edge of the T-square into any two different positions, then lines drawn along side a will be $\parallel$ to each other, and lines drawn along side b will also be $\parallel$ to each other.

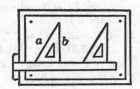

Exercise No. 68

1 $b^2 = c^2 - a^2$, $b = \sqrt{(51)^2 - (45)^2} = \sqrt{2,601 - 2,025} = \sqrt{576} = 24$

2 $A = \dfrac{bh}{2}$; $\dfrac{18(63)}{2} = 567$ sq. in.

3 Perimeter = sum of 3 sides. In isosceles $\triangle$ 2 sides are equal.
   $75 + 75 + 50 = 200$; $200 \times \$2.00 = \$400.00$

4 $c^2 = a^2 + b^2$
   $c = \sqrt{90^2 + 90^2} = \sqrt{8,100 + 8,100} = \sqrt{16,200} = 127.27$

5 Area of $A = \frac{1}{2}bh$; $\dfrac{20(10)}{2} = 100$ sq. ft.

6 $a^2 = c^2 - b^2$, $a = \sqrt{(c)^2 - (b)^2} = \sqrt{(26)^2 - (10)^2} = \sqrt{676 - 100} = \sqrt{576} = 24$

7 Let l = length of ladder, h = height of house, and b = distance from house at base. Then
   $l = \sqrt{h^2 + b^2} = \sqrt{1600 + 81} = \sqrt{1681} = 41$

8 Form the triangle and make the necessary deduction afterward. Let h = height of tree + elevation = $160 + 20 = 180$; l = line from top of tree to opposite shore; d = horizontal distance from tree to opposite shore. Then $d = \sqrt{l^2 - h^2} = \sqrt{500^2 - 180^2} = \sqrt{250000 - 32400} = \sqrt{217600} = 466.47$. Subtracting 100 ft. leaves 366.47 as the width of the river.

Exercise No. 69

1 $AB = AD$, $\angle 1 = \angle 2$ and $AC = AC$ (by identity)
∴ $\triangle ABC \cong ADC$ by s.a.s. = s.a.s.

2 $AD = DC$, $BD = BD$, and $\angle ADB = \angle CDB$ (all rt. ∡ are =)
∴ $\triangle ABD \cong \triangle CBD$ by s.a.s. = s.a.s.

3 $\angle 3 = \angle 5$, $BC = CD$ (bisected line) and $\angle 2 = \angle 6$ (vert. ∡ are =)
∴ $\triangle ABC \cong \triangle EDC$ by a.s.a. = a.s.a.

4 $AB = BD$, $EB = BC$, $\angle 1 = \angle 2$ (vert. ∡)
$\triangle ABE \cong \triangle CBD$ by s.a.s. = s.a.s.
$\angle 3 = \angle 4$ (corr. ∡ of cong. ∆)
∴ $AE \parallel CD$ (two lines are ∥ if a pair of alt. int. ∡ are =)

5 $AD = BC$, $AC = BD$, $AB = AB$ by identity
∴ $\triangle BAD \cong \triangle CBA$ by s.s.s. = s.s.s.
∴ $\angle 1 = \angle 2$ (corr. ∡ of cong. ∆ are =)

6 $AB = CB$, $AD = CD$,
$DB = DB$ by identity
∴ $\triangle ABD \cong CBD$ by s.s.s. = s.s.s.
∴ $\angle 5 = \angle 6$ (corr. ∡ of cong. ∆)
∴ $\angle 7 = \angle 8$ (supp. of ∡ are =)
$DE = DE$ by identity
∴ $\triangle ADE \cong \triangle CDE$ by s.a.s. = s.a.s.
∴ $\angle 1 = \angle 2$ (corr. ∡ of cong. ∆)

7 $AB = EF$, $\angle A = \angle F$ (alt. int. ∡) and $\angle C = \angle D$ (alt. int. ∡)
∴ $\triangle ABC \cong \triangle DEF$ by s.a.a. = s.a.a.
∴ $BC = DE$ (corr. sides of cong. ∆)

Exercise No. 70

1 45°

2 360° (any quad. can be divided into 2 ∆)

3 120° (∡ of equilateral ∆ = 60°, and ext. ∠ = sum of 2 int. ∡)

4 20° and 70° (acute ∡ of a rt. ∆ are comp. ∴ $9x = 90°$, $x = 10°$)

5 52° (supp. 116° = 64°; base ∡ of isos. ∆ are = ∴ $180 - (64° + 64°) = 52°$)

6 $32\frac{8}{11}°$, $49\frac{1}{11}°$, $98\frac{2}{11}°$ (Let x = angle; then $x + \frac{1}{2}x + \frac{1}{3}x = 180°$ and $x = 98\frac{2}{11}°$.)

7 Ratio is 1 : 1 or equal.

8 $\angle 2$ supp. $\angle 1$ and $\angle 3$ supp. $\angle 4$
∴ $\angle 2 = \angle 3$ (Ax. 1, page 103)
∴ $AB = BC$ and $\triangle ABC$ is isos. (if 2 ∡ of a ∆ are = the sides opp. are = and the ∆ is isos.)

9 In $\triangle ABC$ $\angle 1 = \angle 2$ (base ∡ of an isos. ∆ are =)
$\angle 1 = \angle 3$ (corr. ∡ of ∥ lines are =)
∴ $\angle 3 = \angle 2$ (Ax. 1)
∴ $DA = DE$ (if two ∡ of a ∆ are =, the sides opp. are =)

Exercise No. 71

1 Perimeter = sum of 4 sides, and the opposite sides of a rectangle are equal. ∴ $P = 550 + 550 + 390 + 390 = 1,880$

2 Area of a rectangle = $l \times w$. $110 + 40 \times 64 + 40 = 150 \times 104 = 15,600$

3 Area of a square = S^2. $75 \times 75 = 5,625 \times .20 = \$1,125$

4 $4^2 = 16$; $1,024 \div 16 = 64$

5 Diag. of a rectangle makes 2 rt. angles. $c^2 = a^2 + b^2$.
∴ $c = \sqrt{a^2 + b^2}$,
$c = \sqrt{(88)^2 + (66)^2} = \sqrt{4,356 + 7,744} = 110$

6 Side of a square is equal to the square root of the area. $S = \sqrt{A} = \sqrt{288}$. Diagonal makes a rt. triangle in which $c^2 = a^2 + b^2$ or $c = \sqrt{288 + 288} = \sqrt{576} = 24$. By formula, diag. of a sq. = $\sqrt{2A}$ or $\sqrt{2 \times 288} = \sqrt{576} = 24$

7 Perimeter = sum of 4 sides. If area = 81, side = $\sqrt{81}$ or 9; $9 \times 4 = 36$; $36 \times .06 = \$2.16$

8 Area of a trapezoid = $\frac{B + b}{2} \times h = \frac{60 + 30}{2} \times 15 = 45 \times 15 = 675$ sq. ft.

9 Area of a parallelogram equals base times height. $A = bh$. ∴ $A = 24 \times 14 = 336$ sq. ft.

10 To find unknown segment use formula for area of rt. triangle. $c^2 = a^2 + x^2$, or $x = \sqrt{c^2 - a^2} = \sqrt{(10)^2 - (8)^2} = \sqrt{100 - 64} = \sqrt{36} = 6$.

Area of trapezoid = $\frac{B + b}{2} \times h$; $\frac{18 + 12}{2} \times 8 = 15 \times 8 = 120$

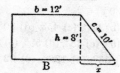

Exercise No. 72

1 $C = \pi d.$ $C = \frac{22}{7} \times 28 = 88$ in.

2 $C = 2\pi r.$ $r = \frac{C}{2\pi}$, $r = \frac{110}{\frac{44}{7}} = 110 \times \frac{7}{44} = \frac{35}{2} =$ $17\frac{1}{2}$ in.

3 $C = \pi d.$ $C = \frac{22}{7} \times 4 = \frac{88}{7}$, $\frac{88}{7} \times 49 = 616$ in.

4 $A = \pi r^2$, $D = 2r$. If $D = 14$, then $r = 7$; $A = \frac{22}{7} \times (7)^2 = 154$ sq. in.

5 Area of ring $= \pi R^2 - \pi r^2$. $D = 128$, $d = 96$, $R = 64$, $r = 48$
$A = \pi(64^2 - 48^2) = \frac{22}{7}$ $(4{,}096 - 2{,}304) = \frac{22}{7} \times 1792 = 5{,}632$; $5{,}632 \times .10 = \$563.20$

6 $A = \pi r^2$, $r^2 = \frac{A}{\pi}$; $r = \sqrt{\frac{A}{\pi}} = \sqrt{\frac{50\frac{1}{4}}{\frac{22}{7}}} =$
$\sqrt{50\frac{1}{4} \times \frac{7}{22}} = \sqrt{\frac{1407}{88}} = \sqrt{16.1}$. Discarding the decimal, $r = 4$; $D = 2 \times 4$ or 8.

7 Since $A =$ constant times R^2, areas are to each other as the squares of their radii, or $A : a :: R^2 : r^2$. If $R = 2$ and $r = 1$, then $A = \pi \times (2)^2$, and $a = \pi(1)^2$, or 4 to 1. Answer is 4.

8 $R = \sqrt{r^2 + r^2 + r^2 + r^2}$
$= \sqrt{(14)^2 + (14)^2 + (14)^2 + (14)^2}$
$= \sqrt{4(196)} = \sqrt{784} = 28$

9 Area $= \pi R^2 = \frac{22}{7} \times 28^2$. Cost is $\frac{22}{7} \times 28 \times 28 \times \frac{1}{4} = 22 \times 28 = \$616$.

10 Area of circle $= \pi R^2$. Side of equal square $= \sqrt{\pi R^2} = \sqrt{\frac{22}{7} \times 28 \times 28} = \sqrt{88 \times 28} = \sqrt{2464} = 49.6$ ft.

Exercise No. 73

1 $\sin B = \frac{b}{c}$, $\cos B = \frac{a}{c}$, $\cot B = \frac{a}{b}$, $\sec B = \frac{c}{a}$,
$\csc B = \frac{c}{b}$

2 $\tan A$

3 $\cot A$

4 $\sec A$

5 $\csc A$

6 $\cos A = \frac{4}{5}$

7 $\sin A = \frac{3}{5}$

8 $\cos A = \frac{15}{17}$

9 $\sec A = \frac{17}{15}$

10 $\cos A = \frac{12}{13}$, $\tan A = \frac{5}{12}$, $\cot A = \frac{12}{5}$, $\sec A = \frac{13}{12}$, $\csc A = \frac{13}{5}$

Exercise No. 74

1 $\cos 64°$

2 $\cot 47°$

3 $\sin 65° 32'$

4 $\tan 1° 10'$

5 $\csc 83° 50'$

6 $\sec 12\frac{1}{2}°$

7 $15°$ ($90° = 5A + A$; $\therefore 90° = 6A$, and $A = 15°$)

8 $45°$ (reciprocals of the cofunctions are $=$, $\therefore \angle A = 45°$)

9 $45°$ ($90° - A = A$; $90° = 2A$; $A = 45°$)

10 $30°$ ($\cos A = \sin 90° - A$; since $\cos A = \sin 2A$, then $\sin 90° - A = \sin 2A$, $90° - A = 2A$; $3A = 90°$ and $A = 30°$)

Exercise No. 75

1	.1392	6	.9063	11	4695	16	15°
2	.6691	7	4.134	12	1.4826	17	35°
3	.8391	8	.9781	13	.8480	18	60°
4	.5095	9	.3839	14	.7071	19	70°
5	1.079	10	6.3925	15	.5000	20	10°

Exercise No. 76

1	.2672	5	1.315	8	$\cos 65° 20'$
2	.9013	6	$\sin 5° 10'$	9	$\cot 49° 40'$
3	1.079	7	$\tan 18° 50'$	10	$\csc 42° 30'$
4	.7674				

Exercise No. 77

1 $a = 54.46$

2 $a = 3.42$

3 $\angle A = 65° 33'$

4 $c = 29.82$

5 $\angle A = 46° 03'$

6 $\frac{a}{c} = \sin A$, $c = \frac{a}{\sin A} = \frac{405}{.2250} = 1{,}800$ ft.

7 $a = c \sin A = 150 \times .7660 = 114.9$ ft.

8 $c = \frac{a}{\sin A} = \frac{12}{.3090} = 38.83$ ft.

9 $a = c \sin A = 200 \times .9455 = 189.1$ ft.

10 $\frac{a}{c} = \sin A = \frac{54.5}{625} = .0872$ which is the sin of 5°

Exercise No. 78

1 $\angle A = 53° 8'$

2 $b = 31.86$

3 $b = 62.08$

4 $\angle A = 60°$

5 $c = 42$

6 $\frac{b}{c} = \cos A = \frac{15}{17} = .8823$ which is the cos of 28°

7 $\frac{b}{c} = \cos A$, $c = \frac{b}{\cos A} = \frac{681}{.8910} = 764.9$

8 $\angle B = 90° - 10° = 80°$, $\cos B = \frac{a}{c}$,
$c = \frac{a}{\cos B} = \frac{125}{.1736} = 720.04$

9 $\cos B = \frac{a}{c}$, $a = c \cos B = 84 \times 6428 = 53.9952 = 54$

10 $\cos A = \frac{b}{c} = \frac{16.5}{100} = .165$ which is the cos of 80°30'

Exercise No. 79

1 36° 52'

2 64

3 45.04

4 18.19

5 15

6 $\dfrac{a}{b} = \tan A$, $b = \frac{1}{2}$ of $280 = 140$ ft., $a = b \tan A$

  $= 140 \times .9325 = 130.55$ ft.

7 $\tan B = \dfrac{b}{a}$, $\angle B = 90° - 10° = 80°$, $b = a \tan B$

  $= 240 \times 5.6713 = 1361.11$ ft.

8 $\tan A = \dfrac{a}{b}$, $b = \dfrac{a}{\tan A} = \dfrac{30}{.3640} = 82.42$ ft.

9 $\angle A = 90° - 15° = 75°$, $\angle A' = 90° - 14° = 76°$
  $CB = b \tan A = 100 \times 3.7321 = 373.21$ ft.
  $CB' = b \tan A' = 100 \times 4.0108 = 401.08$ ft.
  $CB' - CB = BB' = 401.08 - 373.21 = 27.87$ ft.

10 Let x = height of tower
     y = distance from nearer point to foot of
        tower

  From $\triangle ACD$, $\dfrac{x}{300 + y} = \tan 30°$; $\tan 30° = \dfrac{1}{\sqrt{3}}$

  $\therefore y = \sqrt{3}x - 300$

  From $\triangle BCD$, $\dfrac{x}{y} = \tan 60°$, $\tan 60° = \sqrt{3}$ $\therefore y = \dfrac{x}{\sqrt{3}}$

  Equating the values of y, $\sqrt{3}x - 300 = \dfrac{x}{\sqrt{3}}$

  $2x = 300 \times 1.732$, $x = 259.8$

Exercise No. 80

1 $a = 7$, $b = 8.57$

2 $\angle C = 69°$, $b = 58.91$, $c = 58.44$

3 $\angle A = 76° 52'$, $\angle B = 35° 8'$, $c = 20.95$

4 $\angle A = 51° 24'$, $\angle B = 48° 49'$, $\angle C = 79° 47'$

5 $\angle B = 12° 56'$, $\angle C = 146° 4'$, $c = 12.43$

6 $\angle ABC = 97° 44'$
  $\angle BCA = 180° - (67° 31' +$
  $97° 44') = 14° 45'$

  $\dfrac{a}{c} = \dfrac{\sin A}{\sin C}$, $a = \dfrac{c \sin A}{\sin BCA}$

  $= \dfrac{1.83 \times .9241}{.2546}$

  $= 6.656$

  $\sin 82° 16' = \dfrac{x}{6.656}$,

     $x = .9909 \times 6.656 = 6.595 = 6.6$ mi.

7 $\dfrac{b}{c} = \dfrac{\sin B}{\sin C}$, $\sin B = \dfrac{b \sin C}{c}$

  $= \dfrac{985 (\sin 64° 20')}{1460}$

  $= .6081$ which is
    $\sin 37° 27'$

  $\angle A = 180° - (64° 20'$
    $+ 37° 27') = 78° 13'$

  $\dfrac{a}{b} = \dfrac{\sin A}{\sin B}$, $a = \dfrac{b \sin A}{\sin B} = \dfrac{985 \times .9789}{.6081}$

  $= 1585.6$ ft.

8 $A + B = 180° - 50° = 130°$,
  $\frac{1}{2}A + B = 65°$
  $\tan \frac{1}{2}(A - B) =$

    $\dfrac{a - b}{a + b} \times \tan \frac{1}{2}(A + B)$

    $= \dfrac{5.5 - 5}{5.5 + 5} \times 2.145 = .102$

  which is the tan of $5° 50'$
  $\angle A = \frac{1}{2}(A + B) + \frac{1}{2}(A - B) = 70° 50'$
  $\dfrac{c}{a} = \dfrac{\sin C}{\sin A}$, $c = \dfrac{a \sin C}{\sin A} = \dfrac{5.5 \times .7660}{.9446} = 4.46$ mi.

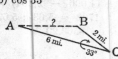

9 By cos law, $c = \sqrt{a^2 + b^2 - 2ab \cos C}$
  $c = \sqrt{2^2 + 6^2 - 2(2 \times 6) \cos 33°}$

    $= \sqrt{19.87}$
    $= 4.46$ mi.

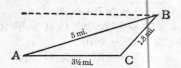

10 By cos law, $a^2 = b^2 + c^2 - 2bc \cos A$
  $\therefore \cos A = \dfrac{b^2 + c^2 - a^2}{2bc}$

  (a) $\cos A = \dfrac{3.5^2 + 5^2 - 1.8^2}{2(3.5 \times 5)} = .9717$

    which is the cos of $13° 40'$

  (b) alt. int. $\angle$s of $\parallel$ lines are $=$;
     $\therefore$ angle of depression $= 13° 40'$

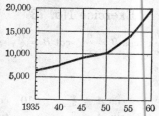

Exercise No. 81

1

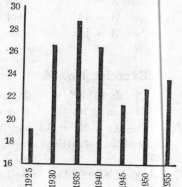

2

3

Ft. lumber	Price
1	$ .08
15	1.20
25	2.00
35	2.80
45	3.60
55	4.40

Price of $36\frac{1}{2}$ feet = $2.92

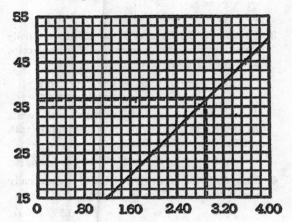

4 $6\frac{1}{2}$ hrs.

5 3,200 ft. Multiply the values shown on the graph by 100.

6

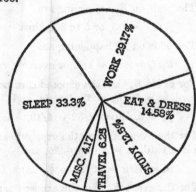

WORK 29.17%
SLEEP 33.3%
EAT & DRESS 14.58%
STUDY 12.5%
TRAVEL 6.25
MISC. 4.17

Exercise No. 82

1 $C(4, 3) = 4$ by count of

$A \& B \& C,$ $A \& B \& D,$

$A \& C \& D,$ $B \& C \& D.$

$P(4, 3) = 24$ by count of

ABC,	BAC,	CAB,	DAB,
ABD,	BAD,	CAD,	DAC,
ACB,	BCA,	CBA,	DBA,
ACD,	BCD,	CBD,	DBC,
ADB,	BDA,	CDA,	DCA,
ADC,	BDC,	CDB,	DCB.

2 $C(4, 3) = \dfrac{4!}{3!(4-3)!} = \dfrac{4}{1!} = 4.$

$P(4, 3) = \dfrac{4!}{(4-3)!} = \dfrac{4!}{1!} = 4 \cdot 3 \cdot 2 = 24.$

3 Since this is a question of grouping without regard to order, it is one of *combinations* with $n = 12$, $t = 5$, and

$$C(12, 5) = \frac{12!}{5!(12-5)!} = \frac{12!}{5!7!}$$

$$= \frac{12 \cdot 11 \cdot 10 \cdot 9 \cdot 8}{5 \cdot 4 \cdot 3 \cdot 2} = 792, \quad \text{Ans.}$$

4 Since different signals can be sent by different arrangements of the same combination of flags, these are questions of *permutations*.

(a) $P(5, 5) = 5! = 5 \cdot 4 \cdot 3 \cdot 2 = 120,$ Ans. (a).

(b) $P(13, 5) = \dfrac{12!}{(12-5)!} = \dfrac{12!}{7!}$

$= 12 \cdot 11 \cdot 10 \cdot 9 \cdot 8$

$= 95,040,$ Ans. (b).

5 (a) $C(n, t) P(t, t) = \dfrac{n!}{t!(n-t)!} \cdot t!$

$= \dfrac{n!}{(n-t)!} = P(n, t),$ as required.

(b) With $n = 12$ and $t = 5$ as in the two preceding examples:

$C(12, 5) = \quad 792$

$P(5, 5) = \quad 120$

$\overline{\qquad 15840}$

$\qquad 792$

$P(12, 5) = 95040,$ check.

6 Regarding the couple as a unit, we have $n = 7$ in the circular-permutations formula

$$P_c(7, 7) = 6! = 6 \cdot 5 \cdot 4 \cdot 3 \cdot 2 = 720.$$

But in each of these permutations the inseparable couple may sit on either side of each other. Hence,

$$2P_c = 2(720) = 1,440, \quad \text{Ans.}$$

7 The 2 vowels can be arranged from 5 in any of

$$P(5, 2) = \frac{5!}{(5-2)!} = \frac{5!}{3!} = 5 \cdot 4 = 20 \text{ ways.}$$

The 3 other letters can be arranged from 21 in

$$P(21, 3) = \frac{21!}{(21-3)!} = 21 \cdot 20 \cdot 19$$

$$= 7,980 \text{ ways.}$$

Hence, all 5 letters can be arranged in

$P(5, 2)P(21, 3) = 20(7,980)$

$= 159,600 \text{ ways,} \quad \text{Ans.}$

8 Here $n_1 = 3$, $n_2 = 6$, $n_3 = 4$, $n = 3 + 6 + 4 = 13$, and

$$P_a = \frac{n!}{n_1! n_2! n_3!} = \frac{13!}{3! 6! 4!}$$

$$= \frac{13 \cdot 12 \cdot 11 \cdot 10 \cdot 9 \cdot 8 \cdot 7}{3 \cdot 2 \cdot 4 \cdot 3 \cdot 2}$$

$$= 60,060, \quad \text{Ans.}$$

9   (a) $N = 4(6) = 24$.   (b) $N = 4(6)(3) = 72$.

10   $N = 2^5 = 32$.

11   $N = 6^4 = 1,296$.

12   $N = 2(6)(4)(9) = 432$ models.

13   Excluding the one case in which *no dot* is raised,

$$N = 2^6 - 1 = 64 - 1 = 63, \quad \text{Ans.}$$

14   This question differs from question 4(a) in that duplications of flags are now possible. Hence, $n = k = 5$, and

$$N = n^k = 5^5 = 3,125, \quad \text{Ans.}$$

15   $M = 2^{16} - 1 = 65,536 - 1 = 65,535$, Ans.

16   (a) We can combine any 2 ranks in

$$C_2^{13} = \frac{13 \cdot 12}{2} = 78 \text{ ways.}$$

And we can combine "a pair" of one rank with "3 of a kind" of another rank in

$$2C_2^4 C_3^4 = 2 \cdot \frac{4 \cdot 3}{2} \cdot \frac{4 \cdot 3 \cdot 2}{3 \cdot 2} = 48 \text{ ways.}$$

Hence a "full house" can be dealt in

$$C_2^{13} 2C_2^4 C_3^4 = 78(48) = 3,744 \text{ ways}, \quad \text{Ans.}$$

(b) In any one suit we can combine 5 cards to form a "flush" in C_5^{13} ways. Hence, with 4 suits in the deck, "any flush" can be dealt in

$$4C_5^{13} = 4 \div \frac{13 \cdot 12 \cdot 11 \cdot 10 \cdot 9}{5 \cdot 4 \cdot 3 \cdot 2}$$

$$= 5,148 \text{ ways}, \quad \text{Ans.}$$

(c) "Any straight" can be dealt with any one rank lowest (or highest) in

$$n^k = 4^5 = 1,024 \text{ ways.}$$

Hence, it can be dealt with any one of 10 possible ranks lowest (or highest) in

$$10n^k = 10(1,024) = 10,240 \text{ ways}, \quad \text{Ans.}$$

(d) By combining the reasoning of (b) and (c), we find a "straight flush" can be dealt in

$$4 \cdot 10 = 40 \text{ ways}, \quad \text{Ans.}$$

(e) $b - d = 5,148 - 40 = 5,108$ ordinary "flushes."

(f) $c - d = 10,240 - 40 = 10,200$ ordinary "straights."

Exercise No. 83

1   The required array and corresponding h values are:

$$h_5 = 4 \begin{cases} h_1 = 1 & H_1 H_2 H_3 & H_1 T_2 T_3 \\ & H_1 H_2 T_3 & T_1 H_2 T_3 \\ h_2 = 3 & H_1 T_2 H_3 & T_1 T_2 H_3 \\ & T_1 H_2 H_3 & T_1 T_2 T_3 \end{cases} \begin{matrix} \\ \\ h_3 = 3 \\ \\ h_4 = 1 \end{matrix}$$

Hence, the corresponding f values are:

$$f_1 = f_4 = 8 - 1 = 7,$$
$$f_2 = f_3 = 8 - 3 = 5,$$
$$f_5 = 8 - 4 = 4.$$

2   $p_1 = p_4 = \frac{1}{8} = 12.5\%$,
$q_1 = q_4 = \frac{7}{8} = 87.5\%$,
$p_2 = p_3 = \frac{3}{8} = 37.5\%$,   Ans.
$q_2 = q_3 = \frac{5}{8} = 62.5\%$,
$p_5 = q_5 = \frac{4}{8} = 50.0\%$.

3   Events E_1, E_2, E_3, and E_4 are all the mutually exclusive different outcomes possible when 3 coins are tossed. Hence,

$$p_1 + p_2 + p_3 + p_4 = \frac{1}{8} + \frac{3}{8} + \frac{3}{8} + \frac{1}{8}$$
$$= \frac{8}{8} = 1, \quad \text{CHECK.}$$

Also, event E_5 is mutually exclusive with events E_3 and E_4, to exhaust the same possibilities with a different grouping. Hence,

$$p_5 + p_3 + p_4 = \frac{4}{8} + \frac{3}{8} + \frac{1}{8} = \frac{8}{8} = 1, \quad \text{CHECK.}$$

4   Since E_5 is the event that either of the mutually exclusive events, E_1 or E_2, happen

$$p_5 = p_1 + p_2 = \frac{1}{8} + \frac{3}{8} = \frac{4}{8} = 0.5 \text{ as before.}$$

5   (a) The odds on E_1 happening are

$$h_1 {:} f_1 = 1{:}7, \text{ or 1 to 7 for.}$$

(b) The odds on E_2 happening are

$$f_2 {:} h_2 = 5{:}3, \text{ or 5 to 3 against.}$$

(c) The odds on E_5 happening are

$$h_5 {:} f_5 = 4{:}4 = 1{:}1, \text{ or even either way.}$$

6   (a) For event E_a that the exposed card be a face card, $w = 52$, $h_a = 3 \cdot 4 = 12$, and

$$p_a = h_a/w = 12/52 = 4/13, \quad \text{Ans. (a).}$$

(b) For the event E_b that the exposed card be a black card, $h_b = 2 \cdot 13 = 26$, and

$$p_b = h_b/w = 26/52 = \tfrac{1}{2}, \quad \text{Ans. (b).}$$

(c) For the event E_c that the exposed card be a black face card, $h_c = 2 \cdot 3 = 6$, and

$$p_c = h_c/w = 6/52 = 3/26, \quad \text{Ans. (c).}$$

(d) Hence, the probability of the partially overlapping event E_d, that either E_a or E_b happen, is

$$p_d = p_a + p_b - p_c = \frac{12 + 26 - 6}{52}$$

$$= \frac{32}{52} = \frac{8}{13}, \quad \text{Ans. (d).}$$

7   The coins can land in $w = n^k = 2^5 = 32$ ways. Of these, only $h = 2$ (1 all heads, and 1 all tails) comply with the condition that all land the same way. Hence, the required probability is

$$p = h/w = 2/32 = 1/16, \quad \text{Ans.}$$

Alternatively regarding the required landing as a multiple event, we can reason that the probability of the first coin landing either heads or tails is $p_1 = 2/2 = 1$ (for certainty), but that the probability of the other coins each separately landing the same way is 1/2 in each case. Hence, $p_2 = p_3 = p_4 = p_5 = 1/2$, and the probability of the specified multiple event is

$$p = p_1 p_2 p_3 p_4 p_5 = 1(\tfrac{1}{2})^4 = 1/2^4$$
$$= 1/16, \quad \text{SAME ANS.}$$

8　Any 2 balls from either box may be combined with any 2 balls in the other box in

$$w = C_2^{10} C_2^{10} = \left(\frac{10 \cdot 9}{2}\right)^2 = 45^2 = 2{,}025 \text{ ways.}$$

But 2 red balls from either may be combined with 2 red balls from the other in only

$$h = C_2^4 C_2^4 = \left(\frac{4 \cdot 3}{2}\right)^2 = 6^2 = 36 \text{ ways.}$$

Hence, the required probability is

$$p = h/w = 36/2{,}025 = 4/225, \quad \text{ANS.}$$

Alternatively, we may regard the drawing of all 4 balls as a multiple event consisting of the 4 separate drawings with the separate probabilities, $p_1 = p_3 = 4/10$ independent of each other, and $p_2 = p_4 = 3/9$ independent of each other but dependent upon p_1 and p_3 respectively. Then, by the multiplication theorem,

$$p = p_1 p_2 p_3 p_4 = \tfrac{4}{10} \cdot \tfrac{3}{9} \cdot \tfrac{4}{10} \cdot \tfrac{3}{9}$$
$$= (2 \cdot 2)/(5 \cdot 3 \cdot 5 \cdot 3) = 4/225, \quad \text{SAME ANS.}$$

9　By the same reasoning, if all 4 balls are drawn from the same box, then

$$p = h/w = C_4^4/C_4^{10} = 1 \left/ \frac{10 \cdot 9 \cdot 8 \cdot 7}{4 \cdot 3 \cdot 2} \right.$$
$$= 1/210, \quad \text{ANS.}$$

Or, alternatively, with each separate event dependent upon those preceding it,

$$p = p_1 p_2 p_3 p_4 = \tfrac{4}{10} \cdot \tfrac{3}{9} \cdot \tfrac{2}{8} \cdot \tfrac{1}{7}$$
$$= \tfrac{1}{210}, \quad \text{SAME ANS.}$$

10　Of the *1,098,240* ways of dealing a one-pair hand, 4/13 of these have pairs of jacks or better. We could add this number to all the numbers of still better hands above it in the *Table* to find h = the total number of hands which have a pair of jacks or better. However, it is arithmetically simpler to find the number of hands which have single pairs less than jacks, or

$$1{,}098{,}240(9/13) = 760{,}320,$$

and add to this the one number of hands in the *Table* still lower than these to find,

$$f = 760{,}320 + 1{,}302{,}540 = 2{,}062{,}860.$$

Then, more quickly,

$$h = w - f = 2{,}598{,}960 - 2{,}062{,}860$$
$$= 536{,}100;$$

and the required probability is

$$p = h/w = 536{,}100/2{,}598{,}960$$
$$= 1 \text{ in } 4.8, \text{ approximately}, \quad \text{ANS.}$$

11　Regardless of the number on which Sloe bets, the mathematical expectation which he obtains for his \$10.00 is only

$$V = A \cdot p = \$360/37 = \$9.73.$$

In other words, all numbers are equally "unlucky" for the player in the long run. The only reason the "house" wins in the long run is that it never puts *any* money up on its "free" number, zero. Moreover, it cannot afford dishonestly to have the wheel "fixed" to come up more frequently on zero, or on any other number, because—quite aside from any question of ethics or good will—the kind of practiced gambler who frequents such houses would soon detect the trend and "break the bank" by placing large bets on the favored outcomes. In other words, whether Sloe bets with or against it, the house will take his money from him most certainly in the long run by keeping the wheel "honest" and Sloe naïvely hopeful. From the theory of probability we learn that, although there may be "systems" which can beat the house that operates a dishonest or accidentally unbalanced wheel, there is no "system" which will long win for anyone but the proprietor on an honest wheel in the long run!

12　The given possibilities are the only distributions with less than 5 cards in any suit. Hence,

$$p_1 = 0.2155$$
$$p_2 = 0.1054$$
$$p_3 = 0.0299$$
$$\overline{ }$$
$$p_1 + p_2 + p_3 = 0.3508 = q,$$

and the required probability is

$$p = 1 - q = 1 - 0.3508 = 0.6492, \quad \text{ANS.}$$

13　One or more can be drawn in any of

$$w = M = n^k - 1 = 2^7 - 1 = 128 - 1 = 127$$

different combinations. Of these, combinations with the possible even numbers of 2, 4, or 6 balls are

$$h = C_2^7 + C_4^7 + C_6^7 = \frac{7!}{2!5!} + \frac{7!}{4!3!} + \frac{7!}{6!1!}$$

$$= \frac{7 \cdot 6}{2} + \frac{7 \cdot 6 \cdot 5}{3 \cdot 2} + \frac{7}{1} = 21 + 35 + 7 = 63.$$

Hence, the required probability is

$$p = h/w = 63/127, \quad \text{ANS.}$$

14 (a) The hour hand is between these marks for only 1 hour out of 12. Hence, the "continuous" probability of event E_a is

$$p_a = 1 \text{ hour}/12 \text{ hours} = 1/12, \quad \text{Ans. (a)}.$$

(b) However, both hands are between these marks for only 5 minutes out of each 12 hours = 720 minutes. Hence, the "continuous" probability of event E_b is

$$p_b = 5 \text{ minutes}/720 \text{ minutes}$$
$$= 1/144, \quad \text{Ans (b)}$$

Alternatively we can reason that the minute hand is between these marks for only 5 minutes out of 60, or for 1 hour out of 12. Hence, the probability of the independent separate event E_m that the minute hand stop between the marks is

$$p_m = p_a = \tfrac{1}{12}$$

And therefore the probability of the multiple event E_b is

$$p = p_a \cdot p_m = \tfrac{1}{12} \cdot \tfrac{1}{12}$$
$$= \tfrac{1}{144}, \quad \text{Same Ans. (b)}$$

15 From the *Mortality Table* on page 170, we learn that the statistical probability of one such person still being alive at age 50 is

$$p_1 = h/w = 69,804/100,000$$
$$= 0.693 = 69.8\%.$$

Hence, the probability of the multiple statistical event that 2 such persons still be alive at age 50 is

$$p_2 = p_1 \cdot p_1 = (0.698)^2 = 0.487$$
$$= 48.7\%, \quad \text{Ans.}$$

TABLE FOR EXAMPLES 1 AND 3, PAGES 46–47

If Form 1040, line 34, is—		And the total number of exemptions claimed on line 7 is—							
Over	But not over	2	3	4	5	6	7	8	9
		Your tax is—							
12,200	12,250	1,103	923	743	570	410	256	116	0
12,250	12,300	1,112	932	752	578	418	263	123	0
12,300	12,350	1,121	941	761	586	426	270	130	0
12,350	12,400	1,130	950	770	594	434	277	137	0
12,400	12,450	1,139	959	779	602	442	284	144	4
12,450	12,500	1,148	968	788	610	450	291	151	11
12,500	12,550	1,157	977	797	618	458	298	158	18
12,550	12,600	1,166	986	806	626	466	306	165	25
12,600	12,650	1,175	995	815	635	474	314	172	32
12,650	12,700	1,184	1,004	824	644	482	322	179	39
12,700	12,750	1,193	1,013	833	653	490	330	186	46
12,750	12,800	1,202	1,022	842	662	498	338	193	53
12,800	12,850	1,211	1,031	851	671	506	346	200	60
12,850	12,900	1,220	1,040	860	680	514	354	207	67
12,900	12,950	1,229	1,049	869	689	522	362	214	74
12,950	13,000	1,238	1,058	878	698	530	370	221	81

If Form 1040, line 34, is—		And the total number of exemptions claimed on line 7 is—							
Over	But not over	2	3	4	5	6	7	8	9
		Your tax is—							
23,600	23,650	3,672	3,392	3,135	2,895	2,655	2,415	2,186	1,976
23,650	23,700	3,686	3,406	3,147	2,907	2,667	2,427	2,197	1,987
23,700	23,750	3,700	3,420	3,159	2,919	2,679	2,439	2,207	1,997
23,750	23,800	3,714	3,434	3,171	2,931	2,691	2,451	2,218	2,008
23,800	23,850	3,728	3,448	3,183	2,943	2,703	2,463	2,228	2,018
23,850	23,900	3,742	3,462	3,195	2,955	2,715	2,475	2,239	2,029
23,900	23,950	3,756	3,476	3,207	2,967	2,727	2,487	2,249	2,039
23,950	24,000	3,770	3,490	3,219	2,979	2,739	2,499	2,260	2,050
24,000	24,050	3,784	3,504	3,231	2,991	2,751	2,511	2,271	2,060
24,050	24,100	3,798	3,518	3,243	3,003	2,763	2,523	2,283	2,071
24,100	24,150	3,812	3,532	3,255	3,015	2,775	2,535	2,295	2,081
24,150	24,200	3,826	3,546	3,267	3,027	2,787	2,547	2,307	2,092
24,200	24,250	3,840	3,560	3,280	3,039	2,799	2,559	2,319	2,102
24,250	24,300	3,854	3,574	3,294	3,051	2,811	2,571	2,331	2,113
24,300	24,350	3,868	3,588	3,308	3,063	2,823	2,583	2,343	2,123
24,350	24,400	3,882	3,602	3,322	3,075	2,835	2,595	2,355	2,134

INDEX